D1594568

Bhakti Religion in North India

SUNY Series in Religious Studies
Harold Coward, editor

Bhakti Religion in North India

Community Identity and Political Action

edited by
DAVID N. LORENZEN

STATE UNIVERSITY OF
NEW YORK PRESS

Barnard
BL
1151.3
.B46
1995
C.2

Published by
State University of New York Press, Albany

© 1995 State University of New York

All rights reserved

Printed in the United States of America

No part of this book may be used or reproduced in any manner whatsoever without written permission. No part of this book may be stored in a retrieval system or transmitted in any form or by any means including electronic, electrostatic, magnetic tape, mechanical, photocopying, recording, or otherwise without the prior permission in writing of the publisher.

For information, write to the State University of New York Press, State University Plaza, Albany, NY 12246

Production by Bernadine Dawes
Marketing by Nancy Farrell

Library of Congress Cataloging-in-Publication Data

Bhakti religion in North India : community identity and political action / edited by David N. Lorenzen.
p. cm. — (SUNY series in religious studies)
Includes bibliographical references and index.
ISBN 0-7914-2025-6
1. Hinduism—Social aspects. 2. Sikhism—Social aspects. 3. Bhakti. 4. Religion and politics—India. I. Lorenzen, David N. II. Series.
BL1151.3.B46 1995
294.5'0954—dc20 93-41538
CIP

1 2 3 4 5 6 7 8 9 10

CONTENTS

PART II: THEOLOGY

PART III: POLITICAL ACTION

A NOTE ON TRANSLITERATION

Diacritics have been used for all Sanskrit and Hindi words *except* the following: (1) names of places, persons and institutions that have "official" English spellings, (2) names of authors, titles and publishers of books and essays in European languages (even when diacritics appear in the original publication), and (3) words that have been absorbed into English (e.g., Krishna, Vishnu, Shiva, yogi, Brahmin, sannyasi, sadhu, Shaivite).

In Hindi words, a final mute *a* appearing after a single consonant has always been dropped. Other cases of mute *a* have been left as the authors of the essays prefer (e.g., Tulsīdās or Tulasīdās, Rāmānand or Rāmānanda). Some words have been written differently in Hindi and Sanskrit (or pan-Indian) contexts (e.g., Rām or Rāma).

A clase nasal *(ṅ, ñ, ṇ, n, m)* has usually been used in place of an *anusvāra (ṃ)* except before *h* and *s* (e.g., *Śaṅkar, siṃha*). Pure nasalized vowels *(anunāsik)* are indicated either by an *anusvāra (yahāṃ)* or by a tilde *(yahā̃)*. The following transliterations are also used: च = *cha;* छ = *chha;* ड = *ḍa;* ड़ = *ṛa;* व = *va* or *wa;* ऋ = *ṛ;* श = *śa;* ष = *ṣa*. In words without diacritics, these last three are usually written as 'ri,' 'sha,' and 'sha' respectively.

PREFACE

The essays in this volume all discuss aspects of medieval and modern Hinduism and Sikhism in North India. All are by scholars working in North American universities. Although this is obviously a vast field of study, the number of scholars working in it in North American universities is still relatively small, even compared to the limited number of scholars working in the related fields of classical and Vedic Hinduism, Tantric religion, and South Indian Hinduism. The scholarly balance between these fields, however, does seem to be gradually coming more into line with their actual historical, religious and social importance.

I was particularly pleased, therefore, when El Colegio de México and the National Council for Science and Technology of the Mexican government agreed to sponsor a symposium on Popular Religion and Sociopolitical Dissidence in North India, held in Mexico City in May, 1991. This symposium brought together a dozen senior scholars working on this field in American, Canadian and Mexican universities, as well as several younger scholars and graduate students. Many of the essays in this book grew out of the papers and discussions of this symposium.

Given the varied nature of the research projects of the scholars working in this field in North America, the topics discussed in this book are necessarily varied. All the essays do, however, address the basic problems of the formation of socioreligious identity and difference in North India and of the nature of the ensuing conflicts between Hindus, Sikhs and Muslims that are daily tearing Indian society apart. As a result, the post-independence Indian state has been forced to resort to ever more desperate efforts to save its administrative structure and territorial unity. Insofar as these efforts have led to systematic abuses of human rights by all sides in the conflicts, including the police and armed forces charged with protecting those rights, it is obvious that a fundamental rethinking of the situation and courageous new political decisions are urgently needed.

My thanks for help in putting together this volume are owed first and foremost to the authors of the essays, who wrote and revised their texts with care and punctuality. Also helpful were many of the comments in the anonymous readers' reports solicited by State University of New York Press. My own essays also benefited from critical comments from various colleagues, especially Susana Devalle, John Hawley and Harjot Oberoi. My wife, Barbara Martiny, graciously gave up time from her own professional work at several critical junctures to give me extra time to work on the project.

How happens it then, said PHILO, if [religion] be so salutary to society, that all history abounds so much with accounts of its pernicious consequences on public affairs? Factions, civil wars, persecutions, subversions of government, oppression, slavery; these are the dismal consequences which always attend its prevalency over the minds of men. . . .

—David Hume,
Dialogues Concerning Natural Religion, 1776

This reality, which mythologies have represented under so many different forms, but which is the universal and eternal objective cause of these sensations sui generis out of which religious experience is made is society. . . .

It is obviously necessary that the religious life be the eminent form and, as it were, the concentrated expression of the whole collective life. If religion has given birth to all that is essential in society, it is because the idea of society is the soul of religion.

—Emile Durkheim,
Les formes élémentaires de la vie religieuse, 1912

INTRODUCTION
The Historical Vicissitudes of Bhakti Religion

David N. Lorenzen

In the context of North India, all Sikhs as well as almost all Hindus may be called followers of bhakti religion since their dominant mode of worship is one of "devotion" *(bhakti)* toward a divine being. Although both the ways of expressing this devotion and the ways of conceptualizing the object of this devotion vary dramatically, all manifestations of bhakti religion do share common historical roots. More specifically, all its sects and currents were heavily influenced in their origins, and many still today, by two Sanskrit texts: the *Bhagavad-gītā* and the *Bhāgavata Purāṇa*. This common heritage gives all its manifestations a family resemblance that is not shared by other religions of India such as Christianity and Islam in which devotion to a divine being also plays a central role.

Since the latter part of the fifteenth century, bhakti religion in North India has been divided into two major streams or currents—*nirguṇī* and *saguṇī*—ostensibly on the basis of a theological difference in the way of conceptualizing the nature of the divine being that is the object of worship. Those who prefer *saguṇ* ("with attributes") bhakti constitute the majority. They worship anthropomorphic manifestations of the divine being, usually forms of the gods Vishnu, Shiva, and the Goddess, and of these gods' close associates or family members. The persons who follow *nirguṇ* ("without attributes") bhakti are fewer in number and generally prefer to worship a divine being who remains mostly unmanifest and non-anthropomorphic. Historically, Sikh religion derives from this *nirguṇī* current of bhakti religion, although it has established a conscious identity as a separate religion. Exactly how and when it did so is still a matter of scholarly debate as Harjot Oberoi's essay in this book demonstrates.

In actual practice, most followers of *saguṇī* religion in North India today direct their devotion especially toward two avatars of the god Vishnu—Krishna and Rāma—and toward the latter's associate

Hanumān. Fewer persons direct their devotion primarily toward Shiva and the Goddess. Those who do generally worship Shiva in the semi-iconic form of a *liṅga*, while the Goddess is most often worshipped as Durgā or Mahiṣamardinī, the killer of the buffalo demon. On the other hand, followers of *nirguṇī* religion, including the Sikhs, generally reject worship of the avatars of Vishnu or any other anthropomophic gods or forms of God. Although *nirguṇī* literature directs the devotee to worship a formless, universal God, this God does take partial embodiment in the Name of God and in the collective Words *(bāṇī)* and the person of the Guru and the saints. Particularly in the case of the Sikhs, the words of the Guru and the saints take the physical form of a holy Book, the *Ādi Granth* or *Gurū Granth Sāhib*.

In this introduction, I will first discuss the relation between religious and social identities in the context of the growth of religious communalism in modern India. Next, I will review the historical development of the social ideologies associated with the traditions of *saguṇī* and *nirguṇī* bhakti. Finally, I will offer some critical comments on the ideas of Max Weber about the nature of low-class religion.

Community Identity and Communalism

Theological differences are not simply the product of historical accident; they are symptomatic and expressive of differences in social identities. Religions are communities of persons who follow, or claim to follow, common systems of beliefs and practices. Even those beliefs and practices that appear to be sociologically and politically arbitrary serve to express and define the limits of any given religious community. In other words, taken together they define the group's identity, its membership and its ideology. This is true even though other factors such as class and caste, gender, ethnic group, language, region, and race generally play important roles in deciding who is likely to become a member of the group.

The Sikhs provide a good example. The essays of Harjot Oberoi and Michael Shapiro in this book illustrate two aspects of the formation of this religious community. Oberoi concentrates on how ritual differences increasingly served to mark and define Sikh identity, while Shapiro shows how distinctive theological features of Sikh religion were woven even into the grammar of the language used in Sikh scripture.

Many religious beliefs and practices are employed not only to define a given community identity but also to provide a utopian vision for the future of the community and of the society of which it forms a greater or lesser part. In other words, these beliefs and practices are normative both in a descriptive, definitional sense and in an ideal, moral sense. Together they constitute, in short, both the identity and the ideology of the community.

The concept of ideology has been given many senses. I prefer to define it as a form of discourse, primarily verbal but also behavioral, that directly or indirectly claims to describe the structure and functioning of society in such a way as either to justify, or to protest against, an unequal distribution of social status, economic wealth and political power among different groups within the society. Although ideologies inevitably have manipulative aspects, their spokesmen for the most part believe what they say, even if they know, deep down, that it is not the whole story. Ideological discourse is not simply cynical propaganda. Propaganda implies a conscious manipulation of the truth to achieve covert economic, social and political ends that benefit certain groups to the detriment of the society at large. Ideology, on the other hand, functions in much more unconscious, and even altruistic, fashion. For its supporters, an ideology represents the proper, and even the natural, arrangement of society.

The classical Marxist argument that each society has essentially only one ideology, to be identified as the "dominant ideology" of its ruling class, is no longer tenable.[1] Still useful, however, is A. Gramsci's idea that the ideology (or ideologies) of privileged classes may exert, by a combination of persuasion and coercion, a "hegemony" over the ideology (or ideologies) of the nonprivileged classes in the same society (Anderson 1976/77). Indeed, it is precisely the distinction between hegemonic and subordinate or subaltern ideological discourse that underlies the distinction between the *nirguṇī* and *saguṇī* devotional movements, as will be argued below (also Lorenzen 1987a). Furthermore, since ideological discourse always claims that its social prescriptions will benefit the society as a whole—even when in fact they serve as much or more to protect the privileges of an upper-class elite—ideological discourse and discourse that defines community identity are always inextricably linked.

In the context of North India, the term "community identity" inevitably invokes the related concepts of *communal* identity and *communalism*. Communalism, particularly as it relates to devotion to the avatar Rām, is the single most recalcitrant and dangerous source of social and political conflict in India today. In this book the essays of Lutgendorf, van der Veer and Devalle all are directly concerned with this problem. Clearly some discussion of the concept and the phenomenon is in order.

Perhaps the most lucid discussion of the varied meanings that the terms "communal" (or "communalist") and "communalism" have acquired in the speech of imperialists, nationalists, and assorted academics is that found in Gyanendra Pandey's book, *The Construction of Communalism in North India* (1990). According to Pandey (1990, 6):

> In its common Indian usage the word "communalism" refers to a condition of suspicion, fear and hostility between members of different religious communities. In academic investigations, more often than not, the term is applied to organized political movements based on the proclaimed interests of a religious community, usually in response to a real or imagined threat from another religious community (or communities).

For Pandey, however, the true "meaning" of communalism as a concept is not to be located in its contemporary Indian usages, but rather in the history of the "discourses"—imperialist, nationalist and academic—in which the concept arose and developed. His aim is (1990, 5–6) "to explore the history of the 'problem' of communalism through an examination of the discourse that gave it meaning."

What Pandey finds in his examination of the historical "construction" of the concept is that (1990, 6) "communalism . . . is a form of colonialist knowledge" since the concept was first developed in the discourse of imperialist administrators who used it as a catchall label for different sorts of social and political unrest. By calling this unrest "religious," these administrators purposely implied that Indian society was fundamentally imbued with religious bigotry and irrationality.

In Pandey's view, nationalists, and to some extent liberal colonialists, have countered this basically racist or "essentialist" interpretation of communalism with another that was more rational and "economistic," but also basically negative (1990, 11): "The nationalists . . . recognize communalism as a problem of recent origins, as the outcome basically of economic and political inequality and conflict, and as the handiwork of a handful of self-interested elite groups (colonial and native), with the mass of people being essentially 'secular'." For both the colonialists and nationalists, communalism has been regarded as an obstacle to the development of a mature nationalism and ultimate self-government. To the extent to which both have shared this bias in favor of nationalism and secularism and the supposed grounding of these "isms" in rational thought, Pandey claims (1990, 13), "both nationalist and colonialist positions derive from the same liberal ideology."

While Pandey's account of the history of the concept does much to illuminate some of the biases and value judgements inherent in its everyday usages, his suggested solution to the "problem" seems to me to be wrong-headed. Rather than to recommend that we simply try to become more conscious of, and thereby correct or modify, the biases and value judgements inherited from colonialist and nationalist discourse, he apparently thinks that it is possible to virtually "deconstruct" the concept of communalism out of existence. In its place, he would prefer that we regard each historical case of conflict between the major religious communities of India on its own terms. For this reason he rejects, in no uncertain terms, the recent historical trend that emphasizes the "continuities" in Indian history, particularly Christopher Bayly's (1985) attempt to identify "The Pre-History of 'Communalism'" in religious conflicts of the eighteenth and early nineteenth centuries. For Pandey (1990, 15), "there is really no sense of context here, not a hint that human beings and their actions, the events of history, derive their meaning from the political, economic, social and intellectual circumstances in which they are placed."[2]

One cannot, however, simply deconstruct communalism out of existence in this postmodernist fashion. The "meaning" of the concept of communalism is not exhausted by an analysis of the biases and value judgements inherent in the discourses in which it arose. One can, I think, fairly invoke the well-worn distinction between what a term connotes and what it denotes. Pandey's "meaning" overvalues the connotations of the term at the expense of its denotation, the latter being roughly equivalent to its contemporary everyday usage. Communalism is a concept, but it is a concept that most people employ to refer to and classify a quite specific range of attitudes and actions. Without such classifying terms and concepts, any discourse is of course impossible. In the case of "communalism," I fail to see that Pandey can offer *any* acceptable substitute.

Pandey may well be correct to reject Bayly's extension of the term communalism to include religious conflicts before 1860, but his charge that Bayly's argument lacks any "sense of context" is unfair. As G. Barraclough has noted (1967), the identification and evaluation of the continuities and discontinuities in society over the passage of time is precisely the principal task that historians undertake. Bayly, of all people, is certainly well aware of the historical context of the examples of religious conflict he has discussed. Where he differs with Pandey is in the much less historically specific meaning he assigns to the concept of communalism. This is the reason Bayly sees continuity where Pandey sees discontinuity.

One vital aspect of any analysis of the phenomenon of communalism is an evaluation of the extent to which it is the product of elite manipulation of popular attitudes and actions. There is little doubt, for instance, that the religious and political elite that control the Rashtriya Svayamsevak Sangh (RSS), Vishwa Hindu Parishad (VHP), and the Bharatiya Janata Party (BJP) have shamelessly manipulated for their own ends the popular religious sentiments invoked by the Rām-janmabhūmi and Bābarī-masjid dispute. It is also clear, however, that these elites have been able to draw from a deep well of popular Hindu discontent and antagonism against the Muslim community with roots going back to medieval times. In his essay here, P. Lutgendorf discusses some of this medieval background to communalism, particularly its relation to Tulasīdās's *Rāmacharitamānas*. P. van der Veer concentrates more on the association between communalism and the nationalist movement, and S. Devalle tackles the problem of the relation of communalism to modern political ideologies and communalist concepts such as *Hindutva*.

Secular nationalists, including Marxists such as Bipan Chandra, have often regarded communal discontent and antagonism as the product of elite manipulation and a typical manifestation of "false consciousness." Chandra (1984, 1) defines communalism as "the belief that because a group of people follow a particular religion they have, as a result, common social, political and economic interests." In this view, such concrete interests do underlie communalism, but they are the interests of elite manipulators, not the common people. If this were in fact true, however, the destruction of communalism would be relatively simple, at least in theory. One need only educate the people to see how their communalist sentiments are in fact based on elite manipulation. It is like the position of the Advaitin who compares illumination to the destruction of an illusory serpent by recognizing that it is *really* a rope.

The chief problem with this point of view is that it underestimates the deep historical roots of the self-identities of the religious communities of India, a subject I will return to shortly. The snake in question is far from illusory. Communalism may well be a comparatively modern phenomenon arising in large measure from elite manipulation, but it is also firmly rooted in community identities that cannot be simply wished away. Furthermore, once created, communal ideology (i.e., one that defines the community in excessively negative, oppositional terms) generates its own social, economic and political reality; it becomes a self-fulfilling prophecy. Once the religious Other is radically excluded from the community, he does in fact become a rival in social, political and economic terms as well as religious ones.

Admitting the reality and practical importance of religious communities, however, need not imply that one should abandon the quest for a secular society. Ashis Nandy (1990) tends in this direction when he attempts to promote a more traditional and religious social identity that is at the same time more tolerant and noncommunalist than the "Hindutva" of the more fundamentalist Hindu nationalists of the RSS, VHP, and BJP. As Peter van der Veer points out in his essay, Nandy can be seen as a post-independence heir to the religious nationalism of Mahatma Gandhi. Somewhat surprisingly, both Gyanendra Pandey (1990, 21–22) and Veena Das (1990) openly flirt with the idea of supporting Nandy's "anti-secularist" position.

Nandy's views and those of Bipan Chandra (1984) provide an instructive comparison, particularly with regard to the evaluation of the role of the state in communal conflict. Both agree that the colonial state played a significant role in fomenting the growth of communalism, but disagree about the role of the state since independence. On the whole, Chandra views the independent state as a relatively neutral arbiter in situations of communal conflict and argues that this positive neutrality is closely linked to the espousal of a secular ideology. Nandy on the other hand regards the "secular" state as often being a source of communal conflict and pins his hopes for avoiding such conflict on the traditional religious tolerance of the majority Hindu community. As van der Veer points out, however, this tolerance is grounded on the doctrine of a hierarchy of religious truths wherein different religions are thought to have received partial revelations of a spiritual reality that is fully manifest only in Hinduism. It is not surprising that the followers of other religions—particularly those that claim virtually exclusive access to God's message such as Christianity and Islam—do not share Nandy's enthusiasm for this doctrine of tolerance.

Chandra's evaluation of the role of religion in communalism tries to make a distinction between "religiosity," which is bad, and "religion," which is good. He defines religiosity as a (1984, 171) "deep and intense emotional commitment to matters of religion and as the tendency to let religion and religious emotions intrude into non-religious or non-spiritual areas of life and beyond the individual's private life, to refuse to separate religion from politics, economics and social life—that is, to be over-religious or to have too much religion in one's life." As van der Veer points out, however, this idea of religion as something personal and separate "from politics, economics and social life" is a quite dubious ideological proposition derived from the European Enlightenment. In Europe and North America religion did in fact to some extent retreat into a more private domain as a result of, first, the necessity of neutralizing the conflict between Catholicism and Protestantism and, second, the rise of the modern nation-state and science. Even in Europe, however, the idea that ethics and values can be empirically (rather than simply logically) separated into personal (religious) and social (political) categories is at best a well-meaning hope that repeatedly flies in the face of reality.

In the case of modern India, Chandra argues that (1984, 167) religious difference was used "to 'mask' the politics of classes and social groups arising in the secular, non-religious spheres." One has to agree with Chandra that communalism represents "too much religion in one's life," but he is mistaken when he argues that this represents an improper overflow of religion into other, nonreligious aspects of life. In large measure religious ethics and values are, in a very basic sense, also expressions of social, economic and political needs and aspirations, as scholars as diverse as Marx, Nietzsche, Durkheim, and Weber long ago recognized. From this point of view, both religions and political philosophies can be regarded as considerably overlapping subsets of the more general category of "ideology."

In its propensity for violence and irrational hatred, communalism has sometimes been called "pathological," an epithet that Pandey (1990, 9–10) and Devalle reject, but that Chandra and Nandy accept (at least implicitly).[3] Provided that this term is understood to be a metaphor, a physiological analogy, it can be of use. The pathology of communalism stems from its exaggerated elaboration of otherwise "normal" aspects of community identity, not the introduction of strange new abnormalities. It is analogous to the pathology of an individual whose commonplace fears, hates or desires—whether rational or not—become obsessive and out of control. In communalism, the defining attributes and ideology of a religious community become obsessively directed against other communities. This obsessive hatred represents a reaction that far outstrips any conceivable objective threat that these opposing communities might pose. The hatred expressed—whether fomented by elite manipulation or not—has become basically irrational and ultimately self-destructive.

If communalism is a pathological condition, an obsessively oppositional form of community identity, it is fair to ask about its causes, the etiology of the pathology. There have been four principal historical factors, I think, that have fostered the development of communalism in South Asia, apart from and in addition to the underlying problem of the existence of several religious communities in one territory.

The first factor is the adoption of the modern ideas of nationalism and popular sovereignty by the Indian elites in the latter part of the nineteenth century and the participation of these elites in nationalist organizations, both secular and nonsecular, as well as in other collective political groups such as caste associations. There is in fact considerable truth to the liberal-secular claim that, as Pandey puts it (1990, 14), "communalism was nationalism gone awry." Both Hindu nationalists and Islamic nationalists insisted that their respective religious communities were also nations or national communities. More recently the advocates of Khalistan have made the same claim for the Sikh community.

A second, related factor is the introduction of the system of electoral politics, first in limited fashion by the British colonialist regime, and later in the democratic parliamentary governments of independent India and Pakistan (the latter remaining democratic only in fits and starts). Electoral politics as a total system—and not simply its directly "communal" aspects such as the issue of separate electorates—inevitably leads to competition between all sorts of communities, including religious ones, for government support in satisfying economic, educational and social goals. As is well known, the British colonial government often cynically and cruelly exploited this competition using the tactic of divide and rule, thereby setting a precedent that is still often followed. The identification of religious communities in the decennial census of the population, an institution closely linked to the development of electoral politics, also contributed much to the growth of communal consciousness.

A third important factor is the demographic explosion which began, or at least became more acute, in the nineteenth century and has continued, only partly controlled, up to the present day. This explosion has helped create dramatic scarcities of agricultural land and other natural resources and made it virtually impossible for the supply of jobs to keep pace with the ever increasing number of job-seekers. The resulting economic and social tensions have been easily channeled into communalist conflicts.[4]

A fourth factor, mostly derived from the others, is the failure of the postcolonial political regime in India to satisfy the hopes of the mass of the population for peace, social order and economic prosperity. Although most national and state governments have made sincere efforts to follow secular policies, the failure to satisfy these hopes have inevitably led to discontents that are easily exploited by Hindu nationalist organizations such as the RSS, VHP, and BJP. Particularly tragic, since it was more avoidable, has been the endless international conflict with Pakistan. Whichever country has been more to blame, and whatever has been the role of the cold war in perpetuating the conflict, the wounds of partition have never healed, and the Muslim community of India remains an easy target for accusations of disloyalty and fifth-column activities by Hindu nationalists. Also significant has been the introduction of a certain amount of communalist propaganda ("playing the Hindu card") by the Congress Party, traditionally the most resolutely secular party, into the general election campaign of 1984, as Devalle notes in her essay. This set a dangerous precedent that may have contributed substantially to the legitimation of communalist parties, particularly the BJP in this and subsequent elections.

Beyond these general, structural factors for the rise and persistence of communalism—factors that largely define communalism as an identifiable historical phenomenon—each specific example of communal conflict must obviously be examined on its own terms and in its own historical context. What were the existing local tensions that made the social terrain ripe for the outbreak of communal conflict? What was the immediate cause of the conflict? How did the conflict proceed? What was the role of the police and government in resolving or aggravating the conflict? What part did existing communal organizations play? Only postmortem examinations of each specific conflict can answer such questions.

It remains true, however, that communalism cannot arise without the prior existence of a religious community. As commonly defined in India, communalism is based on the broadest of all community identities: those of the Muslims, Sikhs and Hindus. Each of these broad communities embodies a full range of social classes and castes as well as an ample number of separate religious currents, sects, subsects, and individual congregations. How is it possible for such heterogeneous communities to create social identities cohesive enough to make possible the pathology of communalism?

Part of the answer undoubtedly lies in the overlap of national and communal identities and the association of each religious community with specific "home" territories: Pakistan and Bangladesh for the Muslims (though this is obviously of dubious value for the Muslim community in India), Punjab for the Sikhs, and all of postindependence India for the Hindus. More important, however, is the fact that each of these communities offers its members a common history (even if often largely imagined), a more or less common set of religious beliefs and practices, and a common social ideology. Each community can also reinforce its group identity by referring to their long histories of mutual conflict and the associated process of self-definition by means of mutual opposition.

For reasons that are not entirely clear to me, a number of contemporary academics have attempted to deny the existence of this long history of mutual conflict and oppositional self-definition among these three religious communities. In particular, they have claimed that in India the very concepts of Hindus and Hinduism as *religious*, as opposed to *ethnic* and/or *geographical*, categories were created in quite recent times. C. J. Fuller's comments in his recent book on popular Hinduism provide a good example (1992, 10):

> Consider the very terms "Hindu" and "Hinduism." The Persian word *hindu* derives from Sindhu, the Sanskrit name of the river Indus (in modern Pakistan). It originally meant a native of India, the land around and beyond the Indus. When "Hindu" (or "Hindoo") entered the English language in the seventeenth century, it was similarly used to denote any native of Hindustan (India), but

> gradually came to mean someone who retained the indigenous religion and had not converted to Islam. "Hinduism," as a term for that indigenous religion, became current in English in the early nineteenth century and was coined to label an "ism" that was itself partly a product of western orientalist thought, which (mis)constructed Hinduism on the model of occidental religions, particularly Christianity. Hinduism, in other words, came to be seen as a system of doctrines, beliefs, and practices properly equivalent to those that make up Christianity, and "Hindu" now clearly specified an Indian's religious affiliation.

In point of fact, the Muslim intellectual al-Biruni (1964) had already clearly delineated the system of religious doctrines, beliefs, and practices of the Hindu community, as opposed to the system of Islam, early in the eleventh century. One can perhaps object that he should be considered a Muslim outsider or an unrepresentative intellectual. Moving ahead to the fifteenth and sixteenth centuries, however, one finds that the poems of virtually all *nirguṇī* saints beginning with Kabīr and Gurū Nānak repeatedly refer to "Hindus and Turks" and "Hindus and Muslims *[musulamān]*" in contexts that clearly show that the authors had in mind religious, and not ethnogeographical, communities. These poems generally follow a pattern in which the Hindus are said to do or believe one thing (worship Vishnu and Shiva, etc.) and the Muslims/Turks another (pray to Mecca, etc.), but neither knows the highest Truth. Medieval *saguṇī* authors more often speak simply in terms of "us" versus the *mlechchhas* or *yavans*, but even these authors can hardly be accused of not understanding the contrasting natures of the religious beliefs and practices of the two communities. Some eighteenth-century Englishmen may have confused ethnogeographical and religious categories, but they did not acquire this confusion from the Indians themselves. Even today Spanish speakers still commonly call all the inhabitants of India *hindúes*, whatever their religious affiliation. Here the confusion clearly stems from ignorance based on a lack of contact, not a conscious resort to an ancient geographical etymology.

All this suggests that in fact the Hindu community of India became much more conscious of its identity as a community under the stimulus of its contact with the Islam of the Turks, Afghans and Mughals who invaded India in the medieval period. Sheldon Pollock (1993) has forcefully argued that the rise of the worship of the avatar Rāma in this same period was in large part a response to the Muslim presence and the Hindu search for a cohesive oppositional identity.

Social Ideologies of Bhakti Traditions

As was noted at the outset of this discussion, the tradition of *saguṇ* bhakti has been dominant in the Hindu community for a thousand years or possibly more. *Nirguṇī* tradition has also exercised considerable influence in North India since about 1500. Except in the Punjab, however, it has remained a subordinate, minority tradition subject to the "hegemony" of the *saguṇī* tradition. Older "orthodox" traditions such as those centered around Vedic recitation and sacrifice, philosophic and yogic enlightenment, and Tantrism, have continued to exist, but none of them remains the principal religious concern of more than a small number of elite practitioners. Even these practitioners have often syncretically combined their traditions with that of *saguṇ* bhakti.

One of the basic functions of the dominant religious tradition of any given society, in the present case *saguṇ* bhakti, is to articulate a social ideology intended to serve as a sort of psychological glue that helps preserve both harmony and privilege within the religious community and within the society as a whole (including its subordinate communities). In practice, however, most ruling elites are forced to resort to direct coercion, or the threat of such coercion, in order to maintain their hegemony over the rest of society. Rarely if ever do the subaltern (Gramsci) or nonprivileged (Weber) classes of society either wholeheartedly accept the ruling ideology or knuckle under elite domination without some form of (usually covert) resistance (see Scott 1990 and Devalle 1985). In North India, *nirguṇ* bhakti has served as one of the more significant forms of ideological resistance of these classes.

Although the contrast between the *saguṇī* and *nirguṇī* traditions is usually defined in theological terms—both by outside observers and by the followers of these two traditions—it is the social ideologies of the two traditions that lie behind and give strength to these differing theologies. And behind the ideologies lie the communities themselves. This is why the obvious theological affinity between *nirguṇī* tradition and orthodox Advaita—an affinity that Sanskritizing intellectuals within the Kabīr Panth such as Hanumaddās (Lorenzen 1981) often cite as a proof of Kabīr's greatness—is ultimately of little significance. However similar the theologies may be, neither the social ideologies nor the communities that have supported the two movements have had much in common.

More significant are the obvious similarities—stemming in part from their shared historical roots—of *nirguṇ* and *saguṇ* bhakti. Some scholars have gone so far as to deny that the differences between the two traditions are significant. John Hawley, who does acknowledge important differences, nonetheless insists (1988, 4) that "we are talking about a single family of saints . . . the family of *bhakti*." Much can be said in favor of this point of view. For example, even though the social bases of two traditions—and the movements within each—can be fairly clearly distinguished, these bases do have considerable overlap. It is also true that the songs and verses of the major poet-saints of both traditions are often loved by the common people in rather indiscriminate fashion. In his essay here, Philip Lutgendorf argues that there is a progressive, *nirguṇ*-like side even to Tulasīdās, who is more often regarded as the maximum champion of a conservative interpretation of *varṇāśramadharma* within the *saguṇī* camp.

John Hawley, in his essay here, points out that many medieval manuscripts contain collections of songs by both *nirguṇī* and *saguṇī* poet-saints. As Hawley has noted elsewhere with regard to the poetry of Sūr Dās (1984, 121–60), however, it is common for most *saguṇī* poets to dedicate some songs to God in his transcendent, *nirguṇī* aspect A much closer examination of the individual songs in these "mixed" manuscripts is needed before we can determine to what extent they do in fact span the theological and social divide between the two traditions.

While some scholars have stressed the common features of *nirguṇī* and *saguṇī* traditions, many well-known Hindi scholars—most notably Pitambar Barthwal, Paraśurām Chaturvedī, and Hazārī Prasād Dvivedī—have emphasized their differences. Most of the mostly American and European scholars in K. Schomer and W. H. McLeod's edited volume *The Sants* (1987) have also emphasized the differences, both theological and ideological.[5] In what follows I will try to explain why I strongly support the view that these differences are more important than the similarities.

Since *saguṇ* bhakti is historically prior to *nirguṇ* bhakti and, more importantly, has come to embody the hegemonic ideology of modern Hindu society, we should begin by looking at how this tradition has been structured. Historically, *saguṇ* bhakti represents a "liberal" reform of an earlier Vedic and *śāstrik* Hinduism that had become the exclusive province of a small, all-male, Brahmin elite who unilaterally barred the rest of the population from any direct eligibility for salvation, or even from hearing the Vedic texts on which the Brahmins' religious authority depended. Even so enlightened a philosopher as Śaṅkarāchārya (c. 750) maintains just such a socially reactionary argument (Lorenzen 1987b).

Without in any way directly challenging the Brahmins' exclusive control over the Vedas, *saguṇ* bhakti did attempt, often somewhat reluctantly, to open the doors of salvation to all persons including women and members of most nonprivileged classes *(varṇas)*. Only the Untouchables *(avarṇa)* were excluded from this right, and even their exclusion was often left ambiguous. Perhaps the earliest, and certainly the most important, statement of this extension of salvation to previously excluded groups is found in the *Bhagavad-gītā* (9.32): "Those who take their refuge in me, O Pārtha, even if they are born from a sinful womb, or as women, Vaiśyas or Śūdras; even *they* will reach the highest goal."

In the *Bhagavad-gītā* this path to salvation through bhakti coexists, somewhat uneasily, with two other paths: that of wisdom or gnosis *(jñāna)* and that of disinterested proper conduct *(karma)*. Several scholars, most recently A. L. Basham (1989), have in fact argued that the *Bhagavad-gītā* chapters propounding the bhakti path represent a later addition welded onto the earlier sections of the text. Many scholars within Hindu tradition have also been well aware of the logical incompatibilities among the paths of bhakti, gnosis and proper conduct and have attempted to smooth over the rough spots with two supplementary doctrines: that of socially appropriate levels of worship and that of the crisis of the Kali Yuga, our present benighted age.

The doctrine of socially appropriate levels of worship maintains that the path of gnosis is appropriate only for learned Brahmins, while bhakti is especially appropriate for lower levels of society including women and Śūdras. In the conservative Advaita version of this doctrine, gnosis is the *only* path that can lead directly to salvation, but sincere bhakti can at least lead to an eventual birth as a learned male Brahmin and hence to salvation. In Mādhava's *Śaṅkaradigvijaya*, a medieval hagiographic life of the Advaita philosopher Śaṅkarāchārya, Śaṅkara is confronted with the dilemma of advising his dying mother on how to approach death. He first offers her instruction about the unqualified Absolute (*nirguṇa-brahman),* but she finds this too difficult to understand. Next he recites a hymn to Shiva, but when this god's messengers appear she rejects them. Finally, Śaṅkara recites a hymn to Vishnu-Krishna, and his mother allows this god's messengers to lead her to the highest heaven.[6]

The second supplementary doctrine is that of the crisis of the present, infernal Kali Yuga. This doctrine claims that in this age the paths of gnosis and proper conduct are no longer available to men (much less to women). In the present age, our intellectual, moral and social condition is simply too degenerate for any path to salvation to function apart from bhakti. It is for that very reason that God (usually identified with Vishnu) introduced the path of bhakti to make salvation available in this Kali Yuga. Often the texts go on to claim that birth in our Kali Yuga is paradoxically the most fortunate birth possible, since in this age God has made available this easy path of bhakti by which everyone—even women and Śūdras—can win direct salvation with little or no effort on their own part, exactly how little effort being an issue for debate among rival theological schools. For example, in the *Bhāgavata Purāṇa* the sage Karabhājana tells king Nimi:[7]

> Noble persons—those who appreciate good qualities and partake of their essence—honor the Kali Yuga. In it all one's aims are realized simply by chanting the name of God *[saṃkīrtana]*. . . . In the Kṛta and other ages, O king, the people long for a birth in the Kali Yuga. Indeed, in the Kali Yuga [good people] worship Nārāyaṇa.

One of the principal innovations of bhakti religion was the central role given to telling stories about the lives of avatars and saints. Here a distinction needs to be made between stories that are basically myths, that is, have little or no historical foundation, and those that are basically legends, that is, involve a mixture of myth and history. Although the dividing line between these two categories is sometimes rather fuzzy, stories about avatars clearly belong to the first category and stories about poet-saints such as Kabīr and Mīrābāī clearly belong to the second. Although this distinction is not openly made in Hindu tradition, it corresponds very closely to the distinction made there between stories about the avatars and saints of former *yuga*s and those about the saints of "our own" Kali Yuga. The term "hagiography" should be limited to such legendary stories about the saints of the Kali Yuga.

The doctrine of the avatars of Vishnu is already present in the *Bhagavad-gītā* (4.7), where Krishna says: "Wherever there is a lessening of dharma, O Bharata, and an increase of non-dharma, at that time I send myself [to earth as an avatar]." The phrase "in every age" in fact implies ages other than the Kali Yuga. Most texts assume that all the major past avatars, with the exception of the Buddha and the future avatar Kalki, were born in earlier yugas. Even though the direct activity of the avatars in the world has long since ended (or not yet begun), the proponents of *saguṇ* bhakti argue that devotion to these avatars can still lead to their intercession on behalf of their devotees and to personal salvation, conceived of as either the end of rebirth and individual existence or as a final birth in Vishnu's heaven.

An important difference between *saguṇī* and *nirguṇī* traditions is that the stories about avatars are a basic defining element of the former, while in the latter usually either the existence of the avatars is denied or their importance downgraded. The few *paurāṇik* stories about avatars and saints that are popular in *nirguṇī* circles—most notably those about Prahlād, Dhruv and Jaḍ Bharat—appear to mostly derive directly from the *Bhāgavata Purāṇa* and to concern legendary saints who are the patient victims of unjust suffering (see Lorenzen 1992).

Nonetheless, both traditions have come to give a prominent place to hagiography, particularly to stories about the founders and principal poets of specific sectarian traditions. These include the *saguṇī* saints Chaitanya, Vallabhāchārya, Sūr Dās, Mīrābāī, Tulasīdās, Narasī Mehatā, and Tukārām, and the *nirguṇī* saints Nāmadev, Kabīr, Raidās, Pīpā, Gurū Nānak, Dādū Dayāl, and Haridās Nirañjanī. To these may also be added the somewhat less historical Nāth saints, Gorakhanāth and Gopīchanda.[8]

The importance of hagiography in medieval and modern bhakti tradition contrasts sharply with the lack of interest in it in Vedic and *śāstrik* Hinduism, where almost the only important hagiographies are a few late medieval texts about Rāmānuja and Śaṅkarāchārya. The inspiration for these texts was probably vernacular hagiographic literature of bhakti religion in any case (Lorenzen 1983). This absence of hagiography in Vedic and *śāstrik* Hinduism ultimately derives from the rejection of historical precedent as a source for spiritual authority by the traditional exponents of Vedic exegesis, particularly the followers of Mīmāṃsā. Philosophers such as Kumārila Bhaṭṭa claimed that the authority of the Vedas and *śāstras*—and hence of the Brahmins that know them—is eternal, revealed and independent of the process of historical creation (see Pollock 1990 and 1989). In this view, religious Truth cannot have a human origin. The ancient sages were only the transmitters of the Vedas, not their authors. These texts, and the Truth they embody, exist eternally outside the realm of time and human effort. The history of specific peoples and individuals belongs to a secondary, mundane realm and has little or no relevance to spiritual Truth.

It should be noted that historical precedent and authority —expressed principally through hagiography and genealogies of teachers and disciples—tends to play a somewhat more prominent role in *nirguṇī* than in *saguṇī* religion. This is particularly true of Sikh tradition in which the historical saga of the ten Gurūs has been indispensible to the formation of Sikh identity. Within *nirguṇī* tradition, the distinction between myth and legend, between the avatars of former yugas and the saints of our Kali Yuga, is sometimes purposely made ambiguous. In her essay here, Uma Thukral discusses the Purāṇa-like hagiographies of the Dharmadāsī branch of the Kabīr Panth in which Kabīr is treated as an avatar. Insofar as this literature mimics *saguṇī* Purāṇas, it can be regarded as a product of Sanskritization, the emulation of higher caste culture. On the other hand, Dharmadāsī hagiography also aims to replace and finally subvert the *saguṇī* Purāṇas. In my own essay on *nirguṇī* hagiographies, I have focused on the extent to which the life stories of various *nirguṇī* saints tend to follow a hagiographic pattern similar to, but not completely identical with, the life stories of *saguṇī* saints.

The doctrine of transmigration and rebirth, called by Max Weber a "theodicy," forms one of the two central pillars of the ethics of *saguṇī* religion. If one behaves properly, one can expect a better rebirth in one's next life, above all a rebirth as a male in a higher caste. Not surprisingly, the followers of *nirguṇī* tradition generally manifest little enthusiasm for this theodicy and for the law of karma in particular. *Nirguṇī* poets do usually accept the idea of the cycle of rebirth tied to the moral character of one's actions, but tend to regard all human births as rare and equally valuable. Kabīr says (1972, *sākhī* 115): "A human birth is hard to get. It won't come a second time. Once a ripe fruit has fallen, it won't reattach itself to the branch." Edward Henry's essay on contemporary *nirguṇī* songs in this volume gives some indication of the continuing vitality of these ideas, as does Schaller's essay on the contemporary movement of the followers of Raidās.

The second pillar of *saguṇī* ethics is, of course, the doctrine of *varṇāśramadharma* (the law of social classes and stages of life). According to this doctrine, one obtains a better rebirth precisely by following the rules of conduct appropriate to the *varṇa* (roughly "class") and *jāti* (caste) in which one was born. The rules of behavior for different *varṇa*s are set out in elaborate detail in the legal texts of Hindu tradition: the *dharmasūtra*s, *dharmaśāstra*s and legal digests. These texts provide sometimes conflicting legal expressions of the social and ethical norms implicit in the doctrines of rebirth and *varṇāśramadharma.* Taken together, these laws and underlying norms constitute the social ideology of *saguṇ* bhakti and other "orthodox" forms of Hindu tradition.

As is well known, the doctrine of the four hierarchically structured *varṇa*s can be traced all the way back to the *Ṛg Veda* (10.90). Even the more detailed legal expression of *varṇāśramadharma* ideology was well established before the appearance of the *saguṇ* bhakti of the *Bhagavad-gītā.* This latter text makes its support for this ideology quite explicit when Krishna explains what he means by "proper conduct" (3.35): "Better is one's own dharma, even if imperfect, than the dharma of another, though well-performed. Better is death in one's own dharma. The dharma of another brings only danger." Later and longer *saguṇī* texts, including the influential *Bhāgavata Purāṇa*, are repeatedly laced with lengthy didactic passages that present elaborate expositions of the doctrines of transmigration and rebirth and of *varṇāśramadharma.*

Apologists for this ideology, including the ancient authors of the *dharmaśāstra*s and modern religious and academic intellectuals, have always been quick to point out that this model of a hierarchically ordered society assigns specific economic and social rights to each *varṇa* and *jāti*. In both theory and practice, however, more and better rights were always given to the social groups with higher social status. For this reason it is logical to ask to what extent does *saguṇ* bhakti's support for *varṇāśramadharma* represent a manipulation of religion for economic, political and status-related ends by the mostly Brahmin elite that wrote the *saguṇī* texts and propagated them among the general population, and by these Brahmins' immediate class allies and patrons, the wealthy landowners and merchants? In Marxist terms: to what extent has *saguṇ* bhakti embodied support for a typical dominant ideology?

Any convincing answer to this question would require the presentation of more empirical evidence than is possible within the limits of this essay. My own opinion is that such ideological manipulation by social elites, particularly by the Brahmin priesthood, is in fact a major element of *saguṇī* religion. The essays here by Lutgendorf, even as he defends Tulasī's social liberalism, and by van der Veer, who more directly attacks the ideology of Hindu nationalist organizations, do, I think, provide evidence that *saguṇī* bhakti has served to justify *varṇāśrama-dharma* and the status and privileges of Brahmins and other upper-caste groups.

This does not mean that *saguṇī* religion is simply Brahmin or upper-class propaganda. As has been noted, ideology and propaganda are quite different concepts. For the most part the supporters of *saguṇī* religion sincerely believe that *varṇāśramadharma* serves the interests of all those who belong to the society, the high and the low, for without it there would be only social chaos, often described as the condition of *matsyanyāya* (the law of the fishes), wherein the bigger eat the smaller.

Even when dominant ideologies such as *varṇāśramadharma* are expounded by upper-class groups with sincerity and good will, however, some element of rational calculation of self-interest is undoubtedly present. Likewise, it is certainly not the case that the lower-classes of society do not to some extent "see through" the class bias of dominant ideologies. When they do so, they sometimes reject these ideologies outright and sometimes reinterpret and refashion them in the light of their own interests and needs.[9]

It is easy to demonstrate that *nirguṇī* religion, particularly in its early stages, has embodied a fairly direct rejection of the ideology of *varṇāśramadharma*. It is somewhat more difficult to identify the ways in which the lower-class and female followers of *saguṇī* religion have reinterpreted its ideology to suit their own interests. In this area, much empirical research remains to be done. Some indication of the ways in which these lower-class followers may pick and choose among different *saguṇī* doctrines is suggested by the ways in which the few *saguṇī* authors who are from non-Brahmin castes or are women do so. The work of Eleanor Zelliot on Chokhāmeḷā (1981 and in this book) and of Parita Mukta on Mirabai and her low-caste adherents (1991) discuss two important examples of this process.[10]

When we come to *nirguṇī* religion, the lower-class and lower-caste identity of most of its followers and many of its leaders and poets is not in doubt. In particular, Brahmins are almost completely absent. In the poetry of the more important early leaders of *nirguṇī* tradition such as Kabīr, Raidās and Gurū Nānak, the outright rejection of the theology, ritual practices, and social ideology of *saguṇī* religion is clear and explicit. Good evidence for the oppositional ideology of *nirguṇī* religion is found here in the essays of Schaller on the Raidāsī movement and Juergensmeyer on the Radhasoamis. Also interesting in this context are Gold's essay on the Naths in Jodhpur and Gupta's on the Kīnā Rāmī. Neither the Naths, nor the Kīnā Rāmī are followers of specifically *nirguṇī* movements, although they are perhaps more *nirguṇī* than *saguṇī*. Nonetheless, both are mostly non-Brahmin and both have fostered social ideologies that generally deny that the Brahmins deserve a privileged status.

The opposition of the proponents of *nirguṇ* bhakti to *saguṇ* bhakti is easy to document, since the *nirguṇī* movement in large measure represents an ideological and religious contestation to *saguṇ* bhakti (at the same time that it appropriates many of the latter's basic beliefs and practices). It should also be noted, however, that some of the proponents of *saguṇ* bhakti have also expressed their opposition to *nirguṇ* bhakti. Tulasīdās's descriptions of the horrors of the Kali Yuga contain several good examples:[11]

> In this Kali Yuga the "devotees" describe bhakti by reciting verses, songs, couplets, stories, and anecdotes while they scorn the Vedas and Purāṇas.
>
> The Śūdras dispute with Brahmins. They cast angry looks and scold: "Are we something less than you? Whoever knows *brahman* becomes a noble Brahmin.
>
> Without any knowledge of *brahman,* women and men speak about nothing else. They are so controlled by greed that for a mere trifle they physically attack Brahmins and gurus.

Max Weber and Lower-Class Religion

Surprisingly few academic scholars have attempted to theorize about the religious traditions and communities of subordinate classes, although the discussions of African-American religion by scholars such as E. Genovese and L. Levine represent an important exception. For a more general theoretical discussion of the problem, however, one must go back to Max Weber's essay "Religion of Non-Privileged Classes" (1963), first published in 1922. Rereading Weber's analysis, one is struck by how dated some of his theories now seem, as well as by how impossibly broad, and sometimes biased, were many of his generalizations. Today it is difficult to take seriously claims such as the following:

> The influence of women only tended to intensify those aspects of religion that were emotional or hysterical. Such was the case in India. (1963, 106)

> It follows that the belief in ethical compensation is even more alien to warriors and to financial magnates who have economic interests in war and in the political manifestations of power. These groups are the least accessible to the ethical and rational elements in any religion. (1963, 97)

> Therefore, the rationalism of the proletariat . . . cannot in the nature of the case easily possess a religious character and certainly cannot easily generate a religion. Hence, in the sphere of proletarian rationalism, religion is generally supplanted by other ideological surrogates. (1963, 100–101)

> The lowest Hindu classes in particular clung to their caste duties with the greatest tenacity as a prerequisite for their rebirth into a better position. (1963, 109)

In spite of such improprieties, however, Weber must still be given credit for attempting to explain how and why the religions of the nonprivileged classes are—in important ways and notwithstanding all their considerable diversity—distinct from the religions of the privileged ("elite," "dominant" or "hegemonic") classes. Weber saw clearly that these differences have a logic that in large measure depends on the specific social, economic and political situations in which these privileged and nonprivileged classes find themselves.

Weber's only important predecessor in the analysis of the social basis of religious movements was Nietzsche. Particularly in his discussion of the sentiment of *ressentiment,* Weber takes Nietzsche as his implicit point of departure. Weber claims that while *ressentiment* played an important role in "Jewish ethical salvation religion," it did not do so "among the Hindus and Buddhists, for whom personal suffering is individually merited." At least as far as *nirguṇī* devotional Hinduism is concerned, Weber is mistaken, for *ressentiment* certainly is present—though the term itself is needlessly negative—in its repeated arguments for social equality and against Brahmins and the gods of *saguṇī* Hinduism.

In his work *The Religion of India,* Weber (1958) begins his discussion of the rise of devotional Hinduism with a hopelessly dated and misguided theory about the "sexual-orgiastic origin of *bhakti* ecstasy." Unfortunately, this hypothesis colors and vitiates the whole of his subsequent analysis of the topic. It is also painfully evident that many of his sources were wrong about basic facts. Only two minor arguments can perhaps be salvaged from the wreckage. First is his claim that the "Islamic foreign domination" (1958, 312) of the medieval period led to a situation in which "the external means of power of the Brahmans decayed and the founders of the sects sought more than ever to join forces with the masses." Second, but somewhat more dubious, is his assertion (1958, 324–25) that "it was first the foreign domination of Islam . . . which gave the development of *guru* power free reign, permitting it to grow to grotesque heights." For the rest, the less said about Weber's discussion of medieval and modern Hinduism the better.

Considerably more useful for a discussion of this same topic are Weber's more general remarks about the religious perspective of artisan and other "lower middle class" groups in his "Religion of Non-Privileged Classes." He first notes (1963, 95) that such groups in fact tend to manifest a great "diversity of religious attitudes." He then claims (1963, 96), however, that despite this diversity, "there is apparent in these lower middle classes, in contrast to the peasantry, a definite tendency towards congregational religion, towards religion of salvation, and finally towards rational ethical religion."

Virtually all the founders—and probably a majority of the earliest followers—of the *nirguṇī* devotional movement of North India came from a variety of artisan and other lower-middle-class groups. The four principal early leaders of the movement comprise a weaver (Kabīr), a minor bureaucrat (Gurū Nānak), a leather-worker (Raidās), and a cotton-carder (Dādū). Almost none of the leaders, or followers, of the movement have come from Brahmin castes. The situation with regard to the *saguṇī* devotional movement in North India is markedly different, since this movement has always been led overwhelmingly by Brahmins. Virtually the only significant exceptions have been Mīrābāī, a royal princess; Tūkārām, a shopkeeper; Chokhāmeḷā, a village servant (Mahār); and Śaṅkaradev of Assam, a clerk (Kāyastha). It should also be noted, however, that in strictly *class* (i.e., occupational) terms a large proportion of Brahmins—excluding those who earned their living directly from traditional religious offices—practised middle- or lower-middle-class occupations as bureaucrats, clerks, teachers, shopkeepers, and the like.

The affinity of the artisan and other lower-middle-class Hindu groups of India for congregational religion can be seen in several characteristic institutions and practices of devotional Hinduism. These include the "association with the good" *(satsaṅga)* for the purpose of religious discussion; the giving and attending public sermons *(pravachan);* group sessions for the singing of religious hymns *(bhajans)* or chanting *(saṅkīrtan);* and the public recitation of the sacred texts of the tradition *(pāṭh)*. (See Thiel-Horstmann 1989, 141–42.) Other institutions and practices, however, are considerably more individualistic. The taking of darshan, for example, is basically an individual transaction between the worshipper and his object of devotion, even when it occurs in a public context. The same may be said of intoning the Name of God *(jap)* and "self-study" *(svādhyāy)*. Other practices typical of devotional Hinduism may be either congregrational or individualistic depending on the social context in which they are performed. These include making various kinds of offerings (*pūjā* of flowers, fruits, *āratī*, etc.) and going on pilgrimage (*tīrthayātrā*, etc.). Many of these practices are characteristic of Hinduism in general, but the congregational ones are definitely much more prominent in the devotional Hinduism of lower-middle-class groups, as Weber suggests.

A single-minded quest for personal salvation characterizes virtually all forms of Hinduism with the possible exception of the most orthodox Vedic cults. As has been noted, devotional Hinduism's quest for salvation is distinguished less by the nature of the goal than by the means to it. For philosophic Hinduism, especially Advaita Vedānta, the means is gnosis or intellectual enlightenment *(jñāna)*. For the practitioners of yoga, the means is a combination of physical and mental control. For devotional Hinduism it is devotion *(bhakti)* combined in various ways with the grace *(prasād)* of God and guru. Another important difference is that devotional Hinduism makes salvation directly available, albeit often rather begrudgingly in *saguṇī* texts, to all persons, including women and members of low castes.

Weber's final (and presumably "highest") characteristic of lower-middle-class religion is its tendency "towards rational ethical religion." The extent to which this trait characterizes devotional Hinduism is debatable. Insofar as most religions (by definition according to some scholars) assert that a supernatural entity or entities play a primary role in both metaphysics and ethics, it is hard for me to understand how any such religion can be said to be significantly more "rational" than any other. By "non-rational" religion Weber apparently has in mind the ceremony and ritual of the Catholic Church and the "magical" practices of primitive and "peasant" religion. At least among anthropologists, however, any attempt to objectively distinguish between magic and religion, a favorite theme from Frazer to Malinowski, has long since been abandoned. Although the distinction continues to have some "common sense" or "rule of thumb" utility, most anthropologists have concluded that calling a practice "magical" rather than "religious" implies more a pejorative judgement than a meaningful distinction. The distinction Weber makes between more and less rational religion is, I think, based more on just such a value judgement than on objective analysis.

Weber's causal explanation for the characteristics of artisan and lower middle-class religion is simply a variant of the basic thesis of his famous essay "The Protestant Ethic and the Spirit of Capitalism." In "Religion of Non-Privileged Classes," he outlines the argument as follows (p. 97):

> Yet it is still true in theory that the middle class, by virtue of its distinctive pattern of economic life, inclines in the direction of a rational ethical religion, wherever conditions are present for the emergence of a rational ethical religion. When one compares the life of a lower-middle-class person, particularly the urban artisan or the small trader, with the life of the peasant, it is clear that

> middle-class life has far less connection with nature. Consequently, dependence on magic for influencing the irrational forces of nature cannot play the same role for the urban dweller as for the farmer. At the same time, it is clear that the economic foundation of the urban man's life has a far more rational essential character, viz., calculability and capacity for purposive manipulation.

If, however, the notion of a radical distinction between magical and "rational" religion can no longer be accepted, it is hard to see how Weber's thesis can continue to be maintained. In any case, the idea that the economic life of peasants is somehow significantly less rational than that of merchants and artisans is, on the face of it, preposterous. What, after all, is so irrational about the techniques of cultivation, the selling of crops, buying seeds, taking credit from money-lenders, hiring laborers, and other regular facets of peasant life? Indeed, peasants must rationally plan for their economic survival over far longer periods than most artisans and merchants.

The basic reason for the primacy of artisans and other, mostly urban, members of lower-middle-class groups in the creation of new religious movements is in fact quite simple. It is the urban or semi-urban environment in which most artisans and small merchants and bureaucrats live. This gives them greater access to a variety of religious preachers, to education, to literacy and books, to a great variety of personal relations, and in general to the greater riches of urban culture. Once such new religious movements of urban artisans and lower-middle-class groups are established, however, they often quickly spread to incorporate the peasant populations of the rural hinterland.

In India, once the *nirguṇī* devotional movements of Kabīr, Raidās, Gurū Nānak, and Dādū were established in more or less urban settings, they made just such a quick spread into the countryside. From quite early times, the backbone of Gurū Nānak's Sikh movement has been the Jāṭ peasantry. Today most followers of Kabīr are low-caste peasants and agricultural workers. On the other hand, the followers of Raidās still come almost exclusively from the caste of leather workers (Chamārs) to which he belonged. They are numerous in both urban and rural areas. The present-day followers of Dādū seem to come mostly from lower-middle-class groups with a relatively high rate of literacy (Thiel-Horstmann 1989, 141). Daniel Gold (1992, 33) claims that there occurred a general "gentrification of sant tradition" in the eighteenth century as more persons from merchant communities such as Palaṭū became *nirguṇī* poets. Juergensmeyer's essay here shows how men from commercial castes have participated in the leadership of the Radhasoami movement. My own feeling is that while merchants such as Palaṭū and Dharmadās have played important roles in some *nirguṇī* sects, they never became a dominant influence in them, except perhaps in a few specific spiritual lineages. In any case, the more important fact is that Brahmin followers have been virtually nonexistent in all *nirguṇī* movements from the beginning until today.

The founders of most *saguṇī* devotional movements also seem to have come from more or less urban environments, but most were from Brahmin castes. The class and caste identities of the followers of *saguṇī* movements and sects, however, are extremely diverse. They include persons from a wide range of castes, from Brahmins to Śūdras, living in cities, towns and rural villages. Untouchables, however, are largely absent. Nonetheless, some Untouchables worship roughly the same gods at their own temples and shrines, a phenomenon that some anthropologists have described as a "replication" of more upper-caste religion (see Moffatt 1979; Lorenzen 1987a).

In some contexts, most notably in the Untouchable communities of South India studied by Michael Moffat and Louis Dumont, the use of this concept of replication may be partly justified. In the context of *nirguṇī* religion in North India, it is not. What *nirguṇī* religion does manifest, however, is a complex combination of borrowing from, imitation of, and rejection of the beliefs and practices of *saguṇī* religion. The essay of Uma Thukral in this book, for example, shows how some of the mostly Śūdra followers of Kabīr constructed a mythology of a series of avatar-like reincarnations of the non-anthropomorphic Satya-puruṣ that culminates in the incarnation of Kabīr, at the same time that these same followers rejected the standard avatars of Vishnu. Elsewhere (Lorenzen 1988), I have described how the Chaukā ritual of the Kabīr Panth borrows many elements from simple domestic rites such as the homonymous Chaukā and the Satya Nārāyaṇa Vrat, but transforms them into a public ritual of homage to the non-anthropomorphic Satya-puruṣ.

The most glaring theoretical weakness in Weber's analysis of the class affinities of religion is the lack of an adequate theory of ideology and the role it plays in determining the beliefs and practices of different religious movements. In this introduction I have attempted to offer some suggestions about the ways in which the articulation of social ideology and the formation of community identity have been key processes in the evolution and definition of *saguṇī* and *nirguṇī* religious traditions in North India. The essays included in this book all discuss topics relevant to these issues. Although the topics of the essays are quite varied, each makes a significant contribution to the understanding of the development of these contrasting religious currents.

Notes

1. Marx and Engels develop this concept in *The Communist Manifesto* and in *The German Ideology*. It has been ably criticized in *The Dominant Ideology Thesis* by Abercrombie, Hill, and Turner (1984). On the concept of ideology in general, I have found John Thompson's *Studies in the Theory of Ideology* (1984) to be quite useful.

2. Presumably Pandey would have much the same opinion of S. Pollock's (1993) more recent attempt to show that the cult of the avatar Rām arose in large part as an expression of Hindu hostility to the conquest and rule of India by Muslim kings.

3. See also the valuable discussion of this and other aspects of communalism and religious conflict by Veena Das in her introduction to *Mirrors of Violence: Communities, Riots and Survivors in South Asia* (1990, 1–36).

4. For a recent discussion of the role of demography in the creation of social and political conflict, see Homer-Dixon et al. 1993. From a somewhat different point of view, the anthropologist Marvin Harris (1991) has also made a case for the role of demography in conflict creation.

5. See Hawley's essay in this volume for a more extended discussion of this point. See also the recent discussion by D. Gold (1992), who emphasizes both sorts of differences and also attempts to distinguish important ideological differences among poets *within* the *nirguṇī* tradition.

6. Mādhava 1915: chap. 14, 29–55. See Lorenzen 1983, 103.

7. *Bhāgavata Purāṇa,* 11.5.36 and 38. See also verses 12.3.51–52. See also the passages on the Kali Yuga from Tulasīdās's *Rāmacharitamānas,* quoted by Lutgendorf in his essay here.

8. For bibliographic information about the hagiographies of all these sixteen saints and more, see my essay in this book.

9. The historians associated with the Annales school in France have produced important theoretical discussions of the ways in which the "popular" classes reinterpret and modify more upper-class culture, especially reli-

gion, in the process of consuming and appropriating it (see especially Chartier 1984).

10. See also Marglin and Mishra 1991; Rao 1991. It is somewhat strange that the historians of the subaltern school of Indian history led by Ranajit Guha have largely steered clear of research on religious movements, although they have done considerable work on the origins of communalism. See, however, the articles by Amin (1988) and Dube (1992).

11. The first of these passages is from a modern collection of his *dohās* (Tulasīdās 1991, 160). It is probably taken from the *Vinaya-patrikā*. In this *dohā* the terms used for "verses and songs" are *sākhī* and *sabadī*, both often used to refer to the verses of *nirguṇī* poets including Kabīr. It is likely that Tulasī is here alluding directly to Kabīr. The remaining two passages are from the *Rāmacharitamānas* (Tulasīdās 1989, 985).

Bibliography

Abercrombie, Nicholas, Stephen Hill, and Bryan S. Turner. 1984. *The Dominant Ideology Thesis*. London: George Allen & Unwin.

al-Biruni. 1964. *Alberuni's India*. Translated by Edward C. Sachau. Two vols. in one. Delhi: S. Chand & Co.

Amin, Shahid. 1988. "Gandhi as Mahatma." In *Selected Subaltern Studies*, edited by Ranajit Guha and Gayatri Chaktravorty Spivak, 288–348. New York: Oxford University Press.

Anderson, Perry. 1976/77. "The Antinomies of Antonio Gramsci." *New Left Review* 100:5–80.

Barraclough, Geoffrey. 1967. *An Introduction to Contemporary History*. Harmondsworth: Penguin Books.

Basham, A.L. 1989. *The Origins and Development of Classical Hinduism*. Edited and annotated by Kenneth G. Zysk. Boston: Beacon Press.

Bhāgavata purāṇa. 1971. Sanskrit text with an English translation by C. L Goswami. Gorakhpur: Gita Press. The translations in this essay are my own.

Bayly, C. A. 1985. "The Pre-history of 'Communalism'? Religious Conflict in India, 1700–1860." *Modern Asian Studies* 19, no. 2:177–203.

Chandra Bipan. 1984. *Communalism in Modern India*. New Delhi: Vani Educational Books (Vikas).

Chartier, Roger. 1984. "Culture as Appropriation: Popular Cultural Uses in Early Modern France." In *Understanding Popular Culture*, edited by Steven L. Kaplan, 229–53. Berlin: Mouton.

Das, Veena. 1990. "Introduction: Communities, Riots, Survivors—The South Asian Experience." In *Mirrors of Violence: Communities, Riots and Survivors in South Asia,* edited by Veena Das, 1–36. Delhi: Oxford University Press.

Devalle, Susana B.C. 1985. "Clandestine Culture of Protest in Colonial Situations." *Canberra Anthropology* 8, nos. 1-2:32–57.

Dube, Saurabh. 1992. "Myths, Symbols and Community: Satnampanth of Chhattisgarh." In *Subaltern Studies VII: Writings on South Asian History and Society,* edited by Partha Chatterjee and Gyan Pandey. Delhi: Oxford University Press.

Fuller, C.J. 1992. *The Camphor Flame: Popular Hinduism and Society in India.* Princeton: Princeton University Press.

Gold, Daniel. 1992. "What the Merchant-Guru Sold: Social and Literary Types in Hindi Devotional Verse." *Journal of the American Oriental Society* 112, no. 1:22–35.

Harris, Marvin. [1977] 1991. *Cannibals and Kings.* New York: Vintage Books.

Hawley, John Stratton. 1984. *Sur Das: Poet, Singer, Saint.* Delhi: Oxford University Press.

———. 1988. *Songs of the Saints of India.* New York: Oxford University Press.

Homer-Dixon, Thomas F., Jeffrey H. Houtwell, and George W. Rathjens. 1993. "Environmental Change and Violent Conflict." *Scientific American* 268, no. 2:16–23.

Kabīr. 1972. *Kabīr-bījak.* Edited by Shukdeo Singh. Allahabad: Nīlābh Prakāśan.

Lorenzen, David N. 1981. "The Kabir Panth: Heretics to Hindus." In *Religious Change and Cultural Domination,* edited by David N. Lorenzen. Mexico: El Colegio de México.

———. 1983. "The Life of Sankaracarya." In *Experiencing Siva: Encounters with a Hindu Deity,* edited by Fred W. Clothey and J. Bruce Long, 155–75. Columbia, Mo.: South Asia Books.

———. 1987a. "Traditions of Non-Caste Hinduism." *Contributions to Indian Sociology* 21, no. 2:263–83.

———. 1987b. "The Social Ideologies of Hagiography: Sankara, Tukaram, and Kabir." In *Religion and Society in Maharashtra,* edited by Milton Israel and N. K Wagle, 92–114. Toronto: University of Toronto, Centre for South Asian Studies.

———. 1988. "El *chauka* del muerto en el Kabir Panth." *Estudios de Asia y Africa* 23:445–68.

———. 1992. "Prahlad the Pious Demon in Saguni and Nirguni Tradition." Unpublished essay.

Mādhava. 1915. *Śaṅkaradigvijaya.* Poona: Ānandāśrama Press.

Marglin, Frédérique Apffel, and Purna Chandra Mishra. 1991. "Death and

Regeneration: Brahmin and Non-Brahmin Narratives." In *Devotion Divine: Bhakti Traditions from the Regions of India. Studies in Honor of Charlotte Vaudeville,* edited by Diana L. Eck and Francoise Mallison. Groningen: Ebert Forsten.

Moffatt, Michael. 1979. *An Untouchable Community in South India.* Princeton: Princeton University Press.

Mukta, Parita. 1991. "Mira among the Subordinated Communities in Rajasthan." Paper presented at the Simposio sobre Religion Popular y Disidencia Sociopolítica en el Norte de la India. Mexico City.

Nābhādās. 1969. *Śrībhaktamāl.* With Priyādās's commentary. 5th ed. Lucknow: Tejakumār Press.

Nandy, Ashis. 1990. "The Politics of Secularism and the Recovery of Religious Tolerance." In *Mirrors of Violence: Communities, Riots and Survivors in South Asia,* edited by Veena Das, 69–93. Delhi: Oxford University Press.

Pandey, Gyanendra. 1990. *The Construction of Communalism in Colonial North India.* Delhi: Oxford University Press.

Pollock, Sheldon. 1989. "Mimamsa and the Problem of History." *Journal of the American Oriental Society* 109, no. 4:603–11.

———. 1990. "From Discourse of Ritual to Discourse of Power in Sanskrit Literature." *Journal of Ritual Studies* 4, no. 2:315–45.

———. 1993. "Ramayana and Political Imagination in India." *Journal of Asian Studies* 52, no. 2:261–97.

Rao, Velcheru Narayana. 1991. "A *Ramayana* of Their Own: Women's Oral Tradition in Telugu." In *Many Ramayanas: The Diversity of a Narrative Tradition in South Asia,* edited by Paula Richman. Berkeley: University of California Press.

Schomer, Karine, and W. H. McLeod, eds. 1987. *The Sants: Studies in a Devotional Tradition of India.* Delhi: Motilal Banarsidass.

Scott, James C. 1990. *Domination and the Arts of Resistance: Hidden Transcripts.* New Haven: Yale University Press.

Thiel-Horstmann, Monika. 1989. ''Dādūpanthī Sermons." In *Living Texts from India,* edited by Richard K. Barz and Monika Thiel-Horstmann, 141–83. Wiesbaden: Otto Harrassowitz.

Thompson, John. 1984. *Studies in the Theory of Ideology.* Berkeley: University of California Press.

Tulasīdās. 1989. *Śrīrāmacharitamānas.* With the Hindi commentary of Hanumānaprasād Poddār. Gorakhpur: Gītā Press.

———. 1991. *Dohāvalī.* With the Hindi translation of Hanumānaprasād Poddār. Gorakhpur: Gītā Press.

Weber, Max. 1958. *The Religion of India: The Sociology of Hinduism and Buddhism.* Translated (from Weber's *Gesammelte Aufsätze zur*

Religionssoziologie, vol. 2) and edited by Hans H. Gerth and Don Martindale. New York: The Free Press.

———. 1963. *The Sociology of Religion*. Translated (from *Wirtschaft und Gesellschaft*, first published in 1922) by Ephraim Fischoff. Boston: Beacon Press.

Zelliot, Eleanor. 1981. "Chokhamela and Eknath: Two Bhakti Modes of Legitimacy for Modern Change." In *Tradition and Modernity in Bhakti Movements,* edited by Jayant Lele, 136–56. Leiden: E. J. Brill.

PART I
COMMUNITY IDENTITY

The Making of a Religious Paradox

Sikh, Khālsā, Sahajdhārī as Modes of Early Sikh Identity

Harjot Oberoi

> Otherwise we must all perish, for behind specific historical and cultural developments, East versus West, hierarchical versus egalitarian systems, individualism versus communism, lies the simple fact that man is both a structural and an anti-structural entity, who grows through antistructure and *conserves* through structure.
>
> —Victor Turner, *Dramas, Fields and Metaphors*

In official Sikh historiography it is commonplace to treat the rise, spread and consolidation of Sikhism as a single unitary whole. Such a narrative, like much else in academic discourse, seeks to dispel disturbing contradictions and synthesize Sikh experience in order to present it as a coherent whole, thus making the Sikh past, to use Nietzsche's illuminating term, "painless" for the minds of those who seek to live by it. A pseudosynthetic historiography comforts contemporary practitioners of faith that their present vision of the world and religious practices are simply a continuity of all that had been enunciated and established by the founders of the Sikh tradition. As a point of departure this essay questions this oversimplified linear growth model and argues for a series of highly complex ruptures, rapprochements and transitions that eventually resulted in what we today recognize as the modern Sikh religious community. In other words, prior to the formation of modern Sikhism in the late nineteenth century Sikh religious tradition traversed various modes of imagination and collective identity, some well known like the Khālsā but others relatively more obscure like the Sahajdhārī. In what follows, I examine these various forms of Sikh identity and their historical articulation, hoping that in doing so we may also begin to notice and document similar processes in the formation and dissemination of other religious communities in the subcontinent.

The dramatic political triumph of the Sikh movement in the second half of the eighteenth century gave the Sikhs a vast empire, but ironically the attainment of power and the process of state formation stalled the crystallization of a uniform Sikh identity. For much of its early history, the Sikh movement, in line with indigenous religious thinking and practices, with the exception of an understandable emphasis on the soteriological teachings of Gurū Nānak, had shown little enthusiasm for distinguishing its constituents from members of other religious traditions and establishing a pan-Indian community. Sikh notions of time, space, corporeality, holiness, mythology, kinship, societal distinctions, purity and pollution, gender, sexuality and commensality were firmly rooted in Indic cultural thinking. The territories the Sikhs lived in, the languages they spoke, the agrarian festivals they participated in, the ritual personnel they patronized and the symbolic universe of their rites of passage, all these were shared by numerous others in the Punjab.

In this sense the history of Sikh tradition is radically different from say, early Christianity, which from the very beginning had a dominant concern with demarcating believers and nonbelievers. Within less then a century of its formation, Christian church leaders had begun to excommunicate those within the church who transgressed its systematic beliefs.[1] Such modes of exclusion and publicizing boundaries of belief and practices were quite alien to the history of early Sikh tradition. However, gradually the elusiveness of Sikh identity begins to disappear and in its place there surface some concrete identity markers under the Sikh Gurūs.[2] Gurū Nānak's fundamental teaching had been that those who were keen on transcending the miseries that the constant cycle of birth and death entailed, should live in accordance with the Will of the Creator and spend their life on earth immersed in *nām simraṇ* or remembrance of the Divine Name. In his paradigm of interior religiosity there was no need for austerities, penances, pilgrimages or formal worship at established religious centers like mosques or temples. Nānak's successors, faced with a rapidly expanding constituency and changing social forces, found it hard to sustain his minimalist teachings. The initial Gurū period, following the death of Gurū Nānak, provided significant axes of identity for the embryonic Sikh Panth: allegiance to the person of Gurū Nānak and his nine successors; identification with their teachings *(bāṇī);* the foundation of congregations *(saṅgats);* the setting up of elaborate pilgrim centers at places like Goindwal and Amritsar; the convention of a communal meal *(laṅgar);* and the compilation by Gurū Arjan of an anthology, commonly known as the *Ādi Granth,* that ultimately acquired the status of a sacred text of the Panth.

This last development took place in 1603–4 and was to have far reaching consequences for Sikh history. Although in our present state of research it is hard to specify the factors that may have prompted the fifth Gurū of the Sikhs to collate an anthology of devotional literature, it is easier to discuss its impact. The production of the *Ādi Granth* turned the Sikhs, in Brian Stock's conceptual terminology, into a "textual community,"[3] that is, a group of people whose social and religious activities are centered around a text, and who seek to order their everyday life in close correspondence to what the text actually prescribes or what they believe it lays down. For such a textual community to exist, it is not essential that everyone be familiar with the contents of the text, as long as there are a few literate persons who can convey to the rest an understanding of the text. Gradually those who are beyond the pale of the text begin to be viewed as outsiders, unable to attain the same level of spirituality as those who imbibed the teachings of the text. Such texts are particularly attractive to those groups "hitherto dependent on oral participation in religion."[4] There were many in the early Sikh movement who for the first time in their lives would be making a transition from an oral culture to the world of a written culture as embodied in the *Ādi Granth.* The popularity of the early Sikh Panth among the unlettered peasants of central Punjab may in part be explained by the existence of a written text. A voiceless sector of Punjabi society could now both interpret and express its life experience through a highly structured written text.

What then constituted Sikh identity during the early Gurū period? A revealing insight into what was demanded of a Sikh and what were the possible meanings of being Sikh in the initial phase is provided by the *vārs* of Bhāī Gurdās Bhallā (c. 1558–1637), a nephew of the third Gurū Amar Dās, maternal uncle to Gurū Arjan, and a close associate of several of the Sikh Gurūs. Well known for his role as a scribe and amanuensis of the *Ādi Granth,* he also wrote exegeses on the compositions of the Sikh Gurūs. There can hardly be a better source for understanding early Sikh identity than the compositions of Bhāī Gurdās written in the late sixteenth and early seventeenth centuries.[5] According to them, it was required that a Sikh should rise before dawn, bathe, and recite the sacred compositions of the Sikh masters. In the early hours of the morning a Sikh should visit a *dharamsālā*, the place used for congregational singing and prayer in the locality, and participate in the activities of the assembled *saṅgat*. Bhāī Gurdās advised the faithful to be humble, courteous and charitable, to eat, speak and sleep in moderation, and, in doing so to transcend the human ego. Unrestrained human energies and chaotic living can lead to sorrow and pain. The ideal way to overcome these afflictions and lead a harmonious life is to practice the precepts of the Gurūs.[6] There are no explicit statements on an independent Sikh identity, but some of the most enduring themes in Sikh consciousness are enunciated: the centrality of belief and abiding faith in the person and utterances of the Sikh Gurūs; the need to visit the *dharamsālā,* and the repeated emphasis on the *saṅgat* as a body of practitioners in faith. Bhāī Gurdās is not completely unaware of boundaries. Frequently in his verse he belabors the point that Muslims are missing the correct path, and Hindus are caught in the snare of empty rituals and social inequalities.[7] The solution for him is a Sikh way of life, a distinctive third path to resolve human problems, and the ideal man is a *gurmukh,* a follower of the Sikh Gurūs and their doctrines.[8] These are not merely metaphysical differences but suggest a new *idiom,* a separate community of believers, and above all a reworking of the social order.

The implicit nature of Sikh identity in the writings of Bhāī Gurdās becomes explicit with the emergence and dissemination of the voluminous *janam-sākhī* literature. *Janam-sākhī* is the name given to mythical life narratives of Gurū Nānak. Although the earliest extant manuscript of this hagiographic tradition can only be dated back to 1658 C.E., it is quite clear from much recent research that these traditional story cycles in their written form go back to the early seventeenth century, and in their oral form they began to circulate as soon as the fame of Gurū Nānak spread by word of mouth in the Punjab.[9] The mythical narratives in the *janam-sākhīs*, while instructing and entertaining the faithful with wonder stories from an imagined life of Gurū Nānak, also simultaneously express the state of the Sikh Panth in the seventeenth century. One of the early anecdotes in the *janam-sākhī* tradition tells how Nānak was commissioned by God to launch his own distinct religious community in the world:[10]

> "Go, Nānak," [answered God]. "Your *panth* will flourish. The salutation of your followers shall be: 'In the name of the true Gurū, I fall at your feet.' The salutation of the Vaiṣṇava Panth is: 'In the name of Rāma and Krishna.' The salutation of the Sannyāsī Panth is: 'In the name of Nārāyaṇ, I bow before you.' The yogis' salutation is: 'Hail to the primal One.' The Muslims' cry is: 'In the name of the One God, peace be with you.' You are Nānak and your panth will flourish. Your followers shall be called Nānak-panthīs and their salutation will be: 'In the name of the true Gurū, I fall at your feet.' I shall bless your panth. Inculcate devotion towards Me and strengthen men's obedience to their dharma. As the Vaiṣṇavas have their temple, the yogis their *āsan*, and the Muslims their mosque, so your followers shall have their dharamsālā. Three things you must inculcate in your panth: repeating the divine Name, giving charity, and regular bathing. Keep yourself unspotted while yet remaining a householder."

Outside this particular anecdote that identifies the Sikh *dharamsālā* and salutations as key markers of communal self-identification, the very vigor and proliferation of this mythological form attests to the growing assertion of Sikh Panth. This hagiographic genre would obviously have not grown enormously during the seventeenth and early eighteenth centuries if there were not a growing awareness of issues of identity.

Having said all this, it must be stated categorically that Sikhs were still in the process of evolution and growth. The category, Sikh, was still flexible, problematic, and substantially empty: a long historical intervention was needed before it was saturated with signifiers, icons and narratives and made to lose its early fluidity. There was still critical space at the center and periphery of the community that had not been appropriated and shaded in with the colors of a dominant religious ideology. At best, the conventions developed during the early Gurū period epitomized what linguists term "denotation." In other words, the label Sikh, designated a section of the population, but this group did not as yet possess a "connotation," a corpus of identical secondary meanings.[11] Even the label Sikh had as yet not become hegemonic. Various categories were used by contemporaries to express an association with the Sikh movement: Nānak-panth, Gurmukh-panth, Nirmal-panth, Gur-sikh and Gurmukh-mārg. While the first term was related to the person of Gurū Nānak, the rest were drawn from his key doctrines. The multiplicitous terminology is a significant reflection of the evolving and unfixed nature of early Sikh identity. Eventually when Sikh identity became standardized all these terms were marginalized: for it is not possible to express a highly uniform consciousness through a plethora of categories.

While protagonists of modern Sikh identity would like to see in the collation of the *Ādi Granth* in 1603–4 under Gurū Arjan, a powerful public declaration of the separation of the Sikh Panth from other religious traditions, historically it is difficult to admit such an interpretation. It was not at all uncommon in medieval India to compile anthologies of devotional literature called *guṭkā*s or *pothī*s.[12] Their compilers and readers did not perceive them essentially to be statements of sectarian intent. While the *Ādi Granth* is the most voluminous and structured of the early-seventeenth-century devotional anthologies, features that may be explained by the institutional successes of the Sikh movement and its growing secular resources, it certainly was neither the first nor the last such collection. In this context the history of the Fatehpur manuscript, virtually unknown in the area of Sikh studies, is most instructive.[13] This anthology of devotional poetry was compiled in Rajasthan twenty-one years prior to the *Ādi Granth*. Although the bulk of it is made up of the compositions of the saint-poet Sūrdās, it also contains the works of thirty-five other poets, including such well-known names as Kabīr, Nāmdev, Ravidās, Parmānand and Kānhā. The *Ādi Granth* shares many features with the Fatehpur manuscript. Like the Fatehpur manuscript, the *Ādi Granth*, besides containing the writings of the Sikh Gurūs, also incorporates the song-verses of twenty-nine other mystics and poets including Sūrdās, Kabīr, Nāmdev, Ravidās and Parmānand. Both collections similarly draw on the works of people from a wide range of social backgrounds ranging from Brahmins to Untouchables, and also note the *rāga*s in which the verses should be sung. While there is no denying the fact that the *Ādi Granth* today has become a key cultural marker of Sikh ethnicity, it would be a gross misinterpretation to view it in the same vein for the early seventeenth century. Its heterodox textuality and diverse contributors were more a manifestation of the fluidity of Sikh identity rather than a signifier of exclusivity. If our objective is to understand the complex nature of the making of the modern Sikh identity, it will not do to mix contemporary Sikh understandings and practices with past patterns. Critically disaggregating the two and locating the precise period of their origins will certainly provide us with a much better feel for the evolution of the Sikh Panth.

The same fluidity and imprint of prevalent traditions that characterizes the *Ādi Granth* is also to be noticed, in fact in a much more amplified form, in the *janam-sākhīs* narrating the life, travels, and teachings of Gurū Nānak. When in the late sixteenth and early seventeenth centuries these mythical texts first came to be recorded in manuscripts, based on a substantial body of oral anecdotes, the mythologists freely borrowed from the rich storehouse of Puranic stories, Sufi hagiographies called *tazkiras* and Buddhist *jātaka* tales. Deploying other peoples' myths is, of course, a poor strategy for those who seek to stake out a bounded religious territory. As a consequence, there is no fixity to Nānak's image in the *janam-sākhī* stories: much like Puranic gods and goddesses, he is always being transformed. In one myth he is represented as an ascetic who lives on sand, in another he becomes a householder who toils for a living. One set of stories transport him to Mecca and another set take him to Hardwar. The Nānak of the *janam-sākhīs* is a saint who delights in mixing his dress code by making his own the styles of Muslim *pīrs* and Hindu ascetics, chooses companions and disciples whose castes and religions do not match and in his social transactions pays no heed to spatial and dietary religious taboos. It is perhaps to keep pace with this kaleidoscopic persona that mythologists, besides calling him Gurū, refer to him by various other religious titles: *pīr, sādh, bhagat, faqīr and darveś*.[14] The underlying logic behind these varied terms of address was to convey the ever transforming personality of Nānak.

Subject to their own historical conditions, Sikh mythmakers of the seventeenth century obviously had no compulsions to disengage themselves from their symbolic universe and concentrate on generating one single image of Nānak. A narrative tradition that represents an image of Nānak in constant flux also had manifold ramifications for early Sikh identity. Just as there is no fixed Gurū Nānak in the *janam-sākhīs*, similarly there was no fixed Sikh identity in the early Gurū period. Mythologists, after all, draw their materials and inspiration from the society they live in. One major impulse in the writing of the *janam-sākhīs* was that seventeenth-century Sikhs would cast their lives in the image of Nānak. But the converse is equally true. Gurū Nānak's mythical life was in part fashioned after the universe of seventeenth-century Sikhs.

It was a universe that was free of fixed identities. If the overall objective of the *janam-sākhī* mythologists is to be construed as the construction of an autonomous Sikh worldview they could not possibly have done a worse job. One *janam-sākhī* episode relates the story of a highly impoverished Sikh who in his efforts to buy food for Gurū Nānak and his companion simply cuts and sells his long hair.[15] Cutting bodily hair was to become one of the central Sikh taboos in the eighteenth century.

Those who argue for a distinct Sikh worldview, right from the initial Gurū period, often quote the following verse of Gurū Arjan:[16]

> I neither keep the Hindu fasts nor the Muslim Ramadan.
> I serve him alone who in the end will save me.
> My Master is both the Muslim Allah and the Hindu Gosāīn,
> And thus have I finished the dispute between the Hindu and the Muslim.
> I do not go on pilgrimage to Mecca.
> Nor bathe at the Hindu holy places.
> I serve the one Master, and none beside Him;
> Neither performing the Hindu worship nor offering Muslim prayer,
> To the formless One I bow in my heart,
> I am neither Hindu nor Muslim.

Taking the last line as the key to this hymn, many have argued that Gurū Arjan is proclaiming that Sikhs are neither Hindus nor Muslims and therefore are a distinct religious community.[17] There are several textual problems with this reasoning. As pointed out by Sahib Singh, the most eminent Sikh exegete of this century, Gurū Arjan wrote this hymn in a definite context: he was reflexively responding to an older verse by the poet-singer Kabīr, included in the *Ādi Granth*:[18]

> I have no disputes,
> For I have renounced the path of both the paṇḍit and the mullah.
> I weave and weave, to make my own way,
> And I sing of the Supreme Being to empty the self.
> All the codes inscribed by the paṇḍit and the mullah,
> Those I absolutely renounce and will not imbibe.
> Those pure of heart shall find the Supreme Being within,
> Kabīr says, in knowing the self, one realizes the Supreme Being.

Gurū Arjan in his exegetical verse cited earlier is thus only further enforcing Kabīr's thought. In line with a dominant theme in medieval *sant* poetics, both Kabīr and Arjan are speaking of rejecting the received Hindu and Muslim orthodoxies, not taking part in their formal modes of worship and pilgrimage, and finally announcing that the mystery of the Supreme Being is to be resolved in one's heart. It is oversimplistic to suggest that they are discounting one set of categories to embrace a new set of labels.

For the unwary, the quest for early Sikh identity can be full of pitfalls. Traditional Indian thought has always spoken eloquently of the impermanence of the world and human endeavors. Sikh Gurūs gave further credence to this very same idea in their vernacular poetry. This belief in the ephemeral nature of the universe has influenced not only the construction of personhood in South Asia, but as Wendy Doniger O'Flaherty has recently shown, also has pervaded its art and literature.[19] In such a cultural milieu, as even the Greeks, Muslims and Europeans who came to India were to realize, it was always difficult for any people to stay apart, and articulate permanent separate identities. But as the initial Gurū period comes to a sudden end with the execution of Gurū Arjan in 1606, the Sikh movement begins to show signs of partly moving beyond existing cultural traditions. A continuous Jāṭ influx into the Sikh movement throughout the seventeenth century and a protracted conflict with an increasingly hostile Mughal state, gradually gave rise to new Sikh cultural patterns.[20]

The Sikhs, to borrow a formulation of Michel Foucault, were faced with a "historical rupture." In the last decade of the seventeenth century, in the month of Baisakh, the last Sikh Gurū, Gobind Singh, instituted the Khālsā order. Due to the paucity of written records, it is hard to specify why the Khālsā order was established and it is even harder to specify the exact nature of the Khālsā under Gobind Singh. But one thing is clear, the Khālsā was instituted to finally end the ambiguities of Sikh religiosity. The Sikhs would henceforth, at least normatively, be able to distinguish between "us" and "others." These distinctions were inscribed through a highly complex cultural repertoire made up of inventive rituals, codes of conduct, mythical narratives and a whole new classificatory code of the body.

The first major signifier of the changing alignments and orientations within the Sikh movement came when the old term *sikh,* derived from the Sanskrit word *śiṣya* meaning disciple, came to be neglected and a new category, *khālsā,* came to the fore. Although in its popular usage today, the term *khālsā,* derived from the Arabic-Persian *khālis*, is seen to signify "pure," in the seventeenth century it was used by the Mughal bureaucracy as part of its revenue lexicon for lands that were under the direct supervision of the Crown.[21] The earlier Sikh Gurūs had appointed officials known as *masaṅds* to take care of rapidly expanding Sikh congregations across northern India. But Gobind Singh decided that these vicarlike officers had turned corrupt and he did away with the institution of *masaṅds*. In abolishing the authority of the *masaṅds* and their status as intermediaries, the Gurū decided to bring all the Sikh congregations directly under his own supervision. Just as the Mughal emperors directly supervised Crown lands *(khālis),* Gobind Singh, following the imperial revenue paradigm, undertook to establish a direct contact with his constituents without what was perceived to be a debilitating mediation on the part of the *masaṅds*. His reservations about the *masaṅds* become explicit when he writes:[22]

> If any one serve the *masaṅds*, they will say "Fetch and give us all thine offerings. Go at once and make a present of whatever property is in thy house. Think on us night and day, and mention not others even by mistake." If they hear of anyone giving, they run to him even at night, they are not at all pleased at not receiving. They put oil into their eyes to make people believe that they are shedding tears. If they see any of their own worshippers wealthy, they serve up sacred food and feed him with it. If they see him without wealth, they give him nothing, though he beg for it; they will not even show him their faces. *Those beasts plunder men, and never sing the praises of the Supreme Being.*

Towards the close of the seventeenth century Gurū Gobind Singh in his *hukam-nāmā*s (decrees) repeatedly asks Sikh *saṅgat*s across northern India to disassociate themselves from the *masaṅds*.[23] In addition, he instructs the Khālsā to maintain unshorn hair and also never to shave facial hair.[24] By the turn of the seventeenth century, the Khālsā was much more than a semantic category analogous to imperial revenue terminology: he was a new person with a concrete identity. His personhood came to be confirmed through an unusual initiation rite called *khaṇḍe kī pāhul,* the like of which had never existed before in South Asia. Most religious sects in the past had initiated their fresh constituents, and this appears to be the case with the Sikh tradition as well, through *charn amrit:* a ritual in which the toe of a guru was dipped into water that was then given to the new initiate to drink. Although we have no contemporary description of *khaṇḍe kī pāhul,* this much is certain, that it involved the use of a heavy double-edged sword and sanctified water. Whatever its precise form and sequence, this new initiation ritual and its distinctive religious imagery, gave the Khālsā a powerful symbolic grid on which to proclaim and affirm their new identity. To this new identity Gobind Singh gave further shape by commanding the Khālsā always to carry arms on his person, and by making hookah-smoking taboo.[25]

Sainapati, a court poet of Gobind Singh and his first biographer, suggests that it was the wish of Gobind Singh that all Sikhs turn Khālsā. There were spiritual incentives for turning Khālsā. In the initial Gurū period, the principal mode to attain deliverance from the miseries of the transmigratory cycle was *nām simraṇ*. Under Gobind Singh this goal could be attained by initiation into the Khālsā. The Khālsā now becomes "the institution of redemption."[26] A new theology comes to inform older Sikh institutions and concepts. The Sikh *saṅgat,* in Sainapati's view, is to be made up exclusively of the Khālsā. Similarly, only those who choose to identify with the Khālsā are *gurmukh*s, the rest are all *manmukh*s. Clearly the ideal Sikh is the Khālsā. Acceptance of Khālsā identity thus became a major yardstick to gauge an individual Sikh's loyalty to the Gurū. Those who were disloyal to the Gurū were susceptible to a series of dangers, including the possibility of never attaining salvation and turning up in hell. Despite the considerable incentives and fear of future accountability for those who did not become Khālsā, not all Sikhs became Khālsā. For instance, we know that some of Gobind Singh's closest disciples did not undergo the Khālsā initiation. Sainapati himself describes at length how in the capital city of Delhi a large number of Sikhs from the Brahmin and Khatrī castes strongly resisted the Khālsā identity. Fearful of becoming marginalized, and wanting to stick to the customary cultural codes of their own lineages and castes, they turned their wrath against their co-religionists who had become Khālsā. The new Khālsā were harassed, their shops were shut down, and an economic boycott imposed on them. In seeking to turn the fluid world of Indic religious identities upside down, the Khālsā from the very beginning found it rough going. Sainapati hints at this when he writes: "On one side stands the Khālsā and on the other the world."[27]

Boundaries and Transgression

While the paucity of sources alluded to earlier prevents a Geertzian "thick description," of the people who came to constitute the Khālsā, it is still possible to delineate the categories of thought, symbolic grids, ritual practices, in brief, the cultural systems of reference that came into prominence following the Khālsā "transformation." The Sikh movement now increasingly turned inward and became preoccupied with securing religious boundaries and distancing all those who were unwilling to accept these new boundaries. Just as in traditional Indian thought each varṇa is supposed to perform its dharma or moral duty, the Khālsā brought forth its own dharma. They gave it their own distinctive name: *rahit*. Texts which list these moral duties accordingly came to be known as *rahit-nāmās*. These codes of conduct cover all domains of human life ranging from such routine matters as how the Khālsā shall eat to laying down the nature of piety. In what follows I use the *rahit-nāmā* literature and allied texts to describe the production and reproduction of Khālsā cultural identity during the first three quarters of the eighteenth century. In tracing the distinctive Khālsā conception of the self, particular attention has been given to five interrelated themes: life-cycle rituals, tabooed behavior, the dynamics of transgression, the constitution of sacred space, and the makeup of the Other. The need for stating the rich cultural universe of the Khālsā has become all the more pressing because there are many who, based on their reading of English language sources such as census reports and army recruitment manuals, have begun to theorize that the Khālsā identity only became dominant in the late nineteenth century under British sponsorship.

Rituals constitute a key element in the construction of religious identity, particularly those that fall under the rubric of rites of passage. In all pre-industrial societies such rites tend to express the relationships between individuals and the society in which they live. Prior to the Khālsā transformation, Sikhs do not seem to have possessed a distinct set of life-cycle rituals. Given the fluid nature of Sikh identity, there was of course no need for such rituals. But in the eighteenth century the Khālsā Sikhs become keenly aware of the absence of distinct life-cycle rituals and took urgent steps to rectify the situation by introducing new rites, particularly to mark a person's birth, initiation and death.[28]

Soon after birth a child was to undergo his first initiation by being administered an initiatory drink made up of sweetened water touched by the feet of five Sikhs. His hair was to be left uncut and the newborn baby was to be given a name from the *Ādi Granth*. On the completion of the naming ceremony, the child was to be bathed in curds. There is an unmistakable quest for an exclusive Sikh identity in these postnatal rituals. I shall have more to say on the import of rituals later in this essay.

The next step, perhaps the most crucial stage, in the construction of an autonomous Khālsā identity was the initiation rite popularly known as *khaṇḍe kī pāhul*. The then accepted time for baptism was early teens, a period before a Sikh's hair had grown to its full length. The initiation ritual was presided over by five devout Sikhs who were recognized for their wisdom and who had been scrupulous in the observance of *rahit*. They were the ones who prepared the sanctified water for initiation by mixing water and sugar confectionary and stirring the preparation with a double-edged sword. All this was done to the recitation of five quatrains from the writings of Gurū Gobind Singh. Once the sanctified water was ready the neophyte was given it five times to drink, and five times it was sprinkled on his eyes and five times on his head. The initiated Sikh then declared: "*Vāhigurū jī kā Khālsā! Vāhigurū jī kī fateh!*" ("Hail to the Gurū's Khālsā! Hail the victory of the Gurū!"). The final part of baptism consisted of the initiate being instructed in *rahit*, particularly his obligation to bear arms and leave his hair uncut.[29]

In the evolution of different religious communities, marriage rituals have often proven useful to express a sense of collective identity. In the eighteenth century, Khālsā Sikhs certainly sensed the powerful potential of marriage rituals to convey separate identity, but seem to have failed in fully harnessing these rituals to their cause. Although the paucity of sources makes it difficult to make a definitive statement on the nature of Khālsā marriage rituals, all available evidence seems to indicate that the sequence of a Khālsā wedding mainly followed old caste and lineage customs prevalent among various sectors of Punjabi society: the bridegroom's marriage procession going to the bride's house after sunset, the performance of numerous wedding rituals under the supervision of Nāīs and Brahmins, and finally the couple to be wed circumambulating the fire, which, as a deity, stood witness to the marriage.[30] The early *rahit-nāmās* certainly do not seem to abolish the age-old marriage practices based on lineage and caste rules, except for a caveat that restricted the choice of bridegrooms to Sikhs alone. The only way a non-Sikh bridegroom was acceptable was if he agreed to undergo an initiation.[31]

The final set of rituals that Khālsā Sikhs appropriated in the eighteenth century were mortuary rituals. The *rahit-nāmās* sternly dictated that a death in the family was not to be followed by public lamentations.[32] The body of the deceased was to be washed and the head was to be left unshaved. During the period of mourning, there was to be a complete reading of the *Ādi Granth,* singing of *kīrtan* and distribution of charitable offerings. A key rite was slowly being suffused with Khālsā doctrines and symbols.

What are the conceptual implications of these newly instituted rites of passage? Ritual enactments are a condensed statement of the most deeply held values of a society. As metaphors of collective consciousness they distinguish between outsiders and insiders by erecting religious boundaries, communicate spatial and temporal notions and endow people with a significant sense of personal identity. The symbols, gestures, formulae and emotions that make up a ritual performance help transform the chaos and vicissitudes of human existence into an ordered and meaningful sequence. More simply put, rituals help people overcome indeterminacy in life, endowing social life with a certainty which it does not otherwise possess.[33] In this sense the Khālsā life-crisis rituals were useful not only in persuading others in the Punjab of the distinct nature of Sikh identity, but also in helping the Khālsā Sikhs to face the unsettled and chaotic conditions of eighteenth-century Punjab, following the decline of the Mughal state and incessant Afghan invasions. The stereotyped, highly repetitive and stylized form of rituals helped generate a sense of orderliness and security among the otherwise highly disordered and dispersed Khālsā. It is worth noting that the meaning of the term *saṃskār,* widely used in lay parlance to denote life-cycle rituals, is to "prepare," "refine" and "complete."[34] In other words these rituals (*saṃskār*s) have a transformative power that distills and completes what is undistilled and incomplete in human life.

The Khālsā rituals at birth, initiation and death were to gradually turn the highly undistilled and fluid Sikh identity into a more distilled and enduring form. For instance, the various steps in Khālsā initiation ritual, the liminal state of an individual before being initiated, the separation of the neophyte from the rest on the occasion of baptism, the preparation of sanctified water, the readings from Sikh scriptures and instructions for future behavior, all these endowed an individual with a new, bounded identity, one that he would only share with others who had been initiated in the same mode and were committed to follow the specific *rahit* code of conduct. The ritual of baptism therefore made it possible for the Khālsā Sikhs to think and act in terms of "us" and "them." Prior to the establishment of this ritual, it had been difficult for Sikhs to demarcate themselves from the rest of civil society. Now they came to establish far more secure communal boundaries.

But the boundaries established by the rites of passage were not sufficient. They were supplemented in the *rahit-nāmās* by a long inventory of tabooed behavior. To qualify for Khālsā Sikh identity an individual had to refrain from certain actions and behavior that may be permitted to others in Punjabi society. The most famous of these tabooed actions was the injunction against shaving hair. Other lesser known actions that were barred consisted of bathing at a spot where washermen washed clothes, sleeping or bathing naked, plucking white hairs, having sexual intercourse with a Muslim woman, speaking while defecating, eating food left by a woman, accepting the authority of a Muslim religious figure, offering prayers at a tomb or a cenotaph and undertaking a visit to a Hindu temple or a Muslim mosque.

While it is possible to find symbolic, religious, or pragmatic reasons for some of these injunctions, they cannot all be fully explained. For instance, the prohibition against consuming the leftovers of a woman can be understood as a precaution against pollution, and the varied injunctions against visiting non-Khālsā religious places was to give shape to distinctive sacred boundaries. But it is not possible to explain each and every item of the vast list of tabooed behavior. It is difficult to understand the ban on speech while a person was defecating. Despite such gray areas, for our purposes what needs to be underscored is that the *rahit-nāmā* literature by prohibiting a section of society from performing certain actions, helped distinguish Khālsā Sikhs from the rest of Punjabi society.

It is hard to sustain separate religious identity without distinctive sacred space. Khālsā Sikhs in the eighteenth century showed deep awareness of this fact. They established firm control over the central shrine in Amritsar and turned it into a major site of pilgrimage. The duties of the Khālsā Sikhs in relation to sacred space and its management were clearly enunciated in the *rahit-nāmās*.[35] Wherever Khālsā Sikhs resided they were expected to set up a *dharamsālā* and assemble there regularly to read and sing from scriptures. On entering a *dharamsālā* a Khālsā Sikh was required to prostrate and make offerings of flowers, fruit or money. There was to be no talking while the scriptures were being read or sung. The person in charge of the *dharamsālā* was to be highly virtuous, celibate and knowledgeable in the scriptures. It was his duty to conduct worship, officiate at religious rituals, and instruct the Khālsā boys in the locality in the contents of the *Ādi Granth* and reading and singing from it.

Khālsā Sikhs in their quest for an exclusive identity and distinct religious boundaries were further assisted by state polity in eighteenth-century North India. In seeking to usurp power from a predominantly Muslim administration, Khālsā Sikhs began to view all Muslims with hostility and suspicion. One mid-eighteenth-century *rahit-nāmā* laid down extensive injunctions against social, cultural or religious contact with Muslims.[36] A moratorium was placed on Khālsā Sikhs' accepting water from a Muslim, eating food offered by a Muslim, or sleeping in their company. In disassociating from the Muslims, Khālsā Sikhs enhanced their sense of separateness and the category Muslim became a powerful signifier of Otherness. Besides Muslims, there were at least twelve other groups with whom the Khālsā Sikhs were to have no contact. Most notable among these reprobate groups were all those who had dared challenge the orthodox line of succession of ten Sikh Gurūs.[37] But it also included others like ascetics who wear caps, naked sadhus who coat themselves with ashes, mendicants who mat their hair, those who shave their heads and those who do not wear turbans.[38] By creating Khālsā identity in opposition to certain groups, a firm distinction could be fostered between "us" and "them."

From the above consideration of Khālsā rites of passage, tabooed behavior, the nature of sacred space and the formation of Others, it is possible to conclude that by the second half of the eighteenth century a distinctive Khālsā normative order had emerged. A considerable distance had to be traversed from being non-Khālsā to a Khālsā Sikh and those who covered this distance in terms of doctrines, rituals, discourses of the body, management of space and negation of various prevalent religious and cultural identities could look upon themselves as a distinct religious formation. Contemporary records—accounts by early Europeans, Persian chronicles and Sikh hagiographic literature—all point towards Khālsā identity gradually becoming hegemonic within Sikh tradition.

The Khālsā cultural formation was not all new. There were elements in it drawn from the early Sikh tradition. Two key Khālsā doctrines of the eighteenth century—the idea of the *Gurū Granth* and the belief in *Gurū Panth*—illustrate very well Khālsā linkages with the past. The Khālsā Sikhs perhaps encountered their first critical test when the line of human Gurūs ended in 1708, with the death of Gobind Singh. No longer was there the possibility of a face-to-face encounter between the master and the disciple. The guiding hand of a supreme religious authority that had played such a creative role in the young Panth's history ceased to function. In the unsettled conditions of the eighteenth century the Khālsā Sikhs were in desperate need of a cohesive principle that would replace the institution of the living Gurūs. Fortunately for them, there had emerged from the time of Nānak the doctrine of an eternal Gurū. This eternal Gurū, as the writings of Aṅgad reveal, was no different from God. In other words, the figure of a Sikh Gurū for their early disciples was an embodiment of God, and ordinary mortals wishing to come into contact with God could do so through the Sikh Gurūs or their mystical utterances popularly known as *bāṇī*.[39] This *bāṇī* was the voice of God, and like a Gurū it could bring man and God together. Since the *Ādi Granth* was a repository of this *bāṇī*, it logically assumed the status of an eternal Gurū. For a social historian, it is unimportant whether Gobind Singh prior to his death formally declared the *Ādi Granth* to be a Gurū or not.[40] If history is a social process, then what is crucial for our purpose is that an older principle of Gurū Granth or scriptural Gurū was successfully put into service by the Khālsā Sikhs in the eighteenth century. In the absence of any clear leadership within the Sikh ranks, the doctrine of Gurū Granth served as a useful substitute for the line of Sikh Gurūs by providing much needed cohesion to a Panth faced with political turmoil and serious internal dissensions.

The highly complex doctrine of Gurū Granth took root in unison with a more simple concept, that of Gurū Panth. This principle too had emerged in the time of the early Sikh Gurūs. With the numerical and geographical expansion of the Sikh movement, it became increasingly difficult for the members of the growing Panth to establish direct physical contact with the Gurū. A way out was found in the belief that the Gurū was present wherever the Sikh *saṅgat* or congregation assembled. Bhāī Gurdās in his influential writings speaks of the presence of the Gurū in the *saṅgat*, and early *janam-sākhīs* also echo the same sentiment.[41] Gurū Amardās suggests that one can find God within the *saṅgat.*[42] By the early seventeenth century, the *saṅgat* had become a focus of Sikh piety, and what was decided within the *saṅgat* was seen to represent the will of the Gurū. This belief in the Gurū working through the *saṅgat* was the direct precursor of the eighteenth-century doctrine of Gurū Panth. When in 1708 at the death of Gobind Singh there was no one to succeed him to the office of the Gurū, the Panth turned into his collective successor. This was to be an abiding belief of the Khālsā Sikhs, one that came to be very useful in waging the eighteenth-century battles for collective survival and political sovereignty.

Paradox: The Khālsā/Sahajdhārī Duality

The increasing political power of the Khālsā allowed it to begin recasting Sikh society after its own image. During the course of the eighteenth century, tens of thousands of Sikhs took to the Khālsā identity, some in pursuit of worldly power and others out of deep religious convictions. The dramatic story of the political triumph of the Khālsā Sikhs begins to unfold in the early eighteenth century with Bandā Bahādur (1670–1716), a prominent disciple of Gobind Singh from his last days in central India. Under Bandā a bloody offensive was launched to uproot the Mughal state in the Punjab.[43] The rural poor, the urban underprivileged and others who persisted on the margins of the Punjabi society readily responded to the Khālsā campaign to turn the existing world upside down. Reflecting on the nature of peasant insurrection under Bandā, Chetan Singh, in his important study of the period, notes:

> Whatever else they may have been, the rebellions of the early eighteenth century were also very obviously an expression of the wrath of the lower classes. Insofar as the Sikhs were concerned, the rejection of the caste differentiation by the Gurūs had attracted a very large number of low caste followers. In their challenge to the established social hierarchy, the Sikhs under Banda, apparently welcomed in their ranks any and every section of society that chose to join them, though these invariably belonged to the lower social orders.[44]

For seven eventful years no efforts were spared by the peasant armies of Bandā to obliterate all vestiges of Mughal control over Punjab.

Armed with hardly anything, except the powerful teachings of the Sikh Gurūs and an ordained sense of victory, they wrote a new chapter in the history of the Khālsā Sikhs. They dismembered a whole range of intermediaries, who extracted the much hated land revenues for the state and often acted as instruments of oppression. Large estates were dissolved and their lands parceled out to the peasantry.[45] It is to this period that we may trace what Clive Dewey calls the "flatness of the Punjabi society."[46]

The newly attained liberties under Bandā did not last for long. By 1716 the Mughal state managed to regain political authority in the Punjab. The Sikh movement suffered a serious setback with the execution of Bandā and his major collaborators. In its post-Bandā phase the Khālsā Sikhs sought to reestablish their power by regrouping into political units called *misl*s. By the mid-eighteenth century there were, according to popular tradition, twelve Sikh *misl*s, of which eleven were concentrated to the north of river Sutlej and only one, the Phulkain, to the south in the Malwa. Unequal in size and resources, each *misl* sought to maximize its territorial possessions. Whenever a *misl* acquired territories, the towns, villages and lands were divided among those who had aided in the conquest. First to be rewarded was the chief, and subsequently each man, in proportion to his efforts and the number of cavalry troops gathered, was given a *pattī* or parcel of land. Each member of the *misl* took his *pattī* as a co-sharer and held it in absolute freedom.[47]

Normally each *misl* acted on its own. When faced with a common danger they acted in unison. Twice a year the leading representatives of all the *misl*s gathered at Amritsar, on the occasion of the Baisākhī and Diwālī festivals. Assembled in the holy city, they deliberated collective action or found solutions to the problems faced by the Sikh Panth. Sikhs who assembled on the occasion of the biannual gatherings passed resolutions called *gurmattā*s, literally meaning "a resolution endorsed by the Gurū," for the Gurū was thought to be present among the faithful when they deliberated in the presence of the *Ādi Granth*.[48] The sacredness of the site where the meetings were held, combined with the presence of the *granth,* endowed the *gurmattā*s with a sacred character. The proceedings at Amritsar were seen to be those of the *sarbat-khālsā* or the corporate body of the Sikhs. Clearly all the Sikhs did not congregate at one point; the meaning of the *sarbat-khālsā* must be found in its ritual significance.

It is essential that historians do not drain ritual practices of all their symbolic content and interpret them only as technical modes to legitimize the fortunes of the Sikh chiefs or charters of aggrandizement. While the *gurmattās* may have served these aims, they also generated through their practice, vision and sacred nature the conditions for the existence of the Sikh Panth. People do not organize all their lives around self-interest alone, as some historians would like to assert. Often individuals seek a purpose and meaning for their lives. The history of Khālsā Sikhs is rich in both instances. We need to proceed with caution when we translate the key ideas or practices of one historical epoch into another. The deep meanings generated by the practices of the *gurmattā* and *sarbat-khālsā* contributed to the consolidation of the Sikh movement. By the 1770s, the Khālsā Sikhs controlled the Mughal *subā* of Punjab and large portions of the provinces of Multan and Shahjahanabad. The solidarity infused through the rituals of *gurmattās* and the *sarbat-khālsā* was a crucial ingredient in the making of the Khālsā Sikhs.

Congruent with the processes of state formation went the trappings of royal power. *Misl* chiefs and those who shared power with them now began to use titles, *khilats* (costumes of honor), kettledrums and banners, the minting of coins, appointment of subordinate administrative and military officials and patronage of musicians and painters.[49] Administrative functionaries in Sikh principalities were rewarded with *jāgīrs*; similar grants were also made to religious leaders, sacred institutions and the much feared Akālīs. By the last decade of eighteenth century Khālsā Sikhs managed to replicate the earlier Mughal state in pomp, power, and ideas of kingship.

In the mid-eighteenth century not all Sikhs were happy with the dramatic triumph of the Khālsā and the Khālsā Sikh identity becoming dominant. In the apocalyptic vision of Kesar Singh Chibber, a Brahmin Sikh, the political power of the Khālsā only spelled doom for the Sikh tradition. Writing in 1769, he prophesied that in another ten years all would be chaos and nothing would be left of the Sikh tradition in the Punjab.[50] Even the *Ādi Granth* would disappear from circulation. For him the newly founded Khālsā principalities were kingdoms of sin. On attaining territorial control, the Khālsā Sikhs had quickly turned their backs to the fundamental teachings of the Sikh Gurūs. For Kesar Singh Chibber power and piety do not go together. Many of the Khālsā Sikhs were deceitful and evil and it was futile to expect them to live up to their commitments or follow any morality. It was certain that they would end in hell. Despite detractors like Chibber and considerable opposition from existing power blocs, Khālsā Sikhs went from one success to another and Khālsā identity continued to attract fresh recruits in increasing numbers.

Paradoxically, with the Khālsā mode becoming hegemonic within the Sikh tradition, it also simultaneously came to be accepted that there were alternate ways of being Sikh. The Sikh Panth was not coterminous with the Khālsā, and it was possible to be a Sikh without being a Khālsā.[51] All those Sikhs who did not turn into Khālsā, and they certainly do not seem to have been in insignificant numbers since the days of Gobind Singh, were often referred to in mid-eighteenth century as *Sahajdhārīs*.[52] Although in our present state of research it is difficult to provide a precise list of those who constituted the Sahajdhārī sector within the Sikh tradition, it can be said with confidence that, among others, it consisted of those called Nānak-panthīs and the Udāsīs.

The Sahajdhārī Sikhs in many ways totally inverted Khālsā categories of thought and religious boundaries. Whereas Khālsā Sikhs maintained unshorn hair, Sahajdhārīs cut their hair; Khālsā Sikhs had to undergo an initiation, Sahajdhārīs did not; Khālsā Sikhs were obliged to carry arms, Sahajdhārīs had no such normative injunction to obey; Khālsā Sikhs were prohibited the use of tobacco, Sahajdhārī Sikhs smoked;[53] Khālsā Sikhs accepted a line of nine successors after Gurū Nānak, Sahajdhārī Sikhs often had a radically different version of the line of succession; and while Khālsā Sikhs began to recognize the *Ādi Granth* as Gurū, Sahajdhārī Sikhs were not given to accept a textual anthology as Gurū and instead favored living human Gurūs.

The recent discovery of a document dating back to 1783 is a good indicator of how the categories Sahajdhārī, Nānak-panthīs and Udāsī overlapped in middle period Sikh tradition. This *gurmukhi* document was compiled by a Nānak-panthī Sikh and was primarily addressed to the head of an Udāsī establishment in Bihar, but it also sought to instruct Sahajdhārī Sikhs. Given the major importance of this document—for it not only exemplifies the close correspondence in the religious identities of Sahajdhārīs, Nānak-panthīs and Udāsīs, but it also illuminates the normative order they all were asked to subscribe to—it is reproduced almost in its entirety below:

> A guidance and direction in the road to salvation, of Bawa Mansha Rām *faqīr,* given to Rāmgarela Rām in 1783. It behooves the

> *mahant* of the Udāsī establishment in Rajgir to remain celibate; be truthful and contented; spread the Panth; share his means with others; recite the Name of the True One with every breath; not to forget the true teachings of the Sikh Gurūs, daily recite *gurbāṇī* [the Gurū's words]; unfold the pages of the granth; not to deviate from the service of the sadhus and the members of the congregation; take the bath early in the morning; repeat the Name; refrain from vices; tell the people of the magnitude of the name of the Gurū; go to the houses of the Sikhs and instruct them to recite the Name; practice charity; perform ablutions; be benevolent and compassionate; observe religious duties; practice contentment and observe the laws of good conduct and morality; root out differences between the high and low; serve the saints and priests of every tradition; observe no discrimination; not to defame any deity; not to obliterate the propriety of conduct towards the Gurū Sikh and the Chelā Sikh; to preserve the dignity of the two *gurpurabs*; continue the distribution of *kaṛāh parśād;* not to stop rendering service to the saints and sadhus on the occasion of the *lound* [intercalary month] fair; to continue the preaching of the Sikh tenets. The first duty of the Sahajdhārī Sikhs is to repeat the True Name and recite the *gurmantara*. The pure Sikh is he who regards the Gurū's words of supreme importance and does not harbor hostility to anyone. No one should remain idle. It is obligatory to learn the *gurmukhī* script. Be not proud and arrogant. Remove the sufferings of the distressed ones. Do not practice deceit and hypocrisy. Give up greed and avarice. The *mahant* of the Udāsī establishment in Rajgir will have to observe these rules. The mahant, who will abide by these rules, will not invite the punishment of the god of death on him, and he will have an easy access to heaven.[54]

If there had been fundamental differences among Sahajdhārī, Nānakpanthī and Udāsī Sikhs, it is highly unlikely that the above quoted text could have ever been written. Both in the sequence of its production and contents, it supports our contention that non-Khālsā Sikhs may be meaningfully considered under the category Sahajdhārī, and where possible we further explore and specify its plural constituency.

The differences between Khālsā and Sahajdhārī categories of thought and concepts of the Sikh person can be better understood by looking in some detail at the Udāsīs, perhaps the most conspicuous and widely patronized segment among the Sahajdhārī Sikhs. Although historians continue to dispute whether the Udāsīs originated with Sirī Chand, the eldest son of Gurū Nānak, or Bābā Gurdittā, the eldest son of sixth Gurū Hargobind, of greater significance here are some of the doctrines, religious practices, and functions of the Udāsīs.[55] The word *udāsī* is derived from the Sanskrit *udās*, meaning detachment, and can signify renunciation or indifference to worldly concerns. The Udāsīs first seem to have come into prominence during the seventeenth century. Early Sikh tradition records ten major Udāsī orders.[56] Members of these orders gradually began to manage key Sikh shrines across northern India, including the Harimandir for a short period of time, and also set up their own establishments in pilgrimage centers like Amritsar, Hardwar and Banaras.

From these rapidly expanding shrines and establishments Udāsīs enunciated a model of Sikhism that was at considerable divergence from that of the Khālsā Sikhs. The differences between the two can be briefly conceptualized by contrasting their attitude at three levels: depletion of hair, dress code and mode of salvation. The Udāsīs did not consider the Khālsā *rahit-nāmās* to be binding on them and accordingly, unlike the Khālsā Sikhs, felt free to cut their hair. Even when the Udāsīs maintained long hair, they would mat it rather than knot it under a turban like the Khālsā Sikhs. Whereas the Khālsā Sikhs laid great emphasis on wearing a *kachh* and sporting arms, the items respected by the Udāsīs were quite different. An inventory of their dress code would include items like a cap, a rosary of flowers, a cotton bag, a gourd vessel, ash for smearing on the body, a chain to tie around the waist and a deer skin to perform *haṭha yoga* on. In appearance perhaps no two persons would have looked more different than a Khālsā Sikh and a Udāsī in the eighteenth century.

Differences in physical appearance invariably reflect much deeper distinctions in thought and modes of being. This certainly holds true for the Khālsā and Udāsī Sikhs. In the worldview of the former, salvation could be attained by living in the world and pursuing secular objectives like political power or accumulation of resources like agrarian land. These secular objectives, however, had to be attained within a particular framework of beliefs and religious practices. Paramount among these beliefs was the Khālsā normative order discussed at length in an earlier section of this essay. Salvation was assured to all those who subscribed to Khālsā identity.

Udāsīs interpreted the issue of salvation differently. For them secular pursuits were not compatible with the goal of human liberation, and to achieve this objective one had to renounce the world. Starting with this postulate the Udāsīs ended up by rejecting a whole series of doctrines and practices which were very dear to the Khālsā Sikhs. In the eyes of the Udāsīs, any individual could become an equal of the Sikh Gurūs by following certain mystical practices. Such heterodox thinking ran contrary to the popular Khālsā belief that no individual could match the divine status of the Sikh Gurūs. Ordinary Sikhs could only emulate the Gurūs, but never themselves turn into Gurūs, for the Gurūs were indistinguishable from God. The Udāsīs, by veering towards a gnostic position, made suspect the orthodox line of succession from Gurū Nānak to Gobind Singh and encouraged figures both within their own tradition and outside it to be viewed as Gurū.[57] But perhaps the most radical attitudinal difference between the two was on the issue of liberation. For Khālsā Sikhs considered *khaṇḍe kī pāhul* and the resulting corporate identity to be a major prerequisite for liberation from the transmigratory cycle. Udāsīs did not endorse this view and encouraged their own esoteric methods to overcome the constant cycle of birth and death.

This description of radical differences between Khālsā and Sahajdhārī modes of identity raises the apparent question: why after the Khālsā transformation was there a duality in Sikh identity? It is not easy to answer this question, as, within Sikh historiography, the post-Gobind Singh history of the Sikhs is supposed to be simply a history of the expansion and eventual triumph of the Khālsā. At one stage or another all Sikhs are supposed to have become Khālsā, and if some did not, official Sikh history suggests that they were simply aberrations, and assumes that there is no particular need for a historian to spend time finding explanations for what, after all, was deviant behavior. Contrary to this conventional wisdom, contemporary evidence points to a different trajectory. During the eighteenth century, there was considerable heterogeneity in Sikh identity and by recognizing and dealing with it, in the end we will have a much better understanding of the complex evolution of Sikh identity.

At a pragmatic level, it is not hard to understand the duality in Sikh identity. The Khālsā Sikhs were a tiny segment of Punjabi society. In their quest for political power they could use all the allies they could get; and what better allies than those who associated with the

Sikh tradition? The Sahajdhārīs may not have subscribed to the Khālsā model, but even the most heterodox among them, for instance the Udāsīs, recognized Nānak as a Gurū, read and recited verses from the *Ādi Granth,* served in large numbers as custodians of important Sikh shrines, and, perhaps most importantly, wrote mythical narratives of Sikh Gurūs and textual commentaries on Sikh scriptures.

On a more conceptual level, the enigma of plurality in Sikh identity during the eighteenth century may be accounted for by the late Victor Turner's suggestion that social life, particularly religious traditions, proceed through a continuous dialectic between two contrasting social models: "structure and anti-structure."[58] One model, according to Turner, is

> of society as a structure of jural, political, and economic positions, offices, statuses, and roles, in which the individual is only ambiguously grasped behind the social persona. The other is of society as a communitas of concrete idiosyncratic individuals, who, though differing in physical and mental endowment, are nevertheless regarded as equal in terms of shared humanity. The first is of a differentiated, culturally structured, segmented, and often hierarchical system of institutionalized positions. The second presents society as an undifferentiated, homogeneous whole, in which individuals confront one another integrally, and not as "segmentalized" into statuses and roles.[59]

There is a constant exchange and play between the forces of structure and antistructure or communitas.[60] While the structure distrusts ambiguities and seeks to generate orderliness and routinization in a society, the antistructure enjoys ambiguity and provides elements for partially reversing the forces of order and for questioning its dominant categories. Out of structure flow rules, pragmatism and a stake in this-worldly activities. On the other hand, those inhabiting the antistructural domain tend to be more unsettled, lax in rules, much more concerned with speculation and philosophical ideas and often manifest an otherworldly attitude, which may easily crystallize into asceticism. This does not mean that antistructure destroys identities or negates society, it simply liberates people from the need to conform to the dominant identity and ideology.

In the dialectic between the force of structure and antistructure, it is not uncommon for one to merge into another, depending very much on particular historical conditions. The exchange between these two models can be highly rejuvenative and enriches a religious tradition. The two do not essentially exist in a pure form and may often coexist. Victor Turner comments: "These contrary processes go on in the same religious field, modifying, opposing, and being transformed into one another as time goes on."[61] The early history of the Sikh movement very well exemplifies these transformative processes and the correlations binding them. The Sikh movement, almost from its inception, but particularly during the eighteenth and much of the nineteenth century, oscillated between structure and antistructure. The interface between the two, if I may simplify, generated much of the middle-period Sikhism, between the end of the orthodox line of Sikh Gurūs with Gobind Singh and the establishment of British rule in the Punjab. Only by recognizing these two poles can we make sense of how two radically different religious identities, that of the Khālsā Sikhs and the Sahajdhārīs, could coexist.

Conclusion

The argument presented here can be summarized as follows. Early Sikh tradition did not seek to fully disengage its constituents from the society they lived in. A few distinctive religious doctrines and cultural practices that did emerge among the Nānak-panthīs or followers of Nānak were in themselves not pronounced enough to push Sikhs towards a separate religious identity. But two major developments in the seventeenth century led to a rupture in the Sikh tradition: first, a massive influx of Jāṭs into the Sikh movement and, second, the Islamic orientation of Mughal polity, particularly under Emperor Aurangzeb (1618–1707). By the early eighteenth century societal forces coupled with the religious initiatives of Gobind Singh had endowed Sikhs with a distinctive religious identity in the form of the Khālsā. Unlike the Nānak-panthīs the Khālsā Sikhs wished to be viewed as a separate religious entity. To achieve this goal, among other things, they formulated their own code of conduct, a novel form of initiation and some new rites of passage. Older Sikh religious resources, like mythical narratives and texts, were quickly tapped and appropriated by the Khālsā Sikhs to proclaim their new identity. The best instance of this act of appropriation is the doctrine of Gurū Granth, a concept which grew out of Sikhs earlier becoming a "textual community."

The political ascendancy of Khālsā Sikhs in mid-eighteenth-century Punjab helped in turning their interpretation of Sikh doctrine, ritual and history into what Michel Foucault most appropriately termed an "episteme." As the Khālsā episteme became hegemonic, its constituents did not seek to abolish other modes of identity within the Sikh tradition. Paradoxically, the increase in number of Khālsā Sikhs did not imply a corresponding reduction in the number of Sahajdhārīs. Our contemporary sources in the form of mythical literature and records of revenue grants to religious establishments, point towards a highly vibrant non-Khālsā tradition. It is this extraordinary fusion of Khālsā and non-Khālsā identities, which mark out the Sikh tradition in the late eighteenth century from what was to follow under colonial rule. This plurality of religious identities seems to have resulted both because of pragmatic and semantic reasons. Khālsā Sikhs in their drive to carve out an empire for themselves soon realized that for their project to succeed they required allies both within and outside the Panth. An internal alliance was quickly forged with the Sahajdhārīs, and their religious culture was conceded to be legitimate for it provided both pragmatic and semantic resources for the expansion of Sikh religion in the Punjab and beyond.

Notes

1. Robin Lane Fox, *Pagans and Christians* (London: 1988), pp. 501–4.
2. The ten Gurūs were: Gurū Nānak (1469–1539), Gurū Aṅgad (1504–52), Gurū Amar Dās (1479-1574), Gurū Rām Dās (1534–81), Gurū Arjan (1563–1606), Gurū Hargobind (1595–1644), Gurū Har Rāi (1630–61), Gurū Har Kriṣaṇ. (1656–64), Gurū Tegh Bahādur (1621–75), and Gurū Gobind Singh (1666–1708). Each took the title and functions of a Gurū on the death of his predecessor.
3. Brian Stock, *The Irnplications of Literacy* (Princeton: 1983). The following theoretical discussion of "textual community" is based on this work, particularly pp. 88–240.
4. Ibid., p. 90
5. Unfortunately, despite the importance of Bhāī Gurdās's writings, as yet there is no major translation into English of his writings. The best way to

access his work is Hazara Singh and Vir Singh, eds., *Vārāṅ Bhāī Gurdās* (Amritsar, 1962).

6. Summary based on ibid., *vārs* 12 (2), 28 (5,6,7,15), 40 (11). The figures in parentheses indicate the respective stanzas for the three *vārs.*

7. Ibid., *vār* 1 (21, 33).

8. The fairly rapid change in the meanings of the word *gurmukh* is an important indication of metamorphosis in early Sikh identity. In the writings of Gurū Nānak the word simply meant an individual whose consciousness is directed towards God. In the compositions of the third and fourth Gurūs, it stands for those Sikhs who are loyal to the person and teachings of the Sikh Gurūs. Bhāī Gurdās too uses the word in its latter meaning. Increasingly the word *gurmukh* was to be identified with the Sikhs alone and non-Sikhs were *manmukh* ("self-oriented"). In making this distinction, I am indebted to Surjit Hans's brilliant work, *A Reconstruction of Sikh History from Sikh Literature* (Jalandhar, 1988), pp. 45, 59–61.

9. The best work on the *janam-sākhīs* is still W. H. McLeod, *Early Sikh Tradition* (Oxford, 1980).

10. Translated and quoted in W. H. McLeod, *The Evolution of the Sikh Community* (Delhi: 1975), p. 30. For the original *janam-sākhī* text of this episode, see Piara Singh, ed., *Janam sākhī Srī Gurū Nānak Dev jī* (Amritsar, 1974), p. 99.

11. For linguistic usages of these two terms "denotation" and "connotation," see John R. Searle, *Speech Acts: An Essay in the Philosophy of Language* (London, 1969), pp. 165–74. According to Searle, in linguistics the proponents of denotation hold that "proper names do not have senses; they are meaningless marks; they have denotation but not connotation" (p. 163). Opposed to this, the theorists of connotation believe that names "must have descriptive content, they must have a sense" (p. 165).

12. I am grateful to Kenneth Bryant for drawing my attention to the incessant outpouring of *guṭkās* and *pothīs* in medieval India.

13. The following description is based on Gopal Narayan Bahura, "Surdas Ka Pada: The Fatehpur Manuscript of 1639 V.S. (A.D. 1582)," in Monika Thiel-Horstmann, ed., *Bhakti in Current Research* (Berlin: 1983), pp. 19–24. Also see, in the same volume, an article by Kenneth E. Bryant, "The Fatehpur Manuscript and the Sursagar Critical Edition Project," pp. 37–52.

14. Background in W. H. McLeod, *Early Sikh Tradition* (Oxford, 1980), and Surjit Hans, *A Reconstruction of Sikh History from Sikh Literature* (Jalandhar: 1988). The particular analysis of the *janam-sākhīs* and their implication for early Sikh identity as presented here is my own.

15. For the text of this story, see W. H. McLeod, ed., *The B-40 Janam-sākhī* (Amritsar: 1980), pp. 50–51.

16. *Rāg Bhairu* 5.3 (*Ādi Granth,* p. 1136).

17. For two prominent instances, see Khushwant Singh, *A History of the Sikhs,* vol. 1 (Princeton, 1963), p. 62, and W. Owen Cole and Piara Singh Sambhi, *The Sikhs* (London, 1978), p. 27.

18. *Rāg Bhairu* 4.7 (*Ādi Granth,* p. 1158). For Sahib Singh's reasoning, see his *Srī Gurū Granth Sāhib Darpaṇ* (Jalandhar), 8:303–4.

19. Wendy O'Flaherty, *Other People's Myths* (New York, 1988), pp. 64–73.

20. The issue of why Jāṭs took to the Sikh movement and the ups and downs of Sikh struggle against the Mughals has been extensively reviewed in recent literature and requires no reiteration here. The best works on these two interelated themes are W. H. McLeod, *The Evolution of the Sikh Community* (Delhi, 1975), particularly chapters 1 and 3; Irfan Habib, "Jatts of Punjab and Sind," in Harbans Singh and N. Gerald Barrier, eds., *Punjab Past and Present, Essays in Honour of Dr. Ganda Singh* (Patiala, 1976), pp. 72–103, and Chetan Singh, "Socio-economic Conditions in the Punjab During the 17th Century," Ph.D. thesis, Jawaharlal Nehru University, 1984.

21. J. S. Grewal and S. S. Bal, *Guru Gobind Singh* (Chandigarh, 1967), pp. 113–15.

22. *Dasam Granth,* p. 716, translated by Max Macauliffe, *The Sikh Religion,* vol. 5, (Oxford, 1909), pp. 322–23 [my emphasis]. The text and pagination of the *Dasam Granth* was standardized in 1895. Since then all the printed editions have always appeared with 1428 pages.

23. See *hukam-nāmās* numbers 46, 50, 51, 52, 54, 55, 56, 57 and 59 in Ganda Singh, ed., Hukamnāme (Patiala, 1967).

24. Sainapati, *Srī Gur Sobhā,* edited by Ganda Singh (Patiala: 1967), p. 22. Although Akali Kaur Singh early this century suggested that this text was written in 1741, there is a growing consensus among scholars that Sainapati wrote this biographical work in 1711. This date in all probability is correct, since there is not even a faint echo of post-1711 history of the Khālsā in this text.

25. J. S. Grewal and S. S. Bal, without specifying the nature of their sources, suggest that early Sikh writings indicate that Gobind Singh asked his disciples to carry five kinds of weapons. See their biography, *Guru Gobind Singh* (Chandigarh, 1967), p.188.

26. Surjit Hans, "Social Transformation and Early Sikh Literature," *Journal of Regional History* 3 (1982): 11.

27. Sainapati, *Srī Gur Sobhā,* p. 46.

28. The following account of life-cycle rituals is based on the *Chaupā Siṅgh Rahit-nāmā*, a text written sometime between 1750 and 1765. I have used the recently published critical edition and translation by W. H. McLeod, *The Chaupa Singh Rahit-Nama* (Dunedin, 1987) [Hereafter referred to as CRN].

29. CRN. 90, 178–79, 181–83. The numerals refers to the specific verses in the Gurmukhī text of the *rahit-nāmā.*

30. For a highly informative essay on the marriage rituals and practices prevalent in eighteenth-century Punjab, see Daljinder Singh Johal, "Institution of Marriage in Medieval Panjabi Literature," *Proceedings of the Punjab History Conference 1982* (Patiala: 1982), pp. 189–98.

31. CRN, p. 16.

32. Ibid., p. 45.

33. Barbara Myerhoff and Sally Falk Moore, eds., *Secular Ritual* (Amsterdam: 1977), pp. 3–24.

34. R. Nicholas and R. Inden, *Kinship in Bengali Culture* (Chicago: 1977), p. 37. W. H. McLeod, *CRN*, pp. 36–37.

35. W. H. McLeod, *CRN,* p. 31.

36. Ibid ., p. 42.

37. For a masterly analysis of these groups, see J. S. Grewal, "Dissent in Early Sikhism," *Proceedings of the Punjab History Conference, 1980,* pp. 109–20.

38. W. H. McLeod, *CRN*, p. 31

39. For further explorations on this point see J. S. Grewal, "Legacies of the Sikh Past for the Twentieth Century," in Joseph T. O'Connell et al., eds., *Sikh Religion and History in the Twentieth Century* (Toronto, 1988), pp. 19–20.

40. For two recent perspectives on this debate, see Harbans Singh, *Berkeley Lectures on Sikhism* (New Delhi: 1983), pp. 24–32, and W. H. McLeod, *Who is a Sikh? The Problem of Sikh Identity* (Oxford: 1989), pp. 52–55.

41. See J. S. Grewal, "Legacies of the Sikh Past for the Twentieth Century," p. 22.

42. *Rāg Sirī* 8 (*Ādi Granth*, p. 26).

43. For an account of Bandā Bahādur and his campaigns based on primary materials, see Ganda Singh, *Life of Banda Singh Bahadur* (Amritsar, 1935).

44. Chetan Singh, "Socio-Economic Conditions in Punjab During the 17th Century," Ph.D. thesis, Jawaharlal Nehru University, 1984, p. 572. Cf. Muzaffar Alam, "Sikh Uprisings under Banda Bahadur 1708–1715," *The Panjab Past and Present* 16 (1982): 95–107.

45. W. Irvine, an English historian, wrote of Bandā and his times: "A low scavenger or leather dresser, the lowest of the low in Indian estimation, had only to leave home and join the Gurū (Banda), when in a short time he would return to his birth-place as its ruler with his order of appointment in his hand. As soon as he set foot within the boundaries, the well born and wealthy went out to greet him and escort him home. Arrived there, they stood before him with joined palms, awaiting his orders. Not a soul dared disobey an order, and men who had often risked themselves in battlefields became so cowed down

that they were even afraid to remonstrate." *The Latter Mughals* (Calcutta, 1922), pp. 98–99.

46. Clive Dewey, "Social Mobility and Social Stratification amongst the Punjab Peasantry: Some Hypotheses," Institute of Commonwealth Studies, University of London, seminar paper, 2 March 1976, pp. 5–6. I am grateful to the author for sharing this paper with me.

47. H. T. Prinsep, *Origin of the Sikh Power in the Punjab and Political Life of Maharaja Ranjit Singh* (Calcutta, 1834; reprinted Patiala, 1970), p. 26. In this same work Prinsep wrote: "The Shah [reference to Ahmad Shah] having thus quitted the field the Sikhs remained the undisputed masters of the Punjab, and spreading over the country occupied it as permanent inheritance, every Sardar according to his strength, seizing what fell in his way, and acknowledging no superior, nor submitting to the control of anybody, nor to any constitutional authority whatsoever" (p. 22).

48. Ganda Singh, ed., *Early European Accounts of the Sikhs* (Calcutta, 1962), p. 16.

49. Background in Andrew J. Major, "Return to Empire: The Sikhs and the British in the Punjab, 1839–1872," Ph.D. thesis, The Australian National University, 1981, pp. 32–39.

50. Kesar Singh Chibber, *Baṅsāvalī-nāmā Dasāṅ Pāt śāhiān Dā* [1769], edited by Rattan Singh Jaggi in *Parakh: Research Bulletin of Punjabi Language and Literature* (Chandigarh, 1972), pp. 199 and 242.

51. Ibid, p. 199.

52. For the past century it has been standard practice to use the term Sahajdhārī for all those Sikhs who are slowly adopting to Khālsā identity. But as W. H. McLeod has recently indicated, the older meaning and usage of the term was quite different. The word *sahaj* in the writings of Gurū Nānak refers to the state of ineffable bliss that could be attained by following the path of *nām simraṇ*. Therefore the compound word *sahajdhārī* refers to those "who accept the *nām simraṇ* teachings of Gurū Nānak " and do not enter the fold of the Khālsā and recognize its code of conduct. For this usage and explanation, see W. H. McLeod, *CRN*, p. 206.

53. For references to smoking, see Sukhbasi Ram Bedi, *Gurū Nānak Baṅs Parkāś*, edited by Gurmukh Singh (Patiala, 1986), p. 448. This fascinating text was written sometime in the early eighteenth century and is an account of Gurū Nānak and his descendants.

54. This document was first located at an Udāsī establishment in Rajgir, Bihar, by historian Ved Parkash. He provides a translation of it in his fascinating book, *The Sikhs in Bihar* (Patna, 1981), pp. 167–68. For readability and clarity, I have made minor modifications to Ved Parkash's translation.

55. For historical background on the Udāsīs, see Randhir Singh, *Udāsī Sikhaṅ dī Vithiā* (Amritsar, 1959), and Sulakhan Singh, "The Udasis under

Sikh rule (1750–1850)," Ph.D. thesis, Guru Nanak Dev University, Amritsar, 1985.

56. The ten orders were: Almast, Balu Hasne, Phūl, Goiṅde, Suthre Śāhī, Bhagat Bhagvānīe, Saṅgat Sāhibīe, Mīhāṅ Śāhīe, Bakht Malīe, and Jīt Malīe.

57. Such a position emerges most clearly in the *Bhāī Manī Siṅgh Vālī Janam Sākhī*, dating back to the eighteenth century. For a perceptive analysis of this work and early Sikh literature, see Surjit Hans, *Reconstruction of Sikh History from Sikh Literature* (Jalandhar, 1988), pp. 206–11.

58. Victor W. Turner, *The Ritual Process: Structure and Anti-Structure* (Chicago: 1969).

59. Ibid, p. 177

60. Victor W. Turner, "Metaphors of Anti-Structure in Religious Culture," in his *Dramas, Fields and Metaphors* (Ithaca, N.Y.: 1974), pp. 279–80.

61. Ibid., p. 275.

The Social Significance of Radhasoami

Mark Juergensmeyer

In recent years there has been a remarkable revival of interest in *guru bhakti* throughout North Indian cities, and among those responding to its appeal have been a considerable number of administrators and office workers in government and business organizations. The Radhasoami movement has flourished in these settings, and has become the largest of the new religious communities in North India. All told, in its various branches and under the several names by which it is known, the Radhasoami community can claim over a million initiates in South Asia, and tens of thousands more in other parts of the world.[1]

The movement traces its origins to Swami Shiv Dayal Singh, who began his public ministry in Agra in 1861. His teachings showed a mix of influences—Kabīrpanthī, Sikh, Nāth yogi, Vaiṣṇava—and they focused on the efficacy of sacred words and the saving power of a spiritual master in transforming the self and achieving access to otherworldly realms beyond. Swami Shiv Dayal advocated a form of yoga that was appropriate for householders as well as sadhus, and his following, largely members of his own urban merchant-caste community, continued to be a lively if increasingly fragmented group after his death. He was succeeded by other spiritual masters, and presently there are at least twenty lineages in the Radhasoami family tree. Some of the branches have prospered. During the 1930s the residential community at Dayalbagh, near Agra, developed an enormous complex of industries, shops, and model farms and dairies; at the same time the colony at Beas, in the Punjab, created something of a utopian city of its own. In the last thirty years Beas has greatly expanded its membership throughout North India, and it and one of its offshoots—the Ruhani Satsang in Delhi—have developed large multicultural networks that are in many ways prototypes for a new kind of international religious organization.

Considering its size and its propensity for social innovation, one might expect Radhasoami to have made a significant impact on the society of North India. This is to some extent true, but because of Radhasoami's particular social stance, the impact is not predictable, nor is it always direct. In this essay I want to explore this perplexing situation, and try to explain why in some ways the movement mirrors the prevailing social attitudes of its predominantly middle-class, managerial membership, and why in other ways it is a radical departure from them.

The Radhasoami Ambivalence toward Society

Radhasoami teachers have had contradictory feelings about the wider society. On one hand they have recognized that Radhasoami followers are intimately linked to the religious cultures around them, to the point that when one of his American initiates asked Charan Singh whether he should leave Christianity behind, it was natural for the Beas master to assure him that since Radhasoami was itself the truest form of Christianity, he should embrace the church with new enthusiasm. On the other hand, Radhasoami teachers retain a certain suspicion of these traditional cultures, and the same master cautioned his American devotee not to take seriously all of the "dogmas, rituals and ceremonies" of the church, for the "priestly class" was out to "exploit" the unwary with its rituals and such. Ultimately, he said, such customs held "no significance"; they paled before the deeper truths.[2]

Most Radhasoami devotees agree with this assessment, but they also have no difficulty with the notion that they can be good Christians, Hindus, or Sikhs and good members of Radhasoami *(satsaṅgīs)* at the same time, since they regard the Radhasoami community as something different from the society around it. Yet they do not think of Radhasoami as being so far beyond ordinary religion that it has no social form at all. In a survey questionnaire I administered to a hundred residents of a Punjabi village, I found that Radhasoami members consistently identified with the social aspects of their religion more strongly than did those who were not *satsaṅgīs*. They said that in times of trouble they would look toward their *satsaṅgī* comrades, whereas the others said they would turn to government agencies or caste associations.[3]

Dayalbagh has tried to capitalize on these feelings of social separation; Beas and the Ruhani Satsang have been more cautious. "We are not here to transform society," Charan Singh told his followers, "but to transcend it."[4] When this statement was made at a gathering of Western followers, some were displeased, others felt it reflected a realistically cautious attitude toward Indian society, and still others accepted his statement as fact: that social issues are irrelevant to religion. In an essentially religious society like India, however, religious values have social implications, and Radhasoami continues to be what most *panthic* movements in Indian history have always been: counterstructures that exist in symbiotic relation to the religious culture of the dominant societies around them.[5]

The *panthic* model is also one that fits comfortably in a modern secular society. Both *dharmic* Hinduism and *qaumic* Islam and Sikhism have recently been at odds with the secular nation-state: these traditional religious communities feel that the secular society intrudes on what had been their domain—a public order for which they provided basic social, spiritual, and political values.[6] As Ainslie Embree points out, one of the greatest challenges of a modern religious organization is to find ways of surviving in, and providing a counterbalance to, the secular nation-state.[7] By creating their own ideal societies, protected from the rest of the society, the Radhasoami communities insulate themselves from the defects of the broader collectivity and offer a new religious alternative to it.

The Radhasoami organization is an alternative to what might be regarded as the only "organization" that traditional Hinduism has had, namely the whole of India's caste society. Perhaps it is significant that the Radhasoami centers have developed in just those places where the old Hindu social order has broken down or is no longer meaningful: in modern urban society. There the creation of religious organizations may be seen as attempts to provide a new dharma, and give to new generations the social stability that earlier generations found in traditional Hindu social order.

The Spiritual Socialism of "Better-Worldly" Dayalbagh

The most utopian attempt to fashion a Radhasoami social alternative was the effort made by Dayalbagh, especially during its heyday in the 1920s and 30s. From the time of its establishment in 1915 to the present, however, there continues to be a broad public interest in what has been known as "the Dayalbagh experiment," and a parade of government officials and social reformers, from Nehru on down, have made their pilgrimage to the colony's headquarters on the outskirts of Agra. "Dayalbagh products came to my notice," said Nehru, so "I came to see with my own eyes the work being done here."[8] What Nehru saw on his visit in 1956 was the efficient use of modern technology by a spiritually dedicated religious community. Other visitors also remarked about this alliance of spiritual and technological power. "What Dayalbagh teaches," a newspaper editor from Lahore exclaimed on visiting Dayalbagh during the 1930s, "is what great miracles can be performed by God force—like other forces of Nature, e.g., steam, electricity, etc.—when building up an ideal structure of human society." The editor went on to state that Dayalbagh was as grand an achievement for the city of Agra in the social realm as the Taj Mahal had been in the architectural.[9]

With interests such as these in mind, many other progressive Indian politicians over the years have kept close ties with Dayalbagh; even Gandhi sent condolences to Dayalbagh at the time of the death of its founder, Anand Swarup.[10] From 1931 on, annual exhibitions of Dayalbagh goods throughout India were inaugurated by government officials. Through government assistance a hydroelectric substation was established in the colony, and government agencies became large purchasers of Dayalbagh products—especially dairy products from Dayalbagh's model farms. During the Second World War, government officials arranged for American troops stationed in Agra to purchase their milk from Dayalbagh in preference to the Indian military's own dairy.[11] In recent years, Dayalbagh leaders have been proud of their relationship with V. V. Giri, who frequently visited their community during his tenure as president of India.

Despite what Indian politicians may have asserted, what makes Dayalbagh effective as a social and economic organization is not any special technique of administration, but a spirit of collective ownership and a sense of common destiny. The members of the Dayalbagh community are joint owners of the community through a legal trust, but the master ultimately "owns" Dayalbagh: it is he who presides over the property and industry of the community. Individuals live and work there at his behest and partake in its ownership only through their relationship with him. In part for tax reasons, the title to Dayalbagh property has from the beginning been in the name of an administrative society, and since 1937 virtually all of the Radhasoami factories have become limited companies and cooperatives, legally owned by the members of the fellowship who work in them. Yet the directives for administering them come from offices at Dayalbagh. At present the leadership team includes G. D. Sahgal, a former judge in the Allahabad High Court, who is president of the society; T. Nath, the general secretary of Dayalbagh; and the present master of Dayalbagh, M. B. Lal, the former Vice Chancellor of Lucknow University. Like his predecessors, Lal provides worldly leadership as well as spiritual direction.

The master is like Plato's philosopher-king, a parallel that was first drawn by Anand Swarup, the founder, who said, "[W]hen I first read Plato's *Republic* I was pleasantly surprised to find . . . many of the ideas I am trying to express here." Swarup's "republic" envisaged a balance between an enlightened constituency and strong leadership, resulting in great civic pride. Swarup described Dayalbagh's ownership as "trusts to be administered in a religious spirit," and explained the differences between it and the more familiar kind of socialism as follows. Although "the farms and colleges are owned by the community," he said in an interview, "this ownership extends to land and houses. . . . Everyone is perfectly free to possess and accumulate whatever money and property he has," and this fact makes Dayalbagh free "from the tyrannies of socialism." Moreover, Swarup concluded, "everything is subordinated to our spiritual ideal."[12]

At Dayalbagh, one's salvation is thought to be affected by the quality of one's social life. Anand Swarup described this ideal of worldly renunciation as "better-worldliness"—a purified, spiritualized form of worldliness that he depicted as superior to the extremes of crass materialism and other-worldly renunciation. Better-worldliness, he claimed, should be the "aim of man's life on this earth."[13] By participating in better-worldliness, a Dayalbagh devotee was contributing to his or her own destiny, and to the destiny of society at large. Involvement in Dayalbagh economic and organizational activities, for example, provided an opportunity for *sevā* on a social scale. The present master reminded a group of his followers who were setting up displays of Dayalbagh products that "the exhibitions are not held for earning profit," but "to inculcate a spirit of cooperation and to work together with love and affection and to earn the Grace of Huzur Radhasoami Dayal."[14]

When Anand Swarup established his first factories, he called them "Model Industries" and intended them to be showpieces of technology and organization. The first product to be manufactured, in

1917, was a simple leather button for British military uniforms. Within ten years Dayalbagh factories were producing surgical instruments, electric fans, textiles, fountain pens, gramophones, and a whole host of leather products. One of the reasons they were successful with leather goods was that Radhasoami residents had no compunction about working with animal hides, thought to be polluting by traditional Hindus, nor were they hesitant about engaging in many other nontraditional areas of work and commerce. After their zenith in the 1930s, however, Dayalbagh industries have been in something of a decline. A steady increase in market competition and alterations in government income tax policies regarding properties owned by religious organizations cut deeply into Radhasoami profits.[15] Under M. B. Lal's leadership, however, there has been a revival of production and sales of Dayalbagh products. In the first ten years of Lal's administration—1975 to 1984—the number of Dayalbagh stores throughout India expanded from 11 to 53, and 22 new production units were established in the same period, manufacturing handloom cloth, soaps, wash powders, and similar products.[16]

Even more dramatic has been the development of new educational institutions under Lal's regime. Although Dayalbagh has had schools and colleges since 1917, soon after it was founded, Lal has been keen on expanding this aspect of Anand Swarup's vision, which was first articulated in one of Dayalbagh's early reports. "Animated by the desire to educate the masses," the report explained, the people of Dayalbagh created schools to "do our little bit in a decent manner." It went on to laud "the kingdom of knowledge, founded, under the aegis of the mighty and unshakeable British Raj, with no selfish motives of any kind."[17] This kingdom of knowledge was explored in cultural evenings at Dayalbagh, in which plays and readings from Shakespeare would enliven the colony's convocations.[18]

This heritage has been revived under Lal's leadership. In 1981 he persuaded the Government of India to authorize a new university at Dayalbagh, one based on its existing colleges. The university—the Dayalbagh Educational Institute (DEI)—was created as a "deemed university" by a special charter of the University Grants Commission of the Indian government. As such it is a national university, rather than a state institution, a status it shares with the Indian Institute of Science, the Tata Institute of Social Sciences, and the Gandhigram Rural Institute, among others. The head of DEI is Mrs. G. P. Sherry, daughter of Lal's predecessor as master at Dayalbagh, Gurcharandas Mehta.

What makes DEI unusual are its four required core courses, intended to inculcate civic values and a sensitivity to the liberal arts. The *Prospectus* for the university describes them as follows:[19]

> 1. Cultural Education (to take pride in the national ethos so that one may not lose one's moorings).
> 2. Comparative Study of Religion: Hinduism, Buddhism, Jainism, Judaism, Christianity, Islam, The "Sant Mat" and modern Religious Movements (to ingrain an attitude of tolerance and a sense of national integration and inculcate moral and spiritual values).
> 3. Scientific Methodology, General Knowledge and Current Affairs (to nurture a scientific temper and be aware of contemporary developments).
> 4. Rural Development: Study of rural society and economy (to foster a fuller understanding of the rural life with a view to appreciate properly the polity and the economy of our country and the social forces at work).

The fourth course also includes a practicum: students must volunteer for participation in a Peace Corps–type rural development project, usually during summer vacation. Also required is participation in physical education classes ("Games") and classes in the arts, such as music, drama, and dance. All this is in addition to the students' major fields of study, which at DEI are primarily in the sciences and technical fields such as commerce and engineering. Mrs. Sherry claims that through this approach DEI creates better persons, not just better students.[20] M. B. Lal, echoing sentiments first expressed by Anand Swarup, states that the educational institutions of Dayalbagh create an environment where children will become "supermen" able to bring into being a transformed, better-worldly society.[21]

Considering the noisy streets of ordinary Indian cities, Dayalbagh appears to have achieved a transformed society already. Its prosperous tree-lined streets caused one American visitor to describe it as "Westernization with a vengeance."[22] From land that was reclaimed when the Jumna River changed its course almost a hundred years ago, Anand Swarup and his successors have created a model city of some five thousand residents. Like Soamibagh, a smaller, rival Radhasoami colony located across the street on the site of the original master's meditation garden, the Dayalbagh colony is legally designated a town. It is a multiregional town, however, and one may find neighborhoods containing Rajasthanis, Punjabis, Biharis, Bengalis, and Tamils as well as people from neighboring Uttar Pradesh. This diverse constituency was attracted to Dayalbagh over the years as Anand Swarup and successive masters went on tour. In general there are fewer Gujaratis and Sindhis in Dayalbagh than in Soamibagh, and more devotees from South India and Bengal. The Bengali, Tamil and Telugu languages are taught in Dayalbagh schools, and there is a major branch of Dayalbagh in Andhra Pradesh at Cocanada, established by P. Sitaramayya, an energetic follower of Anand Swarup.[23]

The cosmopolitan, genteel atmosphere at Dayalbagh befits what Anand Swarup envisaged as a socialism of the elite—the "Aris-Demo" ideal, as he called it. Swarup wanted Dayalbagh's residents to "act as if they were a 'Democratic Community of Aristocrats'—Aristocrats, not on account of wealth, etc., but Aristocrats in Spiritualism." Aristocracy was not meant to imply a life of leisure, however, as Gurcharandas Mehta dramatically showed: he is said to have "denied himself rest and comfort and lived up to the great motto 'Work is Worship.'"[24] At Dayalbagh hard work and a sense of being elite were compatible.

Anand Swarup initially envisaged an ideal city containing not more than twelve thousand residents, the maximum he felt was possible for decent living. Swarup did not want to copy "the monstrous towns of your Western countries; they are overcrowded and therefore breed many undesirable qualities." Instead, he wanted to build "a garden city where people can work and live happily, where they can have plenty of space and air." After completing Dayalbagh, Anand Swarup hoped to create similar model cities all over India, "at least one in each province."[25] With the exception of a colony called Soaminagar, near New Delhi, however, his dream remained unfulfilled until 1984, when M. B. Lal embarked on a program of decentralization intended to expand the sales and production units of Dayalbagh industries, and to create new residential colonies at Lucknow, Roorkee, Vishakhapatnam, and Kanpur; other colonies are planned in Andhra Pradesh, Madhya Pradesh, and Bihar.[26] In a modest way, then, Anand Swarup's plan for the proliferation of Dayalbaghs is being enacted. One English visitor during the time of Anand Swarup thought the Dayalbagh ideal could be replicated throughout India if only there were a hundred leaders of Anand Swarup's quality. Then, he wrote, "how quickly India might become a smiling land, clean, gay, prosperous, dustless and at peace within her borders."[27] The question remains, however, whether even with the Radhasoami community, Dayalbagh's experiment with "better-worldliness" is a viable model for social change.

The Spiritual Kingdom of Beas

The only Radhasoami community larger than Dayalbagh is Beas, located near the city of Amritsar in the heart of the Punjab. It has none of the industrial and educational accoutrements of Dayalbagh, but in some ways it is also a social experiment: like Dayalbagh, it is a city created by and for the master. Sitting by itself on the riverbank at the end of a narrow country road some miles from the nearest railway station, it appears from a distance like a dream city. The towers of the monumental Satsang Ghar float ethereally above the plains, and surrounding it are sturdy brick homes and well-paved, quiet streets. This model city is all the more striking because of the contrast with its rude surroundings. The rough eroded gullies along the banks of the Beas river that were once thought to be inhabited by ghosts became in the 1980s the hideouts of young Sikh terrorists hunted down by the Indian government's armed police. But despite the ghosts and terrorists, many of Beas's visitors think of "this beautiful little dera" as, in the words of one American devotee, "a sacred spot."[28]

As at Dayalbagh, the facilities at Beas are expansive and modern, but even in physical appearance there are substantial differences between the two.[29] Factories and schools dominate the landscape at Dayalbagh, whereas at Beas the Satsang Ghar looms above all else. Offices and product showrooms at Dayalbagh are the busiest areas, while at Beas the liveliest quarters are the publications center and the hostels for international guests. At Dayalbagh one is liable to meet only middle-class, merchant-caste Indians, most of them Hindu. At Beas the scene is much more diverse.

The master at Dayalbagh, Dr. Lal-sahib, a widower, lives in a comfortable but modest bungalow in the center of the colony, easily accessible to the rest of the community. At Beas, by contrast, the residence of master (occupied by the present master, Gurinder Singh, who recently succeeded Maharaj Charan Singh) is almost invisible to passers-by: only one little room on the third floor and a television antenna peek over the high red brick walls that surround the manse he shares with his family. When the master leaves the guarded gate, he does not saunter alone as Dr. Lal-sahib would do at Dayalbagh; in fact, he does not walk at all but is driven in a small gray car even when his destination is only the Satsang Ghar a block away. The reason is a sound one, for the crowd hoping to catch a glimpse of his presence would surely make it impossible for him to walk anywhere other than with a phalanx of guards. At Dayalbagh the guru is treated rather like a revered chairman of the board. At Beas, he is a spiritual king, and this means that the whole colony at Beas takes on more the appearance of a magical kingdom than Dayalbagh, since it is not burdened with the mundane matters of running factories and selling products. Almost all of Beas's permanent residents have come to the colony after retirement, and most volunteer their labor on behalf of an organization that has no reason to exist other than to maintain and expand itself. They are proud to serve at a spiritual court. The honorific title, "Maharaj-ji," given to Charan Singh is in many ways apt, for to many he was the maharaja of Beas. Like the relationships among friends that anthropologists label "fictive kinships" Beas has produced what might be called a "fictive kingship."

As a number of recent films and novels indicate, there is a lingering nostalgia in modern India for the days of the princely states. This is especially true in the Punjab, where until the States Reorganization Act of 1956 small distinctive kingdoms were the dominant form of political organization. Maharajas and maharanis ruled over their dominions with great splendor, leaving the actual administration of the kingdoms in the hands of their chief secretaries, the diwans, whose power was often more palpable than that of the maharajas themselves. It is an interesting fact—perhaps only a coincidence—that Charan Singh is a member of the caste from which most of Punjab's princes were drawn; similarly his office staff comes from the castes that supplied the diwans. And indeed, this latter connection is a real one. Daryai Lal Kapur of Beas was known as "Diwan Sahib" because of his role as judge and finance minister in the princely state of Kapurthala.[30] Shyam Lal of Dhara Sindhu Pratap Ashram served the Gwalior princes, and one of his successors, Thakar Mansingh, worked in the court's bureaucracy. Swami Shiv Dayal himself served in the administration of a princely state, and family members of Radhasoami leaders—including Swami Shiv Dayal—have also served in courtly capacities.[31] At Beas and other Radhasoami organizations these roles are kept alive in a new form.

One of these forms of regal spirituality may be found in the courtly politics of Beas's inner administrative circles. Although the line of command is clearly specified—subcommittee heads report to superiors in higher committees, and the whole structure comes under the review of a general secretary who reports directly to the master—personal relationships count for much. The structure allows some officers to bypass the general secretary: members of the trust committee reported directly to Maharaj Charan Singh, as have regional representatives outside of India.[32] Maharaj-ji's personal secretary and staff also were exempt from the general secretary's command, and certain other individuals ignored the formal structure by going directly to the master with their concerns. These included members of prominent old Radhasoami families and distinguished *satsaṅgīs*, such as professors, politicians, and businessmen. Theoretically anyone can speak directly with the master, but access to him is a privilege obtained easily only by a few. Each of these features revived one aspect of the organization of a traditional Indian kingdom.

The personal authority that the spiritual king provides is an interesting adaptation to the otherwise modern, even meritocratic, pattern of Radhasoami organization. One might say that it is a form of leadership that is peculiarly premodern. Yet it is appropriate for the circumstances of the modern age, for an authority with whom one has an intimate relationship—a father, a spiritual master, or a divinely granted king—is capable of doing much more than adjudicate between the competing interests of individuals: he or she can awaken conscience, command sacrifice, and engender loyalty and love. In premodern societies the institution of kingship served both individual interests and the cause of communal identity by providing a single figure to whom a large group of people could relate, and through the monarch be in touch with one another as well. What made kingship work was a relationship of trust that, as Reinhard Bendix has observed, was virtually always buttressed by religion.[33] The democracies that replaced kingships relied upon a different sort of trust for their authority: a trust in reason, due process, and the good will of civic-minded citizens. It is not surprising that when trust in these elements has been eroded, people embrace an earlier form of public authority, such as the spiritual kings of Radhasoami. The personal relationships that Radhasoami followers form with their leaders allow them to restore their faith in social organization, at least in the protected settings of the Radhasoami communities.

Meritocracy Challenged: Gender and Physical Handicaps

The regal style of administration at Beas has been supplemented by a managerial style, and this may increasingly be the case. When Charan Singh died on 1 June 1990, he was succeeded by his 35-year old nephew, Gurinder Singh Dhillon, who has for years lived and worked in Spain in an import-export business, and who has abjured the courtly politics of the Beas *ḍerā*. Even during Charan Singh's time there was a move towards democratization in the *ḍerā,* marked by a new constitution in 1957 that standardized the process of policy making and made it less subject to personal influence. Charan Singh also shifted the legal title to the property at Beas from his own name to a nonprofit trust managed by senior members of the Beas Satsang. Other aspects of the administration were turned over to the trust as well, and he hoped that in doing so advancement and influence in its structure would be solely determined by one's abilities.[34] One of Beas's leaders called it "true democracy in action."[35] Charan Singh claims to have felt a great sense of relief in abdicating his kingly role for a more contemporary one, that of an administrative advisor.[36]

Yet Beas is still far from being the meritocracy it would aspire to be. Nowhere is this more clear than in its attitudes toward women and people with physical handicaps—even though to a large extent they fare better in Radhasoami society than in the power networks of traditional India. The Beas branch recently listed a "lady doctor" as chairman of its governing society,[37] and the head of Dayalbagh's new university is a woman. At least two Radhasoami masters have been women, as have some of the most loyal and spiritually exalted disciples of other masters. Yet it is also true that these women are rare and unusual exceptions: the "lady doctor" who chaired the Beas governing society was Rani Lakshmibai Rajwade, member of the royal family of a former princely state, and the head of the Dayalbagh university, Mrs. G. P. Sherry, is the daughter of the former master, Gurcharandas Mehta. The annual reports of the Beas Satsang from 1969 through 1984 list only one other woman to have served on the seventeen-member governing society,[38] and there have never been more than two or three women among the fifty members of the managing committee of Dayalbagh.[39] The two women who became masters have done so under unusual circumstances, and not entirely with success.[40] One of the most recent women to be considered for guruship was the Ruhani Satsang's Bibi Hardevi, known as Taiji, "respected aunt."[41] Yet she was never publicly acclaimed the successor of Kirpal Singh, the founding master of the Ruhani Satsang, and some said that the reason was gender: Kirpal Singh had once said that a woman could never become a *sant satguru*.[42]

Although the numbers of women in Radhasoami leadership are small, women are often in the majority at Radhasoami events. They also provide an army of workers to feed the thousands who come to Beas's rallies, and at Dayalbagh, the Mahila Cooperative Association, a women's organization, provides much of the community's income.[43] Radhasoami women are also regarded as stalwarts of spirituality. Perhaps best known are the curious trio—Shibboji, Bukkiji and Vishnoji—who were devoted followers of the first master. Vishnoji was "in constant attendance" on Swami Shiv Dayal, and when he delivered discourses and explained sacred texts "Bukkiji's eyes would become red and tears would flow." While he smoked the *huqqā* (a water pipe) or sat silently reading the scriptures, Bukkiji would "suck His toes for hours and enjoy the nectar of His Feet," which she described as being "like mother's milk." As for Shibboji, she became "so overpowered" in yearning for the Swami's darshan that "she became stark naked" and ran through the marketplace oblivious to the crowds, explaining that she had not noticed anyone aware of her nakedness except Swami Shiv Dayal, in whose eyes there were no secrets.[44] A later telling of this story provides a different rationale for her nudity. According to this account, Shibboji's husband had tried to keep her from leaving her wifely duties and running off to become a devotee of Swami Shiv Dayal. As she strained to leave him, he held on to what he could—her sari—and the garment ripped from her body as she lunged out of the house, through the marketplace, and up to the *satsaṅg* of her spiritual master.[45] This version of the story makes Shibboji a modern-day version of the medieval *sant* Mīrābāī, who is said to have also torn free from her earthly husband to join her real husband, Lord Krishna.

The Great Master at Beas also had three women attending him—Bibi Lajjo, Bibi Rakhi, and Bibi Ralli—who were also model devotees. One contemporary account reported that they rendered "a great service to the Master by preparing his food, doing his laundry, pressing his clothes, and doing his sewing, mending, etc." The report affirmed that these women were "all spiritually minded, advanced souls, and serve with a loving devotion that is rare on this earth." It quickly added, "of course, they get no financial pay." The explanation for their generosity was that "they consider that they are serving the King of Kings."[46]

Bibi Rakhi was particularly famous for giving detailed accounts of her spiritual experiences—"what she saw and heard during her journey through the First, Second and Third regions." It is said that "one could see the light of Truth and joy shining in her face as she told in simple language of the marvels she had seen."[47]

The Radhasoami attitude toward gender is complex. On the one hand its organizations are aggressive, rational, powerful, and efficient, and exhibit what are often thought of as male virtues. On the other hand what is ultimately valued for spiritual purposes are traits of submission, innocence, subtlety, and love—virtues that are often ascribed particularly to women. It is no surprise, then, that Radhasoami men should praise women for doing what men think women do well, and want in some sense to emulate them. This compliment paid to women has its roots in Vaiṣṇava bhakti, where devotees seek to be like Krishna's lady friends, and mimic their love for the handsome lord.[48] Of course, those who do not share the male admiration for what are supposed to be womanly traits may reject its premise as demeaning: the notion that women are inherently less capable of spiritual achievement than men.

The validity of the traditional Indian view—that women are born with a heavier karmic burden than men—is a matter of some debate in Radhasoami circles: some masters say that spiritual achievement is a private matter between oneself and one's master, and that gender is irrelevant; others deny that women have a capacity for spiritual greatness; and still others are circumspect. Charan Singh, for instance, said that women are sometimes less able to progress spiritually because they are "tied down to the world" by the "instinct of devotion," but he noted that the same instinct gives them the ability to move more rapidly in meditation in the initial stages. A man takes longer because "his approach is through logic and reasoning," while "a woman's approach is primarily devotional; she does not bother very much to analyze things."[49] Even so, he affirmed that it is possible for women to reach a high level of spirituality—the *sant,* Mīrābāī, was given as an example—and even the pronoun used to refer to the Absolute could be "He or She, or One."[50] Other masters are more pessimistic about the ability of women to overcome their heavy burden of karma.[51] "On principle," said Anand Swarup, "a female cannot attain the status of a Saint."[52]

Much the same is said about the physically handicapped. The

blind especially are regarded throughout India as having suffered an enormous weight of bad karma, and as a result some within Radhasoami have thought it impossible for the blind to achieve a high degree of spiritual achievement. It is said that once when Kirpal Singh took pity on a blind man and initiated him, the trauma of his assuming the weight of the blind man's karma was so great that the master became physically ill.[53]

The spiritual progress of the blind is also impaired by their inability to visualize the physical form of the master. "The nature of our spiritual practices excludes them," one of the leaders at Dayalbagh explained.[54] For these reasons, some Radhasoami masters have regarded it as futile to initiate the blind at all. Once a British devotee wrote to the Great Master at Beas and urged him to initiate a blind man who earned his living playing the piano, and who "loved him very much." His love failed to persuade the master, however, who responded that initiation was out of the question "because a blind man cannot have the Darshan or sight of the Satguru."[55] The barrier against initiation does not apply to persons who, through accident, have gone blind after birth, however, and the Great Master at Beas is said to have restored eyesight to a *satsaṅgī* who had temporarily gone blind.[56] One successor of Swami Shiv Dayal Singh, Garib Das, was said to have been blind, but he presumably lost his sight through old age rather than as a condition of birth. Because sight is regarded as such a precious gift, Radhasoami leaders have made special efforts to alleviate the problems of those afflicted with eye diseases. At Beas a huge "eye camp" is sponsored each year in order to provide free operations for those whose sight is impaired. But even though it is claimed that true blindness is "not in the loss of eyes, but in keeping away from God," those whose eyesight has been lost from birth continue to be excluded from most of the Radhasoami fellowships.[57]

The Radhasoami Family and the Question of Caste

Despite these seeming inequities, the Radhasoami fellowship is bound together in something like familial love—not necessarily love for one another, at least initially, but love for and from the master. The parental role that the master plays enhances this familial image, and the terms used to designate the followers of a Radhasoami master are the familial ones used throughout Indian culture: *guru-bhāī* and *guru-bahin,* "brothers and sisters in the guru." In the Radhasoami fellowship this sense of camaraderie is even more pronounced; "greater than ties of blood," claims one Radhasoami leader, "are the ties of kinship uniting those who serve the same master."[58]

The contrast between the Radhasoami family and biological families is not usually stressed by Radhasoami teachers, however, most of whom are husbands and householders themselves.[59] To prevent dissension, married women whose husbands are opposed to Radhasoami teachings are often denied initiation. If it is the husband whose wife is hostile to the teachings, however, he is usually accepted, since it is assumed that in a traditional Indian family the wife will eventually bend to the husband's wishes.[60] The masters regret any incidents of family tension caused by Radhasoami membership, and counsel their devotees to "win your estranged family members over to your side with love."[61]

Most Indian devotees are spared these tensions since they join in family units, but the Radhasoami fellowship often poses a different sort of social problem for them: the problem of caste. Radhasoami's community challenges the traditional Indian notion of social order—the linkage of family networks in a caste hierarchy. In the traditional Hindu scheme of things, salvation is closely bound up with one's respect for dharma, the moral system of caste-defined duties that is based upon a religious principle of inequality separating those who have been born into this world pure from those born impure.[62] One's social role thus plays an integral part in the Hindu scheme of salvation, and any theory that alters that view of salvation is apt to have an effect on social organization. Conversely, any movement for social change in India has to deal with, and alter, the religious rationale for caste.[63]

The Radhasoami community has that revolutionary potential. Its soteriology does not rely on dharmic purity, so its own society has no need to bear the marks of hierarchical inequality that are so important to most Hindus. In this respect the contemporary Radhasoami *satsaṅgīs* are much like their *sant* forebears: Ravidās, an Untouchable leather-worker; Kabīr, the low-caste Hindu weaver said to have been adopted by Muslims; Mīrā, a woman; and Sūrdās, said to have been blind. They are often touted in modern Indian writings as India's "first social reformers," and although it is unclear whether they ever intended their ideas of spiritual equality to extend to social relationships, the religious associations that have been established in their names continue to have a reputation of social equality, and are sought after by the less privileged.[64] The modern Radhasoami movement, in holding equality a virtue, keeps this *sant* idea alive.

Caste is not altogether absent in the social divisions within Radhasoami fellowships, but its more oppressive features are largely negated, and there have even been instances of remarkable alliances forged between members of the lowest castes and those much higher. In the Punjabi town of Nabha, for example, the leader is a merchant-caste Khatrī, and as the fellowship developed in the 1950s, most of the new initiates were also Khatrī, with one major exception: a man named Sundar Ram, a Chamar.[65] Chamars are traditionally leatherworkers and are regarded as untouchable, but Sundar Ram was unusual. He had left his traditional caste occupation behind, and by becoming a cloth merchant was a sort of Khatrī by association. He also encouraged many upwardly mobile members of his family and caste to join the Radhasoami fold along with him. Sundar Ram and his caste-mates have continued to be staunch pillars of the Nabha Satsang since those early years: they contributed the land on which the Satsang compound now stands, and one may occasionally see Sundar Ram himself on the podium, seated on the flowered carpet in front of the picture of the master, expounding the tenets of the faith.

Not all of Nabha's proper society approves of this intercaste conviviality, and the disdain that it elicits exemplifies a familiar theme in Radhasoami history. At the beginning, Swami Dayal became embroiled in a brouhaha with the local Brahmins. According to one account, the Swami allowed everyone who came to his quarters to drink the same water, all of it brought from a well on the banks of the Jumna River nearby. The Brahmins were displeased: not only were persons from different castes drinking from the same source, but the well was drawing water from a sacred stream. The Brahmins physically attempted to prevent the Swami's assistants from carrying the water to him, but the Swami commanded them to persist, Brahmins or no. In telling this incident, the Swami's brother followed with a diatribe of his own against the absurdities of Brahminical rules and the injustices of caste.[66]

Swami Shiv Dayal's disdain for caste is also said to have gotten him into trouble with his own people: the caste leaders of the Khatrīs tried to excommunicate him.[67] Stories similar to this are also told about Rai Saligram, who is said to have been threatened with excommunication by the leaders of his Kāyastha caste for consorting with the Khatrī swami; and Brahm Sankar Misra was damned by his Brahmin caste fellows for associating with a religious community that was populated largely by members of merchant castes.[68]

Some of that same spirit of defying caste is to be found in present-day Radhasoami *satsaṅg*s, where the right to worship, to be initiated, or to assume a leadership role is open to anyone. But this stance does not mean that there is a true balance of caste representation. At Dayalbagh, for instance, there are virtually no lower-caste residents except for a few noninitiates who in 1960 embarked on an embarrassingly public strike for higher wages.[69] Until 1957 separate eating places for lower and upper castes were maintained at the Beas *ḍerā*.[70] Much is made in Radhasoami writings about how the late master at Beas, Charan Singh, created "a significant social reform" when he abolished this practice. It is said that when, even after the pronouncement, the Untouchable *satsaṅgī*s huddled together at one side of the dining area, Charan Singh sat down and ate among them, thus establishing forever the precedent of intercaste commensality at the Beas *ḍerā*.[71] The master's egalitarian sentiments are undoubtedly an important factor in shaping the attitude toward caste at Beas, but it is also true that the Indian government attempts to discourage caste through regulations prohibiting caste prejudice at religious places, and by the threat of denying tax-exempt status to institutions that fail to abide by these rules.

Even so, a kind of status inequality continues to persist in many Radhasoami centers. At Beas, for instance, certain eating arrangements are still separate, for in addition to the large free eating grounds there are other, more pleasant restaurants on the premises that offer a finer fare for a small cost. No caste distinctions are made regarding entrance to one or the other but the mere fact of the choice allows for a de facto separation between poorer low-caste devotees and richer high-caste and foreign ones. A similar distinction is made in sleeping quarters: the more luxurious ones are assigned to those who are accustomed to higher standards. These inequalities are based on economic position rather than caste, however, and many *satsaṅgī*s regard the emphasis on merit rather than birth as an improvement on traditional Indian social norms.

The Merchant-Caste Connection

In addition to the question of whether everyone in Radhasoami is treated equally regardless of caste, one might ask how much the values of the dominant caste characterize the values of the movement. What unites all the Khannas, Puris, Mehtas, and Narangs that predominate in the movement—aside from family connections and the similarity in their educational backgrounds, social status, and economic positions—is something that most Indians would immediately detect from their names: they are all Khatrīs. Many of the masters are also Khatrīs, except at Beas, where they are all Jāṭs.[72] Ruhani Satsang masters have all been Khatrīs, as have most of the Agra masters, beginning with Swami Shiv Dayal, and including Madhav Prasad Sinha, Gurcharandas Mehta and M. B. Lal.

Most of the other masters came from similar urban merchant castes: Rai Saligram, Kamta Prasad Sinha and A. P. Mathur, for example, were Kāyasthas, and Anand Swarup was an Ahluwalia. Other gurus have been Aroṛās and Baniyās. The priestly caste is scarcely represented at all. Brahm Sankar Misra, the major exception, brought very few of his caste-mates into the fold. Aside from several Brahmins in attendance at the *satsaṅg*s held at Misra's Radhasoami Bagh in Banaras, and an occasional Brahmin at the other centers, there are almost no Brahmins in the visible ranks of Radhasoami today. As for leaders, the only other Brahmins to have served as masters were associated with the smaller centers: Faqir Chand and I. C. Sharma at Manavta Mandir, for instance, and Anakul Thakar at Pabna, East Bengal.

Among the merchant-caste members both at Agra and Beas is a significant contingent that come from Sindh, the region bordering the lower Indus River in what is now Pakistan. At the turn of the century, Rai Saligram initiated a number of *satsaṅgīs* in the Sindhi cities of Hyderabad and Karachi and attracted them to the Agra branch; Brahm Sankar Misra continued to minister to them after his death.[73] Recently, however, it is the Beas branch that has been recruiting Sindhis, especially those who have settled in Bombay, where Beas maintains a large headquarters. There Charan Singh has sometimes been called the "guru of Sindhis." With the creation of Pakistan in 1947, other Sindhis were scattered to urban centers throughout the world, and Radhasoami's popularity in Indian immigrant communities in Kenya, South Africa, Singapore, England, Canada, and the United States is due in some measure to its being embraced by Sindhis who have settled in those locales.

Many of the descendants of the Sindhis who became Rai Saligram's initiates today reside in Soamibagh. Other Soamibagh residents are Mārwāṛīs, members of a merchant-caste community that originated in Jodhpur, a Rajasthani town not far from Sindh. In the nineteenth century there was a great dispersion of Mārwāṛīs to cities across north India, and in places such as Calcutta they became leaders of industry.[74] A few, such as the Birlas, have become among India's most wealthy families. Wealth of the Birla magnitude is not represented in Soamibagh, but some of the most common Mārwāṛī names, such as Maheshwari and Aggarwal, are represented there.

Who are these urban merchant castes—the Khatrīs and Kāyasthas and Mārwāṛīs—and why do they want to leave the religious customs of their past? The answer to the first part of the question is problematic, for the classical *varṇa* scheme of priests, warriors, merchants, and artisans, followed by Untouchables, is imprecise in defining the many existing castes *(jātis)* in present-day Indian society. Many Khatrīs claim that theirs is a Kshatriya (warrior) caste, as the name itself suggests, and a similar claim has been made by Kāyasthas.[75] Most scholars have disputed these claims, however, regarding such Khatrīs and Kāyasthas as merchant castes who claim a higher status to befit their considerable economic and educational achievements. In the past members of such castes as Khatrīs served as shopkeepers, moneylenders, traders, and teachers. Their reputation for mastering knowledge sometimes extended to the spiritual realm: Gurū Nānak and the other nine founding gurus of the Sikh tradition were Khatrīs, members of the Bedi subcaste. In more recent years Khatrīs have turned to technology and modern organization, where they have risen to high administrative positions.

Their rise in social status, however, has not been commensurate with their economic success. Hindu tradition reserves for Brahmins the role of priestly leadership, and the leadership of the Sikh community has changed over the centuries from Khatrī to Jāṭ. Jāṭs hold most leadership posts in Sikh religious organizations, the major Sikh political party, and in the administration of Sikh educational institutions. It is no wonder, then, that members of Khatrī castes would be attracted to a new religious community that allows them to rise to levels of leadership and status appropriate to the competence they display in society at large.[76] The Radhasoami community belongs virtually to Khatrīs alone, and in the Punjab, where Khatrīs have traditionally been divided between Sikhs and Hindus, the *ḍerā* offers a common meeting ground, uniting Khatrīs of differing religious camps.

The Religion of Managerial People

We return to the question raised at the beginning of this essay, as to how much Radhasoami has been stamped by the attitudes and concerns of its urban, merchant-caste constituency, and to what extent it is akin to the merchant-caste religious traditions, sects, movements and denominations elsewhere in India and in the world: the Arya Samaj, for example, or the Vallabhites.[77] Max Weber argued that the merchant caste values of the Vallabhites made them immune to the "otherworldly" tendencies of Brahminical Hinduism, and he dubbed their almost Protestant emphasis on the sanctity of hard work and the virtues of an upright life an "inner-worldly asceticism."[78] What made the Vallabha group different from other Hindus, he said, was not just that they were merchants, but that they were merchants on the move: socially mobile and acquisitive. Ordinarily rich businessmen regardless of cultural setting have little interest in religion: "skepticism or indifference to religion" have been the attitudes of "large-scale traders and financiers." But an exception arises in the case of groups that are involved in "the acquisition of new capital, or more correctly, capital continuously and rationally employed." These groups, according to Weber, seek a "rational, ethical, congregational religion."[79]

To some extent Weber's description of a merchant caste on the move fits the Khatrīs, and to some extent his description of a "rational, ethical, congregational religion" fits Radhasoami, but there are some differences on both scores. Khatrīs, especially the ones in Radhasoami, are not lonely capitalists, they are socially adept managers; and Radhasoami is not quite a community church: it not only provides "worldly" ethical values but the most "otherworldly" of mystical realms. The question, then, is to what degree the inner- and otherworldly characteristics of Radhasoami are consistent with a managerial mentality.

One of the modern, managerial virtues is an emphasis on individual responsibility and achievement. Radhasoami embraces this value in that it provides a community that all, regardless of caste, may enter, and it offers a salvation free from the fetters of dharma and caste, achievable in one's own lifetime. The industry and knowledge of techniques that are so highly valued in managerial circles are also praised in the Radhasoami community and given a place in its path to salvation: hard work, craft, and scientific knowledge—even knowledge regarding the "science of the soul"—are the main ingredients of both social and spiritual progress. A third managerial value, a sense of public responsibility, is also consistent with Radhasoami attitudes. Radhasoami colonies provide social wholes, and its theology provides a cosmic whole in which individual members may locate themselves and find their moral and spiritual responsibilities.

Although it would seem at first glance that the Radhasoami tradition does give religious expression to managerial virtues, this conclusion does not entirely jibe with the initiates' own perceptions. For many of them, the Radhasoami path is difficult and unfamiliar, requiring a radical transformation of life. "I had succumbed to the modern world," K. L. Khanna testified, "but I abandoned all interests in personal ambition when I fell at the feet of the Master."[80] Although an outsider might interpret Khanna's position as general secretary of the Radhasoami Satsang at Beas as a triumph of personal ambition indeed, from Khanna's point of view his role was only *sevā,* to be exalted no more highly than the work of those who carry baskets of dirt on their heads. The other managerial virtues are similarly qualified: the individualism of Radhasoami's spiritual quest is tempered by the fellowship of *satsaṅg;* the value placed on religious technique is qualified by the assertion that love is a yet more efficacious path; and the sense of responsibility engendered by knowing the whole is belittled by the enormity of the divine responsibility over what cannot be known, the realms beyond human grasp.

It would appear, then, that there are parallel sets of values within the Radhasoami tradition, one confirming the mores of its middle class constituency—its rational, egalitarian efficiency—and the other transforming those values to produce quite a different vision of the suprarational and social ideal. Both are at odds with traditional Hinduism, but they are also to some extent at odds with each other: the Radhasoami vision of a transformed community and a transcendent authority avoids anomie, rootlessness, aggressive and selfish forms of individualism, and many other moral pitfalls of modernity. When Baba Ram Jadoun described his participation in the Dayalbagh community as "taking part in the best of the modern world" and then later claimed that his voyage on the Radhasoami path had been "like setting sail in uncharted seas," he was speaking of these parallel tendencies in Radhasoami tradition: one that endorses the better aspects of modernity and one that seeks to transcend the worst of them.[81] These two dimensions of Radhasoami's world view allow those who possess a modern, managerial outlook to feel confirmed in what they are by their religious lives, but at the same time elevated beyond any worldly identities they know.

Notes

1. See Mark Juergensmeyer, *Radhasoami Reality: The Logic of a Modern Faith* (Princeton: Princeton University Press, 1991), appendix C, for the sources on which I have based this figure. This article is largely adapted from that book.

2. Charan Singh, *Spiritual Heritage* (Beas: Radhasoami Satsang, Beas, 1983), p. 213; and Charan Singh, *The Master Answers to Audiences in America* (Beas: Radhasoami Satsang, Beas, 1966), p. 499.

3. The results of this poll, and an explanation of how it was conducted, are to be found in an appendix to my dissertation, "Political Hope: Scheduled Caste Social Movements in the Punjab, 1900–1970," Department of Political Science, University of California, Berkeley, 1974. It should be noted that this survey was taken long before the current rise of Sikh militarism and the polarization of religious sentiments in the Punjab.

4. Charan Singh, discourse to foreign guests, Beas, 12 November 1980.

5. I explore further the notion of social movements as counterstructures in my *Religion as Social Vision: The Movement Against Untouchability in Twentieth-Century Punjab* (Berkeley: University of California Press, 1982), pp. 278–82.

6. Elsewhere I elaborate on the notion that religion in North India is conceived in three ways: as *dharma, qaum,* and *panth*. See my *Religion as Social Vision,* pp. 2–6.

7. Embree borrows the phrase "ideology of transition" from the sociologist Thomas O'Dea to describe how religion in a secular society can "work to stabilize social institutions" and at the same time "become a vehicle for changing and transforming society" (Ainslie T. Embree, *Utopias in Conflict: Religion and Nationalism in Modern India* [Berkeley: University of California Press, 1990], p. 11).

8. *Souvenir in Commemoration of the First Centenary of the Radhasoami Satsang 1861–1961* (Agra: Radhasoami Satsang Sabha, Dayabagh, 1962), pp. 281–82.

9. Maulana Mohammad Yakub, editorial in *The Light,* 28 December 1936, reprinted in *Anand Sarup As Others Saw Him* (Agra: Radhasoami Satsang, Dayalbagh, 1966), p. 171.

10. *Hazur Sahib Maharaj [Anand Swarup] As Others Saw Him,* p. 176. The message was sent on 25 June 1937.

11. *Souvenir*, p. 327.

12. Quoted in Paul Brunton, A *Search in Secret India* (New York: E. P. Dutton, 1935), pp. 236–37.

13. *Souvenir,* p. 313.

14. *Review of Progress Made by Satsang Institutions During the Last Ten Years (1975–1984)*, supplement to the *Dayalbagh Herald*, 13 August 1985, p. 12.

15. *Souvenir,* pp. 314–19. In 1942, in an effort to prove that the colony was self-supporting and required its enormous assets for spiritual purposes, Dayalbagh made a ruling prohibiting even its own members from contributing to the organization. Nonetheless, tax officials continued to hound the Dayalbagh offices (interview with Ram Jadoun, Dayalbagh, 9 November 1973). For a synopsis of Dayalbagh's nineteen-year dispute with the Indian Government's Income Tax Department—from 1935 to 1954—and the several court settlements in Dayalbagh's favor, see *Souvenir*, pp. 345–48.

16. *Review of Progress*, pp. 9–12.

17. *Radhasoami Educational Institute, Prospectus for 1918, Report for 1917* (Hyderabad, Sind: R. H. Advani & Co., 1918), pp. 3, 14.

18. Interview with J. N. Moudgill, Soaminagar, New Delhi, 5 December 1980.

19. *Prospectus and Application Form*, Dayalbagh Educational Institute, Dayalbagh, Agra, 1986–87 session, p. 16.

20. Interview with Mrs. G. P. Sherry, Agra, 8 December 1986.

21. Interview with M. B. Lal, Dayalbagh, 13 August 1986. Regarding the "supermen" motif, see also *Review of Progress*, p. 15, and *Souvenir,* p. 358.

22. Brunton, *Search*, p. 228.

23. Interview with Ram Jadoun, Dayalbagh, 9 November 1973, and V. Sadyanarayana, Dayalbagh, 13 August 1985.

24. Both quotes from *Souvenir*, p. 358.

25. Brunton, *Search*, p. 236.

26. Interview with G. D. Sahgal, Dayalbagh, 12 August 1985. The new locations are at Kaunool, in A.P.; Khandwa, in M.P., and Murar, in Bihar (interview with G. D. Sahgal, Dayalbagh, 8 December 1986).

27. Quoted from Yeats Brown, *Lancer at Large*, in *Souvenir*, p. 366.

28. Julian Johnson, *With a Great Master* (Beas: Radhasoami Satsang, Beas, 1971), p. 99.

29. My information on the Beas *ḍerā* comes from my visits there in 1970–71, 1973, 1978, 1979, 1980 and 1990; interviews with the general secretary, K. L. Khanna, Beas, 25–26 May 1971, and his successor, S.L. Sondhi, Beas, 12 July 1979; and the published reports of the *ḍerā*.

30. S. L. Sondhi, preface to D. L. Kapur, *Heaven on Earth* (Beas: Radhasoami Satsang, Beas, 1986), p. xi.

31. Pratap Singh Seth, *Biography of Soamiji Maharaj* (Agra: Radhasoami Satsang, Soamibagh, 1978), p. 28. G. D. Sahgal, president of the Dayalbagh Sabha, is the descendent of an administrator in the court of Ranjit Singh, the great nineteenth-century king of Punjab (interview with G. D. Sahgal, Dayalbagh, 13 August 1985). For an interesting discussion of the regal aspects of Radhasoami, see Sudhir Kakar, *Shamans, Mystics and Doctors* (Boston: Beacon Press, 1982), pp. 136–37.

32. Interview with K. L. Khanna, Beas, 26 May 1971.

33. In Bendix's massive study of kingship and the origins of modern democracy in five European and Asian societies, the first generalization made about kings is that their authority "depended on religious sanction" (Reinhard Bendix, *Kings or People: Power and the Mandate to Rule* [Berkeley: University of California Press, 1978], p. 4). In a different vein, Clifford Geertz has remarked that "rulers and gods share certain properties" ("Centers, Kings, and Charisma: Reflections on the Symbolics of Power," in Joseph Ben-David and Terry Nichols Clark, eds., *Culture and its Creators: Essays in Honor of Edward Shils* [Chicago: University of Chicago Press, 1977], p. 152).

34. Interview with Charan Singh, Beas, 4 August 1979. Other reasons given for establishing the Beas trust were for "more efficient management" of *ḍerā* properties and to relieve the master of the time and responsibility expended in administering them (Daryai Lal Kapur, *Heaven on Earth,* p. 413).

35. K. L. Khanna, written answers to my questions, 25 May 1971.

36. Charan Singh, *Light on Sant Mat,* 4th ed. (Beas: Radha Soami Satsang, Beas, 1974), pp . 359–60.

37. *Radhasoami Satsang, Beas: Origin and Growth* (Beas: Radhasoami Satsang, Beas, 1972), p. 8.

38. The other prominent woman at Beas is Sheila Bharatram, whose profession is listed as "housewife" (ibid., p. 9). She became president of the Society in 1979 (Radhasoami Satsang, Beas, Annual Reports, 1979).

39. G. D. Sahgal, president, Radhasoami Satsang Sabha, Dayalbagh, 12 August 1985.

40. The brief and uncertain reign of Maharishi Devi, the sister of Brahm Sankar Misra, is recounted in chapter 3 of my *Radhasoami Reality.* The only other woman to be proclaimed a master was Bibi Rani, who succeeded her father in 1966 as leader of a small offshoot of the Soamibagh line. Radhaji,

wife of Swami Shiv Dayal Singh, was assigned to be a sort of spiritual counselor to the female devotees after the Swami's death, but it is not clear whether she was ever regarded as his successor.

41. Interview with Kate Tillis, Landaur, 30 November 1980.

42. Kirpal Singh, *Spiritual Elixir*, vol. 2 (Delhi: Ruhani Satsang, 1972), p. 33.

43. *Souvenir*, p. 330.

44. *Biography of Soamiji Maharaj*, pp. 83, 81, 79.

45. S. D. Maheshwari, *Bhaktamal of Radhasoami Faith* (Agra: Radhasoami Satsang, Soamibagh, 1979), pp. 50–53.

46. Julian Johnson, *With a Great Master in India*, pp. 126–27.

47. Ibid., p. 30.

48. See an interesting exploration of the gender issue in Vaiṣṇava devotion in the essays in John Stratton Hawley and Donna Wulff, eds., *The Divine Consort: Radha and the Goddesses of India;* in Hawley's *Sur Das: Singer, Poet, Saint* (Seattle: University of Washington Press, 1984), pp. 113–18; and his article in Caroline Bynum, ed., *Gender and Religion* (Boston: Beacon Press, 1986).

49. Charan Singh, *Spiritual Heritage*, p. 186.

50. Charan Singh, *The Master Answers*, p. 16.

51. Interview with Kate Tillis, Landaur, 30 November 1980.

52. *Souvenir*, p. 91.

53. Interview with Kate Tillis, 30 November 1980. Charan Singh is said to have told an audience in London that he would not initiate anyone who did not have the potential of reaching the highest regions within this lifetime, and this excluded the blind, whose karmic weight precluded this possibility.

54. Interview with G. D. Sahgal, Dayalbagh, 12 August 1985. A similar explanation has been given to me by initiates at the Beas, Ruhani Satsang and Soamibagh branches.

55. Rai Sahib Munshi Ram, *With the Three Masters*, 2:17.

56. Julian Johnson, *With a Great Master in India*, p. 31.

57. Kirpal Singh, *Godman*, p. 47.

58. Interview with K. L. Khanna, 25 May 1971.

59. Most of the masters in Radhasoami's Tarn Taran line in the Punjab have been celibate, as was Jaimal Singh, founder of the Beas branch. M. B. Lal, present master at Dayalbagh, has been a widower for many years, and has no children.

60. Interview with K. L. Khanna, 25 May 1971.

61. Charan Singh, discourse to foreign *satsaṅgīs*, Beas, 12 November 1980.

62. The fundamentally religious nature of caste is argued by Louis Dumont, *Homo Hierarchicus: The Caste System and its Implications* (Chicago: University of Chicago Press, 1970), p. 47.

63. See my *Religion as Social Vision*, p. 4.

64. The thesis that the *sants* were democratic reformers is put forth in V. Raghavan, *The Great Integrators: The Saint-Singers of India* (New Delhi: Ministry of Information and Broadcasting, Government of India, 1966), p. 32. The issue of whether the spiritual equality of the *sants* was intended to have implications for social equality is discussed by J. S. Hawley in John Stratton Hawley and Mark Juergensmeyer, *Songs of the Saints of India* (New York: Oxford University Press, 1988), pp. 16–17.

Kabīr and Ravidās, especially, have been brought forth as exponents of lower-caste social protest movements. See David Lorenzen, "The Kabir Panth and Social Protest," in K Schomer and W. H. McLeod, eds., *The Sants: Studies in a Devotional Tradition of India* (Delhi: Motilal Banarsidass, 1987), pp. 281–303; and his "Traditions of Non-caste Hinduism," *Contributions to Indian Sociology* 21, no. 2 (1988): 263–83. See also Hawley and Juergensmeyer, *Songs of the Saints*, pp. 9–23, 35–49; and my *Religion as Social Vision,* pp. 83–91.

65. This account is based on my field visit to Nabha, 15 August 1983, and my interview with Sundar Ram, Nabha, 15 August 1983.

66. Pratap Singh Seth, *Biography of Soamiji Maharaj*, pp. 106–8, 110–20.

67. Ibid., p. 89.

68. *Souvenir*, p. 43, 79–80, 93.

69. Interview with Baba Ram Jadoun, 9 November 1973.

70. Interview with K. L. Khanna, Beas, 25 May 1971.

71. Daryai Lal Kapur, *Heaven on Earth,* pp. 326, 328.

72. Jaimal Singh was a member of the Gill subcaste of Jāṭs, Jagat Singh was a Klare, and Sawan Singh and Charan Singh were both Grewals.

73. (Maharaj Sahib) Misra, *A Solace to Satsangis,* 2d ed. (Agra: Radhasoami Satsang, Soamibagh, 1952), pp. 1–3.

74. Thomas A. Timberg, *The Marwaris: From Traders to Industrialists* (New Delhi: Vikas, 1978), pp. 52–53.

75. See Karen Leonard, *Social History of an Indian Caste: The Kayasths of Hyderabad* (Berkeley: University of California Press, 1978).

76. I pursue further the subject of Jāṭ-Khatrī relations and its role in the political turbulence of mid-1980s Punjab in my preface to *Religious Rebels in the Punjab: The Social Vision of Untouchables* (Delhi: Ajanta Books International, 1989). This is the revised edition of my *Religion as Social Vision.*

77. See Kenneth W. Jones, *Arya Dharm: Hindu Consciousness in Nineteenth-Century Punjab* (Berkeley: University of California Press, 1976).

78. Max Weber, *Religion of India* (New York: Free Press, 1958), pp. 199–201.

79. Quotes from Max Weber, *Economy and Society* (Berkeley: University of California Press, 1978), p. 479.

80. Interview with K. L. Khanna, Beas, 25 May 1971.

81. Interview with Ram Jadoun, Dayalbagh, 9 November 1973.

Sanskritization, Caste Uplift and Social Dissidence in the Sant Ravidās Panth

Joseph Schaller

Ravidās (ca. 15/16th cent. C.E.) was a medieval poet and saint in the devotional or bhakti religious tradition of Hinduism. He and the other saints who worshipped the aniconic, formless *(nirguṇ)* aspect of the Absolute are known as *sant*s. Ravidās was a member of the Chamār caste, an Untouchable caste, whose traditional occupation was removing animal carcasses, particularly those of cows, and tanning the hides of these animals. Today he is widely worshipped or revered throughout North India predominantly by Chamārs and other Untouchable caste groups.

Although they occupy the very bottom of the social hierarchy, the Chamārs and other Untouchable groups who worship Sant Ravidās do not passively accept their inferior status. Their worship of Ravidās is the manifestation of a dissident socioreligious ideology. The primary purpose of this essay is to explore the form, content, and dissemination of this dissident socioreligious ideology and practice as expressed in the poetry of Ravidās, and among the contemporary movement's devotees and leadership.

Oppositional and reform movements centered around low-caste saints such as Ravidās arise partially in opposition to the "institutionalized inequality" embodied in the caste system (Berreman 1971, 20). In order to raise their status within this system, lower caste and Untouchable groups in India have adopted various means including those of religious conversion, as well as varying degrees of Sanskritization. In the context of the *nirguṇ* bhakti tradition of Hinduism, the "teachings of the *nirguṇī* saints" *(sant mat)* has provided the foundation for an often dissident socioreligious philosophy and ideology. It is to this tradition that Sant Ravidās and the contemporary movement centered around him belongs. I shall briefly consider some of the common values of the *sant mat* in the second part of this essay, and how these are expressed in the dissident socioreligious ideology espoused by the contemporary followers of the Ravidās Panth.

In the era surrounding India's independence, the most well-known instance of mass religious conversion was that of the Mahārs of Maharashtra to the neo-Buddhism advocated by Dr. B. R. Ambedkar. The conversion of the Jātavs of Agra, a Chamār subcaste, to the neo-Buddhism of Dr. Ambedkar can be directly traced to the influence wielded by him (Lynch 1969, 130). According to Lynch (1969, 141), the foundation of Dr. Ambedkar's neo-Buddhism was "its unequivocal rejection of Hinduism." Dr. Ambedkar outlined the necessity of completely rejecting Hinduism in a speech intended for the Circle for the Elimination of Casteism (Jāt-pāt Toḍak Maṇḍal) of Lahore in 1936; this speech was later published in 1945 under the title of the "Annihilation of Caste" (Ambedkar 1945, cited in Lynch 1969, 141). In January 1957, a procession was held in Agra to commemorate the death of Dr. Ambedkar just over a month earlier and to install the silver urn containing his ashes at the new Buddhist temple that had been established at Chaki Pat in this city in March 1956. At this event an estimated three thousand Agra Jātav Chamārs were converted (Lynch 1969, 145–46).

In contemporary India, the Jātav Chamārs and other Untouchable groups continue their conversion to other religious traditions in their ongoing struggle for self-respect and socioeconomic and political equality. On 5 September 1990, some one thousand Agra Jātavs of Jaunpur village and nearby settlements were converted to Sikhism following the conclusion of a four-day Sikh convocation *(saṅgam)* held in the area. The mass conversion was said to be a sequel to rioting in Panwari village on 23 June 1990, when some upper-caste Hindus had attempted to halt a wedding procession being taken out by the Jātav Chamār community. Following the rioting, the leaders of this community had decided upon this conversion "as a means to secure social justice" (*Times of India,* 6 Sept. 1990). The conversion was jointly sponsored by the Uttar Pradesh Akali Dal youth wing and the Shiromani Gurudwara Prabhandak Committee of Amritsar. It was led by Bābā Nirañjan Singh, the head priest of the local Guru Katal gurudwārā. Two political leaders, Mr. B. P. Maurya, former Union minister, and Mr. Gulab Sehra, former U.P. transport minister, announced that approximately one million (10 lakh) Untouchables of the Jātav community would convert to Buddhism during September and October of that year (ibid.).

In his landmark study, published shortly after India's independence, M. N. Srinivas developed his concept of Sanskritization. This concept has dominated much intellectual discussion about how middle and lower caste groups within the caste system in South Asia attempt to raise their ritual, that is, socioreligious, status (Srinivas 1952; 1962; 1968). With respect to Untouchable groups, Srinivas himself has pointed out that the "barrier of Untouchability" is one such groups are unable to overcome no matter how thoroughly they Sanskritize their behavior; nevertheless, he argues (1962, 58-59): "The fact that Sanskritization does not help the Untouchables to move up does not, however, make Sanskritization any the less popular [among them]." Srinivas also argues that Sanskritization has served as a safety valve to ventilate the collective frustrations of middle and lower caste groups at the inherent inequality of the caste system, groups which have adopted it as a means of raising their status within this system. In this essay, I shall discuss these assertions and argue that for the Chamārs it is in part the very failure of the adoption of more Sanskritized behavior to improve their socioreligious status that has hastened their embrace of more radically dissident ideologies such as that which is implicit in the worship of Sant Ravidās. And while some examples of Sanskritization can be found among the current devotees of Sant Ravidās, my research suggests this concept possesses little relevance for them as a means of improving their socioreligious status in the context of contemporary India.

In order to elucidate the context in which the adherents of the Ravidās movement struggle to improve their physical and social well being, this essay is divided into two major sections. In the first, I shall discuss Srinivas's ideas about the process of Sanskritization and consider its efficaciousness in raising the socioreligious status of the Untouchable Chamārs. In this discussion, I will draw upon two separate case studies conducted in the two decades following India's independence, as well as the views of my own informants in this regard. In the second section, I will examine the dissident socioreligious ideology espoused by the Chamār and other followers of Ravidās, and some of the main strategies employed for its dissemination.

Sanskritization among Chamār Castes and Subcastes in Theory and Practice

The Theory of Sanskritization

According to Srinivas (1962, 45), there are three axes of power in the caste system: ritual rank, economic resources and political power. On occasion, a disjunction among these different types of power wielded by a particular group may be found, for instance, a caste may possess both economic and political power but low ritual rank. In such instances, the adoption of Sanskritization by the group in question almost always occurred since "without it the claim to a higher position was not fully effective." Thus, the adoption of Sanskritization by a particular caste group served to bring its ritual status into equilibrium with its economic and/or political power.

In his original formulation of the concept of Sanskritization, Srinivas argues that the caste system is not the rigid system its hierarchical structure would make it appear to be. He states the essential tenets of this initial version of Sanskritization as follows (1952, 30):

> The caste system is far from a rigid system in which the position of each component caste is fixed for all time. Movement has always been possible and especially so in the middle regions of the hierarchy. A low caste was able, in a generation or two, to rise to a higher position in the hierarchy by adopting vegetarianism and teetotalism, and by Sanskritizing its ritual and pantheon. In short, it took over, as far as possible, the customs, rites, and beliefs of the Brahmins, and the adoption of the Brahminic way of life by a low caste seems to have been frequent, though theoretically forbidden.

Later, Srinivas himself (1968, 7–10) would reject the above model of Sanskritization as too "Brahminical" and revise it accordingly. I will consider his revised versions of this concept later on in the essay. The necessity of a caste altering its diet and prohibiting the use of intoxicants, however, are central to the ritual status or lack thereof possessed by Chamārs and other Untouchables.

In the Vedic period, textual sources attest to the consumption of beef and imbibing of powerful stimulants like Soma in the performance of Vedic ritual. In the post-Vedic era, however, both of these activities became taboo and ultimately assumed highly pejorative connotations (Srinivas 1968, 24–25). The consumption of beef by the Chamārs has long been considered one of the primary reasons for their degraded status (Briggs 1920, 45); the same is true for other Untouchable groups throughout North India with respect to tending "polluting" animals such as pigs and consuming meat. Whether deserved or not, the widespread belief that Chamārs and other Untouchable groups are also consumers of alcohol and other intoxicating substances negatively influences how they are perceived by higher caste groups in the social hierarchy (Srinivas 1968, 26). Let us now consider the actual effects of the adoption of more Sanskritized behavior by Chamār groups in two different areas of North India.

Sanskritization in Practice: Two Case Studies

During a one-year period in 1952–53, Bernard Cohn (1956) carried out field research in Madhopur village located in the southeastern part of Jaunpur district, Uttar Pradesh (hereafter U.P.). In a paper based upon this research he describes the attempts by the Chamārs of this village, the numerically predominant caste, to raise their social status. Rājpūt landlords are the dominant caste in the village and the second most numerous group. Cohn also notes that the Madhopur Chamārs identify themselves as Raidāsīs. He dismisses the significance of this, however, by drawing upon the work of Briggs (1920) and Grierson (1921) to state (1956, 59): "Raidās does not seem to have founded an organized and enduring sect."

Some thirty years prior to the date of Cohn's study, the Jaiswar Chamārs of the area around Madhopur banded together in an attempt to raise their status by prohibiting two activities: the consumption of beef (from the dead cows it was their traditional responsibility to haul away and skin), and the hauling of manure to the fields of the Rājpūt landlords for whom they worked. In response to the latter action the Chamārs were forced to flee their villages in order to escape the wrath of the landlords. Ultimately, they were permitted to return to the village but were no longer required to perform the work of carting manure they considered degrading. Inspired by this action, the wives of the Chamār laborers took action themselves: they refused any longer to make fuel cakes of cow dung for the homes of the Rājpūt landlords. Ultimately, they too were relieved of this obligation which they perceived as degrading. Cohn notes, however, the Chamārs' attempts at raising their status through these Sanskritizing acts did little or nothing to alter it in the eyes of their upper-caste brethren (Cohn 1956, 73).

My second example is drawn from the work of Owen Lynch (1969), based upon his field research amongst the Jātavs of Agra, a Chamār subcaste. Lynch (1969, 2) notes that in pre-independence India, the Jātavs initiated a systematic attempt to raise their caste status through altering their dietary habits and Sanskritizing their religious practices. Specifically, they stopped eating beef and attempted to adopt many of the ritual practices of more orthoprax Hinduism. The failure of such efforts to achieve their desired aims, however, led the Jātav Chamārs to change their strategy for attaining their objectives in the context of post-independence India. Lynch states (1969, 97):

> The change is due to the fact that Sanskritization is no longer as effective a means as is political participation for achieving a change in style of life and a rise in the Indian social system, now composed of both caste and class elements. The ultimate object of Sanskritization was to open and legitimize a place in the opportunity and power structures of the caste society. It is hoped that the same objectives can now be achieved by active, but separatist political participation.

The experiences, discontents and hopes expressed by my own informants strongly support Lynch's contention that in the context of post-independence India, the focus of low-caste and Untouchable opposition movements is not merely greater social status, but economic uplift and political representation truly representative of their own interests. Srinivas himself notes (1968, 21) that a caste group adopting Sanskritization independent of acquiring economic and political power will fail to improve its social status thereby. Let us now examine how some of these issues are framed in the current discourse among the devotees, ascetics (sadhus), temple officiants *(pujārīs)* and political leadership of the Ravidās Panth as well as Chamār nondevotees.

Sanskritization, Caste Uplift and the Ravidās Panth

The data upon which this and following sections of the essay are based was collected during my field research in North India from December 1989 until April 1991. I was based in Varanasi, U.P., and conducted much of my initial fieldwork at the Ravidās temple in the village of Seer Govardhanpur behind Banaras Hindu University, which is also the subheadquarters of the All-India Adi Dharm Mission (hereafter cited as the ADM). The latter organization sponsors this temple and has headquarters in New Delhi. Extensive fieldwork was conducted at the numerous non-ADM temples, shrines and village communities where Ravidās is worshipped in the areas around Varanasi. Intensive fieldwork was also carried out with the cooperation of the ADM's executive leadership at the several major Ravidās temples they help sponsor both individually and collectively in New Delhi and at the ADM Ravidās monastery *(maṭh)* and temple in Karrapur village, Sagar District, Madhya Pradesh. Finally, during my research I also met with numerous Ravidāsī sadhus, devotees and a temple priest from other parts of U.P. and the state of Bihar.

The next section of the essay is based mainly upon the twenty-five formal interviews I conducted among the Ravidāsī devotees and two Chamār nondevotees. All the respondents are either Chamār by caste or one of its subcastes with the exception of the ADM working-president, who is from the Ahir caste, although he too chose to identify himself as a Chamār. The names of respondents have been changed with the exception of the ADM officials. In response to separate questions concerning their self-ascribed caste background and religious affiliation, respondents answered either with "Chamār" or "Ravidāsī" to the first question, "Ādivāsī," "(not-) Hindu," or "Ravidāsī" to the latter question. The use of the term Ādivāsī has particular connotations in reference to the ADM's goals and ideology which will be discussed later on in the essay. Table 1 displays numerically all respondent's answers concerning their caste background and religious identity.

Table 1: Self-ascribed Caste Background and Religious Status.

Caste Identity	*Religious Identity*		
Chamār	8	7	4[a]
Chamār subcastes:			
Jātav		1	
Jaiswal (1)[b]			
Ravidāsī	3	1	
	Ādivāsī	Hindu	Ravidāsī

[a]One of the respondents identified his caste status as "Chāmar," although his surname is Ahir, which is one of the dominant peasant castes in North India.

[b]One Chāmar, a nondevotee, identified his religious status only as "non-Hindu."

This process of self-ascription is significant, as Steve Barnett states in his study of identity choice and caste ideology in South India

(1977, 394): "Given the rapid and profound changes in caste in this century, Indians can choose amongst a number of identities, and the relation of these choices to caste is central to understanding the operation of ideologies in everyday life."

As noted above, Srinivas regards vegetarianism and abstinence from alcohol as two of the main pillars of the Sanskritizing process. In both the case studies I examined earlier, prohibiting the consumption of beef was one of the primary actions taken by both of the Chāmar groups attempting to raise their status via this process. Among those whom I interviewed, however, while vegetarianism and refraining from the use of intoxicants were considered exemplary, especially for sadhus, it was clear neither of these practices constituted normative behavior for either Chāmar devotees or nondevotees.

From all the devotees and two *pujārīs* questioned on the subject, only one devotee and one *pujārī* indicated they were strictly vegetarian. All of the sadhus indicated they were vegetarians. One of the two Chamār nondevotees thought highly of vegetarianism but was not himself one, while the other consumed meat gladly when it was available. All of the devotees and *pujārīs* stated that virtually all Chamārs who are not devotees will consume meat when it is available, and that among devotees both vegetarians and nonvegetarians are present.

Regarding the use of intoxicating substances, particularly alcohol and hemp *(gāñjā)*, all the devotees and one of the two *pujārīs* indicated occasional use was common. One of the two *pujārīs* explicitly forbade the use of these substances. The use of hemp is highly prevalent among the sadhus of certain ascetic sects, however, and carries no particular stigma as it does among the Ravidāsī sadhus and among the majority of both devotees and *pujārīs*.

Concern for the polluting effects of both eating meat or using intoxicants, however, was expressed by two of the devotees at the Ravidās temple in Varanasi. Both of them indicated that anyone either consuming meat or imbibing alcohol should follow a one-day self-imposed restriction on entering the temple which demonstrates a concern for the sanctity of the enclosure.[1] Nevertheless, it was clear from all the respondents' answers that neither vegetarianism nor moderating the use of certain intoxicants, both of which Srinivas earlier regarded as integral to the Sanskritizing process, are widely practiced among either the devotees of Ravidās or Chamārs in general.

As noted earlier, Srinivas concluded that his original formulation of the Sanskritization concept was too "Brahminical." In later essays, he would revise this concept in order that it might encompass groups further down in the caste hierarchy who were seeking to improve their socioreligious status via its adoption. According to one of these later revisions, this concept is reformulated as follows (Srinivas 1968, 6): "Sanskritization is the process by which a 'low' Hindu caste, or tribal or other group, changes its customs, ritual, ideology, and way of life in the direction of a high, and frequently, 'twice-born' caste."

Thus, in addition to altering its dietary habits, Srinivas also suggests a low caste will adopt the worship of more highly Sanskritized deities and ritual practices in order to raise its status. Historically, another major cause of the Chamārs' low status has been their worship of non-Sanskritic deities and the performance of non-Brahminical religious rites. This includes a belief in ghosts and a world of spirits, and the practice of animal sacrifice. According to Briggs (1920, 125–36), goats were used by the Chamārs for divination while the worship of non-Sanskritic deities was related to the control and cure of disease.

The Ravidāsī devotees and Chamār nondevotees split evenly on the question of worshipping non-Sanskritic deities with half saying that they did so and the other half saying they did not. Those who did worship them gave a variety of reasons for doing so, the foremost being for the relief of bodily pain or distress as well as protection from potentially malevolent forces. All the sadhus, except one, and both *pujārīs* stated they worshipped only Guru Ravidās.

Regarding animal sacrifice, all the devotees and *pujārīs* said such acts were no longer performed by their caste group. Half the devotees at the Ravidās temple in Varanasi, however, admitted that such sacrifices used to occur there regularly, primarily for the purpose of warding off disease, until some twenty-five years ago when the construction of the temple began. Interestingly, both of the nondevotee Chamārs admitted such sacrifices were still regularly performed by their caste fellows although neither of them participated in such rites. Mr. Sohan Singh Ahir, the current ADM working-president who is employed as an official in the Indian civil service, said to me in this context (interview 20 February 1990): "Yes, some Chamārs still do these things, but as one's education increases these beliefs vanish." As his statement suggests, the extent of such practices is clearly related to the very diverse levels of class and other forms of socioeconomic status existing among this group as a whole in contemporary India. Nevertheless, the worship of non-Sanskritic deities and performance of animal sacrifices by some Chamār devotees, and especially nondevotees, suggests the failure of Sanskritization to spread among a very large proportion of the Chamār population.

These two practices are not, of course, exhaustive of all the forms of ritual and worship prevalent in this caste. In Hindu social and religious life one passes through certain rites of passage *(saṃskār)* depending upon his/her stage in life. Some of these rites such as marriage virtually all Hindus will undergo, while some such as the investiture of the sacred thread *(upanayan)* are confined to the twice-born castes. How extensive the performance of such rites are and who performs them in the Chamār community provides further evidence for the adoption or lack thereof of Sanskritizing practices by this community.

In the interview, the respondents were asked to describe in detail their worship practices. As might be expected, all of the devotees described themselves as following the path of *nirguṇ* devotion just like Guru Ravidās did and were devoted mainly to him (almost all devotees also revered and/or worshipped Dr. Ambedkar as well). Eleven of the thirteen sadhu respondents indicated they worshipped Guru Ravidās exclusively; one admitted to being a practicing Vaishnavite in addition to worshipping Guru Ravidās and one did not respond. Among both groups, the singing of devotional songs *(bhajan)* or concentrating upon the lord's name or image *(jap)* were the most widely preferred forms of worship.

All of the devotees, both *pujārīs*, and one of the two nondevotees indicated they and their families all celebrated the *saṃskārs* relevant to their socioeconomic status and caste affiliation. All of them, including both Chamār nondevotees, indicated one of their own caste fellows and not a Brahmin pandit would officiate over the ceremony in question.[2] In the case of the Ravidāsīs in Seer Govardhanpur village, this would be one or both of the two temple *pujārīs* who officiated in a wedding during my period of fieldwork there. One of the devotees in this village did state that a few of his caste fellows employed Brahmins to conduct their ritual performances as they believed the rites would be conducted more efficaciously *(sahī)* thereby.[3] There was little evidence, however, to suggest that this occurs on a large scale.

Finally, all the respondents were almost evenly divided on the question of the cause of their Untouchable status in this birth. Just over half indicated it was a consequence of their actions or karma in a previous birth; the other half argued that in reality caste does not exist and all humankind is unconditionally equal. While the opinion of the former provide some evidence for the spread of Sanskritic ideas amongst the Chamārs, I would argue this influence is limited at best for reasons such as their being denied access to Sanskritic texts and education. The opinion of the latter half indicates their acceptance of one of the central tenets of the ADM ideology, which I shall discuss at greater length shortly.

Both of the case studies examined earlier highlight the almost total failure of Sanskritization to significantly enhance the Chamārs' ritual status which Srinivas argues is the primary benefit it offers. My own research calls into question not only the efficacy of the Sanskritizing process in this regard, but its relevance both to the Untouchable Chamārs of the contemporary Ravidās movement *(panth)* and especially non-devotee Chamārs, given the quite limited extent to which it has been adopted among these two branches of the Chamār community. Again, I reiterate here Srinivas's claim that while for Untouchable groups the barrier of Untouchability would appear to be insurmountable no matter to what extent such groups Sanskritize their behavior, this does not serve to diminish the popularity of its adoption among these and other low-caste groups (see note 9). Accompanying Srinivas's later revision of this concept quoted above, he states (1968, 7): "Sanskritization results only in positional changes in the [caste] system and does not lead to any structural change." Yet, such structural change is exactly what is being demanded by the Chamār followers of Ravidās and other organized Untouchable and low-caste groups. Accompanying these demands for change is an underlying dissident socioreligious ideology which intends to subvert, if not overturn, the social, economic, and political prerogatives of the upper castes in the hierarchical caste order.

I shall now explore the development of this dissident socioreligious ideology in the context of the devotional religious tradition, and how this ideology is expressed in Ravidās's poetry, among his contemporary devotees, and by the ADM organization which claims to speak for the Ravidās movement as a whole. Some of the strategies employed by the ADM for gaining control of this movement and extending the range of its influence will also be considered.

Dissident Social Ideology in the (Nirguṇ) Bhakti Tradition and the Ravidās Panth

The devotional religious tradition of Hinduism is amenable to a variety of interpretations. This tradition is comprised of two distinct, though not mutually exclusive, schools: the *nirguṇī* and *saguṇī*. While a scholar such as Hawley (1988, 3–8) is careful to demarcate the opposing theological positions of each of these schools, he nevertheless emphasizes the inclusion of each school's members in a united family of saints. Jayant Lele (1981, 5–6) argues persuasively that a tradition such as the bhakti movement contains seemingly contradictory elements of hegemony, oppression, and liberation all at once: the hegemony of tradition, the embodiment of this hegemony in an oppressive social order, and yet the existence within this tradition of liberating, dissident, and reformist elements as well. In a recent article on Mīrābāī and the bhakti movement, Kumkum Sangari (1990, 1464) too notes the liberalizing and dissident aspects of this tradition, and interprets them as joining together in it "as a powerful force which selectively uses the metaphysic of high Hinduism in an attempt to create an inappropriable excess or transcendent value grounded in the dailiness of a material life within the reach of all." While these scholars clearly recognize the competing hegemonic and reformist aspects of the bhakti tradition, most scholars of this tradition have tended to emphasize its egalitarian aspects, which are perceived as fostering social reform and helping to dissipate the tensions inherent to the social hierarchy of the caste system. In embarking upon my fieldwork, I took this conception of the bhakti movement as an operating assumption the validity of which I wished to test among the predominantly Chamār devotees of Ravidās. My research into his poetry, the composition of his contemporary followers, and the messages of protest implicit in much of their worship, however, has lent support to an opposing interpretation of the contemporary Ravidās Panth and, by extension, of the socioreligious movements centered around other low-caste saints of the *nirguṇī sant* movement.

With respect to the *sant* tradition as a whole, Charlotte Vaudeville (1987, 22) has commented that in general the *sants* are nonsectarian and share no common body of doctrine. She states further that in spite of this, they share certain common characteristics which distinguish them from both "educated" poets as well as poets affiliated with various religious sects. One of these is the strong anti-Brahminical tone that pervades much of *sant* poetry. And if orthodoxy in the Hindu context is defined as accepting the authority of the Vedas and the Brahminical tradition which flourished and reigned supreme long into the post-Vedic era, then Hindu, and particularly Muslim *sants*, may be regarded as "heterodox" or "heretics" in this context. The label of heterodox or heretical is not applicable to the Maharashtrian Vārkarī saints, however, who retain strong ties with the Bhāgavat or nonsectarian tradition of Vaishnavism (Vaudeville 1987, 22–23). In the conclusion to her essay, Vaudeville acknowledges the much more radical position adopted by the northern *sant*s, particularly Kabīr, in comparison with other bhakti saints (1987, 38): "The northern Sants . . . seem to have gone a step or two further than even the most liberal of the ancient Bhāgavats and of the southern Sants as a whole by actually breaking with the Brahminical tradition altogether."

Recent work by David Lorenzen (1987; 1987a; 1987b) has challenged the conventional interpretations of the bhakti movement by highlighting the competing approach and emphases of this movement's two schools. He argues that the contemporary followers of Kabīr use Kabīr's teachings—whatever their original intent or function—in order to reject the marginality assigned them in the hierarchical caste order (1987, 283):

> The basic hypothesis of this paper is that the strong element of social and religious dissent in Kabir's teachings, whatever its original intent and function, has been used by the adherents of the panth—mostly marginal groups such as Shudras, Untouchables and Tribals—to express their rejection of certain aspects of hierarchical caste ideology. . . . [T]he more egalitarian ideology of the Kabir-panth does provide them with a positive self-image, one which rejects the innate and absolute character of the inferior status to which they are relegated by more orthodox Brahminical Hinduism.

Similarly, the contemporary adherents of the Ravidās panth who are overwhelmingly from Chamār or other Untouchable and marginal caste backgrounds, utilize the elements of socioreligious dissent expressed in Ravidās' poetry and teachings to formulate their own message(s) of protest against the iniquitous position they occupy in the caste hierarchy.

Bhakti is the love of and devotion to God. A boundless love and devotion to God is the pervasive theme of Ravidās's poetry; it also forms the basis for his egalitarian social philosophy, according to which all who practice selfless devotion are rendered equal thereby, no matter their caste affiliation or other status. In his poetry, Brahmins, who are usually portrayed as lacking such devotion, are caricatured as hollow figures pumped up with false pride and hypocrisy; the endless rituals they perform are disparaged as empty in comparison with the power and salvific potentialities inherent in loving devotion.[4] Finally, he upholds the path of *nirguṇ* devotion as supreme for attaining liberation from the endless cycle of birth and rebirth.[5] I have selected just one poem *(pad)* from the *Raidās-vānī* (hereafter *RV*) to exemplify these themes:

Refrain:

rẽ chit chẽt achet kāhe bālak ko dẽkh re.
jāti te koī pad nahĩ pahũcha Rām bhagati bisekh re.

O mind! Come to your senses! Why are you unconscious?
Look at the child!
By caste alone no one has obtained liberation; devotion to
Rām is incomparable.

1. *khaṭkram sahit je bipra hote Haribhagati chit driḍh nāhī rẽ*
Hari kī kathā suhāy nāhĩ Supach tūlai tāhi re.

There are Brahmins who perform the six rituals daily, still
their hearts are not resolute in devotion to Hari.
The stories of Hari are not pleasing to them; they are just like
that Chaṇḍāl Supach.

2. *mitra śatra ajāt sab tẽ antar lāvai het rẽ.*
lāg vā kī kahā̃ jānai, tīn lok pabet rẽ.

He brings love in his heart for all whether friend, enemy or
one of low caste.
Who knows the location of that love which pervades the
three worlds?

3. *Ajāmil gaj janikā tārī kāṭī kuñjar kī pās re.*
aise durmat kīye to kyõ na tarai Raidās re.

He ferried across the Brahmin Ajāmil, an elephant and a prostitute, and cut the elephant's noose.
He liberated such fallen ones: so why has Raidās not been liberated?

Rāg Soraṭhā 48

Time and again in his poetry Ravidās upholds devotion as the sole determinant of one's true worth and as the most efficacious means of obtaining ultimate liberation: the power and status accruing by virtue of one's position at birth in the Hindu caste order is rejected.

As noted above, p. 103, the singing of bhajans is the preferred mode of worship among the Ravidās devotees, sadhus, *pujārīs* and Chamār nondevotees I met. As part of my fieldwork, I collected a total of some eighty-five bhajans sung by them. By category, these bhajans are divided as follows:

1) Thirty-five bhajans (41 percent) are in praise of the Guru.
2) Twenty-eight bhajans (33 percent) are based mostly upon the hagiographical tales of Ravidās's life.
3) Eighteen bhajans (21 percent,) describe the hypocrisy of the world and/or the inevitability of death.
4) Sixteen bhajans (19 percent) exhort their listeners to seek liberation on the Guru's path steadfastly.[6]

The remainder can be grouped thematically according to the headings of: songs of entreaty *(bintī)* to the guru (12); songs patterned after verses in the *Raidās-vānī* (6); songs dedicated to the memory of Dr. Ambedkar (4); songs which use or refer to Tantric vocabulary or technique (2). The total number of bhajans shown exceeds eighty-five due to some being listed in multiple categories.

The terms *kīrtan* and *satsaṅg* ("devotional song/singing" and "good company") are the terms most often used by devotees to refer to a bhajan singing session. Often, brief didactic stories or moral exhortations are interspersed with the songs and are recited by the singer him/herself or someone nominally in charge of the gathering. The source for the longer exhortations or stories are often excerpts drawn from the stories of Guru Ravidās's life and draw their moral authority from this as well. Noting the role played by Smārta Brahmins in leading a devotional cult in Madras centered around the worship of Rādhā and Krishna, many of whose members are from the lower two twice-born castes, Milton Singer suggests the bhajans sung by this group serve two possible functions (1966, 1214): "(1) providing an easier path to salvation in an age when the paths of strict ritual observances, religious knowledge, and ascetic withdrawal have become difficult or inaccessible, and (2) reducing the consciousness of caste, sect . . . and the tensions generated by this consciousness."

Singer upholds the interpretation, discussed earlier, of bhakti as an integrative force. While the predominant message of most of the bhajans I recorded was the unity of all who practice true devotion, they also often serve as a medium of protest for the devotees of the Ravidās movement against the injustices they and other Untouchables have suffered in occupying the lowest strata of the hierarchical caste order.

These bhajans praise Guru Ravidās in terms of reverence and adoration. He is depicted as the locus of inestimable grace, power and majesty who helps ferry his devotees over the ocean of existence. In those bhajans drawing upon the hagiographical tales of his life, the Brahmins often arrayed against him are generally portrayed as hypocritical and dishonest opponents who are incapable of defeating him no matter what ruse they might employ. Just one such bhajan is cited below which elucidates these themes and articulates the feelings of many of Ravidās's contemporary devotees forcefully and elegantly.

The author of this bhajan is Jagatnāth Rām, a lifetime resident of Varanasi. He states he has been a Ravidās devotee throughout his life like his father before him. Jagatnāth worked as a minor civil servant until his retirement in 1987. He claims to have over one hundred disciples in and around Varanasi. He never sings himself but does play percussion instruments during bhajan sessions on occasion (interview, 25 January 1991). The bhajan was actually sung by one of his disciples, Gwālanāth of Lahartara village, just outside Varanasi proper. Gwālanāth is of course also a devotee of Guru Ravidās.

> By accepting any religion which was created with feelings *(bhāvnā)* of high and low, humanity feels shame.
>
> That religion which does not judge *(chinhe)* one by his actions, has given us great sorrow. It has given us great sorrow.
>
> Even though devoid of good qualities the fair-skinned Brahmins [are highly regarded], while Śūdras though wise, skillful and of good character are disregarded.

That religion which is expounded in the *Rāmāyaṇa*, has given us great sorrow.
We were forbidden from studying the Vedas and were blinded for doing so.
Those of us who listened to them were caused to go deaf.
You established the tradition that a Śūdra is not a human being; this was established by you and not a demon like Rāvaṇa.
You have taken away our means of livelihood by force; and have stolen all of our rights.
Having needlessly become Hindus, our deeds met with frustration—this religion has caused us great sorrow.
Who is more knowledgeable than Vyāsa *muni* about the *Mahābhārata*?
Is there any other creator like Vālmīki of the *Rāmāyaṇa*?
The sages Supach, Kumbhaj and Parashar were the light of knowledge, but Cheta and Ravidās were not their inferiors in wisdom.
O great Manu! You didn't do justice: you didn't behave like a human being.
That religion which does not know the internal mysteries of the *sant*s has caused us great sorrow.
What did the glorious Guru Droṇacharaj [Sanskrit: Droṇāchārya] do with his disciple?
Eklavya did not obtain any instruction from him.
Having cut off his thumb you snatched away his knowledge of archery by force; and you became pleased having distributed this knowledge amongst your best disciples.
You made the Kauravas and Pāṇḍavas very pleased, and set yourself on the sinful path.[7]
You set yourself on the sinful path; and you treated the Kauravas brutally.
That religion has caused us great sorrow.
In Rām's reign Sambūkh did not do anything to lessen Rām's glory.
He was a Śūdra practicing asceticism; he was not committing any sin.
Why did Rām ultimately have to punish Sambūkh with death?
From the Śūdra's austerities a crisis arose in this hypocritical religion.
Consider the recent story of Baba Sahab Ambedkar: has any man been born who was more law-abiding than him?
When everyone heard that he had switched religions they burned [with anger].
Shit in water will not remain submerged for long; this pot of sin will certainly be filled.
Find a way to create a little love immediately.
This religion has caused us great sorrow.
This religion has caused us great sorrow.

In this bhajan, tales drawn from the two great Indian epics, the *Mahābhārata* and *Rāmāyaṇa,* are interpreted from the perspective of the Chamār devotees of Guru Ravidās. Instead of revering the predominantly high-caste heroes of these stories as men of great wisdom or manifestations of the divine (avatars), upholding the sanctity and moral rectitude of the *varṇāśramadharma* order, the author emphasizes the injustice and suffering meted out to the Untouchable and low-caste victims as heroes. He refers contemptuously to semidivine figures such as Manu who established this order and the inhumanity it fosters towards those lowest in it.

The opposition of the Ravidās devotees to and their contempt for the hierarchical social order of the caste system expressed in their songs of devotion contradicts the conventional interpretation of the bhakti movement as an integrative force mitigating the worst aspects of casteism. Rather, many of Sant Ravidās's contemporary followers express a dissident socioreligious ideology which challenges the hegemonic power of the dominant castes who are often perceived and portrayed by these devotees as their oppressors. This ideology is most coherently articulated and systematically propagated by the ADM organization which founded the Ravidās temple at Varanasi and which seeks ever greater control over this expanding movement.

The next section of the paper is based upon three primary sources, two of which are ADM pamphlets: one of them contains their constitution and bylaws, the second concerns the "aims and objectives" of the movement.[8] The third is the interviews I conducted with the leaders of the ADM organization at their headquarters in New Delhi and the Ravidās temples they control in the capital, at Seer Govardhanpur in Varanasi, and the monastery temple at Karrapur village, Sagar District, M.P.

The forerunner of the ADM was the Ādi-dharm, later renamed the Ādi-dharm Maṇḍal ("Society of/for the Original Religion") founded in 1920 by Maṅgu Rām of Mugowal village, Hoshiarpur District, Punjab (pamphlet 2:2).[9] More about this organization's history and efforts, especially on the campaign against Untouchability in the Punjab, can be found in Mark Juergensmeyer's work on the subject (1982). The ADM was formed in the year 1960 under the leadership of Banta Rām Ghera, who has been the mission's president since its founding. The ADM defines itself as "a non-political and socio-religious organization, working for the dissemination and promotion of [the] cultural heritage of so-called downtrodden (Scheduled Caste/Scheduled Tribe) people in India and abroad" (pamphlet 2:6). According to Mr. Khuśī Rām (interview, 19 February 1990), the ADM's longtime general secretary and current vice-president, some fifteen years before its formal organization the mission was responsible for organizing the first procession celebrating the birth of Guru Ravidās, which is believed to have occurred on Māgh Pūrṇimā (the full moon day in the month of Māgh, i.e., February-March). At all the Ravidās temples currently under its control the celebration of Guru Ravidās's birth (Ravidās Jayantī) is now held at this time annually and constitutes the largest and most prominent festival of the movement.

In an earlier section of this essay, I discussed Srinivas's concept of Sanskritization and its failure to increase the ritual, that is, socioreligious, status of Chamār groups who had altered their patterns of behavior in accordance with it. Recognizing the failure of a low-caste group's attaining significant improvement in their ritual status solely by means of adopting more highly Sanskritized behavior, Srinivas continued to revise this concept in later essays. In one of these essays, he states (1962, 57):

> Sanskritization does not automatically result in the achievement of a higher status for the group. The group concerned must clearly put forward a claim to belong to a particular varna, Vaishya, Kshatriya, or Brahmin. They must alter their customs, diet, and way of life suitably, and if there are any inconsistencies in their claim, they must try to "explain" them by inventing an appropriate myth.

The ADM does indeed advance an appropriate myth to legitimate their demands. If accepted, however, this myth would reverse entirely the hierarchical caste order to place the Untouchables on top in accord with the status which was once theirs according to the ADM. This myth's content is as follows.

Almost three thousand years ago, those who are today known as the Scheduled Castes (Ādi-dharmīs) and Scheduled Tribes (Ādivāsīs) were the original inhabitants and rulers of India, which was then a very prosperous country. At that time in central Asia there was a drought which had lasted for many years, causing a terrible famine. So the people of central Asia who were known as Aryans began to migrate to India. Initially, the Ādi-dharmīs and Ādivāsīs resisted their advance and killed almost half of those attempting to migrate. Finally, the

Aryans begged the Ādi-dharmīs and Ādivāsīs for permission to stay in India until the drought and famine in their own country ended.

Most of the Aryans were robbers and liars (pamphlet 1:4), whereas the Ādi-dharmīs and Ādivāsīs of India were truthful, benevolent, helpful, and meditated continually upon God through his true gurus. Seeing the bad habits and character of the Aryans, the indigenous peoples "began to call them Hindu, which means dishonest man" (pamphlet 1:4). Over time, the Aryans by their cunning were able to divide the Ādi-dharmīs and Ādivāsīs into smaller and smaller groups and thereby gain control of the country, which they named Bhāratvarṣ. They obliterated the literature and other artifacts of the indigenous peoples' civilization and replaced these with treatises *(smṛti/śāstra)* among which the *Laws of Manu* was the most significant. By these laws the indigenous peoples were stripped of all their former rights and privileges and even education was denied them.

The Aryans launched their own religion and wiped out the remaining vestiges of the religion practiced by the Ādi-dharmīs and Ādivāsīs. In order to save them, God sent the sage Supach in Krishna's time, Guru Vālmīki in Rām's time, and Guru Ravidās, Gurū Nānak and Kabīr Sahab in the fifteenth century. These gurus preached the equality of all humankind, and taught the worship of the one, true God. These gurus also left behind their teachings in written form, which were destroyed by the Aryan usurpers (pamphlet 1:3–5). Thus, the ADM was formed to collect the literature and other cultural artifacts of the pre-Aryan age, and to disseminate the teachings of the gurus Vālmīki, Ravidās, Chokāmeḷā and others in order to bring the Ādi-dharmīs and Ādivāsīs who have adopted other religions back onto the true path (pamphlet 1:5).

Such is the basic mythology and raison d'être of the ADM. But the ADM does not stop here. They also advance a theory of the origin of Untouchability (pamphlet 2:3–4); prescribe strict codes of behavior governing the holding of religious festivals and the manner in which ritual acts *(saṃskār)* are to be performed (pamphlet 1:5–8); and state the religious symbols to be displayed and formalities to be observed at any center of Ravidās worship under their control (pamphlet 1:32–33). In addition, just over half of the second pamphlet (pp. 9–23) is devoted to chronicling the achievements of the ADM research committee in determining the basic history of Guru Ravidās's life with avowed certainty. The members of this committee are part of the executive leadership committee of the ADM. Sant Kāśī Dās is the research committee's chief secretary and is in charge of its work, including the compilation of the teachings and sayings of all the gurus (*Guru-vāṇī)* mentioned in the ADM myth of the Ādi-dharmīs' origin. The research committee's most significant finding thus far has been the "discovery" of the village of Seer Govardhanpur in Varanasi as the birthplace of Sant Ravidās. This discovery occurred in 1963, and the foundation stone of the Ravidās temple there was laid in 1965 (pamphlet 2:9). Many of the other sites in the area of Varanasi associated with major events in Ravidās's life as well as his travels to other parts of India are chronicled in the following pages of this pamphlet.

This unified mythology propagated by the ADM is a paradigmatic example of what Eric Hobsbawm (1983) terms an "invented tradition." Hobsbawm distinguishes between custom versus tradition and old versus new traditions as follows. Invariance is both the object and hallmark of traditions, whether newly invented or long established ones. Traditions in this sense are clearly distinguishable from "custom" which predominates in "traditional" societies. In such societies, custom serves a dual function. On the one hand, custom allows for change and innovation up to a certain point, although this is substantially limited by the requirement that such change or innovation appear compatible or even identical with precedent. On the other hand, what custom imparts to a desired change, or in certain cases resistance to innovation, is (p . 2) "the sanction of precedent, social continuity and natural law as expressed in history." One marked difference between old versus invented traditions is readily apparent: whereas (p. 10) "the former were specific and strongly binding social practices, the latter tended to be quite unspecific and vague as to the nature of the values, rights and obligations of the group membership they inculcate." Hobsbawm classifies "invented traditions" according to three overlapping types (p. 9):

a) those establishing or symbolizing social cohesion or the membership of groups, real or artificial communities,
b) those establishing or legitimizing institutions, status or relations of authority, and
c) those whose main purpose was socialization, the inculcation of beliefs, value systems and conventions of behavior.

With respect to invented traditions of type A, the ADM conflates the separate and internally heterogeneous communities of the Scheduled Castes and Scheduled Tribes, and represents them both as the original inhabitants and rulers of India whom they term Ādi-dharmīs and Ādivāsīs respectively. This in turns legitimizes the existence of the ADM organization itself, which assumes the right to represent both these groups in attempting to regain a share of their former power and glory. I described above the strict prescriptions of the ADM in the areas of religious symbolism, formalities, and ritual permitted in all the Ravidās temples, monasteries and sites of worship under their control. This emphasis on conformity in religious belief and practice serves a twofold purpose: to increase the ranks and potential sources of economic and political support of the ADM, which in turn will provide the organization further legitimacy and strengthen its claim to speak for an ever-growing constituency.

Srinivas's notion of "spread" is also operative here (1952, 213–14). According to this idea, the veneration of common deities and other objects of worship results in greater solidarity than the adoption of common ritual and cultural forms. Moreover, an inverse relationship exists between the degree to which common ritual and cultural forms are shared and the size of the area of worship: the larger this area the less common shared ritual and cultural forms will be and vice versa. Sant Ravidās is worshipped under various names throughout most of the states of the Hindi-speaking belt of North India, especially in the states of U.P., Bihar and M.P., and also very widely in the state of Punjab. Thus, by establishing Ravidās as the central focus of worship, the ADM can solidify its control of the movement even if it cannot enforce orthopraxy among all its members.

A brief note of caution should be sounded here regarding the extent of the ADM's influence over the Ravidās movement as a whole. As with any large-scale movement of a religious or other nature, internal tension(s) and dissension are natural outgrowths of its development. Within the ADM itself, its current vice president, Mr. Khuśī Rām, disagrees sharply with the rest of the leadership regarding the exact extent of territory over which the ADM exercises direct control (interview, 19 February 1990). Nevertheless, the ADM is the most organized and best financed group in India working actively to promote the worship of Ravidās throughout the country. It is registered with the Indian government (pamphlet 1:3), and currently controls directly five major Ravidās temples and/or monasteries: the Seer Govardhanpur temple in Varanasi; two temples in New Delhi, excluding another major one in the city under the control of another group; a temple at Khuralgarh, Hoshiarpur District, Punjab; and a monastery and temple at Karrapur village, Sagar District, M.P.

Conclusion

What I have attempted to demonstrate in this essay is that considerations of power and politics are inseparable from religious concerns for the contemporary followers of Ravidās. Relegated to the very bottom of the caste hierarchy, their worship of Ravidās is not only a religious phenomenon, but a vehicle of social, religious and political protest against the inequitable distribution of power and wealth in this social order. In a recent article, Nicholas Dirks (1989, 72) argues "that structures of power play a central role in the social organization of caste and kinship, that politics is fundamental to the process of hierarchilization and the formation of units of identity." In Owen Lynch's study of the Jātav Chamārs of Agra (1969, 159–60), their ultimate adoption of Dr. Ambedkar's neo-Buddhism served not only a religious purpose, but also as a dissident socioreligious ideology and model of social equality which would eliminate the privileged status of the dominant castes. The worship of Ravidās serves many of these same purposes for his contemporary Chamār and other followers.

Notes

The research for this paper was financially supported by a Junior Research Fellowship (1989–90) from the American Institute of Indian Studies. I also wish to thank Professors Linda Hess and David Lorenzen for their careful readings of earlier drafts of this manuscript. Many thanks and appreciation are also due to the numerous devotees, ascetics, and leaders of the Ravidās Panth as well as nondevotees cited without whom this could not have been written.

1. Interviews with Kishan Lāl and Rāi Kumār, 10 January 1991.
2. Interview with Pannu Lāl, Chamār nondevotee and resident of Citturpur

village (Varanasi), 15 July 1990; interview with Vikram Prasād, Chamār non-devotee and resident of Sigra (Varanasi), 13 January 1991.

3. Interview with Vinod Dās, Ravidās devotee, 6 February 1991.

4. *Śrī Gurū Granth Sāhib,* 4 vols., translated by Gurbacan Singh Talib in consultation with Bhai Jodh Singh (Patiala: Punjabi University Publication Bureau, 1984–90): Rāg Gaurī Bairāgan, vol. 1 (1984: pp. 731–32); Rāg Vilālav 2, vol. 3 (1987: pp. 1772–73); Rāg Rāmkalī 4, 1, vol. 3 (pp. 1997, 1998); Rāg Kedārā 1, vol. 4 (1990: pp. 2285–86); Rāg Basant 1, vol. 4 (pp. 2416–17); Rāg Malār 1, 2, vol. 4 (pp. 2601–2).

Raidas, *Raidās kī Vānī* (Allahabad, Belvedere Press, 1988): Rāg Rāmkalī 1, 21, 24; Rāg Āsāvarī 35; Rāg Soraṭhā 48; Rāg Vilālav 62; Rāg Gaur 67. This is the version of the *Raidās-vānī* I am currently using. It was jointly translated by myself and Mr. Avadesh Mishra, director of the American Institute of Indian Studies Language Training Program in Varanasi. Mr. Virendra Singh, who works with the Wisconsin College-year Abroad Program, also assisted with some of the translations.

Dr. Winand Callewaert of Belgium was for many years engaged in producing a critical edition of the *Raidās-vānī* manuscripts. A doctoral student in the University of London, Peter Friedlander, has completed a translation and linguistic study of this text based upon Prof. Callewaert's manuscripts. This work, jointly written by them, is currently in press.

5. See *Śrī Gurū Granth Sāhib:* Rāg Soraṭhā 1, vol. 2 (pp. 1378–79); Rāg Dhanaśrī, vol. 2 (pp. 1447–48); also see *Raidās kī Vānī :* Rāg Rāmkālī 4, 9; Rāg Soraṭhā 53, 54; Rāg Bhairo 57; Rāg Kedārā 72.

6. Percentage figures shown here exceed 100 percent due to some bhajans being listed in multiple categories.

7. Literally: "placed your feet in the direction of sin."

8. *Constitution of the All India Adi Dharm Mission (ADM): Rules and Regulations of the Mission, 1970–71* (New Delhi: ADM Central Managing Committee) [hereafter cited in text as "pamphlet 1"]; *All India Adi-dharm Mission: Aims and Objectives, 1988* (New Delhi: ADM Executive Committee) [hereafter cited in text as "pamphlet 2"].

9. According to Mark Juergensmeyer (1982, 39–42), the correct date here should be 1926.

Bibliography

All India Adi-dharm Mission: Aims and Objectives, 1988. New Delhi: ADM Executive Committee. 24 pp.

Ambedkar, B. R. 1945. "Annihilation of Caste." Bombay: Bharat Bhusan P. Press.

Barnett, Steve. 1977. "Identity Choice and Caste Ideology in Contemporary South India." In *The New Wind: Changing Identities in South Asia*, edited by Kenneth David, 393–417. Paris: Mouton.

Berreman, Gerald. 1971. "The Brahmanical View of Caste." *Contributions to Indian Sociology* 5:16–23.

Briggs, G. W. 1920. *The Chamars*. Calcutta: Association Press.

Cohn, Bernard. 1956. "The Changing Status of a Depressed Caste." In *Village India: Studies in the Little Community*, edited by McKim Marriott, 53–78. Chicago: The University of Chicago Press.

Constitution of the All India Adi Dharm Mission (ADM): Rules and Regulations of the Mission, 1970–71. New Delhi: ADM Central Managing Committee. 35 pp.

Dirks, Nicholas B. 1989. "The Original Caste: Power, History and Hierarchy in South Asia." *Contributions to Indian Sociology* 23, no. 1:59-78.

Grierson, George A. 1921. "Shiva Narayanis." In *Encyclopedia of Religion and Ethics*, edited by James Hastings, 11:579. New York: Charles Scribner's Sons.

Hawley, John. 1988. *Songs of the Saints of India*. New York: Oxford University Press.

Hobsbawm, Eric. 1983. "Introduction: Inventing Traditions." In The Invention of Tradition, edited by Eric Hobsbawm and Terence Ranger, 1–15. Cambridge: Cambridge University Press.

Juergensmeyer, Mark. 1982. *Religion as Social Vision: The Movement against Untouchability in Twentieth-Century Punjab.* Berkeley: University of California Press.

Lele, Jayant. 1981. "The Bhakti Movement in India: A Critical Introduction." In *Tradition and Modernity in Bhakti Movements,* edited by Jayant Lele, 1–15. Leiden: E. J. Brill.

Lorenzen, David. 1987. "The Kabir-Panth and Social Protest." In *The Sants: Studies in a Devotional Tradition of India,* edited by Karine Schomer and W. H. McLeod., 281–305. Delhi: Motilal Banarsidas.

———. 1987a. "The Social Ideologies of Hagiography: Sankara, Tukaram and Kabir." In *Religion and Society in Maharashtra*, edited by M. Israel and N. K Wagle, 92–114. Toronto: University of Toronto, Centre for South Asian Studies.

———. 1987b. "Traditions of Non-caste Hinduism: The Kabir Panth." *Contributions to Indian Sociology* 21:264–83.

Lynch, Owen. 1969. *The Politics of Untouchability: Social Mobility and Social Change in a City of India.* New York: Columbia University Press.

Raidās. 1988. *Raidās kī Vānī.* Allahabad: Belvedere Press.

Sangari, Kumkum. 1990. "Mirabai and the Spiritual Economy of Bhakti." *Economic and Political Weekly*, 7-14 July, 1464–75/1537–52.
Śrī Gurū Granth Sāhib. 1984–90. 4 vols. Translated by Gurbacan Singh Talib in consultation with Bhai Jodh Singh. Patiala: Punjabi University Publication Bureau.
Singer, Milton. 1966. "The Radha-Krishna Bhajanas of Madras City." In *Krishna: Myths, Rites and Attitudes,* edited by Milton Singer, 90–139. Chicago: The University of Chicago Press.
Srinivas, M. N. 1952. *Religion and Society among the Coorgs of South India*. Oxford: Clarendon Press.
———. 1962. *Caste in Modern India and Other Essays*. New York: Asia Publishing House.
———. 1968. *Social Change in Modern India*. Berkeley: University of California Press.
Vaudeville, Charlotte. 1987. "*Sant Mat:* Santism as the Universal Path to Sanctity." In *The Sants*, edited by Karine Schomer and W. H. McLeod, 21–41. Delhi: Motilal Banarsidass.

Interviews

Jagatnāth Rām, Ravidās devotee and bhajan author, 25 January 1991
Khuśī Rām, former ADM general secretary and current vice-president, 19 February 1990
Kishan Lāl and Rāi Kumār respectively, Ravidās devotees, 10 January 1991
Pannu Lāl, Chamār nondevotee and resident of Citturpur village (Varanasi), 15 July 1990
Sohan Singh Ahīr, current ADM president, 20 February 1990
Vikram Prasād, Chamār nondevotee and resident of Sigra (Varanasi), 13 January 1991
Vinod Dās, Ravidās devotee, 6 February 1991

The Instability of the King

Magical Insanity and the Yogis' Power in the Politics of Jodhpur, 1803–1843

Daniel Gold

In the summer of 1843, Mahārājā Mān Singh of Jodhpur, a major Rājpūt kingdom, had taken himself to live in barren seclusion in a desolate spot outside his capital. Wrapped only in a thin cloth, his hair matted, he appeared to the British political agent, Captain J. Ludlow, like an ordinary "religious mendicant."[1] The maharaja had already abandoned his palace the year before, earlier receiving Captain Ludlow in a "wretched" tent he was occupying outside a small house in Jodhpur City.[2] Mān Singh had long been known for his religious idiosyncrasies, so it was less the visible signs of the maharaja's unusual behavior that disturbed Ludlow then than its immediate cause: the resurgence in Jodhpur of the political influence of Nāth yogis. Often rough and awesome in appearance, the Nāths had achieved considerable power in Jodhpur during the forty years of Mān Singh's reign, the maharaja himself formally adopting a Nāth guru within a year of his accession.[3] The political influence of the Nāths, although apparently accepted by the populace, was an object of envy among factions of the gentry and of abhorrence to British colonial officers, who complained of the Nāths' abuse of power and lackadaisical administration.[4]

In September of 1839, the British had used a show of armed force to persuade Mān Singh to remove the Nāth leaders from positions of political power and expel them from Jodhpur with most of their followers. Ludlow took charge of a council of nobles who governed together with the maharaja. The new regime seemed to be working effectively, and in the autumn of 1841, Ludlow went on tour to some neighboring territories. When he returned in January, however, he found that the Nāths had returned as well, and had regained their active influence over the maharaja. Now living in his tent in the city, Mān Singh refused to go back to the palace unless the Nāths were restored to their former positions. He would abdicate, he said, and when this had no effect declared that he would go live in the great Nāth temple of Jodhpur and refuse to do any state business. The British responded by seizing some Nāth leaders and sending them off to the British headquarters at Ajmer.

At this Mān Singh "threw dust upon his head, rolled on the bare earth, and tore his beard."[5] When the British refused his demands to release the captured Nāths, he inflicted more austerities on himself, finally walking barefoot and bareheaded to an open canvas shelter, smeared with ashes like a yogi. Eventually he moved to a spot about six miles outside the city, where Ludlow finally found him sitting underneath a tree. Unable to be persuaded to return to the palace, the maharaja was also unable to endure the austerities he had inflicted on himself, and on September fifth succumbed to an attack of seasonal fever that was then ravaging his realm.[6]

The figure of Mahārājā Mān Singh brings together cultural types that frequently appear in opposition within Hindu tradition. On the one hand, Mān Singh was born into a lineage of Rājpūts, the "sons of kings" who ruled in Western India; and Rājpūts have traditionally valued outward dominion, which they demonstrated in part through ostentatious display. On the other hand, he was initiated into an order of religious practitioners—*sādhūs* in Hindi—heir to a long tradition of Indian ascetics who have valued inner control, which was demonstrated in part through renunciation. Although the maharaja has been recognized as exceptional in Indian history, the very possibility of his emergence brings into question any radical distinction between warrior-kings and ascetic yogis in postclassical India. At the same time, the difficulties of Mān Singh's reign suggest some limitations on the convergence of the two socioreligious roles.

Vulgar Sadhus, Ascetic Warriors, and Rājpūt Ideals

The Nāth sadhus with whom Mān Singh identified were a rough lot, initiated into their order through the painful drilling of holes through their cartilages for thick earrings.[7] Consisting of householders as well as ascetics, they found characteristic religious goals not in a blissful absolute but in a physically conceived immortality and in magical powers that they would not hesitate to use for material ends. In fact they seem to exemplify a type of vulgar sadhu that reveals another dimension of the vagabond warrior ideal cherished by Rājpūts.

Paid employment in military service, as Dirk H. A. Kolff has recently demonstrated,[8] was an important means of livelihood for the peasants of certain areas of late medieval North India, developing distinctive forms of organization, codes of honor, and genres of folklore. Recruiting young men *(javāns)* from the countryside, military leaders maintained their own independence, fighting for the prince who would reward them the best, and entering into changing alliances that might be marked by exchanges of women. The recruits themselves saw their service as a temporary affair. They looked forward to settling down in midlife with their family and enjoying the fruits of their military wages, which played an important part in the economy of Eastern Hindustan. In its enforced separation from family, then, military life might be depicted in folk songs as a kind of asceticism, but it was an asceticism of limited duration, finding its fulfillment in the return home.[9]

Perhaps the most controversial aspect of Kolff's picture is the revised meaning given to the concept of the Rājpūt in fifteenth- and sixteenth-century India. Being a Rājpūt then meant not being a member of a closed descent-group: one of the "thirty-six races of Rājpūts" that continue to be heralded in Western India. In earlier centuries, says Kolff, "Rājpūt" was a more ascriptive term, referring to all kinds of Hindus who lived the life of the adventuring warrior, of whom most were of peasant origins.[10] The understanding of a Rājpūt as a member of a genealogically based caste developed later under the relative stability of Mughal rule, when opportunities for independent adventuring became fewer and established groups began guarding their prerogatives.

Now the ascriptive identity that Kolff attributes to the first Rājpūts is particularly characteristic in medieval India of certain religious groups: joining a Hindu sect or becoming an ascetic was typically a voluntary, individual affair, open to people of diverse castes. And whatever the final verdict on Kolff's view of Rājpūt military bands in pre-Mughal India, later Mughal times certainly witnessed the activities of bands of militant ascetics. By the eighteenth century we have reports of militant ascetic leaders functioning like military leaders,[11] making their own changing alliances with princes. By this time too, with the Rājpūts of Western India clearly existing as a closed caste, a new sectarian religious identity was more easily accessible to adventurous peasant youth than was a Rājpūt one. But even after joining a religious order, these military recruits, like others, might consider their active militant asceticism to be temporary, and eventually marry and have children. To these new householders of peasant background, a yogic identity could still remain religiously and economically attractive, while old caste ties, once implicitly renounced, were not always easy to renew. With children growing up in yogic communities needing a recognizable social identity, a militant ascetic order could also grow to function as a Hindu caste.

The Jodhpur Nāths, then, as a militant ascetic tradition, had attributes of both an open, ascriptive fellowship and a closed, genealogical caste, types of organization that by late Mughal times were characteristic of sectarian religious orders and mundane social orders respectively. Both their open, sectarian and closed, mundane attributes contributed to their numerical strength. By Mān Singh's time, the Jodhpur Nāths contained a core of members born into the order who recognized kin-networks among themselves, but continued to accept new recruits, too. Just as significantly, both types of attributes contributed to their practical power. For even as high Nāth gurus in Jodhpur maneuvered for political influence and a share of the kingdom's wealth, they could also maintain a supernatural aura, with their material successes seen to derive in part from their psychic powers. To achieve their practical ends, Nāths could understandably find it useful to project themselves as the spiritual strongmen of Hinduism, with their physical gruffness and military prowess backed by a corresponding psychic weight. Thus complementing the references to the ascetic Rājpūt warriors of early medieval lore pointed out by Kolff, we also get continuing images of the belligerent vulgar ascetic—coarse, powerful, and materially effective.

Some of the most vivid stories of the Nāths as spiritual strongmen have been told by the Nāths themselves. As did other groups of married yogis throughout North India, many Nāths of Rajasthan maintained a bardic tradition, singing heroic tales of legendary yogis of the past. In the Rājasthānī epic of the Gopī Chand, Nāths act like other political and military leaders: accompanied by large groups of followers, they compete with one another and plot to get what they want. Using magical and physical power together, they conquer rivals and degrade them.[12]

Nāth Power in Jodhpur

In an imaginative world where sadhus behave forcefully like Rājpūts and psychic power is used for political domination, a continuing practical alliance between sadhus and princes can seem entirely in order. To bring one into reality in nineteenth-century Jodhpur needed only the conjunction in extreme conditions of two powerfully imaginative personalities: Rājā Mān Singh and his guru Ayas Dev Nāth. Both politically and religiously, Mān Singh's meeting with Dev Nāth appears as a turning point in his life. Certainly, it is represented as such in *Tawārīkh Mānsingh*, a manuscript history of Mān Singh's reign found in the Rajasthan State Archives at Bikaner, which begins with a detailed narrative of the crucial encounter between the two men.

In 1803, Mān Singh was a young man of twenty, fighting what seemed to be a losing battle for succession against his cousin Bhīm Singh. For more than two years he had been besieged in Jalor, the seat of a great fort about seventy-five miles south of Jodhpur. Jalor was the fiefdom of Mān Singh's adopted mother, Gulāb Rāī, herself the favorite courtesan of the last maharaja, Vijay Singh. Mān Singh had lost his natural mother when he was six and his father, Vijay Singh's fifth son, when he was ten.[13] He had then been raised by Gulāb Rāī, who persuaded the raja to name him heir. Since many of the nobles had already united behind Bhīm Singh, Mān Singh was sent for safety to Jalor.

Near Jalor fort was a large temple to Jālandhar Nāth, who is treated like a deity in some Nāth traditions. Reigning as guru at the temple was the yogi Dev Nāth, who, among his other powers, was reputed to be able to prophesy the future.[14] During the long siege of the fort, Dev Nāth offered Mān Singh both psychological and logistical support. When faced with an ultimatum from Bhīm Singh, Mān Singh was advised by Dev Nāth—who, according to *Tawārīkh Mānsingh,* had received an inner order from Jālandhar Nāth—not to leave until a certain date a few weeks later.[15] Two days before the date prophesied Mān Singh's rival cousin suddenly died, the siege was lifted, and Mān Singh advanced to Jodhpur. Colonel Tod, the British chronicler, suggests that Dev Nāth's prayers were made effective through the skilful use of poison.[16]

In Mān Singh's new regime, Dev Nāth played an extremely influential role. In addition to the spiritual authority he continued to hold for the raja, Dev Nāth also managed to dominate Indarrāj, Mān Singh's chief administrator *(mukhtārī)*. "Business was sanctioned through Dev Nāth's order." says *Tawārīkh Mānsingh*, "Indarrāj would work according to his command."[17] In the ritual protocols that marked the hierarchies of Rājpūt society, Dev Nāth's position was recognized as high indeed. When Dev Nāth came to court, the maharaja touched his head to the floor.[18] And when the raja went to Dev Nāth's establishment, as he did every Monday,[19] he carried no arms and the drum-beating that customarily accompanied him was to stop two hundred feet away.[20] Special occasions, too, saw unusual honors given to Dev Nāth. After a long siege of Jodhpur fort by the forces of Jaipur, Mān Singh's first ceremonial act was to escort Dev Nāth down from the fort to Mahāmandir—himself riding "in the back, having seated the guru up front."[21] At the birth of Dev Nāth's son, Lāḍū Nāth, a measure of raw sugar was distributed to every house in Jodhpur City.[22]

The public celebration of the birth of Dev Nāth's son was merely representative of the honor accorded to the rest of his family. Dev Nāth was born into an established lineage of yogis: *Tawārīkh Mānsingh* remembers both Dev Nāth's father and his grandfather as Nāths, with Dev Nāth as the middle of three "older" brothers who also had two "younger" ones.[23] All were quickly well provided for, through temples, or land grants, or both. Moreover, as further redistribution occurred during the reign "Dev Nāth's brothers and nephews received a great deal of land-grants."[24]

But the beneficence of Rājā Mān Singh went beyond Dev Nāth's family line to Nāth sectarian tradition as a whole. Mān Singh engaged in a program of temple-building that covered all the districts of his realm.[25] In Jodhpur, special temples were dedicated to the nine legendary Nāths and another to the eighty-four Siddhas, a related tradition.[26] To the images of Hindu deities at Mandor, Mān Singh added figures of Jālandhar Nāth and Gorakh Nāth.[27] Both symbolically and practically, Nāth power became associated with the authority of Jodhpur state. Writing the name of Jālandhar Nāth over official correspondence,[28] Mān Singh explained that this merely indicated his personal devotion, not the institution of Nāth tradition as a state religion. But in fact the power wielded by the raja's Nāth gurus was considerable—waxing, despite occasional reversals, until the very last years of his reign.

Nāth influence in Jodhpur became pervasive. Exercised largely through the Nāths' ability to influence administrative appointments, which often went to the managers of their temples,[29] it was resisted by certain elements of the population. These included at times the merchants, who protested in 1835 against new taxes and in 1841 called a strike to protest the arrest of some among them who defied the Nāths.[30] Leaders of the old noble houses, too, often found themselves displaced, and particularly during the end of Mān Singh's reign had to ingratiate themselves with the Nāths to maintain an active role in state polity.[31] At the same time, powerful Nāth householders began to adopt high-caste Hindu ways. Thus, although contemporary Rājasthānī householder Nāths like most peasant castes have allowed widow remarriage and even forms of divorce, Laxmī Nāth, the priest at Mahāmandir, in 1841 forbad the practice vehemently. When he heard that a distant widowed relative of his was going to marry another Nāth, he sent an armed force to have them both killed. Just as Brahmins and respected landlords should not make such marriages, he declared, neither should respected Nāths.[32]

The role of Nāths in the state was now at least as much political as it was military. Nāths remained an element in the Jodhpur armies, but their role as strongmen became more oriented toward internal enemies. We see them at this point as urban enforcers, moving about in bands with power to arrest people.[33] No longer merely asserting a monarch's authority through awesome prowess in battle, the Nāths with their reputed magical powers appeared as a pervasive institutional presence in his realm.

Mān Singh as Raja and Nāth

As religious preceptors, moreover, the Nāths elicited from Mān Singh a devotion that seemed more than perfunctory. A man of poetic sensibilities, Mān Singh sponsored literati at court, collected manuscripts, and himself wrote verses—largely verses of devotion to his guru and illustrious Nāths of the past. His impressive library, which continues to be maintained at Jodhpur fort, is a vast depository of Nāth devotional lore. Mān Singh in his glory thus seems to have been able to play the role of beneficent, cultured monarch. But he played it out in a peculiar fashion, seeing himself as the disciple of a yogi and calling his kingdom an offering *(arpan)* to the Nāths.[34]

Mān Singh's alliance with the Nāths was vital to both his political and religious identity. Publicly, it represented a change not only in intensity of royal sectarian affiliation but also in type. Mān Singh was raised within *Puṣṭimārgīya* Vaiṣṇava tradition, which features a line of hereditary priests who at that time had followers among the gentry of Mān Singh's realm. During the reign of Mān Singh's grandfather, Vijay Singh, Vaiṣṇava temples had enjoyed state support. In the first few years of his own reign, however, Mān Singh asserted himself against the previously established Vaiṣṇava socioreligious elite. *Tawārīkh Mānsingh* describes encounters first with a Gosāīṃ, as Puṣṭimārgīya priests are called, and then with a Vaishnavite noble—perhaps the same Gosāīṃ's disciple.[35] In both instances the Vaiṣṇavas are asked to acknowledge formally the new religious alignment of the royal house, with their refusal leading to serious political repercussions for them.

Taking a temple tour during the same Indian year of his accession (*samvat* 1860), the raja reached a shrine to Krishna, which he attempted to enter wearing a mark of ash on his forehead in the style of Nāth yogis. The Gosāīṃ, invoking the old maharaja, wouldn't let him pass: "'You're Vijay Singh's grandson . . . ,' he said, 'don't come into my temple with ash on your forehead.' From that day on his highness stopped going to the temple; and whatever villages the temple had, were confiscated. . . . The Gosāīṃ went off to Vraj [a center of Krishna worship]."[36] Under ordinary circumstances, a wealthy, well-born Hindu with ash on his forehead could very conceivably have been permitted to enter a Vaiṣṇava temple. But given the conjunction of courtly and religious protocols in a royal temple visit, the new raja's gesture was taken as the challenge it was no doubt meant to be. Although Mān Singh was apparently ready to incorporate the old religious order into the new, he would do so only on his own terms.

While asking other spiritual leaders to acknowledge him as a Nāth, Mān Singh also asked his courtiers to treat his Nāth guru with the respect due to a spiritual leader. Within a year of Mān Singh's encounter with the Gosāīṃ he told all his headmen, officers, and mistresses to go "hear the name" from his guru Dev Nāth. Although this expression can sometimes mean taking formal initiation from a preceptor, here the public context suggests that it meant not much more than listening to a generalized instruction and reciprocating with a modest gift—a public mark of respect to a holy person many Hindus would offer. The *ṭhākur* of Chandaval, however, whose name was Bisan Singh, claimed that his allegiance to his Gosāīṃ would not permit him to participate. Mān

Singh would brook no exception: "Everyone heard the name and gave offerings. Wearing cloths were given, and Bisan Singh made this petition: 'I've already heard the name from my respected Gosāīṃ, and my ears won't hear any other.' His highness told him specifically: 'Then hear it even while your heart does not accept it.' [Bisan Singh] came to the pavilion wearing a crazy look, stubborn and under duress, and then went off to Chandaval."[37] Bisan Singh then fell out of favor, and his younger brother gained control of the ancestral lands.

A person like Mān Singh who can ask someone else to listen politely to a spiritual instruction even while not accepting it at heart might well recognize in himself the capacity to do so, too. At several places in *Tawārīkh Mānsingh,* we find the presupposition that as in the world at large, so particularly in the maharaja's case, outward religious observance might not always match inward religious attitudes. Two critical periods of Mān Singh's life have been particularly perplexing in their complex juxtaposition of inward attitude and outward religious poise. One of these, with which we introduced this study, occurred at the end of the raja's life, when he appeared as a somewhat unbalanced renunciate, while probably harboring a desire to rule together with his Nāths. This behavior was presaged, however, by events that happened three decades earlier, when, after the death of his guru Dev Nāth, Mān Singh began to act insane.

Dev Nāth was assassinated in 1815 together with the minister Indarrāj, the result of factional politics. Understood to be a vital event in Mān Singh's life, the scene is given detailed description in *Tawārīkh Mānsingh*, appearing as one of the most elaborately narrated in this generally terse text. We see Dev Nāth and Indarrāj, encircled in the palace, shot with carbines by Pathan troops loyal to Mār Khān, one of Mān Singh's sometime allies. The maharaja, after obstructions by the plotters, finally arrives on the scene: "Don't let those murdering Turks get away," he shouts.[38] Through entreaties from Dev Nāth's younger brother Bhīm Nāth, however, Mān Singh soon reconciled himself to political and military realities and released the Pathan troops.[39] Finally realizing the scope of the plot, he adopted reclusive, bizarre behavior that appeared to many to be insane.[40]

Providing him a persona for almost three years, Mān Singh's bizarre behavior was instigated by events that could understandably have been experienced as a genuinely unbalancing shock. Certainly, to someone as actively involved with his guru as was the maharaja, the latter's sudden demise could be severely unsettling. The maharaja may also have experienced some guilt over the affair: he had brought his guru to court and may have been apprised of the plot against Indarrāj, if not against Dev Nāth himself.[41] Who knows, moreover, what the maharaja thought about the lingering presence of Dev Nāth after his death. The crown prince, at least, was told that Mān Singh's insanity was caused in part by the continuing existence of Dev Nāth's magical powers *(jantra mantra)*.[42]

Yet Mān Singh's behavior has also been interpreted as a mere pose of insanity, capable of being diminished and heightened at will. About a year into the period of infirmity Mān Singh was able to consecrate the crown prince "with his own hands" and when the latter died after a year and a half Mān Singh was able effectively to resume power. Moreover, Mān Singh's eccentricities during this period, if sometimes appearing paranoid, do not seem to have been without design. Mān Singh kept pigeons, we are told, which he used to test against poison in his food, losing a couple of birds in the process.[43] When his wives visited him, he would keep quiet and feed the pigeons; and when the crown prince's mother came "he would display even more craziness."[44]

The apparently insane behavior of Mān Singh after Dev Nāth's assassination is in many ways consonant with the apparently ascetic behavior preceding his own death. The recurring description of the maharaja's symptoms in *Tawārīkh Mānsingh* is "The Raja didn't meet anyone"—an example of the gruff, incommunicative behavior that is also characteristic of the reclusive ascetic. Similarly, the maharaja's rough visage that *Tawārīkh Mānsingh* presents as insane is also characteristic of the tough sadhu: "His highness maintained his craziness. He didn't shave, he didn't bathe, he didn't get his clothes washed."[45] Mān Singh in addition presented his act of ceding the rule to his teenage son as one of religious renunciation: "I'll just pray to the Lord; you [subjects] take the prince."[46] Certainly, adopting the guise of the somewhat crazed ascetic, retreating from the scene and "not meeting anyone" in fact proved to be an effective means of survival in an intractable political situation. But this guise may not have been totally feigned, for it was also consistent with the raja's personal identity. Throughout his reign, Mān Singh saw himself as a king and yogi too, and if his princely authority was threatened, he could at least assert his yogic role.

Yet as a raja, a yogi, and an individual, Mān Singh was obviously unstable. He bore little resemblance to any of India's exemplary divine kings such as Ayodhya's Lord Rām or Krishna in the *Mahābhārata*, figures idealized in Hindu civilization as their counterparts are in many others. For even though in India royal warriors and ascetic sadhus were *ordinarily* likely to follow norms that appeared to diverge, pervasive Indian ideas of homologies and intersections among all planes of existence found fruit in images of the great royal person, the *perfect* ruler who could serve as a pivot between spiritual and temporal worlds: distant, unique, and exemplary.

Indeed, ideals of divinely inspired rulership have remained powerful in India through the present day, evoked most forcefully by Mohandas Gandhi—who, like Mān Singh, was idiosyncratically spiritual in his politics, manipulated an ascetic image for calculated ends, and was even ready to challenge the British by undertaking fasts. Gandhi's fasts, however, were politically effective, in part because for Gandhi the roles of worldly politician and ascetic sadhu converged in a lofty moral truth. From that lofty moral ground Gandhi was able to integrate his political and ascetic roles into an exemplary ideal that resonated beyond a specific Hindu cultural world. For Mān Singh, by contrast, both political and ascetic identities were rooted in material power. With no high moral ground that integrated the two, Mān Singh instead seemed to shift between them, moved as much by political circumstances as by his personal religious state. With his Nāth bureaucrats and royal excesses, Mān Singh's divine and kingly identities diminished as much as they complemented each other, leaving the raja to be remembered as an idiosyncratic, complex, and creative personality, not as an exemplary wielder of spiritual or material power.

Notes

1. Zabar Singh, *The East India Company and Marwar (1803-1857 A.D.)*, (Jaipur: Panchsheel, 1973), p. 82.
2. Ibid., p. 81.
3. *Tawārīkh Mānsingh* (Manuscript at Rajasthan State Archives, Bikaner), p. 56. Man Singh was initiated on 23 September 1805. See Padmaja Sharma, *Maharaja Man Singh of Jodhpur and his Times (1803–1843 A.D.)* (Agra: Shiva Lal Agarwala and Company, 1972), p. 156.
4. Zabar Singh, *The East India Company*, pp. 63–67.
5. Ibid., p. 82
6. Ibid., p. 83

7. George Weston Briggs, *Gorakhnath and the Kanphata Yogis*, 2d ed. ([Calcutta, 1938] Delhi: Motilal Banarsidass, 1973) remains the classic Nāth ethnography. The fullest account of Nāth oral traditions is given by Ann Grodzins Gold, *A Carnival of Parting: The Tales of King Gopi Chand and King Bharthari as Sung and Told by Madhu Natisar Nath of Ghatiyali, Rajasthan, India* (Berkeley: University of California Press, 1992), which gives a comprehensive bibliography of recent scholarship on the Nāths. For the Nāths in their postclassical religious context, see Shashibhusan Das Gupta, *Obscure Religious Cults*, 3rd ed. ([1946] Calcutta, 1969), pp. 211–55. Relevant shorter studies include Catherine Champion, "'A contre courant' *(ulta sadhana)*. Tradition orale du norde-est de l'Inde: l'exemple des récits chantés bhojpuri," in *Living Texts from India*, edited by Richard K. Barz and Monika Thiel-Horstmann (Wiesbaden: Otto Harrassowitz, 1989); and Daniel Gold and Ann Grodzins Gold, "The Fate of the Householder Nāth," *History of Religions* 24 (1984): 113–32.

8. Dirk H. A. Kolff, *Naukar, Rajput and Sepoy: The Ethnohistory of the Military Labour Market in Hindustan, 1450–1850* (Cambridge: Cambridge University Press, 1990), pp. 71–158.

9. Ibid., pp. 74–82.

10. Ibid., p. 183.

11. See David N. Lorenzen, "Warrior Ascetics in Indian History," *Journal of the American Oriental Society* 98 (1978): 61–75; W. G. Orr, "Armed Religious Ascetics in Northern India," *Bulletin of the John Rylands Library* 24 (1940): 81–100; Daniel Gold, "The Dadu Panth: A Religious Order in its Rajasthan Context," in *The Idea of Rajasthan: Explorations in Regional Identity*, edited by Lloyd Rudolph et al. (Riverdale, Md.: Riverdale Press, 1992); and Sir Jadunath Sarkar, *A History of the Dasnami Naga Sannyasis* (Allahabad: Shri Panchayati Akhara Mahanirvani, 1958).

12. See Ann Grodzins Gold, *A Carnival of Parting* (note 7 above).

13. Sharma, *Maharaja Man Singh*, p. 24.

14. Ibid., p. 154

15. *Tawārīkh Mānsingh*, pp. 5–6.

16. Lieut.-Col. James Tod, *Annals and Antiquities of Rajast'han; or, The Central and Western Rajpoot States of India*, 2 vols. ([1829–32] New Delhi: M.N. Publishers, 1978), 1:565.

17. *Tawārīkh Mānsingh*, p. 187.

18. Sharma, *Maharaja Man Singh*, p. 162.

19. *Tawārīkh Mānsingh*, p. 87.

20. Sharma, *Maharaja Man Singh*, p. 162

21. *Tawārīkh Mansingh*, p. 174.

22. Ibid., p. 222.

23. Ibid., p. 56. These may have been the children of different wives: Dev Nāth's brothers and half-brothers.

24. Ibid., p. 187.
25. Dr. Rāmprasād Dādhīch, *Mahārājā Mānsingh: Vyaktitva evaṃ kṛtitva* (Jodhpur: Rājasthānī Śodh Saṃsthān, Chaupāsnī, 1972), p. 51.
26. Sharma, *Maharaja Man Singh,* p. 251.
27. Ibid., p. 252.
28. Ibid., p. 161.
29. Ibid., p. 204.
30. Ibid., p. 208.
31. Ibid., p. 181
32. Notes Ludlow: since "De[v]onath['s] family . . . has risen to rank and influence the females have been *purdah nusheen* [secluded] and hence the imputed criminality of the second alliance" (Zabar Singh, *The East India Company,* p. 155).
33. Sharma, *Maharaja Man Singh,* p. 208.
34. Zabar Singh, *The East India Company,* p. 85.
35. The generic *gusāījī* is used to refer to both personages.
36. *Tawārīkh Mānsingh*, pp. 72–73.
37. Ibid., p. 96.
38. Ibid., pp. 257–59.
39. Ibid., p. 262
40. Ibid., pp. 264–65.
41. Sharma, *Maharaja Man Singh,* p. 105, cites a contemporary letter implicating Mān Singh in the plot against Indarrāj, but he dismisses it.
42. *Tawārīkh Mānsingh*, p. 270.
43. Ibid., pp. 292–93.
44. Ibid., p. 294.
45. Ibid.
46. Ibid., p. 281.

The Kīnā Rāmī

Aughaṛs and King in the Age of Cultural Contact

Roxanne Poormon Gupta

The term *aughaṛ* refers to someone who has taken up the lifestyle of a Shaivite sadhu but has not necessarily taken formal initiation into any particular order. The British census takers of the nineteenth century accurately used the term *aughaṛ* to describe someone who is affiliated to a Nāth sect but who has not undergone the formal, ear-splitting initiation of a *Kānphaṭā*.[1] The Aughaṛs among the Kīnā Rāmī, the followers of the sect founded by Kīnā Rām, are not affiliated to the Nāth *sampradāya,* but, like the followers of the sects of the related *sant* tradition, they are heavily influenced by Nāth culture.

The question of whether or not the Kīnā Rāmī are Tantric is a separate but important issue. The ascetics of the Kīnā Rām sect refer to themselves as Aughaṛs and deny that they are Tantrics, even though they are most often believed to be Tantrics by outsiders, and this for very good reasons. This essay is not about that discussion. Let it suffice to say that the distinction between Tantrics and Aughaṛs is in my view great enough for me to use the term preferred by the Kīnā Rāmīs, while accepting that there is some overlap between Aughaṛs and Tantrics in both symbolism and practice.

Perhaps because of the Tantric connection of many of those who call themselves Aughaṛs, it is extremely rare to find an orthodox Daśnāmī sannyasi who will refer to himself as an Aughaṛ. For the most part, Daśnāmīs do not associate with Aughaṛs.[2] This is at least in part because Aughaṛs generally reject the social ideology of *varṇāśrama-dharma*. They do not accept the idea that one becomes a sadhu as a life stage. Because many Aughaṛs are drawn from the lower castes, there is no question of a student stage of life followed by a householder stage and eventually the ashram of the forest dweller. Many become Aughaṛs as young men and some may even later marry without abandoning their Aughaṛ lifestyle.

With this as a prelude, I would like to begin with a brief tour of the Kīnā Rām *sthala,* the headquarters of the Kīnā Rām sect, one of the most enigmatic religious movements in North India, located in New

Colony, Banaras. With its gates flanked by giant skulls, the site is a burial ground for more than sixty Aughaṛs who have taken *samādhi* (attained immortality). The largest tomb or *samādhi* is that of Kīnā Rām, the seventeenth-century *sant* for whom the Kīnā Rām sect is named, while the other tombs are those of the successors of his lineage. The bodies have been buried in an upright seated position *(padmāsan)* and it is believed that the souls of the Aughaṛs are accessible to devotees who come to worship them and gain their assistance in solving various problems. The *samādhi*s are marked by Shiva *liṅga*s where devotees make offerings of water, flowers, including datura flowers, and even alcohol. Each of the graves is covered with a highly ornate domed roof in typical Indo-Persian style. On the grounds there is also a large pond used for bathing, a tamarind tree covered with bats, a well whose water is believed to have curative properties, and a fire where unburnt logs from Hariśchandra cremation ground perpetually smolder. Each of these features of the site are associated with myths and rites of healing and/or deliverance. Every morning and evening the souls of the Aughaṛs are awakened and put to sleep with the deafening clanging of bells, cymbals and kettledrums and the offering of incense, a ceremony that is attended by small groups of devotees.

To approach the *samādhi* of Kīnā Rām, devotees must climb a steep set of stairs that encircle a round raised structure on which the tomb rests nearly twenty feet above the ground. On the way up, one has the darshan of Kīnā Rām in a painting that is most often used to depict him. In this painting, a white-haired, bearded Kīnā Rām sits on a throne wearing only a loincloth and a string of *rudrākṣa* beads, smoking a hookah. His guru Kālu Rām stands in the background holding a trident and *kamaṇḍalu* (water pot), while his disciple Bījarām plays sitar at his feet, and another disciple holds out a glass of liquor. The floor appears to be a decorated parquet floor built in a garden setting.

In this painting, as well as in the architecture and ambience of the *sthala* or headquarters itself, one cannot help but notice the Moghul mood. There is a sense of princely leisure rather than stark asceticism in the lifestyle of these *bābā*s. While this atmosphere is unusual, it is not surprising in light of the caste background of these ascetics. Like their founder, most Kīnā Rāmīs come from Rājpūt communities and their ascetic lifestyle reflects the imprint of a Rājpūt ethos. Their representation of rulership is not based on Brahminical ritual but rather opposed to it. For them rulership seems to be based not on divine right or heredity, but on a commonsense justice as embodied in, and mediated by, a powerful and charismatic ruler. The image of power and strength proper to the Kṣatriya ruler is refracted through the medium of the Shaivite ascetic. This image also reveals an element of intentional irony as these ascetics act out the part of kings, sitting on thrones in palaces located in the middle of graveyards.

According to the official records of the sect, their founder Kīnā Rām was born in 1608 and left his body in 1779 (making him 171 years old, not an unusual life span in Indian apocrypha).[3] One of the most often repeated stories about Kīnā Rām makes him a contemporary of Rājā Chet Singh (who ruled 1770–81).

The story goes like this. One day as Rājā Chet Singh was entertaining some guests with music on the verandah of his palace, Kīnā Rām walked by.[4] He was dressed in tatters and had some bells tied to his leg. The maharaja, disturbed by the sound, asked, "What does a sadhu have to do with dancing bells?" Kīnā Rām, insulted, replied, "What do you have to do with ruling the kingdom?" Kīnā Rām went on to curse the maharaja for neglecting his duties as a ruler, pronouncing that his lineage would be barren and that one day this magnificent palace would be empty except for the pigeons that would defecate all over the marble floors. Today informants point out that all these things came to pass. Chet Singh had no son, and even up until the current generation no maharaja of Banaras has been able to produce an heir.[5] All have been forced to adopt sons. Chet Singh was forced to abandon his palace when Warren Hastings came to arrest him in 1781. Today it is still empty except for the defecating bats and pigeons.

Other stories about Kīnā Rām place him much earlier, during the time of Tulsī Dās, Shāh Jahān and others. For our purposes, what is more important than the actual dates of Kīnā Rām's life span is the quasi-historical focus of many of the legends about him. These stories all share a common theme of the empowerment of the rejected and the despised. It appears that at the interface of myth and history, the Kīnā Rām sect used powerful religious imagery for distinctly political purposes.[6]

I would like to suggest that we can read the myths, images and symbols of the Kīnā Rām sect as a complex and creative response to the social and political conditions of the past few centuries. Unlike the eighteenth-century Nāths depicted in Daniel Gold's paper—who sought political power for their own wealth and prestige or to gain patronage for their sect—among the Kīnā Rāmī the involvement with political power has served as a platform to mount a social and political critique: a challenge to Brahmin domination and the economic oppression it entailed.

While many of the *sant* figures of the seventeenth and eighteenth centuries used their spiritual charisma to effect some degree of political reform, no other figure has absorbed such a wide range of social and religious projections as Kīnā Rām. Depending upon who one talks to, Kīnā Rām may be described as a saint, a Rājpūt hero, a Shaivite, a Śākta, a Vaiṣṇava,[7] a Tantric, a protector of sadhus, a champion of the people, a poet, the founder of a *sampradāya,* and a benefactor or chastiser of rulers.

But the dominant image of Kīnā Rām resides in the term most often used by informants: Kīnā Rām Aghorī. The very notion of an *aghorī* saint seems on face value to be an oxymoron, for no other term carries such a horrific connotation in Indian society as *aghorī*. An *aghorī* is an ascetic who practices *aghor sādhanā*—Shaivite Tantric practices that use imagery of death and transcendence in order to invoke various forms of the goddess and gain her power.[8] These rituals often take place in cremation grounds and involve the offering of dangerous and polluting substances such as dead bodies, bones or skulls, liquor and cannabis, sexual fluids and excreta.[9] *Aghor sādhanā* has the reputation of being India's most radical and archaic religious path, one that informants claim is used to achieve supernatural power. As an *aghorāchārya*, a master of this sadhana, Kīnā Rām is believed to have possessed many miraculous powers. These include the ability to fly, to walk six inches above the ground or move underground at breakneck speed, to see events at a distance, to appear at several places at once, to empower wells and ponds with healing properties, to possess the *vāch siddhi* that enabled him to deliver curses or boons, to make barren women fertile and empty storehouses full, to make fish jump out of the water and into the fire, to raise the dead, turn water into wine and vegetables into fish and back again.[10] He is said to have drunk wine out of the skull of a Brahmin, and, like Shiva, to have smoked tobacco, cannabis, and datura.

During my research I noticed varying attitudes towards the reputation of Kīnā Rām as an *aghorī*. Informants (mostly upper caste) warned me to be careful while researching the sect. A Vaiṣṇava Brahmin pandit begrudgingly admitted to me that such a path was a legitimate part of Hinduism, but indicated that he nonetheless found it disgusting, inferior, and unnecessary. Many people were frightened of the tales of strange happenings that had taken place over the years inside the gates of the *sthala*—how the Tantric *bābā*s had drunk liquor, wandered naked and had used prostitutes for their rituals. Others (usually lower-caste or Kṣatriya informants) focused less on the *aghorī* practices and more on the power gained, describing Kīnā Rām in humorous and irreverent stories as a champion of the underclasses who taught lessons to corrupt Brahmins, unjust kings, and proud sadhus.

Echoing the earlier tradition of Gorakhnāth and the sixty-four Siddhas, it may be said that Kīnā Rām and his followers are largely feared and respected by the upper castes and classes and championed by the lower ones. Unlike the Nāth ascetics who chose to ally themselves with powerful kings, however, the Kīnā Rāmī, in true Rājpūt form, acted out the role of kings themselves in small kingdoms of their own creation.

Within a 150-mile radius of Banaras proper, eight monastic centers were established where Kīnā Rāmī Augharṣ (renunciants) or *mūḍiyas* (semi-renunciants) played out the role of "Aughaṛ kingship." Headed by a *mahant* chosen as the resident "Kīnā Rām," despite, or perhaps because of, their radical reputations, the Augharṣ operated as village zamindars, local arbiters of justice, and healing and ritual specialists.[11] Moving from village to village on elephants, they collected taxes in the form of grain or money and when necessary took up arms to protect the villagers from outside looters.

Challenging not only Brahminical notions of pollution and ritual hierarchy but the very cosmology by which these were legitimized, the Kīnā Rāmīs built their movement on the religious power bases of the lower and excluded castes. Their headquarters were built in geographic proximity to, and incorporate the worship of, *bīr*s, *pīr*s, *māyi*s, *mazār*s, trees, *satī* stones and *nāga*s.[12] They legitimated these forms of worship that were traditionally rejected as superstitious within the Brahminical system. At the same time they consolidated their own power, both spiritual and political, by encompassing and establishing a dominion over the spirits inherit in these forms. This was done by accepting the label, the imagery, and at least some of the practices of the *aghorī*s, who were traditionally believed to have power over the dead. By seeming to advocate the ritual eating of human flesh on the cremation ground, the Kīnā Rāmī openly defied the Brahminical worldview that judges men primarily by what they eat. By handling human feces, they rejected the very notion of untouchability and defilement.

Although their methods were religiously and culturally radical, the agenda of the Kīnā Rāmī was basically reformist. While they were opposed to Brahminical domination, they were not antihierarchical. They instead sought to establish a new hierarchy in which the rulership rights of the Rājpūts would be consolidated not through force or even ritual, but through an ideology of a just and inclusive religious and social community.

Similarly, the Kīnā Rāmī did not oppose the idea of a central administration as set up by the Mughals and later the British, but rather sought to symbolically emulate and encompass its power. This is wonderfully symbolized by one of the most incongruous objects of worship at the Kīnā Rām *sthala* in Banaras, a large wooden desk-*cum*-seat. Located in its own separate shrine inside the courtyard of the complex, it has two tiers and is supported by claw feet. Five drawers on each side are said to have once held the papers and writing materials of Kīnā Rām. It is called a *takhta* (throne) and is believed to have miraculous powers as the seat on which Kīnā Rām sat to deliver speeches.

One's first reaction to this strange object of devotion might be that it is an all too appropriate religious symbol in a country where the bureaucracy wields so much power. In fact, the symbolism of Kīnā Rām as a ruler literally sitting on top of a desk of papers highlights the rising importance of written records, especially land deeds, under the Moghul and British rule, not to mention in India since independence. The *takhta* is, then, a symbol of Kīnā Rām's mastery over the administrative power of the rulers, a power that is closely linked to the ownership of land. By sitting on top of the *takhta*, Kīnā Rām stakes a claim to the power of the secular rulers.

Despite the manipulation of such symbols, within the larger Hindu context, the Kīnā Rāmī were, like many of the *Sant*-inspired movements, radically iconoclastic. They also display several affinities with Islam. It can be argued that their Kṣatriya ethos of just rulership is closer to Islamic notions of transcendence than to Hindu Brahminical ritualism. In the same vein, Augharṣ were closer in lifestyle to the Sufi sects than they were to upper-caste Hindus or even to the highly organized and wealthy Daśnāmī sadhus who had become consummate merchants and landlords.[13] In the stories of Kīnā Rām, it is more often the Muslim rulers who gain the boons and the Hindu leaders who get the curses. It was also from a Muslim ruler that Kīnā Rām accepted patronage. According to legend, the Moghul ruler Shāhjahān issued a copper plate granting that one pice and one unburnt log from each funeral pyre at Hariśchandra Ghāṭ in Banaras be donated for the maintenance of the Kīnā Rām sect. To this day it is from Hariśchandra that members of the sect drag the wood to keep the perpetual fire burning at the *sthala*. In accepting the patronage of a Muslim ruler, the message may be that Kīnā Rām prefers the pollution of the Muslim to the purity of the Brahmin. He is also playing the role of Shiva, who drank the world's poison and was not destroyed. In the practice of *aghor sādhanā,* from pollution comes power.

The partially burnt wood from the cremation ghāṭ, collected from Hindu funeral pyres, is tantamount to taking *prasād* from the Ḍoms, who are the lowest and most defiled of all castes by virtue of their occupation as handlers of corpses. By creating a sacred fire from wood from cremation fires and offering oblations into it, the Vedic *yajña* is turned on its head and Brahminical power is overthrown. It is interesting to note here that at the yearly ritual of Lolarak Chasthi, Brahmin priests from the major (Shaivite) temples of Banaras, including the temple of Viśvanāth, chant the *Black Yajurveda* in the presence of this fire in order to recharge their mantras with its power.[14]

In true Kṣatriya style, Kīnā Rām's predominant characteristic has been his dominion over the powers that be, sacred or secular. Power became the means by which Kīnā Rāmīs, as Kṣatriyas, superseded the Brahminical hierarchy—which they perceived as impotent, elitist, and corrupt. Yet when they played out the role of temporal rulers, it was with more than a little ironic flair. As half-naked sadhus sitting on thrones, smoking hookahs, and drinking alcohol in prodigious quantities while musicians played and dancing girls performed Kathak, they presented a transgressive and macabre vision of the order they emulated. From the realm of Yama, the Lord of Death, they mocked temporal rulers even as they appropriated for themselves the role of protectors of justice.

Today most Kīnā Rāmī centers barely survive. Land ceilings in the post-independence period led to the confiscation of zamindari holdings, and impoverishment has forced the centers to sell most of their remaining lands. The secular power of these centers has also been severely circumscribed by the diminishing Augharṛ population, modernization, and the increasing power of the government bureaucracy.

At the same time, the Kīnā Rām sect is now in the process of a reformation under the leadership of a charismatic leader named Avadhut Bhagwan Ram.[15] Although Bhagwan Ram was initiated into this sect at an early age, he declined the opportunity to officially head the sect at the time of his guru's death. Instead he went on to found his own organization called Sri Sarveshwari Samooh, which he stresses is not a religion but a social service movement dedicated to such humanitarian activities as opening leprosy hospitals and free medical dispensaries, and performing low-cost and dowry-free marriages.[16] The Sri Sarveshwari Samooh has in recent years overshadowed the traditions of the Kīnā Rām sect and has worked to erase the old reputation of the Kīnā Rām *sthala* as a hangout for Augharṣ and *gañja*-smoking outcastes. But at the same time, the sect has retained its powerful traditional religious imagery. There has been a shift in emphasis from a Shaivite to a Śākta-centered worship with a corresponding emphasis on the importance of the role of the feminine in religion and society. These changes are understood within the Kīnā Rām sect to serve as a way of updating the message of Kīnā Rām to administer to the needs of the common people in the modern age. The vision for this reformation is centered in the person of Bhagwan Ram who, by his disciples, is referred to as "Sarkār," "Ṭhākur," "Mālik," or "Mahārāj"[17] and is worshipped by some as an incarnation of Kīnā Rām himself, by others as a form of the goddess Sarveśvarī,[18] and by yet others as an *aghoreśvar*, one who has achieved extraordinary powers through the practice of *aghor sādhanā*. For the more secular-minded, he is seen as an enlightened saint with a salvational social vision.

The interface between politics and religion characteristic of the Kīnā Rām sect continues today as politicians flock to Bhagwan Ram as a source of inspiration, guidance and sheer power. In November of 1990, Chandrashekhar, a close disciple of Bhagwan Ram, briefly became national prime minister after the fall of the V. P. Singh government. In Delhi, his rise to power was seen as the result of a highly unusual combination of political flukes. In the Banaras region, even in the newspapers, it was attributed to the blessings of his guru. During the Guru Pūrṇimā celebrations the previous July, attended by more than fifty thousand people, Bhagwan Ram had invited Chandrashekhar to be a keynote speaker. Similarly, many of the stories informants told me about the guru Bhagwan Ram dealt with other major political figures of contemporary India. The general theme of these stories was the way in which the guru wields power over even the power brokers of modern India. This echoes the role that Kīnā Rām is believed to have played in relation to the rulers of his time and establishes a continuity with that tradition despite the moral reforms that Bhagwan Ram is imposing on the sect.

The Kīnā Rām sect, in its history and current reformation, provides an interesting case study of the relationship between politics and religion in the context of social change. Kīnā Rām can be viewed as the most radical of the sociopolitical dissidents to have arisen out of the North Indian *sant* traditions. In addition, his life sheds light on the role of Tantric or heterodox lineages within the history of Indian religions and, above all, on the fascinating relationship between Tantric practitioners and secular rulers, between Augharṣ and kings.

Notes

1. See William Crooke, *Tribes and Castes of the Northwest Frontier,* vol. 1 (1895), p. 29.
2. See Surajit Sinha and Baidyanath Sarasvati, *Ascetics of Kashi* (Varanasi: N. K. Bose Memorial Foundation, 1978).
3. Amar Singh, *Aghor Peetha and Baba Kina Ram* (Varanasi: Sri Sarveshwari Samooh, 1988)
4. This story takes place at the Chet Singh Palace on the banks of the Ganges near Godolia Crossing in Banaras.
5. Another story tells how the current maharaja managed to get the curse removed. In this story the current head of the Kīnā Rām sect, Bhagwan Ram, plays a central role. See my forthcoming dissertation, "The Politics of Heterodoxy and the Kina Rami Aghoris of Benares," Syracuse University.
6. By "political" I here mean activity that concerns itself with the mobilization of people and resources to effect material and social change. For further discussion of this point, see my forthcoming thesis (previous note).
7. It is perhaps difficult to understand how Kīnā Rām can be called a Vaiṣṇava, but he is traditionally credited with founding four "Vaiṣṇava" and four "Aghor" monasteries.
8. For some definitions and descriptions of aghorīs in early British scholarship, see James Hastings, ed., *Encyclopedia of Religion and Ethics*, vol. 1, p. 210; H. Balfour, "Life History of an Aghori Fakir," *Journal of the Anthropological Institute* 26 (1897): 340–57; J. C. Oman, *The Mystics, Ascetics and Saints of India* (London: T. Fisher Unwin, 1905).

9. For a "firsthand" account of such a rite, see Robert Svoboda, *Aghora: On the Left Hand of God* (Albuquerque, N.M.: Brotherhood of Life, 1986).

10. For an "official" account, see Lakṣmaṇ Śukla, ed., *Aughaṛ Rām Kīnā Kathā,* 2d ed. (Varanasi: Sri Sarveshwari Samooh, 1978).

11. The rituals they performed were simple and catered to the needs of the villagers they served. Because the Kīnā Rāmī were a Kṣatriya group opposed to Brahmin domination, I would argue that these rituals reflected an appropriation of the Brahmin's ritual privileges over lower-caste groups.

12. For a discussion of these forms of worship and their relationship to *sant* sects of North India, see Shukdeo Singh, "The Development of Nirgun Religion in Medieval India," unpublished manuscript.

13. For a description of the lifestyles of the Daśnāmīs in the eighteenth century, see Kamala Prasad Mishra, *Benaras in Transition: 1738-1795* (New Delhi: Munshiram Manoharlal, 1975).

14. I witnessed this in September of 1988 and 1989. My first impression was that these priests were somehow legitimizing the *samādhi* of Kīnā Rām with their Brahmin presence. Guru Bhagwan Ram later asserted, however, that the situation was just the reverse: the Brahmins attend the ceremony every year to draw power from Kīnā Rām's fire.

15. Avadhut Bhagwan Ram died in November 1992.

16. See Bali Ram Pandey, *An Introduction to Sri Sarveshwari Samooh* (Varanasi: Sri Sarveshwari Samooh, 1988).

17. All honorific titles often used for Kṣatriyas.

18. One of the more fascinating aspects of this sect, not covered in this paper, is the transsexual dimension of the worshipping of a male guru as the incarnation of a female deity. See my forthcoming thesis (note 5).

PART II
THEOLOGY

The Theology of the Locative Case in Sacred Sikh Scripture (Gurabāṇī)

Michael C. Shapiro

This paper arises as an outgrowth of close textual studies of the language of sacred Sikh scripture *(Gurabāṇī)* that I have been carrying out for several years. In these studies I have been examining both the specific linguistic correlates of *Gurabāṇī* as well as the ways that the Sikh Gurūs whose compositions are included in the *Gurū Granth Sāhib* (or *Ādigranth*) employ language in carrying out their religious, moral, doctrinal, and poetic ends. In the course of conducting this close reading of Gurabāṇī I have been struck by how often particular verses and series of verses are structured around words or phrases that are in one way or another "locative." Although not all of these uses can be seen to have weighty intentions behind them (i.e., some locatives are merely locatives), in a surprising number of instances the use of these constructions can be shown to be linked to the religious or doctrinal significance of the verse or verses in question. So frequent and conspicuous is this linkage in Gurabāṇī in general, and the *Gurū Granth Sāhib (GGS)* in particular, that I do not believe it can be considered accidental. It is for this reason that I believe it a useful exercise to enumerate locative usages in sacred Sikh scripture and to speculate on why they occur where they do. In carrying out these ends, I will refer primarily to compositions by Gurū Nānak, but I will also refer to verses by the fourth and fifth Gurūs, Rām Dās and Arjan, respectively.

Linguistic Data

The language of the core sections of the *GGS*[1] possesses a wide variety of constructions that are in one way or another locative. They include the following: (1) special locative case forms of nouns, adjectives, pronouns, and occasionally postpositions, in both the singular and plural numbers; (2) a locative case of the infinitive; and (3) a so-called "locative absolute" construction, based upon the past participle. A summary of representative locative case forms in Gurabāṇī, as described by Shackle (1983), is given below.

NOUNS

Declension	Direct singular	Locative singular standard	Locative singular extended	Locative plural
		(masculine)		
I.	*manu* 'mind, heart'	*mani*	*mane/mani*	*manī̃*
	nā̃u 'name'	*nā̃i*	*nā̃e/nā̃ī*	*nā̃ī̃*
II.	*mā̃gatā* 'beggar'	*mā̃gatai*		*mā̃gatā̃ī̃*
III.	*pāpī* 'sinner'	*pāpī*		*pāpīī̃*
		(feminine)		
IV.	*deha* 'body'	*dehi*	*dehai*	*dehī̃*
V.	*rāti* 'night'	*rāti*		*rātī̃*

ADJECTIVES

Declension	Direct singular	Locative singular	Locative plural
I.	(m.) *niramalu* 'pure'	*niramali/niramala*	
II.	(m.) *kūṛā* 'false, untrue'	*kūṛai/kūṛe*	*kūṛī̃*
	(f.) *kūṛī*	*kūṛī*	*kūṛīī̃*
	Possessive postposition *kā*		
	(m.) *kā*	*kai/ke*	*kī̃*
	(f.) *kī*	*kī*	*kī̃*

PRONOUNS

Sample listings only: *āpi/āpe* from *āpu* 'oneself'; *itu/etu/aitu* from *ihe/ehu* 'this'; *titu* from *so* 'he, she, it'; *jitu* from rel. pro. *jo; kitu* from interrogative *kavaṇu* 'who'; *kitai* from indefinite *ko/koī/koi* 'someone or other'; *ik(ki)/ ek(k)i/ik(k)atu/ek(k)atu* from *ik(k)u* 'one'; *sabha/sabhatai* from *sabhu* 'all'.

VERBS

Locative infinitive

dir. *ākhaṇu* 'to say', loc. *ākhaṇi;* dir. *jāvaṇu/jāṇu* 'to go', loc. *jāvaṇi/jāṇi.*

Locative absolute

Stem	past participle (masculine singular)	locative absolute
su- 'hear'	*suniā*	*suniai*
kari- 'do'	*kītā*	*kītai*

In addition to single words that are in an overt locative case, the language also makes use of diverse locative phrases in which a noun in a generic oblique case is followed by what can be called a locative postposition. Thus the language expresses the concept "in the mind/heart" either by a first declension noun in the locative singular *(mani)* or by a two-word locative postpositional phrase *(mana vichi).*

In discussing the use of the locative case in Gurabāṇī, it is important to bear in mind that the language does not make use of a morphologically distinct instrumental case, and that the locative is used for some functions that would be expressed by the instrumental in Old Indo-Aryan. Thus an expression such as *hukami* can be rendered in English both as "in God's will/order" or "through God's will/order." This distinction between semantically locative and semantically instrumental applications of the locative case is important as there are many places in the *GGS* where, I believe, the correct reading of a verse hinges upon the distinction, or where a verse can be read variously depending upon whether a locative form is to be read as having instrumental or locative force.

Uses of the Locative in Gurabāṇī

The uses of the locative case or locative phrases that are crucial for my purposes in this paper are those in which the locative element is the framing element of a verse or series of verses. It is important to note that the locative element in such verses usually occurs in the initial position in the line or half line, in what can be thought of as the slot of highest profile. The locative word is iterated frequently, this iteration producing a highly pronounced *ostinato* musical effect. The verses in which these repetitions take place generally have a highly intricate internal structure, and display such formal unifying principles as antithesis, parallel or symmetrical clause structures, multiple words derived from the same underlying root or stem, and word or sound play of diverse sorts.[2] These verses are often elliptic, and the non-occurrence of finite verbs is quite common. The most common syntactic patterns exhibited in these locative usages is what I refer to as a "predicate locative" type in which a proposed locative word or phrase is starkly juxtaposed with a nominal phrases of one type or another. In many instances the locative word or phrase around which a verse is structured may be prefigured by occurrences of the same word or phrase in earlier verses or echoed by other locative expressions later.

A representative example of the sort of textual phenomena to which I refer can be seen in *Japujī* 6:

hukamī hovani ākāra hukamu na kahiā jāī.
hukamī hovani jīa hukami milai vaḍiāī.
hukamī utamu nīchu hukami likhi dukh sukh pāīāhi.
ikanā hukamī bakhasīsa iki hukamī sadā bhavāīāhi.
hukamai ādari sabhu ko bāhari hukama na koi.
nānaka hukamai je bujhai ta haumai kahai na koi.

All forms exist in/through the will [of the Lord], ineffable though that will be.
All living things exist in/through the will [of the Lord] [and] greatness obtained in/through his grace.
In/through [his] will [is the differentiation] of high and low; by/through his will [do people] obtain woe or joy.
For some, grace is bestowed through [his will]; some are made to wander eternally through [his] will.
Within his provenance is everything; nothing is outside his provenance.
Oh Nānak, if one understands [God's] order, then one does not speak [words] of egoism.

We see in this verse the profiling of locative forms of the noun *hukamu*, which is paralleled in the fifth line by the locative postpositional phrase *hukamai ãdari.* The locative expressions in question occur at the beginnings of short terse clauses that often incorporate dichotomies or formal antitheses. In addition, the word *hukamī* is linked to iterations of the same word both in previous and following verses of the same text.

It is important to note that long sections of text in the *GGS* consist of sequences of verses, each beginning with a locative expression, with some of these expressions carried over for several verses at a time. The most dramatic and well-known example of this technique is in the *Japujī*, where long strings of verses are structured around a chain of locative framing phrases. These phrases, and the numbers of the verses in the *Japujī* in which they occur, are as follows:

ādi 'in the beginning' (1, 28–31)
sochai 'through introspection' (1)
chupai 'in/through silent [meditation]' (1)
hukami/hukamī/hukamai ãndari 'in/through accordance with [God's] will' (1–3)
tīrathi 'in/at [a] place of pilgrimage' (6)
mati vichi 'in the heart/mind' (6)
suṇiai 'through having heard [the Word]' (8–11)
mannai 'through having accepted [the Word]' (13–15)
ākhaṇi 'in/through speaking/saying' (32)
karamī̃ 'through [one's] actions' (34)

The order of locative phrases in this sequence is quite important. After the initial assertion of the timelessness of Truth *(ādi sachu jugādi sachu)*, Gurū Nānak proceeds to a statement of the impossibility of attaining true spiritual awareness through introspection (*sochai)* or through meditation *(chupai)*. After denying the efficacy of certain means for achieving ultimate enlightenment, Nānak turns inevitably to a discussion of the nature of the highest truth, which is revealed both in and through God's will/order *(hukamī)*. Understanding of this truth is internalized through first hearing *(suṇiai)* the Word, accepting it *(mannai)*, and verbalizing it *(ākhaṇi)*, through which progression one has been led unawares into a state of sympathetic vibration with the highest principle, which is equated with sound *(sabad, ikõkār)*.

Although the *Japujī* contains the most stunning use of verses linked sequentially by preposed locative phrases, it is by no means the only place in the *GGS* where such structures can be found. They are characteristic of the longer set compositions by Gurū Nānak in general. The use of these structures is also, I believe, particularly well suited to the genre of the *vār*, which by its very internal structure, built around *pauṛīs* "rungs of a ladder" by a single Gurū, to which are added one or more *salok*s by various Gurūs, favors compositional techniques establishing linkages across disparate verses.[3] *Āsā kī vār,* in particular, displays several dramatic instances of verses framed around locative phrases such as *kudarati* "through the power [of the Gurū]" (3.2), *bhai vichi* "in/through fear" (4.1), *haü vichi* "in/through pride/egoism" (7.1), and *satiguri miliai* "when the Satguru is obtained" (8, *Pauṛī).* In other places in *Āsā kī vār,* such as in the following *salok* by Gurū Nānak in verse 15, verses are structured around syntactically parallel locative expressions:

nai manniai pati upajai sālāhā sachu sūtu;
daragaha ādari pāīai tagu na tūṭasi pūta.

Through accepting the Name, honor is engendered; in/through acts of praise [is obtained] the true [sacred] thread;
When it is obtained in the court [of the Lord], that sacred thread for the son [??] will not break.

Despite the fact that the Gurūs after Nānak do not use locative phrases for framing and linking purposes with anything like the same frequency as Nānak, their use of these architectural devices is still quite evident, particularly in longer compositions. Gurū Arjan, for instance, employs them to telling effect in the *Sukhamanī* in Rāga Gāuṛī:

sãta kai dūkhani[4] *ārajā ghaṭai.*
sãta kai dūkhani jama te nahī chhuṭai.
sãta kai dūkhani sukhu sabhu jāi.
sãta kai dūkhani naraka mahi pāi.

(Rāga Gāuṛī, Sukhamanī, Mahalā 5, 13.1)

In/through reproaching the saints [one's] lifetime is diminished.
In/through reproaching the saints [one does not obtain] freedom from Death (i.e., from Yama).
In/through reproaching the saints all happiness disappears.
In/through the suffering of the saints [one falls] into hell.

Sometimes particular locative phrases are used almost formulaically as topic markers. Phrases such as *haŭ vichi, bhai vichi,* or *satiguri miliai* need only to be invoked as the initial phrases of a verse to initiate or continue a discourse on a particular theological point that has been of concern to the Gurūs or their followers. An excellent example of this can be found in a *salok* by Gurū Rām Dās to the *vār* in Rāga Vaḍahāsa:

bhai vichi sabhu ākāru hai nirabhau hari jīu soi.
satiguri seviai hari mani vasai tithai bhaŭ kade na hoi.
(Rāga Vaḍahāsa kī vār, Mahalā 4, 2.1)

Through fear [comes into existence] all material creation; only Hari exists without fear.
When the Satguru is served, Hari dwells in the heart; there is never any fear at that place.

In discussing the importance of locative expressions within the overall context of Gurabāṇi, it is important to bear in mind that these usages do not occur by themselves, but are a part of a wider sentential or clausal syntax. For the most part, verses framed around locative expressions are constituted of simple equational structures in which a locative expression is first announced and then followed by a listing of elements that are equated with or derivative of the state or activity represented by the locative phrase. This type of syntactic construction is well illustrated by *Japujī* 8–11, where the majority of half lines consist of the word *suṇiai* "by/through hearing [the Name]" followed appositionally by an enumeration of entities brought into being through the process of hearing the Name:

suṇiai sidha pīra surināth; suṇiai dharati dhavala ākāsa.
suṇiai dīpa loa pātāla; suṇiai pohi na sakai kāla.
nānak bhagatā sadā vigāsu; suṇiai dūkha pāpa kā nāsu. (8)

suṇiai sarā guṇā ke gāha; suṇiai sekha pāra pātisāha.
suṇiai ādhe pāvāhi rāhu; suṇiai hātha hovai asagāhu.
nānaka bhakatā sadā vigāsu; suṇiai dūkha pāpa kā nāsu. (11)

Through hearing [the Name are brought into being] siddhas, pīrs, and the lords of the gods; through hearing [the Name] are brought into being the earth, Dhavalu [the bull that supports the earth], and the sky.

Through hearing [the Name are brought into being] the continents, the worlds, and the nether regions; through [hearing the Name] Death has no power.
O Nānak, the bhaktas are ever happy; through hearing [the Word is brought about] the destruction of grief and sin.

Through hearing [the Name is brought into existence] praise of an ocean of qualities; through hearing [the Name are engendered] shaikhs, pīrs, and emperors.
Through hearing [the Name] the blind find their way; through hearing [the Name] one can touch bottom in the depths (??).
O Nānak, the bhaktas are every happy; through hearing [the Word is brought about] the destruction of grief and sin.

A further example of preposed locative phrases in equational or "predicative" structures can be seen in a *Sabad* by Gurū Nānak in Sirī Rāg:

lekhai bolaṇu bolaṇā lekhai khāṇā khāu.
lekhai vāṭa chalāīā lekhai suṇi vekhāu.
lekhai sāha lavāīāhi paṛe ki puchhaṇa jāu.
(Sirī Rāg, Mahalā 1, Sabad 3)

Through one's fate [is determined] what one says; through one's fate [is one given] food to eat.
Through one's fate one's way/path is made; through one's fate does one hear and see.
Through one's fate are breaths taken; what purpose is there in going to ask an educated person?

In this verse a word in the locative case *(lekhai)* is first exposited and then has things predicated of it. Whereas in other examples discussed this predication has been accomplished by nouns or adjectives, in this one it is also achieved by finite verbs (e.g., *sāha lavāīāhi*).

Functions of Verses Built around Locative Phrases

If, as I have argued, it is the case that the *GGS* has a greater number of verses structured around locative phrases than can reasonably be ascribed to chance, then one might inquire as to why this should be the case. It would be reasonable to inquire as to what message or theological point is advanced or served by such linguistic means.

From my reading of selected corpora of Gurabāṇī I have been able to ascertain several distinct theological points that are enhanced by the use of the grammatical structures of the type I have just described. In describing these functions it is important to note whether the locative phrase around which a verse is structured denotes an activity or state that is judged positively or negatively. When denoting something viewed positively, as, for example, hearing or accepting the Word, the bestowing of Grace by the Lord on an individual, or existence or abiding in God's court, the use of locative-based syntax serves to enumerate serially a class of entities that are brought into existence as a result of the state, condition, or activity represented by the form in the locative. In effect, the use of this structure establishes what can be considered chains of causation and statements of first principles. For example, when in *Āsā kī vār* 3.2 Gurū Nānak states "*kudarati vedā purāṇā katebā kudarati saraba vichāru,*" he is in essence establishing an ontological chain in which the existence of the Vedas, Purāṇas, Koran, etc. is subordinated to the more fundamental power *(kudarati)* of the Gurū. In the exposition of the hierarchy implicit in such a chain, no explicit grammatical connecting material is needed or desired. Many other examples of such ontological chains can be found in the *Sukhamanī* of Gurū Arjan, as, for instance, in the third *salok* of the first *asaṭapadī:*

prabhu kai simarani ridhi sidhi nau nidhi.
prabhu kai simarani giānu dhiānu tatu budhi.

By/through remembering the Lord [are obtained] psychic powers [and] the nine treasures.
By/through remembering the Lord [are obtained] knowledge, meditation, and the essence of wisdom.

In many other examples found in Gurabāṇī the expression appearing in the locative describes action or state that is undesirable or that has negative consequences. In such instances, the inverted predicate locative syntax is used to enumerate a range of phenomena, all in some way negative, illusory, or undesirable, that arise from the action or state appearing in the locative. This is illustrated by the first half-line of the excerpt from *Vaḍahãsa kī vār* cited earlier:

bhaï viche sabhu ākāru hai nirabhaü hari jīu soi.
satiguri seviai hari mani vasai tithai bhaü kade no hoi.

Through fear [comes into existence] all material creation; only Hari exists without fear.
When the Satguru is served, Hari dwells in the heart; there is never any fear at that place.

Our understanding of what is being accomplished by means of the first half-line of this verse is enhanced when we observe how that half-line stands in contradistinction to the following half-line and next full line, in which we are told both of the lack of fear of Hari, and the good consequences that ensue from serving the Satguru. It should be noted that the sense "when the Satguru is served" is expressed by the locative absolute phrase *satiguri seviai.*

An additional example of scripture structured around a repetitive locative expression describing a state from which multiple negative consequences ensue is to be found in verse 4 of *Āsā kī vār*. This section of text is structured around repeated clause-initial instances of the words *bhai vichi* "in/through fear" and describes a succession of phenomena that are in some sense derivative of fear of God:

bhai vichi pavaṇu vahai sada vāu; bhai vichi chalāhi lakha darīāu.
bhai vichi agani kaḍhe vegāri; bhai vichi dharatī dabī bhāri.
bhai vichi indu phirai sira bhāri; bhai vichi rājā dharamu duāru.
bhai vichi sūraju bhai vichi chandu; koha karoṛī chalata na antu.
bhai vichi sidha budha sura nātha; bhai vichi āḍāne ākāsa.
bhai vichi jodha mahābala sūra; bhai vichi āvāhi jāvāhi pūra.

In/through fear the wind [comes to exist] and the breeze blows eternally; in/through fear flow hundreds of thousands of rivers.
In/through fear is fire compelled to do its work; in fear is the earth weighed down by its burden;
In/through fear does Indra move about with his head burdened; in/through fear does Dharmarāja, the divine portal, exist;
In/through fear exists the sun; in/through fear exists the moon; they travel crores of *kosa*s without end;
In/through fear exist the Siddhas, Buddhas, Suras, and Nāths; in/through fear were the heavens spread out;
In/through fear are the warriors, brave heroes; loads of them come and go.

An extraordinary example of how points of great theological significance are expressed in Gurabāṇī by poetry centered around a locative phrase (*haü vichi* "in/though egoism") is a *salok* by Gurū Nānak to verse 7 of *Āsā kī vār:*

haü vichi āiā haü vichi gaïā; haü vichi jammiā haü vichi muā.
haü vichi ditā haü vichi laiā; haü vichi khaṭiā haü vichi gaiā.
haü vichi sachiāru kūṛiāru; haü vichi pāpa punna vīchāru.
haü vichi naraki suragi avatāru; haü vichi hasai haü vichi rovai.
haü vichi bharīai haü vichi dhovai; haü vichi jātī jinasī khovai.
haü vichi mūrakhu haü vichi siāṇā; mokha mukati kī sāra na jāṇā.
haü vichi māiā haü vichi chhāiā; haümai kari kari jāta upāiā.
haümai būjhai tā daru sūjhai; giāna vihūṇā kathi kathi lūjhai.
nānak hukamī likhīai lekhu; jehā vekhahi tehā vekhu.

In egoism [one] came; in egoism [one] departed; in egoism [one] was born; in egoism [one] died.
In/through egoism [is something] given; in/though egoism [is something] taken; in/through egoism [is something] accumulated; in/though egoism [is something] spent.
In/though egoism [does one become] truthful or deceitful; in/through egoism [arises] the differentiation of sin and merit.
In/through egoism [does one have] birth in hell or heaven; in/through egoism does one laugh; in/through egoism does one cry.
In/through egoism is [one] covered [with pollution]; in/through egoism does [one] cleanse oneself; in/through egoism [is one assigned] a category based upon birth and in/through egoism are such categories erased.
In/through egoism arises [the distinction between being] a fool and [being] clever; [so also arises] an awareness of *mukti* and *mokṣa*;
In/through egoism arises illusion and shadow; creatures are engendered when egoism is enacted.
[When] egoism is understood then the gate [of salvation] comes to mind; in the absence of [this] knowledge [of the nature of egoism??], one becomes agitated in trying [over and over again] to describe it [i.e., the nature of egoism (??)].
Nānak says, [only] through the Divine Will is [one's] fate written; things take form in accordance with God's will [??].

It is hard to imagine a verse in which a higher profile is assigned to locative expressions. One of the central points of this verse is that the various dualities of material existence come into existence as a consequence of egoism *(haümai)*. This point is expressed by the use of an extended chain of small clauses in each of which the topic, the condition of being in a state of egoism, is first asserted and that followed by a terse predicate that describes the false dichotomies that arise in or through egoism. The use of formal antitheses (e.g., *haü vichi āiā haü vichi gaïā)* iconically mirrors the point that both of the members of sets of polar opposite phenomena in the real world (e.g., going and coming, being born and dying, laughing and crying) are derivation of an delusional first cause. It should be noted that when Gurū Nānak ends the listing of derivatives of the state of egoism and moves to a statement of the ultimate cause of good and true consequences, the key word shifts to *hukamī* "in/through [God's] will/ provenance," which is also in the locative case.

The widespread occurrence in Gurabāṇī of locative expressions of the type discussed in this paper has not just been a matter of abstract interest. The failure to identify, analyze, and understand fully the linguistic aspects of these constructions and the reasons for their employment has caused translators of Sikh scripture into English and other languages to produce translations that do not do full justice to the sense of the original. I say this with full understanding of the inherent difficulty of rendering into languages such as English of structures involving a terse predicative linking of one or more nouns with a locative phrase. Even Macauliffe, in many ways one of the most careful and thoughtful translators of Gurabāṇī, occasionally translates text in a way that, because of a failure to properly assess the import of locative syntax, misses an important theological point. For example, he renders the line "*bhai vichi sidha budha sura nātha; bhai vichi ādāne ākāsa*" as "In fear are the Siddhs, the Budhas, the demigods, and the Nāths; in fear are the stars and the firmament."[5] Macauliffe's translation is, I believe, inaccurate because it fails to explicate the function that the locative phrase *bhai vichi* has. What this verse does, if my analysis of it is correct, is posit a series of mental states or conditions out of which, through which, or as a result of which, other nonabiding and ultimately illusory phenomena in the real world come into existence. These mental states are placed in contradistinction to other mental states and/or processes from which can be derived abiding truth and contentment. Let me just note that I believe the verse in question, as well as the full *vār* of which it is a part, is as much about first principles as it is about fear of God.

Conclusion

When I first started reading Gurabāṇī several years ago one of the first things I learned about it was the claim, made frequently by pious commentators, that the entire contents of the *Gurū Granth Sāhib* is encapsulated in the *Japujī*, which is in turn encapsulated by the *Mūl Mantra*, itself epitomized by the word *ikõkār*. It will be recalled that the last word of the *Mūl Mantra* is *guraprasādi* ("through the Grace of the Gurū"), which is in the locative case, and which is appended to a chain of nominal forms that stand in apposition to the phrase *ikõkār*. There is certainly a sense in which claims concerning the epitomizing nature of *Japujī* and *Mūl Mantra* are supported by what I have been saying about locative formations in Gurabāṇī. Although I do not wish to overstate my case, I do believe that there is some legitimacy in the claim that the use of the word *guraprasādi* in the *Mūl Mantra* prefigures the use of locative framing structures throughout the entire *Japujī* and even the entire *GGS*. I would also add that I do not believe it to be accidental that so many words of theological or doctrinal significance within the discourse of the Sikh Gurūs (e.g., *guramukhi, guraprasādi, hukamī*) are grammatically locative. Given that so much scripture in the *GGS* is posed in the form of propositional chains having the logical sense "X brings about Y," but stated as "in/through X [occurs] Y," it is only natural that linguistically locative case forms expressing semantically locative or instrumental functions, would be used extensively.

In concluding this essay I would just like to note that one of the most exceptional characteristics of Gurabāṇī, and especially of the compositions by Gurū Nānak, is the interrelatedness between the external form of particular texts and the messages expressed by these texts. Much of Gurabāṇī exhibits an internal unity in which the formal aspects of texts, including their metrical, poetic, and linguistic structures are fully at one with their content. Works of scripture such as *Japujī* and *Āsā kī vār* are highly complex and profound works that cannot be simply characterized as being only about one or a few things. Nevertheless, it can be argued that both of these words are prolonged meditations that are deeply concerned with, inter alia, the nature of Divine Grace, the means of achieving awareness of higher realities through progressively hearing, accepting, and speaking the true Word, and means for differentiating between things that are ultimately false and those that are true. These texts also concern inner mental and spiritual states, as well as about other states, qualities, and phenomena that are derivative of these inner states. It should not be surprising, therefore, to find that these texts attach particular importance to words or phrases that denote either states in which or means through which higher awareness is obtained. It is in this sense that the claim, implicit in the title of this paper, that there exists a "theology" of the locative case in Sikh scripture, may be seen to have a modicum of validity.

Notes

1. In several important studies, Shackle (1977, 1978a, 1978b) has demonstrated how the language of the Gurūs as incorporated in the *GSS* can be analyzed as containing a homogeneous core, as well as "southwestern," "Persianized," and "Sahaskriti" strata. For descriptions of the grammatical properties of this core, see also Sāhib Siṅgh 1976, Shackle 1981 and 1983, and Shapiro 1987a.

2. An extended discussion of the operation of these unifying structures in the *Japujī* is given in Shapiro 1987b. For descriptions of the use of comparable unifying techniques in other Indian literary texts, see Salomon n.d. and Tubb 1985.

3. For a discussion of the formal structure of the *vār*, see Kohli 1961, 69–76, and Sāhib Siṅgh 1962–64, 3:604–10.

4. This phrase alternately can be rendered as "through/by means of the suffering of the saints."

5. Macauliffe 1909, 1:222.

Bibliography

Gurbachan Singh Talib, trans. 1984–88. *Sri Guru Granth Sahib*. Patiala: Punjabi University.

Kohli, Surendar Singh. 1961. *A Critical Study of the Adi Granth*. Delhi: Motilal Banarsidass.

Macauliffe, Max Arthur. 1909. *The Sikh Religion: Its Gurus, Sacred Writings and Authors*. Oxford: Oxford University Press.

McLeod, W. H. 1968. *Guru Nanak and the Sikh Religion*. Oxford: Oxford University Press.

Sāhib Siṅgh. 1962–64. *Srī Gurū Granth Sāhib Darpaṇ*. Jullundur: Rāj Publishing.

———. 1976. *Gurabāṇī viākaraṇ*. Amritsar: Siṅgh Brothers.

Salomon, Richard. n.d. "The poetic structure of the *Saundarananda*." Chapter in unpublished manuscript, "Asvaghosa's *Saundarananda:* Literary, cultural, and linguistic studies." Seattle.

Shackle, C. 1977. "'Southwestern' elements in the language of the *Adi Granth*." *Bulletin of the School of Oriental and African Studies* 40, no. 1:36–50.

———. 1978a. "Approaches to the Persian loans in the *Adi Granth*." *Bulletin of the School of Oriental and African Studies* 41, no. 1:73–96.

———. 1978b. "The Sahaskriti poetic idiom in the *Adi Granth*." *Bulletin of the School of Oriental and African Studies* 41, no. 2:297–313.

———. 1981. *A Guru Nanak Glossary*. London: School of Oriental and African Studies, University of London.

———. 1983. *An Introduction to the Sacred Language of the Sikhs*. London: School of Oriental and African Studies, University of London.

Shapiro, Michael C. 1987a. "Observations on the core language of the *Adigranth*." *Berliner indologische Studien* 3:181–93.

———. 1987b. "The rhetorical structure of the *Japuji*." Paper presented at the Second Berkeley Conference on Sikh Studies, Berkeley, California, February 1987.

Tubb, Gary A. 1985. "Principles of organization in the *Sisupalavadha*: The structure of Canto Four." Paper presented at the 14th Annual Conference on South Asia, University of Wisconsin at Madison, 2 November 1985. To appear in *Journal of South Asian Literature*.

The Nirguṇ/Saguṇ Distinction in Early Manuscript Anthologies of Hindi Devotion

John Stratton Hawley

When we use the term *nirguṇ* to identify one of the great traditions of North Indian religion, one important point of departure is a basic discrimination that has been made between two types of voices emerging from the "classical" period of bhakti literature in North India. In writing about this period—the so-called devotional period *(bhakti kāl),* extending from roughly the fifteenth through seventeenth centuries—historians of Hindi literature commonly make quite a sharp distinction between poets of the *nirguṇ* persuasion and those of the *saguṇ* camp. In the standard *Hindī Sāhitya kā Bṛhat Itihās,* for example, two volumes are devoted to the *bhakti kāl*, the first (volume 4) dealing with *nirguṇ* bhakti and the second (volume 5) taking up *saguṇ* bhakti. Poets included in the former volume include the iconoclasts: *sant*s such as Kabīr along with their Sufi counterparts. Poets discussed in the latter volume are the imagists: Sūr, Tulsī, and company. These are categorized, for the most part, according to whether they are thought of as poets of Krishna or of Rām.[1] Table 1 presents a quick, schematic representation of this way of approaching the *bhakti kāl,* and contains a very short list of the major poet-saints involved:

Table 1. *Nirguṇ* and *Saguṇ* in *Bhakti-kāl* Hindi Poetry.

School	"Without attributes" *(nirguṇa)*	"With attributes" *(saguṇa)*
Deity	(nameless), Rām	Krishna, Rām
Saints	*sant*s	*bhakta*s
	Ravidās	Sūrdās, Tulsīdās
	Kabīr	Mīrābāī

Most scholars, including those who write in European languages, have accepted this fundamental distinction between *nirguṇ* and *saguṇ* orientations. Obviously I include myself in this number, since the diagram I have just produced is a very slightly altered version of one that I prepared for an earlier publication.[2] But I am hardly alone. Charlotte Vaudeville and W. H. McLeod are two influential scholars who consider that a coherent *nirguṇ* or *sant* tradition can be rather easily separated from the *saguṇ* persuasion that one otherwise finds in "classical" Hindi bhakti,[3] and most contributors to the important collection of essays entitled *The Sants* take this discrimination as foundational and noncontroversial.[4]

As contributors to the present volume press the *nirguṇ* theme further, however, it is worth asking just how true-to-life this dichotomy is. How long has it actually been felt? As Karine Schomer observes in her introduction to *The Sants*:[5]

> The concept of *'nirguṇa* bhakti' as a distinct devotional mode contrasting with *'saguṇa* bhakti', and of the Sants constituting a separate devotional tradition, is relatively new. The idea that there is a coherent body of Sant teachings *(sant mat)* and that individual Sants belong to a common spiritual line of descent *(sant paramparā)* distinct from that of sectarian Vaishnavas did not become fully crystalized until the mid-nineteenth century.

In pointing to the mid-nineteenth century as a possibly crucial juncture, Schomer is apparently thinking of the origins of the Radhasoami movement, within which the concept *sant mat* came into prominent usage.[6] But Radhasoama thinkers took this term to be simply descriptive, nothing novel or of their own invention, and their publications in the early decades of the twentieth century suggest that they did not understand the word *sant* to designate an entirely exclusive *nirguṇ* category.[7] The idea that there was a true dichotomy between *nirguṇ* and *saguṇ* poet-saints may have come into strict usage as late as the 1930s, with the publication of a book from within the Radhasoami camp: Barthwal's *Nirguna School of Hindi Poetry*.[8]

My purpose here is not to pursue this problem in the history of ideas from the nineteenth century backward, though that would be an important and fascinating exercise. Instead, I wish to approach the issue from the opposite end in time. In this essay, I will ask to what degree we can see a clear distinction being made between *nirguṇ* and *saguṇ* paths in the *bhakti kāl* itself. Can one find it in writings that emerge from North India in the "classical" period—fifteenth to seventeenth century—or must one assume that it was the result of sectarian definitions that grew strong as the centuries passed?[9] If the former, there is no reason to question the rubrics that we have come to accept in describing the religious poetics of the *bhakti kāl*. If the latter, we will need to learn to use a good deal more caution than we have done in the past, and the historical background against which many essays in this volume are cast will have to be seen in a somewhat different light.

Resource A: Internal Evidence

One way to investigate the point is to give closer attention than has normally been done to compositions of the *bhaktas* themselves—that is, to poems that can be shown to have existed in their own time, or not long thereafter. A growing arsenal of critical work begins to make this possible.[10] I know the terrain with Sūrdās far better than elsewhere, and can say that early poems bearing his name show less careful attention to the *nirguṇ/saguṇ* dichotomy than do those added to the Sūr corpus later on. True, there are all those famous and eloquent *bhramargīt* poems ridiculing the *nirguṇ* persuasion. But on the other side of the issue, especially in the *vinaya* genre, there is a broad band of themes, tropes, and language that Sūr shares not just with Tulsī and Mirā but with Ravidās and Kabīr.

I have written about this on an earlier occasion,[11] so I will not belabor the point here. Rather, let a single poem suffice to show the sort of thing I mean. This composition, listed as number 115 by the Nāgarīprachāriṇī Sabhā, is first attested to early in the seventeenth century, having almost certainly emerged in the sixteenth:[12]

अपनै जान मै बहुत करी

कौंन भांति हरि भगति तुम्हारी सु कछु न स्वामी समुझि परी

गए दूरि दरसन कै कारन ब्यापक की बिभुता बिसरी

मनसा वाचा कर्म अगोचर सो मूरति नहि ध्यान धरी

बिनु गुन गुन बिनु रूप रूप बिनु नाम नाम कहि राम हरी

कृपा सिंधु अपराध अपरमित छिमहु सूर पै सब बिगरी

1 Much I was able to grasp on my own,
2 But Hari, my master, the act of loving you was something I could never understand.
3 I traveled great distances to have a glimpse of you, forgetting that you reign everywhere.
4 Inaccessible to thoughts, words, and deeds: that was the image I never thought to see.
5 Its traits are no traits; its form, no form; its no-name name they call Hari-Rām.
6 Ocean of mercy, forgive the unbounded impertinence that has made Sūr spoil it all.

The fourth and fifth lines are those that particularly bear remembering. There the renowned *saguṇ* poet, as if to contest that very designation, describes the search for images *(mūrati)* as misguided. He goes on to say that the true image has the trait of being traitless *(binu gun gun)* and the form of being formless *(binu rūp rūp)*. As for a name, it has an unnamable name *(binu nām nām)*. In the presence of lines such as this, it seems an understatement to observe that the *nirguṇ/saguṇ* distinction does not seem to work very well for Sūrdās. In fact, as I have tried to show, it took an invented conversion in his hagiography to make this notion plausible at all. Sūr became a pupil of Vallabha, the sectarians said, and forswore this kind of poem, thereafter producing only poems in the approved *saguṇ* mold.[13]

Resource B: Hagiography

That is indeed the next resource for tracing the history of the *nirguṇ/saguṇ* distinction: hagiography. But the problem with hagiography, as we see in the example I have just cited, is that the early hagiographies themselves seem to have been creations of writers with specific sectarian associations. They were often written precisely with the aim of establishing lines of affinity and affiliation that would give to received tradition a greater—or at least different—coherence than it formerly had. W. H. McLeod has certainly shown this to be the case in the Sikh *janam sākhīs*,[14] and Vallabhite texts such as the *Chaurāsī Vaiṣṇavan kī Vārtā* and the *Śrī Nāthjī ke Prākaṭya kī Vārtā* seem to evince the same pattern.[15] With Nābhādās and Priyādās, perhaps, one has a somewhat more catholic approach—we await a close analysis of the text of the

Bhaktamāl on this point—but they too had their sectarian loyalties.[16] And David Lorenzen would give considerable weight to the sectarian associations ascribed to Anantdās, though I myself am somewhat more skeptical about how accurately they reflect Anantdās's own historical position.[17]

Another means of approaching the *saguṇ/nirguṇ* question in a hagiographic vein would be to amass references to a sense of lineage in texts attributed to the poet-saints themselves, and there is a certain harvest to be reaped. The results are best on the *nirguṇ* side of the divide: Ravidās, for example, refers to Nāmdev, Kabīr, Trilochan, Sādhanā, and Sen.[18] *Saguṇ* poets, by contrast, tend to refer themselves to a different sort of lineage, a mythological variety rather than a human one. Sūr and Tulsī set themselves up as heirs to a tradition of divine grace that affected Gajendra, Ajāmil, Ahalyā, and the like. The strictly human connections—that Sūr came to Tulsīdās to ask his blessing on the *Sūrsāgar*, or that Tulsī carried on a sort of "Dear Abby" correspondence with Mīrā (he was Abby)—are hagiographical inventions.[19]

Yet here too the lines are more blurred that the current *nirguṇ/saguṇ* taxonomy would lead one to expect. Consider the case of Sūr—or rather, to be more precise, the corpus of poems attributed to Sūr that would have been known in the sixteenth century. Within this corpus Sūr does, on one occasion, cite another poet, and it is Nāmdev. He alludes to the story of Vishnu's appearing to cover Nāmdev's hut with thatch. Here is the reference (NPS 4):

1 That ocean of mercy: the deeds he has done simply cannot be described.
2 Even for touching him with falsified love the bird-woman won a mother's prize.
3 The Vedas and Upanishads have sung his praise, calling him the Formless One,
4 Yet he's taken form as Nanda's boy and allowed himself to be roped down.
5 In an instant he rescued the master of Braj from being caught in Varuṇ's snare,
6 Just as he hurried to the elephant king when he learned what pain he bore.
7 When he heard of Ugrasen's sad state—the suffering he endured—
8 He made him king by killing Kaṃs, and he himself bowed his head before him.

9 When Nāmdev appeared in the present world-age, he covered his hut with thatch,
10 But what of the appeal that Sūrdās makes? Who will make him listen to that?

This alignment between Nāmdev and Sūrdās is an intriguing one, for of all the great Maharashtrian poets, Nāmdev is perhaps the hardest to situate firmly on one side or the other of the *saguṇ/nirguṇ* line.[20] Furthermore, the way in which Nāmdev is introduced—namely, at the end of a list of figures we would call mythological—suggests that Sūr may not have seen the sorts of distinctions that buttress our conception of the *saguṇ/nirguṇ* split. He may not have recognized the distinctions we take for granted between myth and history, and between gods and humans, although his reference to the Kali age certainly goes some distance toward marking a separation between the divine and the human realms.

So far, then, we have looked at two resources for estimating the force of the *saguṇ/nirguṇ* distinction as felt in "its own" time: the words of the poet-saints themselves and the hagiographies that soon developed around them. On both scores, the *nirguṇ/saguṇ* distinction survives with only mixed success.

Resource C: Anthologies

Now it is time to introduce a third resource, one that to my knowledge has never been tapped in trying to deal with the question we have before us. This third resource is provided by early anthologies of the utterances of *sant*s and *bhakta*s.[21] It is no surprise that this body of material has been neglected as a scholarly tool: of all the early texts, these are in many ways the most difficult to approach. They are the scrapbooks—and, indeed, the scraps—of the field. They are often the hardest genre to locate in catalogues and indexes of manuscript libraries, and once one finds them, the work has only begun. Often one actually has to go through them to see what poets these anthologies contain. For a catalogue is apt to give such amorphous descriptions as *Dādū jī ke pad, Kabīr jī ke kṛt, ādi* ("Dādū's poems, Kabīr's Poems, and so forth")[22] or simply to list the contents of such collections as *sphuṭkar pad* ("miscellaneous pads"). Because the more "miscellaneous" sort in particular are not high-prestige documents—no name recognition, you know—their contents tend to be poorly catalogued, and for the same reason they are often in worse physical shape than the *Sūrsāgar*s and *Vinayapātrikā*s of this world. Frequently they are slimmer, smaller in physical size, and more haphazardly inscribed than the great named corpora. Finally, and for our purposes crucially, they are less apt to possess a dated colophon.

For all these reasons, many of the leading manuscript libraries of North India seem to have placed a low priority on collecting anthologies of *pad*s, the genre that most commonly spans the *nirguṇ/saguṇ* gap. Remarkably, I have been able to find only one dated manuscript entitled *sphuṭkar pad* in the massive library of the Nāgarīprachāriṇī Sabhā in Banaras, to which, however, I would add two other collections noted among the manuscripts described below.[23] The Jaipur branch of the Rajasthan Oriental Research Institute also has only one *sphuṭkar pad,* and it too is late (V.S. 1953).[24] The Vrindaban Research Institute, a library located squarely in the middle of *pad* country, has only two (dating to V.S. 1825 and 1893). Even the Anup Sanskrit Library in Bikaner, a wonderfully rich collection, lists only ten dated manuscripts out of a total of sixty Hindi documents described as *phuṭkar kavitā* (miscellaneous poetry). Of these ten, seven predate V.S. 1800, the period with which we are concerned.[25]

It is a shame that early anthologies of *pad*s have been so sparsely preserved; I find it hard to believe there really were so few. It is much to be hoped that others will emerge from private collections in the future. For the nonce, however, we must deal with the early dated anthologies we have, and ask what they reveal. In these collections, who was put alongside whom? Does the *saguṇ/nirguṇ* distinction emerge?

We can get a sense of this by classifying the anthologies in question into three groups relevant to the subject at hand. In the first group let us place manuscripts that seem clearly to espouse a *nirguṇ* perspective. (Rām bhakti often abuts rather closely on this *nirguṇ* point of view, so we may have to admit poems of that sort to this list.) Into a second group let us put manuscripts that fall patently on the other side of the divide: *saguṇ* manuscripts containing the outpourings of Krishna *bhakta*s. These two groups should reinforce the *nirguṇ/saguṇ* classification. But what if still other manuscripts are left over? Then we will need a third group, to comprise manuscripts where *nirguṇ* and *saguṇ* voices are set side by side—or at any rate, allowed to nestle between the same two covers. Needless to say, it is this third group that we will watch with particularly strong interest.

Before listing the manuscripts I have found that can be grouped by means of this threefold categorization, I must point out how partial my sample is in relation to the territory that really ought to be covered. The field is vast. All I can report on are *pad* anthology manuscripts that I myself kept notes on—and in some cases, photographs. Not surprisingly, it was my doctoral dissertation (and its seemingly everlasting *Nachlaß*) that initially drove me to it. In the later stages of the project, happily, Kenneth Bryant and I did some of the work together, with Bryant gaining access to what is undoubtedly the most important early anthology of them all, the Fatehpur manuscript of 1582 (V.S. 1639) housed in the royal collection at Jaipur. As for myself, I tried to keep an eye out for anthologies as I went from library to library, and sometimes house to house, in Uttar Pradesh, Madhya Pradesh, and Rajasthan, searching for early collections of the poetry of Sūrdās. For the Sūr work, I took 1700 C.E. as my approximate cut-off date—V.S. 1763, to be precise—so what I have to report here will also fall more or less within that span. Specifically, I shall limit myself to manuscripts written or copied before V.S. 1800 (that is, 1743 C.E.).

The first limitation on my sample is therefore time. Obviously, later dated manuscripts are also relevant, and undated ones provide a particularly important additional challenge. But they are beyond the scope of what I can consider here.

A second limitation is geographical. I was primarily following leads about Sūr manuscripts. These were rather extensive leads, to be sure, but they were specialized for Sūr nonetheless.[26] I was looking for early dated *pad* anthologies in the hopes that they would reveal poems of Sūr that had hitherto been overlooked. (Luckily, they sometimes did.) This search led me to certain sections of North India rather than others. I tried to extend my list of the libraries to be visited as much as I sensibly could, but I can hardly claim to have been everywhere, even everywhere in northwest and north-central India. Moreover, my records for collections outside of India are particularly weak. Let me give a list of the libraries and institutions from which my survey of dated *pad* anthologies is drawn:

Libraries Consulted

Agra Hindi Vidyapith
Allahabad Museum
Anup Sanskrit Library, Bikaner
Library of the Government Degree College, Datia
Hindi Sahitya Sammelan, Allahabad
Jiwaji University, Gwalior
K. M. Hindi Institute, Agra University
Maharaja Man Singh Pustak Prakash Research Centre, Jodhpur
Maharaja Sawai Man Singh II Museum, Jaipur
Mathuradhis Temple, Kota
Nagaripracharini Sabha, Banaras
Rajasthan Oriental Research Institute
    Bikaner
    Jaipur
    Jodhpur
    Kota
    Udaipur
Rajasthani Shodh Sansthan, Chaupasini, Jodhpur
Library of the Tilakayat Maharaj Sri, Srinathji Temple, Nathdvara
Sarasvati Bhandar, Kankarauli
Vrindaban Research Institute

With the preliminaries now stated, we have before us the task of depositing the manuscripts I found into the recepticles we have created. As I have hinted, readers may be disappointed to see how few there are. Considering the size of the sample, we can only guess what contours ultimately will emerge from a more careful and extensive study. But that, I think, we can do.

In the list that follows, I give the manuscripts by accession number, prefixed by serial numbers where necessary. The numbers refer to the Hindi collections of the institutions named, except in cases where the collections are not subdivided by language and manuscripts. There, obviously, the number refers to the whole collection. I list documents by date, the oldest first. It is important to note—and this is yet another important caveat—that specifically sectarian collections such as the *Pañchvāṇī* and *Sarvāṅgī* of the Dādū Panth and the Sikhs' *Ādi Granth* are omitted from consideration. Otherwise the list would be much longer—and its first category, certainly, much larger, though Rajjab's *Sarvāṅgī* strays a bit into Vaiṣṇava terrain. Readers should set what they learn from the list that follows against the background of these better-known, better-published collections.

Here, then, is a description of early Hindi devotional anthologies that I have surveyed. Gaps in my knowledge will be quickly apparent, and there is no real defense for them. I can only plead that at the point I surveyed many of these manuscripts, I had in mind quite a different purpose from the present one, and that I have often not been able to consult these manuscripts since.

Group 1: Nirguṇ (and Rām Bhakti) Manuscripts

(a) No. 3322, Maharaja Sawai Man Singh II Museum, Jaipur, V. S. 1717. Regrettably, my data are not complete, so I cannot say at what point the various sections of this manuscript were conjoined or whether the colophon applies conclusively to all of them, as is implied by the catalogue of the Jaipur royal *pothīkhānā*.[27] I also do not know the size of the manuscript or its full contents. I can say with confidence, however, that *pads* attributed to Kabīr, Gorakhnāth, Datta (presumably Dattātrey), Pīpā, Santā̃, and Haraṇvant are included.

(b) Serial no. 2379, accession no. 1602/933, Nāgarīprachāriṇī Sabhā, Banaras, V.S. 1742. It contains *vāṇīs* and *sabadīs* of Gorakhnāth, Bharatharī, Dattātrey, Mahādev, Chirpaṭ, Hālīpāv, and others, in 101 folios. This collection seems to be a product of the Nāth Sampradāy.

(c) Serial no. 74, accession no. 773/48, Nāgarīprachāriṇī Sabhā, Banaras. Because this manuscript is a composite, of which only one part—the last and apparently latest—is dated, one may refer to its date as *terminus ad quem* V.S. 1757. It contains *pads* of Raidās, Kabīr, and, as the catalogue says, "so forth" *(ādi)*.[28]

(d) No. 30587, Rajasthan Oriental Research Institute, Jodhpur, V.S. 1788. The manuscript contains *sākhīs* of Dādū and Kabīr.

I wish I could say I have actually examined all these manuscripts. I have not. With this set, I am working from catalogues only, so I do not know, for example, whether on inspection the Jodhpur manuscript (d) would prove to be a standard *Pañchvāṇī*. It is not so called in the catalogue, and that may say something. This Jodhpur manuscript certainly seems the easiest to associate with a definite *sampradāy*. It, like quite a number of others in the Jodhpur collection of the Rajasthan

Oriental Research Institute, is a product of the Dādū Panth. One of the Banaras manuscripts (b) seems similarly to have been compiled under the auspices of a particular community, in this case the Nāth Sampradāy. The remaining two (a, c), however, are not so easily assigned, and may not reflect the work of any sect as such.

Group 2: Saguṇ (and Krishna Bhakti) Manuscripts

This second group is somewhat larger than the first, but let us not forget that this may reflect the fact that I was searching especially for Sūr, and that fixed, well-known sectarian anthologies have been excluded from the first group. The manuscripts in the second group are as follows:

(a) No. 1057, K. M. Hindi Institute, Agra University, dated V.S. 1713. Although the hand is uneven, the various sections of this manuscript are consecutively numbered, suggesting that the manuscript was assembled at a time at least approximately contemporary with the part that does bear a date. This colophon comes after the *daśamaskandh* (i.e., *rāspañchādhyāyī*) of Nandadās, the third section in the manuscript, and includes the date 1713. Preceding that are an incomplete *Hit Chaurāsī* and some five hundred *pad*s of Sūrdās. Following it is a brief *ṣaṭu rāg svarūp varṇan,* one folio in length, and thirty-five folios of *pad saṅgrah* enticingly entitled *malla akhāḍo.* The poets represented are Nandadās, Sūrdās, Mānkavi, Govindsvāmī, Kiśordās, Caturbhujdās, Kṛṣṇadās, Mādhodās, Bakhatāvar, Jagannāth, Tursī *[sic],* Annadās, Hit Harivaṃś, Girathardās *[sic]*, Narasiṃhdās, Rāmdās, and Sundarkuṃvari. Although the words *śrī gorakh* have been inserted on what seems to have been a previously blank space just after the colophon, the whole collection is distinctively *saguṇ*. It is notable, however, that it crosses *sampradāyak* lines, beginning with Hit Harivaṃṣ and proceeding to many of the (Vallabhite) *aṣṭachhāp* and beyond. If the parallel to manuscripts of the Dādū Panth could be trusted, this would seem to mean that the scribe or his patron held Hit Harivaṃś in special veneration, but the length of the Sūrdās section and the fact that the place of composition is given as Meḍtā make one wonder how this could have been so.

(b) No. 30346, Rajasthan Oriental Research Institute, Jodhpur, entitled *phuṭapadāḥ* (that is, *sphuṭkar pad)* and listed in the catalogue as bearing the dates V.S. 1713–14. In a brief examination, however, I was unable to verify the dates or to discover the relevant colophon(s). The manuscript is in two sections, of 110 and 91 folios respectively, and is written in at least two different hands. Agardās (elsewhere, Agradās), Kiśordās, Mādhodās, and Mīrā are among the signatures I saw in a brief look at these *pads*, and I noticed an enticing reference to the *vallabh kul.* The *pads* seem universally to be in the *saguṇ* mode.

(c) No. 2469, Rajasthan Oriental Research Institute, Udaipur, entitled *virah līlā,* dated V.S. 1731. This is a brief collection, comprising merely eleven folios.

(d) No enumeration, private collection of Dr. Nareś Chandra Bansal, Kasganj, *pad saṅgrah*, sections of which bear the dates V.S. 1740 and V.S. 1750. The main portions of the manuscript, which are numbered consecutively, are in the same hand and comprise chiefly the oldest dated *kīrgan praṇālī* (hymn book) of the Vallabh Sampradāy that I have seen. The V.S. 1750 colophon comes at the end of this section, following pads arranged according to the seasonal *(varṣotsav)* and daily *(nitya sevā)* calendars, with a few additions at the end. Then follows a more casual Vallabhite *pad saṅgrah* in the same hand. A briefer *pad saṅgrah* in a different hand precedes the main section, and there are various short sections in Gujarati interspersed. Like *kīrtan praṇālīs* in current use, the *pads* that appear are largely of the *aṣṭachhāp,* augmented by later sectarian poets, but one also finds the occasional verse from Narasī Mehtā in this manuscript of Gujarati provenance. This is definitely a *saguṇ*, Krishna bhakti collection. The few poems appropriate to Rām Navamī are also of a *saguṇ* nature.

(e) No. 2437, Maharaja Sawai Man Singh II Museum, Jaipur, a large manuscript written in different parts, with sections on the poetry of Priyādās and Nāgarīdās dated V.S. 1783 and that representing Sūr dated V.S. 1784.

(f) Serial no. 3258, accession no. 3477, Rajasthan Oriental Research Institute, Kota, entitled *kīrtan janmāṣṭamī rādhāṣṭamī kīrtan chaupaḍī,* with individual poems bearing dates ranging, in a puzzling fashion, from V.S. 1780 to V.S. 1810. Many are of Nagadhardās, but a substantial number of other poets are represented also, in a total of forty folios.[29]

(g) The next oldest sectarian collections of *pads* that I have seen bear dates later than V.S. 1800 and therefore fall "off the map" from the point of view of this presentation. Yet I might mention that the Vrindaban Research Institute has a Rādhā-vallabhī *varṣotsav ke pad* dated V.S. 1893 (serial no. 752, accession no. 4400). The library of the Tilakāyat Mahārāj Śrī at Nathdvara contains only three dated collections of *pads* used in daily worship (called in the catalogue *nitya kīrtan* and *nitya ke pad),* and these are more recent than the group under consideration here, since they bear the dates V.S. 1834, 1886, and 1890. Libraries of other Vallabhite *gaddīs*, such as those at Jatipura and Kamban, which I have not yet been able to survey, may of course provide earlier manuscripts, but if my somewhat schematic notes on the well-known collection at Kankarauli are an accurate forecast, one should not hold out too great a hope.

On the basis of the evidence at hand it is indeed surprising that a larger number of early, dated *kīrtan praṇālīs* has not appeared. One obvious explanation is that such volumes would have been in sufficiently frequent use that the oldest among them long ago deteriorated, to the point of needing to be replaced by more recent copies. One sees this preference for recently "copied" versions even in the present day, at least in the Vallabh Sampradāy, for printed editions have quickly replaced manuscripts in temple use. Families known to have been singers *(kīrtaniyā)* in the *sampradāy* for many generations—at least the ones I have visited—do sometimes work from manuscripts, but these too look comparatively recent, certainly less than two centuries old.[30]

Group 3: Manuscripts that combine Saguṇ and Nirguṇ poems

We now come to the group of manuscripts that is for our purposes the most interesting, namely those that span the gap between *saguṇ* and *nirguṇ* bhakti (if indeed the latter category makes sense, a question that Charlotte Vaudeville has forcefully raised).[31] The first entry in this group has a distinctly *saguṇ* bias—so much so that it has most often been referred to as a *Sūrsāgar*—but closer examination reveals that it belongs in this group of what would seem from a later point of view to be "hybrid" manuscripts. It is:

(a) The manuscript written at Fatehpur, near Jaipur, and published in facsimile as *Pad Sūrdāsjī kā/The Padas of Surdas* by Gopāl Nārāyaṇ Bahurā, with an introductory essay by Kenneth E. Bryant. It is housed in the royal collection of the Maharaja of Jaipur.[32] The manuscript is complex in its organization. It is divided into two broad sections. The first section, comprising 284 poems, is a true anthology, showing a strong preponderance of poems by Sūr near the beginning (it opens with an unbroken sequence of 35) and ending with a concentration of poems by Kānhā̃dās. The second section, which bears the colophon, is written in a different hand and contains the remaining 126 poems. This section is organized by *rāg*, and is devoted entirely to Sūrdās. Some *pad*s that appear in the first section are repeated in this second collection-within-a-collection.

As we have seen, it is in the first part of the manuscript, the anthology, that one encounters poets other than Sūr. Among these are such *saguṇ* poets as Paramanāndadās and Nāmdev (though there is some doubt about how he should be classified), but also, on the other hand, *nirguṇ* figures such as Kabīr, Sundardās, Ravidās, Kīlhadās, and the *vinaya* poet Kānhā̃dās. After Sūr, Kānhā̃dās is the poet who appears most frequently.

(b) No. 209, Anup Sanskrit Library, Bikaner, dated V.S. 1668. The manuscript consists of assorted *dohā*s and *savaiyā*s—228 of the former, 132 of the latter. I have photographed the manuscript, but the prints, many of which are inadequate in their present version, remain to be closely examined. A quick survey, however, shows a considerable range of subjects and poets—all the way from cautionary dohās of the *nirguṇ* type to *pad*s dedicated to Krishna.[33]

(c) An unnumbered manuscript from the collection of Harihar Nivās Dvivedī, now in the collection of Jiwaji University, Gwalior, where it is described as *bhajan ādi*. The portion bearing the colophon, dating it to V.S. 1727, contains thirty-nine folios. The collection begins with *dohā*s and proceeds to *pad*s. Both *nirguṇ* and *saguṇ* poems appear, but aside from Kabīr no well-known poets are represented.

(d) No. 6992, Rajasthan Oriental Research Institute, Jodhpur, entitled *phuṭ pad saṅgrah sūr ādi* and containing at various places the dates V.S. 1736, 1742, and 1744. The poets represented are primarily Vaiṣṇava—Nandadās, Tulsīdās, Agardās, and Paramānand, and there is a *sūr pachīsī*—but Kabīr is also included.[34]

(e) No. 992, K. M. Hindi Institute, Agra University, dated V.S. 1762, is a large (340 folios) Dādūpanthī collection that begins with substantial collections of Dādū (with an internal colophon of V.S. 1660), Kabīr, Nāmdev, Raidās, Har[i]dās, and Garībdās. It then proceeds to a *pad saṅgrah* before returning to Bakhnā̃, whom one would expect in a Dādūpanthī collection of this sort, and there is a final untitled *pad saṅgrah* section in which the colophon appears. In the *pad saṅgrahs*, *saguṇ* poets are represented. Six poems of Sūr, for instance, appear on folios 260–61.

(f) No. 2062, Rajasthan Oriental Research Institute, Udaipur. This *pad saṅgrah* is undated, but it is bound together with a *prahelikā saṅgrah* (collection of riddles) bearing a colophon dating it to V.S. 1754. It seems a reasonable likelihood that both sections belong to the same period. In the *pad saṅgrah,* Krishna poets such as Sūr are interspersed with others such as Raidās, Tulsīdās, and less familiar figures such as Ahmad and Gaṅgā.

(g) No. 2511 (1), Rajasthan Oriental Research Institute, Udaipur, entitled *phuṭkar kavitā* and in sections bearing various dates extending from V.S. 1777 to V.S. 1791. The manuscript consists of seventy folios, numbered from 21 to 90, representing such poets as Kabīr, Keśav, Navaraṅg, and Tursī (?Nirañjanī).

Conclusion

I set out by saying I wanted to find some means to assess how high the wall between the so-called *nirguṇ* poets and their *saguṇ* cousins was felt to be in their own time. That is, I wanted to find ways to determine how firm the *saguṇ/nirguṇ* divide might have seemed in the sixteenth and seventeenth centuries, up as far as V.S. 1800. I suggested there were various materials we could use to address the problem: internal references in the poetry of these *sant*s and *bhakta*s; perspectives expressed in their hagiographies; and finally divisions—explicit or implicit—observed in early anthologies of their verse. The beginnings of an estimate can now be made.

It seems to me that each of these yardsticks teaches us to exercise caution when we speak of the great contrast between *nirguṇī*s and *saguṇī*s in the early or "classical" period of North Indian bhakti, the *bhakti kāl.* The most influential sectarian anthologizers certainly saw the force of this distinction, but even there it sometimes took a while to sand down the rough edges, as in the case of the *Ādi Granth.* Mīrā and Sūr, whom some put in, were cast out by others.[35] In addition one has to reckon with the fact that even among *nirguṇ* anthologies there was a range of personality. As Karine Schomer and Linda Hess have so nicely shown, there is a difference between the flinty Kabīr of the *Bījak;* the hearty, domestic Kabīr of the *Ādi Granth;* and the softer, more mystical Kabīr of the *Pañchvāṇī*.[36] And then there is the fact that as the Kabīr Panth itself branched out, Kabīr branched with it.[37]

Even so, if one works from the great sectarian anthologies the *nirguṇ/saguṇ* distinction largely works. From this vantage point the theological conclusions assumed by the editors of the *Hindī Sāhitya kā Bṛhat Itihās* and similar works—and the organizational strategies they pursued—make tolerably good sense. Yet there are other kinds of evidence, and other anthologies in particular, that need to be taken into consideration. The anthologies I have described here are only a part of the literature that deserves to be surveyed, but they do seem clearly to suggest that the *nirguṇ/saguṇ* distinction only reveals part of the truth about how poets of the *bhakti kāl* were viewed in documents that we can be sure were written within a century or so of the poets' own time.

It is true that, among the anthologies I have presented, there are some that bear a clear *nirguṇ* stamp—and some that bear a *saguṇ* stamp too. But there are also a considerable number of manuscripts that cannot be forced to either side of the *nirguṇ/saguṇ* divide. If my sample is any indication, this last group—the hybrids—is a substantial one, and as I have remarked, I suspect it may have been even more substantial in the sixteenth and seventeenth centuries than we might guess on the basis of the documents that have survived to our own time. Broadly speaking, then, we seem to be dealing with a period and a tradition that did see differences of theological slant, social perspective, and literary mood between *nirguṇ* and *saguṇ* poets. As we know, sectarian boundaries were early erected to enshrine those differences, though earlier in some instances (the Sikh Panth, for example) than in others. Yet at the same time there seem to have been many settings in which the sectarian divisions that later came to loom so large were not—or not yet—regarded as determinative. In such settings the *nirguṇ/saguṇ* division was often honored, if it was honored at all, in the breach.

Notes

1. Paraśurām Caturvedī, ed., *Hindī Sāhitya kā Bṛhat Itihās*, vol. 4 (Varanasi: Nāgarīprachāriṇī Sabhā, V.S. 2025 [1968 C.E.]; Dīnadayāl Gupta, Devendranāth Śarmā, and Vijayendra Snātak, eds., *Hindī Sāhitya kā Bṛhat Itihās*, vol. 5 (Varanasi: Nāgarīprachāriṇī Sabhā, V.S. 2031 [1974 C.E.].

2. Reproduced from J. S. Hawley and Mark Juergensmeyer, *Songs of the Saints of India* (New York: Oxford University Press, 1988), p. 5.

3. E.g., Charlotte Vaudeville, *Au Cabaret de l'Amour: Paroles de Kabir* (Paris: Gallimard, 1959), pp. 7–9; Vaudeville, *Kabir*, vol. 1 (Oxford: Clarendon, 1974), pp. 97–110; W. H. McLeod, *Guru Nanak and the Sikh Religion* (Oxford: Clarendon, 1968), pp. 151–58.

4. Karine Schomer and W. H. McLeod, eds., *The Sants: Studies in a Devotional Tradition of India* (Berkeley, Calif.: Berkeley Religious Studies Series; Delhi: Motilal Banarsidass, 1987). Notably, however, Kenneth E. Bryant, in another collection, has outlined a scheme that would justify the distinction between *saguṇ* and *nirguṇ* poets on rhetorical—that is, strictly literary—rather than theological lines. See Bryant, "Sant and Vaisnava Poetry: Some Observations on Method," in Mark Juergensmeyer and N. Gerald Barrier, eds., *Sikh Studies: Comparative Perspectives on a Changing Tradition* (Berkeley, Calif.: Berkeley Religious Studies Series, 1979), pp. 65–74.

5. Schomer, *The Sants*, p. 3.

6. In regard to Tulsī Sāhib's role here, see Mark Juergensmeyer, "The Radhasoami Revival of the Sant Tradition," in Schomer and McLeod, eds., *The Sants*, p. 337.

7. In particular, Mīrābāī is included among the "Sants" listed as having been previously published by the Belvedere Press in its *Santbānī Pustak-mālā* series. See [no editor named] *Santbānī saṅgrah* (Allahabad: Belvedere Pless, 1915). Mīrā is also included among the *sant*s in the collection represented by the *Santbānī saṅgrah* volume itself. Mīrā's putative initiation at the hands of Ravidās might have provided a justification for her inclusion within the *sant paramparā*. It is noteworthy that *Santbānī saṅgrah* also contains a section where Vaiṣṇava poets such as Sūrdās, Narasī Mehtā, and Tulsīdās are anthologized, but in that case the designation *dūsre mahātmā* ("other great souls")—as against those *mahātmā*s who had actually been included in the *Santbānī Pustak-mālā* series—is introduced to explain the apparent confusion or expansion of categories (*Santbānī saṅgrah*, p. 2).

8. Pitambar D. Barthwal, *The Nirguna School of Hindi Poetry: An Exposition of Medieval Indian Santa Mysticism* (Banaras: Indian Book Shop, 1936).

9. Cf. Wilfred Cantwell Smith, "The Crystallization of Religious Communities in Mughul India," in Mojtaba Minori and Ijar Afshar, eds., *Yadname-ye Irani-ye Minorsky* (Tehran: Tehran University, 1969), pp. 1–24.

10. In particular, Rupert Snell, *The Eighty-four Hymns of Hita Harivamsa, An Edition of the Caurasi-pada* (Delhi: Motilal Banarsidass, 1990); W. M. Callewaert and Mukund Lath, *The Hindi Songs of Namdev* (Leuven: Departement Orientalistiek, 1989); Mātāprasād Gupta, *Sūr Sāgar* (Agra: K. M. Hindī tathā Bhāsavijiñān Vidyāpīṭh, Agra University, 1979); Gopāl Nārāyaṇ Bahurā and Kenneth E. Bryant, *Pad Sūrdās jī kā/The Padas of Surdas* (Jaipur:

Maharaja Sawai Man Singh II Museum, 1984); K. E. Bryant and J. S. Hawley, *The Poems of Surdas* (Cambridge: Harvard University Press, forthcoming); J. S. Hawley, *Sur Das: Poet, Singer, Saint* (Seattle: University of Washington Press; Delhi: Oxford University Press, 1984); Gurinder Singh Mann, "The Making of Sikh Scripture," Ph.D. diss., Columbia University, 1992; Pāras Nāth Tivārī, *Kabīr Granthāvalī* (Allahabad: Prayāg Viśvavidyālay, 1961); Shukdeo Singh, *Kabīr Bījak* (Allahabad: Nilābh Prakāśan, 1972).

11. Hawley, *Sur Das*, pp. 121–60.

12. Here and below "NPS" (Nāgarīprachāriṇī Sabhā) numbers are used to locate a poem of Sūr's in relation to the most widely known edition, that of the Nāgarīprachāriṇī Sabhā: *Sūrsāgar*, edited by Jagannāthdās "Ratnākar" et al. (Banaras: 1934, 1972, 1976). The actual text translated, however, which appears just below, is the one established by Kenneth Bryant for his forthcoming *The Poems of Surdas*. The earliest dated manuscript in which this poem appears (B2) was written by a scribe in the entourage of the maharaja of Bikaner in 1624 (V.S. 1681); he claims to be copying from an earlier manuscript.

13. See Hawley, *Sur Das*, pp. 18–22.

14. McLeod, *Early Sikh Tradition* (Oxford: Clarendon, 1980).

15. Charlotte Vaudeville, "The Govardhan Myth in Northern India," *Indo-Iranian Journal* 22 (1980): 1–45; J. S. Hawley, *Sur Das*, pp. 14–22, and "The Sectarian Logic of the *Sur Das ki Varta*," in Monika Thiel-Horstmann, ed., *Bhakti in Current Research, 1979–1982* (Berlin: Dietrich Reimer Verlag, 1983), pp. 157–69.

16. R. D. Gupta, "Priya Das, Author of the *Bhaktirasabodhini*," *Bulletin of the School of Oriental and African Studies* 32, no. 1 (1969): 61–69; Philip Lutgendorf, "Krsna Caitanya and His Companions as Presented in the *Bhaktamala* of Nabha Ji and the *Bhaktirasabodhini* of Priya Dasa," M.A. diss., University of Chicago, 1981, pp. 25–29.

17. David Lorenzen, in collaboration with Jagdish Kumar and Uma Thukral, *Kabir Legends and Ananta-das's Kabir Parachai* (Albany: SUNY Press, 1991), pp. 9–18. The principal problem, as I see it, has to do with the historical status of Rāmānand, who figures importantly in the *guruparamparā* of Anantdās, as apparently claimed by himself in his *Pīpā parachaī*, though the evidence is not yet entirely clear (Lorenzen, *Kabir Legends*, p. 10n). Rāmānand's symbolic import as a conduit between later North Indian bhakti and earlier South Indian forms—and his legitimating force, therefore—is sufficiently great to make me feel uneasy about too great a trust in the historicity of legends and lineages associated with him. His usefulness as entrepôt between South and North, and between *sant* and Vaiṣṇava, is simply too great, and the use to which legends associated with him are put by a hagiographer such as Priyādās makes me doubly cautious.

18. See Hawley and Juergensmeyer, *Songs of the Saints,* p. 24. The poem translated there is number 33 in Padam Gurcharan Siṃh, *Sant Ravidās: Vicārak aur Kavi* (Jalandur: Nav-Cintan Prakāśan, 1977).

19. Hawley and Juergensmeyer, *Songs of the Saints,* p. 158. The hagiographical text involved is the *Mūl Gosāī̃ Charit (dohās* 29–32 and the accompanying *chaupāīs)* attributed to Benī Mādhavdās, as found in Kiśorīlāl Gupta, *Gosāī̃-Charit* (Varanasi: Vāṇī-Vitān Prakāśan, 1964), p. 285. In regard to the status of the text, see Philip Lutgendorf, "The Quest for the Legendary Tulsīdās," paper presented to the American Academy of Religion, Los Angeles, November 1985.

20. I confess that on the basis of the awkward meter used in this poem and its lack of any great poetic adornment, I wonder whether the "real" Sūrdās—I am convinced there was one—composed this poem. Its manuscript pedigree is not the absolute best (A1, B2, B3, B4, G1, J4, U, U2, V1), but it is sufficiently strong to suggest very powerfully that this poem was known in the sixteenth century. The use of the word *pragaṭ* in verse 9 raises the question as to whether an avatar theory of saints, such as the one expressed in Mahipati's *Bhaktavijaya*, was assumed by the poet. The text, as edited by Kenneth E. Bryant, is as follows:

करनी करुणासिंधु की कहत न बनि आवै
कपट हेत परसे बकी जननी गति पावै
बेद उपनिषद जसु करै निर्गुनहि बतावै
सोइ सगुन ह्वै नंद कै दांवरी बंधावै
बरून पास ते ब्रजपती छिन मैं छुटकावै
दुषित गजेंद्रहि जानि कै आपुन उठि धावै
उग्रसेन की दीनता सुनि सुनि दुष पावै
कंस मारि राजा कियौ आपुन सिर नावै
कलि मै नामा प्रगटियौ ता की छानि छवावै
सूरदास की बीनती कोइ जाइ सुनावै

21. If, for a moment, we accept that distinction. To the contrary, see Hawley, *Sur Das*, pp. 141–48.

22. Catalogue of the Rajasthan Oriental Research Institute, Jodhpur, in reference to Hindi manuscript 30587 (V.S. 1788).

23. The *sphuṭkar pad* manuscript is accession no. 773/48, dated in the NPS register to V.S. 1757, as a *terminus ad quem*. The additional two are listed in Group 1, below.

24. From this point onward, in referring to manuscript anthologies, I will frequently cite only the *vikram saṃvat* (V.S.) dating that one finds in the manuscripts themselves. The comparable dating according to the Julian calendar can usually be determined by subtracting 57 from the V.S. number.

25. Rawatmal Saraswat and Dinanath Khatri, *Catalogue of the Rajasthani Manuscripts in the Anup Sanskrit Library* (Bikaner: Maharaja of Bikaner, 1947), pp. 50–71. The category *phuṭkar pad* covers poems described as being *dohās*, *sorațhās*, *savaiyās*, and *kavitts*. The last-mentioned term is apparently used as a designation large enough to include *pads* within its span.

26. I refer to the various *Khoj Reports* of the Nāgarīprachāriṇī Sabhā and to the earlier manuscript survey coordinated by Mātāprasād Gupta.

27. This manuscript is not listed among the *pad saṅgrah (sphuṭ)* listed as such in Gopal Narayan Bahura, *Literary Heritage of the Rulers of Amber and Jaipur* (Jaipur: Maharaja Sawai Man Singh II Museum, 1976), p. 168.

28. Regrettably, my notes contain no information as to the number of folios.

29. The manuscript has been photographed, and awaits further examination.

30. E.g., Śyāmsundar Kīrtankār of Kota or Rādheśyām Kīrtankār of the "second *gaddī*" in Nathdvara.

31. Vaudeville, "*Sant Mat:* Santism as the Universal Path to Sanctity," in Schomer and McLeod, eds., *The Sants*, pp. 27–29.

32. Jaipur: Maharaja Sawai Man Singh II Museum, 1982 (actually published 1984). I am grateful to Gurinder Singh Mann for enlightening discussions about the shape of the Fatehpur manuscript.

33. At this point I omit a manuscript that would seem from its catalogue description to belong at this point in the list. It is accession no. 39687 in the Jodhpur branch of the Rajasthan Oriental Research Institute, entitled *Guṭkā sant vāṇī saṅgrah*. The catalogue states that its date of composition is V.S. 1710, but the colophon page—now, at least—is missing, hence no date can reliably be assigned. It seems notable that a *"nirguṇ"* poem of Sūr's, the "Sūr pachīsī," is included, given the general *sant* designation.

34. This manuscript was photographed by Kenneth Bryant on 12 December 1980.

35. A recent statement in regard to this issue can be found in Pashaura Singh, "The Text and Meaning of the *Adi Granth*," Ph.D. diss., University of Toronto, 1991, pp. 186–90. That, in turn, is superseded by Gurinder Singh Mann, "The Making of Sikh Scripture," pp. 171–74, 181–86.

36. Karine Schomer, "Kabir in the *Guru Granth Sahib:* An Exploratory Essay," in Juergensmeyer and Barrier, eds., *Sikh Studies*, pp. 75–86; Linda Hess [and Shukdev Singh], *The Bijak of Kabir* (San Francisco: North Point Press, 1983), pp. 6–7.

37. David N. Lorenzen, "The Kabir Panth: Heretics to Hindus," in D. N. Lorenzen, ed., *Religious Change and Cultural Domination* (Mexico City: El Colegio de México, 1981), pp. 151–71.

The Lives of *Nirguṇī* Saints

David N. Lorenzen

Whatever theological and ideological differences may characterize the *nirguṇī* and *saguṇī* traditions of bhakti religion, both traditions incorporate an emphasis on hagiography, the legendary lives of important saints, that is not found in Vedic and *śāstrik* Hinduism. In the introduction to this book, I suggested that this absence of hagiography in Vedic and *śāstrik* Hinduism has to do with the rejection of historical precedent and individual illumination as sources of religious truth in schools of Vedic exegesis, especially Mīmāṃsā. All religious truth is embodied in the Vedas, texts that are eternal and independent of all human agency. The only proper role for religious specialists, an occupation limited by law to male Brahmins, is that of transmitting and explaining the timeless truth of these texts.

In bhakti religion, however, both historical precedent and the religious authority of specific persons do become matters of primary concern. *Saguṇī* bhakti does continue to express faith in the authority of the Vedas and the Brahmins, but the religious emphasis shifts first to the myths about the gods Vishnu and Śiva, particularly to those about Vishnu's avatars Krishna and Rāma, and later to the life stories of the saintly founders and principal poets of various sectarian movements. In North India, these *saguṇī* saints include Mīrābāī, Chaitanya, Sūr Dās, Vallabhāchārya, Narasī Mehatā, Tulasīdās, and Tukārām.[1] In Nāth tradition—which is neither *saguṇī* nor *nirguṇī,* but closer to the latter—the stories of Gorakhanāth and Gopīchanda assume a similar importance.[2]

A key role in the early development of hagiographical literature about both *nirguṇī* and *saguṇī* saints was played by the Rāmānandī Sampradāy. In about 1600, the Rāmānandī author Nābhādās wrote his well-known *Bhaktamāl* (1969), a text of individual verses about the lives of hundreds of *saguṇī* and *nirguṇī* saints. Its verses about the more important saints were later expanded into full-fledged hagiographies by the commentator Priyādās in 1712. Also in about 1600, the

Rāmānandī author Anantadās wrote a series of hagiographic narrative poems called *parachaī*s about several important *nirguṇī* saints.

In *nirguṇī* tradition per se, the religious authority of the Vedas and their Brahmin exponents are actively contested, while the authority of the words and lives of the key saints of the tradition are correspondingly highlighted. The lives of seven of these saints—Nāmadev, Kabīr, Raidās, Pīpā, Gurū Nānak, Dādū Dayāl, and Haridās Nirañjanī—assumed a special importance and will be used as the basic sources for this essay. I had originally intended to include the lives of other *nirguṇī* saints such as Dhanā, Sen, Sadanā, and Trilochan, but their "lives" consist of only one or two parables or episodes and belong more to the category of Christian *exempla* or Sufi *tazkira*s than that of full hagiographies.

Most modern academic studies of the lives of Hindu saints have not attempted to make systematic comparisons between the lives of different saints. The life of each saint has been treated as a more or less independent topic. Most scholarly effort has been instead directed at extracting from each set of legends a minimal historical biography. From this point of view, the more mythical elements of these legends—the material the legends of various saints are likely to have in common—are mostly viewed as an obstacle to the discovery of the historical "truth." For example, C. Vaudeville (1974, 46), after extracting what she feels are the genuine historical elements of the Kabīr legends, relegates the rest of his legendary life to "well-known patterns of Indian hagiography." In my own work on these Kabīr legends (1991), on the other hand, I have tried to show that the legends about Kabīr's life contain ideological "messages" that have their own historical importance, independent of whether or not the stories tell us what actually happened. Neither approach, however, addresses the problems of determining to what extent the lives of Kabīr and other *nirguṇī* saints do in fact follow Vaudeville's "well-known patterns" and, assuming they do, of identifying the specific features of these patterns.

For the most part, only those early saints whose disciples organized an important religious movement seem to have acquired a full legendary biography. Nonetheless, two of the saints used in this study are exceptions to this rule. Nāmadev is claimed as a famous forerunner both by the tradition of the Vārakarīs, which combines *saguṇī* and *nirguṇī* elements, and by the *nirguṇī* tradition of Kabīr, Raidās and Dādū. In spite of his importance, however, his followers never organized a Nāmadev

Panth. Similarly, Pīpā's followers never established a significant Pīpā Panth. In addition, Pīpā's "life" is somewhat truncated. Although it includes many episodes, it does not contain stories of his birth, death, or childhood.

The principal sources used for this essay include Anantadās's (1989; 1982; Lorenzen 1991) *parachaīs* of Nāmadev, Kabīr, and Raidās, written about the end of the sixteenth century; Priyādās's commentary of 1712 C.E. on Nābhādās's (1969) *Bhaktamāl*, with a modern Hindi paraphrase by Sītārām Śaraṇ Bhagavān Prasād Rūpakalā; Chaturadās's commentary of about 1800 C.E. on Rāghavadās's (1969) *Bhaktamāl*, with a modern Hindi paraphrase by Svāmī Nārāyaṇadās; Abbott's and Godbole's English translation of Mahipati's (1982) Marathi *Bhakta-vijaya* (1762 C.E.); Rāmasvarūp Sonī's (1984) recent life of Haridās Nirañjanī; Winand Callewaert's edition and English translation of Jan Gopāl's (1988) early seventeenth-century life of Dādū Dayāl; and various works on the life of Gurū Nānak by W. H. McLeod: his translation (1980a) of the B40 *Janam Sakhi*, his *Guru Nanak and the Sikh Religion* (1968), and his *Early Sikh Tradition* (1980b). Since the lives of Pīpā and Haridās do not seem to be available in English, German or French, I have added two appendices to this essay that give summaries of them.

Since the principal aim of this essay is to discuss the general pattern of these saints' lives, and not to analyze specific episodes in the lives of specific saints, I have mostly ignored the many differences among the various retellings of each saint's life. Later retellings often introduce many elements not found in the earlier versions. Often they include additional "factual" details, specific names of people and locations, didactic passages, and miracles, that lend a false impression of historicity to the stories. W. H. McLeod (1980b, 124–27) has closely analyzed these typical changes in the context of the hagiography of Gurū Nānak. From a comparative perspective, it should also be noted that the more recent retellings generally make the life of each saint more closely resemble that of other saints, the addition of specific details notwithstanding.

Rather unexpected is the fact that the main episodes in the life of each saint are pretty much the same, with only minor though interesting differences, whether that life is told by a *nirguṇī* or a *saguṇī* storyteller. This undoubtedly reflects the fact that only *saguṇī* storytellers deeply sympathetic to *nirguṇī* tradition such as Anantadās and

Priyādās chose to tell the lives of *nirguṇī* saints. In the case of the *nirguṇī* saints, no hostile "unauthorized" biographies such as the Jain version of the life of the Vīraśaiva saint Basava have survived.

Another notable aspect of the hagiographies is that—in addition to the similarity of their general pattern and thematic structure—they also share many of the same folkloric motifs. Sometimes even whole episodes, virtually identical, are told of two or more different saints. The motif of the disappearance of the saint's corpse and its replacement by flowers, for instance, is told of Kabīr, Dādū and Nānak (and others). The motif of the saint causing a dry stick to sprout green leaves is told of Kabīr, Dādū and Pīpā (Rāghavadās 1969, 264–65, 674, 202, 214), not to mention Mahatma Gandhi (Amin 1988, 328–30). Many other such examples could be cited.

Examples of whole episodes that are told of two or more saints are less numerous but not uncommon. The story of Samman and Seu is also told of Kabīr and Kamal (Lorenzen 1991, 52–54). The story of Pīpā, his wife Sītā, and the libidinous merchant (Rāghavadās 1969, 205–7) is also told of Kabīr and his wife (Lorenzen 1991, 49–50). The story of the highwayman Haridās Nirañjanī and his guru Gorakh (Rāmasvarūp Sonī 1984, 1–3) is retold as that of the highwayman Bholā and Gurū Nānak (McLeod 1980a, 42–45; 1980b, 122–24). A story quite similar to that of Kabīr and the *paṇḍā* of Jagannāth (Lorenzen 1991, 29–32) is told about Pīpā and a festival in Dvaraka (Rāghavadās 1969, 215). The story of Kabīr helping Rāmānanda put a garland round the neck of an idol (Lorenzen 1991, 25) is also told of Pīpā and his nephew-disciple Śrīraṅga (Rāghavadās 1969, 213–14).

It is tempting to view the changes and additions found in later versions of the stories as arising from some unmanifest or latent model text of *nirguṇī* hagiography (perhaps even of pan-Indian or universal hagiography), a hidden transcript or deep structure that steers empirical examples of life stories in the direction of a single uniform story. For me, however, such "superorganic" cultural constructs involve supra-empirical assumptions about the existence of unconscious or divine archetypes or Platonic ideal forms that are unacceptable. I prefer to regard such narrative convergence as stemming from a combination of factors including mutual historical influences among the stories, the gradual forgetting and dropping out of historical specifics (as opposed to invented details), and the shared psychological and ideological needs of the tellers and listeners of the stories.

The basic pattern of the life stories of these *nirguṇī* saints is quite straightforward and uniform, although all of the parts of the pattern are not included in the life stories of all of the saints. In very general terms, the pattern resembles a somewhat simplified version of the archetypical life story of legendary heroes as analyzed by O. Rank, Lord Raglan, A. Dundes, and others.[3] In somewhat more specific terms, the pattern closely resembles the life stories of saints in general and Hindu saints in particular. There are also, however, narrative elements that seem to be quite specific to *nirguṇī* saints. The typical life pattern of *nirguṇī* saints is outlined below. The reader who wishes to see how each part of the pattern is reflected in the life of each of the seven saints (Dādū, Haridās, Kabīr, Nāmadev, Nānak, Pīpā, and Raidās) should refer to table 1. The extent to which any one of these stories corresponds to historical reality is at best difficult to determine. For present purposes, their historicity, or lack of it, is basically irrelevant.

The major elements of the typical pattern are the following:

1. The saint has an unusual birth. Often the evident aim of the birth story is to mitigate or deny the saint's low-caste and/or Muslim origin and to claim him to be somehow directly related to God (as a part or full avatar of Vishnu or as a manifestation of the more abstract *nirguṇ* Brahman, Rām or Satyapuruṣ). The saint is sometimes found by his foster parents floating in a pond or river (e.g., Nāmadev, Kabīr, Dādū). One or more stories about the high-caste status of the saint in his previous life or lives may also be recounted in connection with the birth story.

2. The saint displays his religious vocation, supernatural power, or outright divinity at a young age. This is more true of Śūdra and Untouchable saints than of Kṣatriya saints, who generally adopt a religious vocation only after meeting their first guru.

3. He has a life-changing encounter with his first guru and/or a celestial voice or vision. At this time he may or may not receive some sort of initiation from the guru, and he may be either a child or a mature adult when the encounter takes place.

4. He may be either a celibate ascetic or a married person. Early versions of the legends may assume that the saint is married, while later versions may claim that he is a lifelong celibate ascetic. He may acquire children either by natural or supernatural means. He may also eventually abandon his riches, his profession or occupation, and his family life in favor of the life of a wandering ascetic.

Table 1. Life Patterns of *Nirguṇī* Saints

Name	Caste and occupation	Previous lives	Unusual birth	Early religious vocation	Encounter with guru/sky-voice/ divine vision	Marriage and children
Dādū Dayāl	Dhuniyā (cotton carder)	—	Yes: three versions	Yes: age 11	Yes: age 11 (guru) age 18 (God)	Perhaps: some say 2 sons & 2 daughters
Haridās Nirañjanī	Sāṅkhalā Kṣatriya (Rājpūt thief)	—	—	No: thief until age 44	Yes: age 44 meets guru Gorakh	?Yes: abandons family
Kabīr	Julāhā (weaver)	Yes: various births & legends	Yes: various versions	Yes: at age 20 or as a child	Yes: sky-voice and guru Rāmānanda	Yes: adopts (?) Kamāl & Kamālī
Nāmadev	Chhīpī (tailor)	Yes: incarnation of Uddhav	Yes: two versions	Yes: age 5	Yes: at age 5 gets God to drink milk	Yes: wife is named Rājabāī
Nānak	Bedī Khatrī (bureaucrat)	—	Yes: heaven & earth celebrate	Yes: age 5	Yes: age 37(?) goes to heaven from river	Yes: 2 sons
Pīpā	Rājpūt (minor king)	—	—	Yes: about age 18	Yes: at age 18 Devī tells him to go to Rāmānanda	Yes: wife Sītā, no known children
Raidās	Chamār (leather worker)	Yes: Brahmin in in former life	Yes: refuses mother's milk	Yes: from birth	Yes: sky-voice tells Rāmānanda to go to Raidās	Yes: children uncertain

Table 1. Life Patterns of *Nirguṇī* Saints (continued)

Name	Encounters with petitioners	Encounters w. animals/ gods/ghosts	Encounters w. Brahmins or Baniyās	Encounters with *qāzīs* or mullahs	Encounters with kings	Naming of successor	Unusual death
Dādū Dayāl	Yes	Yes	Yes	Yes	Yes	Yes: after Dādū's death	Yes: age 59–60 1544–1603
Haridās Nirañjanī	Yes	Yes	Yes	—	—	—	No: age 88 ?1455–1543
Kabīr	Yes	Yes	Yes	Yes	Yes	Yes: competing versions	Yes: age 120 1398–1518
Nāmadev	Yes	—	Yes	—	—	—	No: age 80 1270–1350
Nānak	Yes: (many)	Yes	Yes	Yes	Yes	Yes	Yes: age 70 1469–1539
Pīpā	Yes: (many)	Yes:	Yes	—	Yes	—	No: died about ?1465
Raidās	—	—	Yes: Brahmins only	—	Yes	—	No: Age 120 contemporary of Kabīr

5. He has a number of encounters, often during his travels to various towns and villages, with others who may belong to a variety of different categories. These others may include his own mother, his wife, ascetics and yogis, *qāzīs* and mullahs, Brahmins and pandits, Baniyās and other merchants, wild animals (elephants, lions, snakes), kings and sultans, gods and ghosts, goddesses and nymphs, and ordinary devotees. The saint's encounters fall into two basic categories, differentiated principally by the nature his relation to the others he meets. These categories are as follows:

a. The others may be petitioners who request the saint's assistance in solving some difficulty or simply wish for his blessing in exchange for his accepting a gift. Invariably the saint solves their difficulty, often by miraculous means. The saint may also subject the petitioner to a test to teach him or her a lesson. Once the petitioners' requests are granted, or they submit to the test, they often become the saint's disciples.

In the hagiographies of Gurū Nānak, he has many relatively friendly dialogues on religious topics with various Muslim and Hindu holy men, whom he treats virtually as equals, although inevitably they do most of the asking and Nānak the explaining. Most of these dialogues belong to the literary forms that McLeod identifies as "narrative discourses" and "heterodox discourses."[4]

b. In most cases the others are the saint's rivals and opponents. They generally put *him* to some sort of test. This may take the form of a theological debate, a miracle contest, or one or more ordeals. Sometimes these opponents do not test the saint directly but enlist the aid of a king or official to test or punish him. The king's/official's attitude toward the saint is, initially at least, usually relatively neutral. The saint always wins or escapes unharmed, sometimes with the help of a direct intervention on his behalf by God in divine or human form. The rivals or opponents and their royal agents either leave the scene begrudgingly acknowledging their defeat, or they repent and become the saint's disciples.

6. In the case of the saints whose followers sooner or later organized themselves into a sect, the legends may tell how the saint named his successor and/or instructed his followers to carry on the tradition after his death (Kabīr, Nānak), or tell how the community of followers named a successor after the saint's death (Dādū). As is to be expected, such episodes generally occur only in rather late, sectarian versions of the saint's life story.

7. The saint has an unusual death, often at a very advanced age.

This unusual death may include a bodily ascent into heaven, a meeting with the many gods and sages living there, and/or a direct vision of supreme Vishnu in *saguṇ* form.

Although this narrative pattern is quite similar to that of the lives of *saguṇī* saints, particularly at the more abstract level of thematic structure, a few significant differences between *saguṇī* and *nirguṇī* saints' lives can be noted. For example, in *saguṇī* lives the stories of the saints' births rarely attempt to deny their low origins for the simple reason that most *saguṇī* saints are Brahmins, whereas most *nirguṇī* saints come from artisan or minor Kṣatriya castes. For this same reason the encounters between *saguṇī* saints and their opponents much less often involve subjecting the underdog saint to unfair tests by the arrogant representatives of "official" religious and political authority. Kings are more often portrayed as the *allies* of *saguṇī* saints, while their opponents may either be fellow Brahmin philosophers (with whom they have mostly polite intellectual debates) or low "heretics" who are generally dispatched by force (either by the saint's magical power or by the physical power of his royal ally).

It is possible, however, to note the existence of a few exceptions to the rule that *nirguṇī* saints are from artisan and Kṣatriya castes and *saguṇī* saints are Brahmins. For example, Dharmadās and Surat-gopāl, two of Kabīr's leading disciples, were from Vaiśya and Brahmin castes respectively. Palaṭū Sāhab was another important *nirguṇī* saint from a Vaiśya caste. In *saguṇī* tradition, the Vārakarī saints Chokhāmeḷā and Tukārām were from Untouchable and Vaiśya castes respectively, while Mīrābāī was a royal princess from a Kṣatriya family. On closer examination, however, the stories of such *saguṇī* Untouchables and Kṣatriyas and *nirguṇī* Brahmins and Vaiśyas generally turn out to be the exceptions that "prove the rule," since the legends about them explicitly recognize their exceptional caste status. Taking the stories as a whole, one cannot help but note the existence of an alliance of *nirguṇī* poor laborers and rulers against *saguṇī* merchants and priests. Is it too farfetched to see these alliances as early precursors of the curiously similar political alliances of present-day India between the social base of the Congress and Janata Dal Parties (richer peasants, Untouchables, poor laborers, and Muslims), on one side, and the social base of the Bharatiya Janata Party (merchants and traders, lesser peasants, and many white-collar professionals), on the other?

It is for these reasons that the contrasting caste and class origins of *nirguṇī* and *saguṇī* saints cannot simply be regarded as a historical "accident" that does not seriously affect the basic character of the narratives. These social origins are an intrinsic part and source of the religious and social ideologies purveyed by these two movements. These differing ideologies get more directly expressed in the individual episodes that make up the life stories of the saints and in the didactic sermons espousing differing social ideologies that are often found in the actual narrative texts. I have treated these two topics elsewhere.[5] Although these two aspects of hagiographic stories pass beyond the more structural analysis of this essay, it is important to note that in actual practice they represent nearly invariable elements that sharply distinguish *saguṇī* and *nirguṇī* hagiographic narrations.

Although most modern scholars have neglected the systematic study of the common patterns of Hindu hagiography, A. K. Ramanujan is an important exception. In his article on the legendary lives of women saints, he has stressed the common psychological and religious patterns in these stories. At the same time, however, he has clearly recognized that the stories also embody an important social dimension (1982, 316):

> There are significant differences of life pattern between upper-caste and outcaste male saints, and between upper-caste male saints and all women saints. For upper-caste male saints the *bhakti* point of view effects a number of reversals when compared with normative Hindu views such as those represented in Manu's *Dharmaśāstra*. According to Manu the female is subordinate to the male and the outcaste to the upper-caste, but in the lives of the *bhakti* saints "the last shall be first": men wish to renounce their masculinity and to become as women; upper-caste males wish to renounce pride, privilege, and wealth, seek dishonor and self-abasement, and learn from the untouchable devotee.

Ramanujan argues that there exist analogous "reversals" in the life patterns of the women saints discussed in his article. What he does *not* do is to clearly distinguish between the social and the psychological dimensions of these reversals as they apply to each of the different categories of saints: male and female, high-caste and low-caste.

What distinguishes the reversals in the life patterns of upper-caste male saints from the reversals in the lives of women (and low-caste male) saints is that the former engage in a temporary "playing the role" of female and low-caste persons, whereas the latter commit themselves to a permanent change of social status. When the psychological role-playing is over, the upper-caste male saints can safely return to their original social identities. For a short while they behave *as if* such social distinctions are unimportant, but they in fact never permanently reject or abandon either their "true" social identities or the hierarchical norms that legitimize them.

For female and low-caste devotees, however, to "play the role" of upper-caste males would obviously be both practically impossible and logically absurd. Upper-caste males can engage in social "slumming" in this way without major consequences. If female and low-caste devotees were to dare to engage in any analogous "king for a day" role-playing behavior, this would inevitably lead to their permanent social and economic ostracism and even put them in direct physical danger. In such circumstances, any temporary psychological consolation produced by such behavior—consolation such as I. M. Lewis (1971) finds in ecstatic cults popular among women in many parts of the world—simply cannot compensate for the direct risk to their economic and physical well-being.

Ramanujan (1982, 317) identifies the main reversal found in the legendary life pattern of female saints as "the way in which Indian women saints invert and even subvert the traditional ideals of womanhood embodied in such mythic figures as Sītā and Sāvitrī, adopting different patterns altogether." Up to this point, his analysis cannot be faulted. I cannot agree with Ramanujan, however, that this permanent *social* reversal is simply "another aspect of the same configuration" as the temporary *psychological* reversals found in the lives of upper-caste male saints. Once women saints such as Mīrābāī abandon their homes to follow a religious vocation, they can never return to husband and family. The reversal is permanent, forever irreversible.

As a result of his conflation of these two types of reversals, Ramanujan is left with no alternative but to seek a parallel psychological explanation for the permanent social reversal found in the life pattern of the women (and low-caste male) saints (1982, 324):

> The [upper-caste] males take on female personae: they are feminine, yearning, passive toward a male god. Before God all men are women. But no female saint, however she may defy male-oriented "relational" attitudes, takes on a male persona. It is as if, being already female, she has no need to change anything to turn

> toward God. Like the untouchable and the low-caste saint, she need shed nothing, for she has nothing to shed: neither physical prowess, nor social power, nor punditry, nor even spiritual pride. She is already where she needs to be, in these saints' legends.

If, however, all the women saints—and the "untouchable and low-caste" saints as well—have to do is to be themselves, why do their lives involve a profound and permanent challenge to the dominant socio-religious authority and norms of upper-caste males? The very existence of women and low-caste saints and their followers implies a social reversal that traditional upper-caste males (and females) have generally regarded as a religious and social rebellion that threatens the whole fabric of the hierarchical *varṇāśramadharma* ideology of Indian society. The psychological, role-playing reversals in the lives of upper-caste male saints, on the other hand, represent little more than a psychological spur for discovering their own humanity. This is undoubtedly a laudable goal, but, with good reason, such behavior never provoked the same social outrage as that of women saints such as Mīrābāī and low-caste *nirguṇī* saints such as Kabīr and Raidās. The legendary lives of these saints express the desires of the women and subaltern groups of Indian society both to fulfill their own full and equal humanity and, more importantly, to have it recognized and accepted by all others in that same society.

I would like to close this essay with a favorite quote from Anantadās's legendary biography of the Julāhā (weaver) saint Kabīr in which Kabīr's upper-class enemies, Muslim as well as Hindu, clearly identify the nature of the threat to the basic values of Brahmanical Hinduism and elite authority that Kabīr's *nirguṇī* religion represents. One day, when the Muslim sultan Sikandar comes to Banaras, the Baniyās, Brahmins, *qāzīs*, and mullahs—and even Kabīr's own mother—go to demand that Sikandar punish Kabīr. Sikandar asks, "What has he done, brothers? Has he snatched away a village or a district?" The petitioners reply as follows (Anantadās 1991, 165–67):

> He hasn't taken a village or a district. The Julāhā has done an unconventional thing. He has abandoned the customs of the Muslims and has broken the touchability rules of the Hindus. He has scorned the *tīrtha*s and the Vedas. He has scorned the nine planets, the sun and the moon. He has scorned the gods Śaṅkar and Mother Durgā. He has scorned the gods Śāradā and King Gaṇapati. He has scorned the rites of the eleventh day of the fortnight, of

homa and *śrāddha*. He has scorned the Brahmins, whom the whole world worships. He has scorned service to one's mother and father, sisters, nieces and all the gods. He has scorned the hope of all dharmas, the six systems of metaphysics and the rites of the twelve months. In this way he has corrupted everything. He has separated himself from both the Hindus and the Muslims. For that reason no one respects us while this Julāhā remains in Kashi.

Appendix A: The Life of King Pīpā

As far as I know, the cycle of legends about Pīpā, the king of Gāgaron, is available in English only in a short summary by John Hawley (1987, 63–66) and in a translation of the few episodes narrated in Mahipati's Bhaktavijaya *(1982, 1:406–14). The important early sources in Hindi include Anantadās's still unpublished* Pīpā parachaī *(c. 1590* C.E.*), Priyādās's commentary (1712* C.E.*) on Nābhādās's* Bhaktamāl *(1969), and Chaturadās's commentary (c.1800* C.E.*) on Rāghavadās's* Bhaktamāl *(1969, 195–213). The following is a free and slightly abridged translation of the relevant sections of Nārāyaṇadās's modern Hindi paraphrase of Chaturadās's commentary. The episode of the libidinous shopkeeper is also told about Kabīr. That of Pīpā getting his hand black putting out a fire in Dvaraka is very similar to that of Kabīr and the* paṇḍā *of Jagannāth in Puri. The episode of Pīpā helping Śrīraṅga tie the garland around the neck of the idol is also told about Kabīr helping Rāmānanda.*

Pīpā was a Rājasthānī king of Gāgaron. In British times this was in the Jhālāvaṛ kingdom. Pīpā was a worshipper of the Goddess, a *Śākta*. He worshipped her for twelve years in order to obtain salvation. One day there was a special festival at the temple of the Goddess. To this a big group of [*nirguṇī* Vaiṣṇava] sants arrived. Part of the food reserved for the Goddess and her worshippers was given to the sants. They offered it to Lord Vishnu. That night the king had a dream. A ghost *(bhūt)* overturned the king's bed and threw him to the ground. The king woke up frightened and went off to the temple of the Goddess. The Goddess appeared and offered him a boon. He said: "Give me salvation." The Goddess answered: "You will get what you want. You should go to Banaras and become a disciple of Rāmānanda and do bhakti."

After having his dream the king acted strangely and the people feared he had become mad. When he made preparations to visit Rāmānanda in Banaras, they knew he had recovered. In Banaras, when he tried to enter the ashram to see Rāmānanda, the doorkeeper stopped him and said: "First we must ask Rāmānanda's permission. If he agrees to see you, you may go in." Rāmānanda said: "What do we care about lovers of royal pomp?" The doorkeeper told Pīpā and sent him away. Pīpā then quickly gave away all his royal accoutrements and returned to the ashram. He asked the doorkeeper to tell Rāmānanda what he had done and to repeat his request for an audience. Rāmānanda said that Pīpā should go jump into a well. Pīpā did so. The servants pulled him out and brought him to Rāmānanda.

Rāmānanda made Pīpā a disciple. He put his hand on Pīpā's head and filled him with the Name of Rām. After a few days, Rāmānanda told Pīpā: "Return to your capital and give away your wealth for service to the sants. When the sants arrive here in Banaras, they will inform us. Then we will go to visit you."

Pīpā returned home and did as his guru had requested. Pīpā then wrote a letter of invitation to Rāmānanda: "Be true to your word and come to visit us." Rāmānanda accepted the invitation, and he and forty sants, including Kabīr and Raidās, set off for Gāgaron. When Pīpā learned that they were arriving, he ordered a luxurious palanquin and went with a large crowd to greet his guru. He then pleased his guru and the sants with his service to them. Rāmānanda said: "If you keep doing bhakti to the Lord like this, then there is no need to abandon your palace. Stay and do bhakti." Pīpā ran and fell at his guru's feet. By this he implied that he preferred to stay with his guru and abandon his kingdom. The guru said: "It is good."

Pīpā's twelve queens learned that he was abandoning the kingdom and made their own preparations to leave with him. Pīpā could not convince them to stay. Then he tore up a blanket and said: "If you really want to come, then take off your fine clothes and jewels and put on this rag." The queens looked at each other and ran off crying. But the youngest queen named Sītā took off her clothes and wrapped the piece of blanket round herself. Pīpā asked his guru if it were acceptable that Sītā should come like this.

Rāmānanda said: "Sadhus don't even keep a blanket. They remain naked. She should take this off as well." Sītā then took off the blanket and threw it away. She stood in the middle of the court completely naked. The guru then hugged her and said to Pīpā: "This Sītā is not an obstacle to your spiritual progress. She will be a help. Take her with you."

At the time of leaving, the other queens made a plot to stop them. They said to a Brahmin of the court: "If you can stop the king, you will get 1900 rupees." The Brahmin was required to eat poison and fall down dead in front of the sants. Pīpā was frightened by this, but Rāmānanda returned and brought the Brahmin back to life. The Brahmin was made to return to the court and the troop of sants left on their way to Dvārakā.

Pīpā stayed with his guru at Dvārakā for many days to benefit from the *satsaṅg*. When the guru set off for Banaras, Pīpā asked for permission to stay in Dvārakā. He had heard that the true Dvārakā was in the ocean. There Krishna has his home. Pīpā had a strong wish for a darshan of Lord Krishna. With this in mind the king and Sītā jumped into the ocean. The Lord pervades everything. The devotee who has faith will meet Him anywhere.

As Pīpā and Sītā jumped into the ocean, Krishna sent a servant to bring them to Him. Pīpā and Sītā then had a darshan of the true Dvārakā and of Krishna Himself. The Lord showed them much kindness. They stayed for seven days, playing in the many gold palaces. Then the Lord said: "Now you should return." But Pīpā was so happy he begged to stay. The Lord said: "Wherever you go, you will remain sunk in meditation on my true form. It you don't go, however, your body will drown and die. This should not happen. It would be a disgrace." Pīpā was overwhelmed by the thought of leaving Krishna but realized that he must. Krishna gave him a seal *(chhāp)* and they left together. Krishna went with Pīpā and Sītā a ways but finally left them. They then came out of the water. As they did the people recognized them and were astounded. They then gave the seal to the priest of the Lord and said to him: "The Lord gave us this and told us that it should be used to remove the sin of living beings.

When Pīpā saw the people coming for darshan he said to Sītā: "We should now move on to the forest." Sītā agreed and they both set off. Ten kilometers into the forest they met an evil Pathan bandit. He grabbed Sītā and took her away. Sītā asked the Lord: "Lord, make him let me go. Please hurry." The Lord appeared in the guise of a hero *(vīr)*. He killed the Pathan and freed Sītā. Pīpā, knowing what the Lord wanted him to do, sat in a lonely place worshipping. The Lord brought Sītā to Pīpā and then vanished.

Pīpā said: "Look what sort of trouble we are getting into. This life is dangerous for women. It will be better if you return home." Sītā said: "You don't know Rām the protector. I have seen my protector Rām in person. He is always with me. There is no danger." In this way Sītā reassured Pīpā. Pīpā opened his heart to her and said: "I was just testing you. I now have proof of your resoluteness and great love of Hari."

They left the road and took another. A bit further on a lion appeared in front of them. Seeing it coming Pīpā said to it: "In a previous life you sinned and now you are suffering the consequences. But you are still killing sinless beings. Stop your killing and do bhakti." The lion accepted Pīpā's words and gave up killing. He then died from hunger and was reborn as the devotee Nṛsiṃha Mahatā [= Narsī Mehtā].

Pīpā then went to Dhaner village to get the darshan of the [idol of] the Lord Vishnu lying on the cosmic serpent. There he met a man who was selling bamboo staffs. Pīpā asked him for the gift of a staff. The man said: "Cut a bamboo from a bamboo grove and bring it here." Pīpā agreed. At that instant the man's dry staffs took root and became green. Pīpā then cut one for himself.

Pīpā one time heard about the devotee named Chīndhaṛ Chhaulī and went to see him. When Chīndhaṛ and his wife saw Pīpā and Sītā, they were very pleased. Chīndhaṛ said to his wife: "Sītā and Pīpā have arrived. Make arrangements for their supper." His wife said: "There is no food in the house." Then she took off her own clothes and gave them to him. Being naked, she sat and hid. Chīndhaṛ sold her clothes and bought some food. He returned and said to Pīpā: "You will have to prepare the food." His wife had hid herself and was unable to help. The food was prepared. They offered it to the Lord and then sat down to eat. Pīpā said to him: "You and your wife should take the *prasād* of the Lord with us." Chīndhaṛ said: "After you have dined, we will eat the *prasād* that remains." Pīpā insisted: "We will eat only if you eat with us." Even so, Chīndhaṛ's wife still did not come out. Then Sītā went inside and saw that the devotee's wife was completely naked.

Sītā asked: "Where is your garment?" Chīndhaṛ's wife said: "When you sants came here, we were overjoyed. Salvation comes from serving the sants. My clothes were sold for food for you sants. One should have no other care than that of serving the sants. It is all I want." Sītā was overwhelmed. She tore her own garment in two and gave half to Chīndhaṛ's wife. She said: "Let's tie this round your waist." Sītā tied it and took her hand to bring her out to eat. After dinner, Sītā thought:

"We are called devotees, but in fact these are the real devotees." Then she said to Pīpā: "They have nothing, not even enough for clothes to cover the woman's body. They should at least have enough to eat. We should bring them something from somewhere and give it to her." Pīpā agreed.

Sītā said: "Now I must take up the role of a prostitute. By this means I will get money and give it to Chīndhaṛ's house so that they can live." There was a good-sized town not far from Chīndhaṛ's house. Sītā went to the grain market and sat there. Pīpā sat nearby. Sītā was beautiful. All the young men who passed by looked at her with lust in their eyes. They each asked: "Who are you?" Sītā replied: "I am a prostitute *(pātārī)* and this is my pimp." When the young men heard this, their lust knew no bounds. But the older persons and devotees realized that this was Sītā and Pīpā. So what happened? A pile of coins, grain and other supplies appeared. They sent all the materials to Chīndhaṛ. But that day 500 sadhus came to his place. He fed all the sadhus and kept nothing for himself.

Chīndhaṛ Chhaulī finally bid farewell to Pīpā and Sītā. They then traveled on to Ṭoḍā village. On the way there was no food, so they went hungry. They arrived at Ṭoḍā and began to stay there. One day Pīpā went to bathe. At the bathing place he found a pot full of gold coins buried in the earth. He left it there and went away. At night some thieves arrived at his place. For their benefit, Pīpā said to Sītā that he had seen a pot of money at his bathing place. Sītā said to him: "Don't go there now. Take your bath somewhere else." The thieves heard what was said and went there and dug up the pot. When they opened it, they heard the hiss of a snake. When they saw the snake, they thought: "He wanted to get us killed by the snake. Let's throw it in his hut so that he will be bitten and die." They took that illusion to Pīpā's place and fled. What Pīpā found was 720 gold coins. Each coin was big and heavy.

After this whoever came to Pīpā's door was given a full meal. Pīpa invited innumerable sants. In this way the money was quickly spent. The king of the place, Sūrya Sen Malla, heard about Pīpā. He took Pīpā's darshan and was pleased. He bowed and made a request: "Please give me your teachings and initiation. This is what I most want." Pīpā said: "The first teaching is this. One should become detached." The king said: "Ask whatever you wish. It will be done." Pīpā said: "Bring all your wealth and your queen and offer them to me." The king did what was asked. He brought his money and his queen. Pīpā tested King Sūrya Sen Malla. He gave him teachings and then gave him a mantra of the Lord. Finally Pīpā returned everything to him saying: "All this is now mine. You are its manager. Keep managing it properly." To the queen he said: "Don't keep purdah with the sants."

The king insisted that Pīpā keep the money. Pīpā did keep some for feeding the sants and said to the king: "O king, be without pride and worship Rām." Sūrya Sen Malla's brothers heard that the king had become Pīpā's disciple and had offered all his wealth and his queen to Pīpā. They became very angry, but Pīpā's inner force was very powerful. They could do nothing.

A trader *(banjārā)* came to Ṭoḍā to buy a bullock. Bad men said to him as a joke: "The devotee Pīpā has lots of bullocks. Take one from him." The trader went to Pīpā and said: "You have very good bullocks. Give them to me. I will give you a down-payment of 500 rupees. Afterward I will give you more according to the number of bullocks I take. Pīpā realized that he had been misled by bad men and said: "Right now they are all in the village. Come tomorrow at eleven and you can take as many as you like." Pīpā then invited all the nearby sants for a meal and spent the trader's 500 rupees for the feast. While the sants were eating the trader arrived and asked about the bullocks. Pīpā said: "My business is with these bullocks. Take whichever one you like." When the trader saw all the sants eating his heart was filled with bhakti. He ordered cloth and gave some to each of them.

One day Pīpā mounted a horse and went to bathe at the tank. He tied the horse to his own stick after sticking it in the ground and entered the tank to bathe. Meanwhile a bad man took the horse from there and tied it up at his own place. But when Pīpā came out of the water, the Lord made the horse return there to him.

Sūrya Sen Malla called Pīpā to help in settling a quarrel. Pīpā went there. Meanwhile some sants arrived at his ashram. Sītā bid them to sit, but there was no food to feed them. Sītā thought: "A meal must be made for the sants. I will go and bring it." In the village there was a libidinous shopkeeper. Seeing such a beautiful woman, he was tempted. As fate would have it, Sītā went and asked him for food on credit. He said: "If you return at night to be with me, you can take anything you like." Sītā was a *mahāsatī*. She had faith that if the sants ate the shopkeeper's food, then he would be purified. She accepted his proposition and took the food.

Pīpā arrived at the ashram as the sants were eating. Pīpā asked Sītā: "We had almost no food. Where did you get it from?" Sītā told him of her arrangement with the shopkeeper. Pīpā knew that it was inevitable. He said: "It is well done. The sants got fed. All will be OK." That night Sītā got dressed and ready to go. Then it began it rain. Pīpā said: "Your feet will get dirty in the mud and your clothes will get wet. Cover yourself with a blanket and sit on my shoulders. I will take you to the shopkeeper." Then he brought her to the shop.

The quarrel for which Pīpā had gone to Sūrya Sen Malla's place was this. A traveler and his beautiful wife had arrived at the tank. Another unknown man also came there and said: "This is my woman." The quarrel was brought to Sūrya Sen Malla. Since there was no reliable witness the king and his advisors were in a tizzy. They were unable to reach any decision. Then they called Pīpā. Pīpā realized that one of the men was a ghost *(pret)*. Pīpā asked that several nested caskets with a lock be brought. He then gave an iron bottle and its top to a strong man *(vīr)*. He said to the two men who were quarreling: "Whichever one of you can stay for a half-hour in this bottle will be known as this woman's husband." One of the men kept quiet, but the other said: "I will enter the bottle." When he disappeared, Pīpā had the strong man put the top on the bottle. Then he put the bottle in the smallest casket, that casket in the bigger one, and that in the bigger ones one after another. Finally he put the lock on it and said: "This is not a man. It is a ghost. If he gets out, he will cause trouble." Then they buried the caskets and gave the woman back to the man who had kept quiet.

Meanwhile, Pīpā sat at the bottom of the stairs and sent Sītā up to the shopkeeper. When he saw that Sītā's feet were dry, he asked: "Lady, by what path did you avoid getting your feet wet?" Sītā said: "My husband put me on his shoulders and brought me." The shopkeeper asked: "Tell me. Where is he now?" Sītā said: "Sitting down below." The shopkeeper went down and fell at Pīpā's feet. Pīpā said: "Do what you like. Don't be afraid. You made a bargain and gave the food." The shopkeeper was filled with shame. He couldn't speak. His eyes were full of tears. Pīpā realized that he had been purified. Pīpā gave him teachings and established Hari in his heart. By Pīpā's kindness the shopkeeper became a pure sant.

The news about what Pīpā had done reached the royal assembly. The Brahmins met and said to the king: "This is something repugnant. It is not proper for you to have a person like this as your guru." The king was not very intelligent. He didn't realize that Pīpā had done this to turn the libidinous shopkeeper into a devotee.

One day Pīpā went to the king's place to give him teachings. When he arrived, someone said to the king: "Pīpā has arrived." The king said: "Tell him that the king is performing worship *(sevā-pūjā)*. When they told him this Pīpā said: "He is standing in the hut of the saddle-maker having a saddle made. What do you mean he is performing worship?" The man went and told the king what Pīpā had said. At that moment the king was thinking to himself: "I have had my horse's saddle repaired several times, but it is still not right. I must go to the saddle-maker's place and tell him exactly what to do." He realized that Pīpā knew what he was thinking. He came out and fell at Pīpā's feet. Pīpā said: "How can you insult your own guru and allow your mind to wander at the time of performing worship? What sort of behavior is this? This is not the way to find the Lord."

One of Sūrya Sen Malla's queens was beautiful but barren. Pīpa requested that the king give her to him. The king agreed, but he did not really want to do it. The king went to his harem to get her, but found a lion seated in front of the entrance. He could not go forward for fear of the lion, nor back without doing what he had promised. Then the lion, who was really Pīpā in disguise, vanished. When the king reached the queen, he saw a newborn child playing with her. He realized that this child was a product of Pīpā's great power *(prabhāv)*. The king bowed before Pīpā [in the form of the child] and said: "It is difficult to know the extent of your greatness. Be merciful.'' Then Pīpā made the child vanish and gave his darshan to the king in his own form. Rebuking the king, he said: "Where did the sentiment *(bhāv)* go that you had the day you became my disciple?" The king said: "Forgive my mistake. Make me your slave. My sentiment is still the same." Pīpā gave teachings to Sūrya Sen Malla and purified his heart. The king again followed the rule of service to the sadhus and bhakti to God. Pīpā was pleased and set off for his own ashram.

Then an evil man who was dressed as a devotee came to Pīpā and said: "Give Sītā to me for one night." Pīpā said: "Take her." The false devotee said to Sītā: "Run away with me." Sītā followed his advice quite literally and started running. She ran all night, and he never got what he wanted. In the morning Sītā said: "My master commanded me [to go with you] for one night. Now I won't move." She sat down and wouldn't budge. The false devotee conceded defeat and went to get a palanquin from the next village. [When he returned] he saw Sītā sitting in front of every house. By this miracle his mind was put right. His lust vanished and he came to look on Sītā as a guru. He bowed before her and said: "Mother, I will now return you to your own ashram."

One day four lustful rogues in the disguise of sants requested Pīpā to give them Sītā. Pīpā said: "Go ahead. She has put on makeup and is eagerly waiting for you in that room. Go have some fun." The four went to the door of the room and looked in. They saw a lioness coming to eat them. Since they were dressed as sants, however, she did not do so. The rogues were all frightened and ran off to Pīpā. Angrily they said: "You tricked us by having a lioness sit there in her room ready to kill us." Pīpā said: "You should reflect on your own sentiments. One reaps the consequences of one's own thoughts." The rogues realized that this was the truth and their sentiments became pure. Sītā gave them her darshan and sent them to Pīpā. They fell at his feet and became his disciples, saying "Rām, Rām."

One day the sants said to Pīpā: "Today we should make an offering of curd to the Lord." Soon afterwards a milkmaid arrived there bringing curd. Pīpā took it from her and gave it to the sants to drink. The milkmaid asked for twenty-six *ānās*. Pīpā accepted her price and said: "Right now I don't have this amount. But whatever offerings arrive today, you can have them all." After some time a devotee of Pīpā arrived. He gave an offering of goods worth 400 rupees. All that Pīpā gave to the milkmaid. She, however, would not accept it. She went and got some more money of her own and gave it to feed the sants.

A Brahmin, who was a devotee of the Goddess, prepared a feast and sent out an invitation to all the sadhus and Brahmins. Pīpā said: "We will come if an offering is made to Rām before the one made to the Goddess. The Brahmin, out of respect for Pīpā, agreed. The offering was made and Pīpā and all the sants ate. That night the Goddess angrily said to the Brahmin: "Today I remained hungry." The Brahmin said: "Today a great deal has been offered." The Goddess said: "The offering was made to God. The servants took me out of the temple." The Brahmin said: "If they obstructed the offerings to you, why don't you kill them?" The Goddess said: "My power doesn't work on them." When the Brahmin heard this, he and his family gave up Goddess worship. They became Pīpā's disciples and began to worship the Lord.

One day a very beautiful woman oil-seller came by crying: "Get your oil! Get your oil!" Pīpā told her that she should instead cry "Rām! Rām!" The oil-seller replied: "Devotee, why don't you think before speaking? Women who cry 'Rām! Rām!' are those are grieving for the death of their husbands." Pīpā said: "Very well. If your husband were to die, then you would cry 'Rām! Rām!'" When she arrived home, a roof beam fell on her husband's head and killed him. As she took him to the cremation ground, she began to cry "Rām! Rām!" Pīpā said to her: "Now you are saying 'Rām! Rām!'" She fell at Pīpā's feet and said: "You have killed my husband." Pīpā said: "If you say 'Rām! Rām!' day and night your whole life long, then by the grace of Rām your husband will return to life." She said: "As you command, we will say 'Rām! Rām!' Return him to life." Pīpā revived the oil-man. The man and his wife fell at his feet and became his disciples. They sang bhajans for the rest of their life and found God.

King Sūrya Sen Malla gave Pīpā a buffalo that gave good milk. It grazed in the forest and came back to the ashram at night by itself. They milked the buffalo each day. After churning the butter, they gave the buttermilk to the sants. One day thieves began to steal the buffalo, but left its calf. Pīpā called after them: "Take the calf with you. If you don't, how will it give milk." They then asked him: "Who are you?" Pīpā said: "They call me Pīpā." When the thieves heard this they fell at his feet and became his disciples and practiced devotion.

When the crowds in Ṭoḍā became too big, Pīpā and Sītā went to live in a more isolated village. A devotee arrived there and gave Pīpā a cart full of food and some gold coins. That same day some thieves came and took away all the food. Pīpā ran after them and said: "Brothers, you have left the gold coins. Take them. They will be of use to you." Then they asked who he was. He said: "They call me Pīpā." Hearing his name, they fell at his feet and asked his forgiveness. They returned the food and became his disciples. They also made an offering of a buffalo with its calf. Sītā was angry that they had become encumbered with so many things, but Pīpā said: "They will be of use for the sants."

One day invitations came from five different villages, all for the same time. Meanwhile some sants arrived at the ashram. Pīpā was kept busy serving them. Then to please those who had sent the invitations, he took on five duplicate bodies and went to all five villages at once. In one village Pīpā had two female disciples from the cotton-carder *(kaṇḍerinī)* caste. They took Pīpā's darshan and fell at his feet. Early the next day Pīpā abandoned his duplicate body and the people in the village cremated it. His two disciples were very sad. They set off for Ṭoḍā to tell Sītā what had happened. On the way they passed another village where they were cremating another of the duplicate bodies. In this way they saw him being cremated in five places. Finally they came to Ṭoḍā. There they saw Pīpā still alive. Their grief ended. Pīpā was serving the sadhus. For this, he had borrowed food from a shopkeeper. One day the shopkeeper said: "Look at this account. You owe me 700 rupees." He gave Pīpā the bill and demanded his money. But Pīpā had nothing. He said: "Some gift will turn up. When it does, I will give it to you." The shopkeeper was not satisfied with this. He took the bill to the village council and said: "Many rupees have been offered to the saint, but he doesn't pay back anything. The five councillors looked in the shopkeeper's account book, but the page was blank. Pīpā's name was not there. This made the shopkeeper worried. His mouth got dry. Pīpā heard about this and send a message: "I have the shopkeeper's rupees, but he is demanding his payment too soon." The shopkeeper pleaded with Pīpā. Meanwhile a merchant arrived. He gave Pīpā many rupees. The shopkeeper got all his money back.

One day Pīpā said to Sītā. "Let's leave this house. Listen to these words and understand them well. We should go about living on alms and meditating on Hari." There was much wealth in the house, but they left it and went on their way. Within three days, the people had looted everything. Pīpā and Sītā went and stayed in a deserted village. A crowd of sannyasis arrived there, however, and that place also became full.

A Brahmin once killed a cow. The Brahmin came to Pīpā and told him what had happened. The Brahmin said: "I have come here after bathing and the Ganges. I have prepared a feast with fried food and am ready to give a feast to the people of my caste. But the Brahmins are not willing to take me back into their caste." Pīpā said: "Bring the food here and feed them. The Lord will remove your sin." Then the Brahmin fed the Brahmins, sadhus and sannyasis at Pīpā's place. All sat in the same eating-line. Pīpā gave the Brahmin his foot-water and said: "Your sin is now expunged." But the dogmatic Brahmins did not take him back into their caste. Pīpā said to them: "When will you accept him as purified?'' They said: "When Hanumān dines on food from his hand." Pīpā had the disgraced Brahmin offer food to Hanumān. When the curtain had been closed, Pīpā said to the god: "If this Brahmin has become purified by taking the foot-water of God's grace and feeding the sants, then you should eat the food." When they opened the curtain everyone saw that Hanumān had taken the food. When the Brahmins saw this, they accepted the cow-killer as being purified.

One time King Sūrya Sen Malla had not had a darshan of Pīpā for many days. He sent horsemen here and there to find Pīpā. After twenty days one of the horsemen found Pīpā and told him that the king wished to see him. Pīpā said: "I knew what the king wanted and was just coming to see him." He wrote a letter announcing his intention and gave it to the horseman. At that instant, Pīpā and Sītā went to the king's place. The king gave them gifts and money.

One day Pīpā had gone to another village for some festival. A good man *(sādhu)* came to Sītā and said: "My daughter is a maiden; give me money for her wedding." Sītā gave him all the money she had in the house, and was very pleased.

Śrīraṅgajī was [Rāmānanda's *saguṇī* disciple] Anantānanda's disciple and Pīpā's nephew-disciple. He lived in Dausā village. He sent Pīpā a letter requesting him to come for a visit. Pīpā then went to this devotee's house in Dausā. Pīpā saw that Śrīraṅga was seated meditating on Hari. Then he began to perform *pūjā* [to a mental image of the Lord]. When he tried to put a garland on the Lord, it got stuck on the idol's ear. Śrīraṅga got flustered and thought to himself: "What should I do now?" Pīpā saw that there was a problem in Śrīraṅga's mental *pūjā* and said: "Concentrate on what you are doing. It the garland is too small, then open the knot and tie it on the Lord's neck." Hearing this, Śrīraṅga was surprised. He thought: "How did he know what I was thinking? This must be a sant." He left his *pūjā* and went to Pīpā: "Who are you?" Pīpā said: "They call me Pīpā."

Pīpā began to give Śrīraṅga teachings. Śrīraṅga said: "Let's go to the garden." They went to the garden. There a crowd of devotees with musical instruments assembled. They all returned to Śrīraṅga's house with much fanfare. After staying there for some time, Pīpā said: "Let's go stay at Geṭolāv Tāl.

While Pīpā was at Geṭolāv, two beautiful cotton-carder *(kaṇḍerinī)* girls came there to gather dung cakes. Pīpā said to Śrīraṅga: "Although these two girls are very beautiful they are doing [the menial work] of collecting dung. They should be offering devotion to Rām. I will instruct them and make them devotees." He called them over and said: "Even though you have such beautiful bodies, you still gather dung. Perform devotion to the Lord instead." He gave them the mantra of initiation and made them disciples. Because of this, their home-folk got angry with them. They decided to go on pilgrimage. They came to Ṭoḍā and began to live with Pīpā as devotees of the Lord.

A group of people passed by bringing *bhārīs* of bamboo. Pīpā said: "Give us a pole." They refused and began to laugh at him. Then they stood up the bamboos and went for a drink of water. The bamboos immediately took root and sprouted.

A Brahmin passerby called for help. Pīpā asked: "Brother, what is troubling you? Why are you calling?" The Brahmin said: "My daughter is of marriageable age and there is no money in the house." Pīpā said: "Come with me. I will get someone to give you money." He had the Brahmin's head shaved, had him dressed as a sadhu and said: "Don't say anything. I am going to take you to the king and offer you *pūjā*." Pīpā took him to the king's palace. He said to the king: "Offer *pūjā* to this sadhu. You should know that he is the equal of our guru." The king gave him costly gifts. Pīpā said: "Go on back to your village."

On one eleventh-day [of the bright fortnight], an all-night *kīrtan* was being held in the presence of King Sūrya Sen Malla. Pīpā suddenly stood up in the middle of the group and began to rub his hands. Everyone saw that his hands had become black. The king asked why this was so. Pīpā said: "In Dvārakā a similar festival is taking place. There the lamp set fire to the canopy over the idol of the Lord. I pounded it with my hands and put it out. That is how my hands got black." The people did not believe him. They wondered: "How can this be true?" The king sent a rider on a rapid camel to Dvārakā to verify the story. It turned out to be true. The people in Dvārakā said: "The night of that eleventh day the canopy began to burn and Pīpā put it out. Pīpā comes here for every eleventh-day *kīrtan*.

One day, Pīpā went to bathe. There an upset Brahmin said to Pīpā: "To cultivate my crops I need a bullock. Find someone to give me one. Without a bullock we'll starve to death." At that time a son of an oil-man came by to give water to his own bullock. Pīpā grabbed the bullock's nose-rope and gave it to the Brahmin, saying: "Go and cultivate your crops." The son of the oil-man went home crying. His father went to Sūrya Sen Malla to complain. The king said to him: "Go talk to Pīpā." The oil-man came and fell at Pīpā's feet. Pīpā said: "Your bullock is at your own home. Go and look." The oil-man went home and saw the bullock tied up at his own door.

In 1563 C.E. there was a famine. Because of the lack of food, there was much social unrest. Many were dying of hunger. Pīpā felt much compassion. He organized a daily distribution of alms. He gave food and clothes to everyone. At that time, by the grace of God, he found several hoards of money buried in the ground. He spent all that in feeding and clothing the hungry. He kept nothing for himself.

Appendix B: The Life of Haridās Nirañjanī

A summary of the life of Haridās Nirañjanī is also unavailable in English. He is not mentioned in Nābhādās's Bhaktamāl *(1969). Rāghavadās's* Bhaktamāl *(1969) does have two verses (681-82) about him, but Chaturadās wrote no commentary on them. Nārāyaṇadās's modern Hindi commentary does give a fairly extensive summary (ibid., pp. 794–805), but this is probably mostly based on Maṅgaladās Svāmī's modern study (1962). The summary given below is based on a modern pamphlet by Rāmasvarūp Sonī (1984) of the Nirañjanī Panth. The key episode of Haridās's abandoning his life as a thief is also told about a disciple of Gurū Nānak named Bholā.*

Haridās Nirañjanī is said to have been born in the year 1455 C.E. in Kāpaḍaud village near the town of Didwana. He belonged to the Sāṅkhalā Kṣatriya caste. His original name was Harisiṃha. He and his brothers fed their families from what they earned as thieves. He lived like this until the age of forty-four. Finally he caught a wandering sadhu named Gorakhnāth. Gorakhnāth told Harisiṃha to ask his family members who would be willing to share the guilt of his evil actions. Harisiṃha asked his family but no one was willing. He then abandoned his family and became a disciple of Gorakhnāth. Having taken the name Haridās and dumping his weapons in the Khosalyā well, he went to Tīkhalī Ḍuṅgarī hill to take up life as an ascetic. On the hill he became a Siddha by virtue of his meditation and mystically experienced his identity with Brahman, also called Rām. The basis of his religious practice was yoga and *nirguṇ* bhakti.

At some point a man named Gāḍhājī took charge of feeding him, Gāḍhājī was a resident of Didwana, a long three *kos* away. Every day Gāḍhājī brought him food and water. One day, just as he reached the hill, Gāḍhājī slipped and the water jug broke. He took the food to Haridās and told him what had happened to the water. Haridās said: "Maybe you made a mistake. Go back and look." Gāḍhājī went and found that the jug was unbroken and full of water.

Gāḍhājī was old and had no children. The daily trek of three *kos* back and forth was too much for him. Haridās agreed to grant him two favors. Haridās moved to Didwana and stayed under a *pīpal* tree. Today this spot is known as the Pīpalī temple. Later Haridās moved to a place in the jungle to the north of town. Gāḍhājī had a well dug there known as the Gomatī well. Fifty-two *bīghās* of land were attached to the site. Haridās's *samādhi* was set up at this site, now known as the Gāḍhā-dhām. Gāḍhājī's wish for a child was rather ambiguously granted. Haridās told him: "Your name will go on in age after age."

One day Haridās was walking through town asking for alms. At the place where he formerly had stayed a house was being built. The Vaiśya builder was debating whether or not to cut down the *pīpal* tree. Haridās told him that the *pīpal* would grow no further. But if he cut it, his own family would not grow. The Vaiśya did not cut it and his family prospered and grew.

One time Haridās went to the town of Nāgaur, ruled by Rāṭhāṛ Kṣatriyas. On the way he stopped at a tank infested by ghosts *(bhūts)*. A ghost tried to scare Haridās but ended up having to ask his forgiveness. On this occasion Haridās recited his first hymn: "The Praise of Brahman." Hearing it the ghost escaped from his bad birth.

Haridās went to Pushkar and Ajmer, cities under the control of Muslims *(yavanas)*. Haridās stayed outside Ajmer where today Daulat Bāg is located. There a jealous Hindu ascetic sent a wild elephant to attack him. The elephant instead put his head at Haridās's feet. The townsfolk built a stone elephant at this site, now known as Hāthībhāṭā.

Leaving Ajmer, Haridās stayed at a village with a famous bard *(chāraṇ)*. He taught the bard and wrote a text called the *Bārahapadī jog granth*.

Haridās then went to Ṭoḍārāyasiṃha. There he set up his place over a snake hole. The snake was guarding some treasure. At night the snake came out, but seeing Haridās in yogic trance *(samādhi)*, it did not bite him. Haridās taught the snake and told him to put his treasure to good use. The snake's mind was enlightened and he escaped from his unfortunate birth.

Haridās went north from there. He learned about a yogi named Āis Siddha on the way. Haridās went to see him. Āis had foolishly taken the form of a lion to test Haridās. Haridās knew this and called him an "ass" *(khar)*. Āis turned into an ass. His pupils came looking for him after a few days. Haridās then agreed to change him back into a yogi.

Haridās went to Jobaner and stayed outside the village. A local

Vaiṣṇava holy man was not pleased. He sent Haridās a pot of poisoned water, saying it was *prasād* from Haridās's own guru Gorakhnāth. Haridās knew the truth. Nonetheless he drank the water. The Vaiṣṇava thought that Haridās would die that night. Haridās was still alive and meditating in the morning. The Vaiṣṇava asked for forgiveness, gave away all his wealth to the sants, and became Haridās's disciple.

Haridās went from Jobaner to Āmer (Jaipur), at that time controlled by the Kachhavāhas. Haridās sent up his camp on a remote hill, full of lions and tigers. A lion came there. As soon as Haridās looked at him, the lion's carnivorous instincts were quelled. It sat there a while and then moved off. The people learned what had happened and begged Haridās to leave that dangerous place, but he refused.

From there Haridās came to Khetaḍī. Many people came to see him, including a crippled Brahmin. Haridās told him: "Stand up." The Brahmin was cured and began to walk.

From Khetaḍī Haridās went to Siṅghāṇā. Many people came to see him every day. One day the only son of his lay disciple, Śāhajī, suddenly died. At that moment, Haridās was going to eat at someone else's house. When he learned what had happened, he stopped at Śāhajī's house and said to the dead boy: "Why are you sleeping? Get up!" The boy got up.

From Siṅghāṇā, Haridās returned to Didwana by roughly the same route. He traveled about five years (1522–27 C.E.). He died on the sixth day of the bright fortnight of the month of Phālgun in 1543 C.E. There is now a celebration in Didwana on this day.

Notes

1. For modern studies about these *saguṇī* saints and their hagiographies, see especially S. K. De 1961 on Chaitanya, R. Barz 1976 on Vallabhāchārya, J. S. Hawley 1985 on Sūr Dās, H. Goetz 1966 on Mīrābāī, P. Lutgendorf 1990 on Tulasīdās, J. N. Trivedī 1972 on Narasī Mehatā, and V. Śarmā 1957 on Tukārām.

2. For these and other Nāth saints, see A. G. Gold 1992.

3. See O. Rank et al. 1990. This book contains Rank's *Myth of the Birth of the Hero;* Lord Raglan's *Hero: A Study in Tradition, Myth, and Drama, Part II;* A. Dundes's "Hero Pattern and the Life of Jesus"; and a new introduction by R. A. Segal.

4. McLeod (1980, 82–105) divides the materials found in the Sikh *janam-sākhī*s into five "forms": narrative anecdotes, narrative discourses, didactic

discourses, heterodox discourses, and codes of discipline. He subdivides the category of narrative anecdotes into moralistic anecdotes, chimeric fairy tales, devotional legends, and aetiological legends. In my opinion, the criteria that McLeod employs to construct this typology are too diverse for the typology to be logically consistent. The criteria include thematic, historical, and literary factors.

5. In a book on Kabīr legends (1991), I have attempted to extract the ideological "messages" inherent in individual episodes of Kabīr's life, and in an essay on the *saguṇī* and *nirguṇī* versions of Prahlād's story (1992), I have discussed the didactic "advertisements" that almost invariably accompany the differing texts that narrate this hagiographic myth.

Bibliography

Amin, Shahid. 1988. "Gandhi as Mahatma: Gorakhpur District, Eastern U.P., 1921–22," in *Selected Subaltern Studies*, edited by Ranajit Guha and Gayatri Chakravorty Spivak, 288–348. New York: Oxford University Press.

Anantadās. 1989. *Nāmadev parachaī*. Edited and translated in Winand M. Callewaert and Mukund Lath, *The Hindi Padavali of Namdev*. Delhi: Motilal Banarsidass.

———. 1982. *Raidās parachaī*. Edited by B. P. Śarmā in his *Śrī guru Ravidas charitam*. Chandigarh: Śrī Guru Ravidās Saṃsthān.

Barz, Richard. 1976. *The Bhakti Sect of Vallabhacarya*. Faridabad: Thomson Press.

De, Sushil Kumar. 1961. *Early History of the Vaisnava Faith and Movement in Bengal*. Calcutta: Firma K. L. Mukhopadhyay.

Goetz, Hermann. 1966. *Mira Bai: Her Life and Times*. Bombay: Bharatiya Vidya Bhavan.

Gold, Ann Grodzins. 1992. *A Carnival of Parting: The Tales of King Bharthari and King Gopi Chand*. Berkeley: University of California Press.

Hawley, John S. 1987. "Morality Beyond Morality in the Lives of Three Hindu Saints." In *Saints and Virtues*, edited by John S. Hawley, 52–72. Berkeley: University of California Press.

Hawley, John S., and Mark Juergensmeyer. 1988. *Songs of the Saints of India*. New York: Oxford University Press.

Jan Gopāl. 1988. *The Hindi Biography of Dadu Dayal*. Edited and translated by Winand M. Callewaert. Delhi: Motilal Banarsidass.

Lele, Jayant. 1981. "The Bhakti Movement in India: A Critical Introduction." In *Tradition and Modernity in Bhakti Movements*, edited by Jayant Lele, 1–15. Leiden: E. J. Brill.

Lewis, I. M. 1971. *Ecstatic Religion: An Anthropological Study of Spirit Possession and Shamanism.* Harmondsworth: Penguin Books.

Lorenzen, David N. 1992. "Prahlad the Pious Demon in Saguni and Nirguni Traditions." Unpublished essay.

———. 1991. *Kabir Legends and Ananta-das's Kabir Parachai.* Albany: State University of New York Press.

———. 1987a. "The Social Ideologies of Hagiography: Sankara, Tukaram and Kabir." In *Religion and Society in Maharashtra,* edited by M. Israel and N. K. Wagle, 92–114. Toronto: Centre for South Asian Studies, University of Toronto.

———. 1987b. "Traditions of Non-caste Hinduism: The Kabir Panth." *Contributions to Indian Sociology* 21:264–83.

Lutgendorf, Philip. 1989. "Ram's Story in Shiva's City: Public Arenas and Private Patronage." In *Culture and Power in Banaras: Community, Performance and Environment, 1800–1980,* edited by Sandria B. Freitag, 34–61. Berkeley: University of California Press.

———. 1990. "La búsqueda del Tulsidas legendario." *Estudios de Asia y Africa* 25, no. 1:8–29.

McLeod, W. H., trans. 1980a. *The B40 Janam-Sakhi.* Amritsar: Guru Nanak Dev University.

———. 1980b. *Early Sikh Tradition: A Study of the Janamsakhis.* Oxford: Clarendon Press.

———. [1968] 1976. *Guru Nanak and the Sikh Religion.* Delhi: Oxford University Press.

Mahipati. 1982. *Bhaktavijaya.* Translated by Justin E. Abbott and Narhar R. Godbole as *Stories of Indian Saints,* 2 vols. in 1. Reprint; Delhi: Motilal Banarsidass. Translation first published in 1933. Marathi text written in 1762 C.E.

Maṅgaladās Svāmī, ed. 1962. *Śrī mahārāj Haridāsa jī kī vānī saṭippanī vā apār Nirañjanī mahātmāoṃ kī rachanā ke aṃśāṃśa.* Jaipur: Nikhil Bhāratīy Nirañjanī Mahā Sabhā.

Nābhādās. 1969. *Śrībhaktamāl.* With the verse commentary of Priyādās (1712 C.E.) and a modern Hindi prose paraphrase of both the text and commentary by Śrīsītārām Śaraṇ Bhagavān Prasād Rūpakalā. Lucknow: Tejakumār Press.

Rāghavadās. 1969. *Bhaktamāl.* With the verse commentary of Chaturadās (c. 1800 C.E.) and the modern Hindi paraphrase of both the text and commentary by the editor, Svāmī Nārāyaṇadās. Jaipur: Śrī Dādū Mahāvidyālay.

Ramanujan, A. K. 1982. "On Women Saints." In *The Divine Consort: Radha and the Goddesses of India,* edited by John S. Hawley and Donna Marie Wulff, 316–24, 365–67. Berkeley: Berkeley Religious Series.

Rāmasvarūp Sonī. 1984. *Śrī Haripuruṣa jī mahārāj kī jīvan jhāṅkī.* Didwana: Svāmī Paramānanda.

Rank, Otto et al. 1990. *In Quest of the Hero.* Princeton: Princeton University Press.

Śarmā, Vinayamohan. 1957. *Hindī ko Marāṭhi saṃtoṃ kī den.* Patna: Bihār-Rāṣṭrabhāṣā-Pariṣad.

Trivedī, Jeṭhālāl Nārāyaṇ, ed. 1972. *Narasī ro māhero.* Jodhpur: Rājasthān Prāchyavidyā Pratiṣṭhān.

Zelliot, Eleanor. 1981. "Chokhamela and Eknath: Two Bhakti Modes of Legitimacy for Modern Change." In *Tradition and Modernity in Bhakti Movements*, edited by Jayant Lele, 136–56. Leiden: E. J. Brill.

Chokhāmeḷā: Piety and Protest

Eleanor Zelliot

The songs of the fourteenth-century saint-poet Chokhāmeḷā and his family are the first authentic voice of the Untouchable in Western India. It is the only Untouchable voice from the Marathi-speaking region that we have until the nineteenth century, although the six-hundred-year-old bhakti *panth* to which Chokhāmeḷā belonged is still a very important part of the Maharashtrian tradition and has admitted into its fold all castes and creeds. Chokhāmeḷā was a Mahār, a caste which performed village service duties ranging from carting away dead animals and bringing fuel to the funeral pyre to adjudicating boundaries and caring for the horses of traveling government officials. Some of Chokhāmeḷā's *abhaṅgas* refer to Mahār work, just as almost all bhakti poets use their personal experience as symbols in their songs. The legends of his birth and death are told within the context of Mahār duties. Chokhāmeḷā himself is very conscious of Mahār social status, and mixed with his piety is protest both of his birth and the very concept of purity and pollution. We have a less than authentic fourteenth-century text, but it is clear that we have here an authentic Untouchable voice.

While many of Chokhāmeḷā's songs express pure joy in the worship of Viṭhobā of Pandharpur, god of the Maharashtrian bhakti *panth*, and in the fellowship of other *bhaktas*, several of whom were his close friends and admirers, it is his life and his voice as an Untouchable that move us today. A few of the *abhaṅgas* of his wife Soyrābāī and his son Karmameḷā add to the intensity of that voice.

Chokhā's birth was miraculous, and although a Brahmin is involved in the legend, his mother and father were acting as Mahār village servants at the time of his birth. In contrast to some of the legends about the northern Untouchable saint-poet Raidās, the stories of Chokhāmeḷā's birth do not made him a Brahmin born as an Untouchable. The legend tells that Chokhāmeḷā's parents were traveling to the capital at Bedar on the orders of the village headman, carrying mangoes. The God Viṭhobā, disguised as a Brahmin, begged a fruit from Chokhā's mother-to-be, tasted it, told her it was sour and returned it to her. When the mangoes were delivered, the bitten mango, tucked in the folds of Sudāmā's sari, had become a lovely child, Chokhāmeḷā.

Another miracle relates to Chokhāmeḷā's death, and like the birth legend, it refers to Mahār work. While Chokhāmeḷā was working on the repair of the wall of Mangalvedhe, a town near Pandharpur, it collapsed, burying him and the other Mahār workmen. Nāmdev, Chokhāmeḷā's devoted friend and a great *bhakta*, went to the village to claim his body and when he found the bones that murmured "Viṭṭhal, Viṭṭhal," he took them to Pandharpur, the home of the temple of Viṭhobā and the focal point of Maharashtrian bhakti. Ranade comments that the legend "shows that devotion to the Name of God had penetrated to the very bones of Chokha."[1] Nevertheless, no Untouchable could go into the temple of Viṭhobā at Pandharpur until independence, but had to stop at the *samādhi* of Chokhāmeḷā at the foot of the temple stairs.

Many of Chokhāmeḷā's *abhaṅgas* seem to be without reference to caste, and these are the ones which are most popular. However, at times there may be some ambiguity, as in the use of the word "pure" in the following song, and at times a Mahār word can be found in a song which seems to be simply an expression of pure joy. In the last line of this song about the pilgrimage to Pandharpur (here called Pandhari), Chokhāmeḷā's "cry" is a *dauṅḍī*, the call given by the Mahār to villagers to gather for the headman's instructions:

> Sound the cymbals raise the flags, take the road to Pandhari.
> The marketplace of Pandhari is the market of joy!
> Pilgrims meet there in ecstasy.
> So many flags they cannot be counted!
> The banks of the Bhima resound with joyous shouts.
> Let unbelievers come;
> Let them go back pure.
> Chokhāmeḷā gives this cry from his heart.
>
> *Abhaṅg* 28

Chokhāmeḷā was indeed a devout Wārkarī (pilgrim to Pandharpur), and is today an honored saint-poet in the bhakti pantheon for the great numbers who perform the yearly pilgrimage to Pandharpur. A very popular *abhaṅga* of Chokhāmeḷā and one of Soyrābāī, his wife, reveal their humble approach to God and, in subtle fashion, the place the Untouchable Chokhāmeḷā holds still in the bhakti movement. Irawati

Karve tells of the singing of this Chokhāmeḷā *abhaṅga* as the *diṇḍī* she joined wended its way on the pilgrimage to Pandharpur:[2]

> The cane is crooked, but the sugar is sweet;
> The river is winding, but the water is pure;
> The bow is bent, but the arrow is straight;
> Chokhā is uncouth, but his devotion is not.
> *[chorus]:* Why be fooled by outward appearance?
>
> *Abhaṅg* 125

Soyrābāī's best known *abhaṅga* (which has been used as an introduction to at least one modern scholarly book on religion) is equally self-deprecating:

> We'll place a leaf before you
> and I will serve you family food.
> O God, it's not fit for you,
> but imagine it sweet and accept it.
>
> *Abhaṅg* 1

Both these *abhaṅga*s reflect the strong bhakti tradition that even an Untouchable can experience the fellowship of God, and in many *abhaṅga*s Chokhāmeḷā sings within this belief. In others, however, his low place is less acceptable to him, and even less to his son Karmameḷā.

Both Chokhāmeḷā and his son use the image of eating leftover food, which was one of the stated "rights" of the Mahār, as a metaphor in their songs. Chokhāmeḷā begins this song with the salutation the Mahār was required to use, *johār* (rather than *Rām Rām* or *namaste*) in his address to God as Mother-Father:

> *Johār, Māy Bāp, Johār*
> I am the Mahār of your Mahārs.
> I am so hungry I have come for your leaving.
> I am full of hope; I am the slave of your slaves.
> Chokhā says: Here's my bowl for your leftover food.
>
> *Abhaṅg* 190

Karmameḷā uses the same image but in a very different, far more bitter way, chiding the god who, according to legend, came begging to eat in their home, and addressing him simply as "you":

You made us low caste.
Why don't you face that fact, Great Lord?
Our whole life—leftover food to eat.
You should be ashamed of this.
You have eaten in our home.
How can you deny it?
Chokhā's Karmameḷā asks:
Why did you give me life?

Abhaṅg 3

Both Chokhāmeḷā and Karmameḷā mourn their caste, but here also Karmameḷā's voice is the more troubled. Chokhā is still respectful in his address to God:

O God, my caste is low; how can I serve you?
Everyone tells me to go away; how can I see you?
When I touch anyone, they take offense.
O my Govinda, my Gopāla.
Chokhā wants your mercy.

Abhaṅg 88 (Kadam)

But Karmameḷā sings:

Are we happy when we're with you?
O Cloud-Dark One, you don't know!
The low place is our lot; the low place is our lot; the low place is our lot,
King of Gods!
We never get the good sweet food.
It's a shameful life here for us.
It's a festival of bliss for you and misery written on our faces.
Chokhā's Karmameḷā asks, O God, why is this our fate?

Abhaṅg 4

Needless to say, Karmameḷā's *abhaṅga*s are not much sung as the happy pilgrims walk toward Pandharpur.

The theme of purity is one that seems constantly on Chokhāmeḷā's mind. Here he seems to challenge the idea of pollution in a way that I think refers to caste:

The only impurity is in the five elements.
There is only one substance in the world.

Then who is pure and who is impure?
The cause of pollution is the creation of the body.
In the beginning, at the end, there is nothing but pollution.
No one knows anyone who was born pure.
Chokhā says, in wonder, who is pure?

Abhaṅg 279 (Kadam)

While many *bhaktas* have little use for orthodox texts or formal religious concepts, Chokhāmeḷā puts his castigation in clear terms of pollution:

The Vedas are polluted; the Śāstras are polluted; the Purāṇas are full of pollution.
The soul is polluted; the oversoul is polluted; the body is full of pollution.
Brahmā is polluted; Vishnu is polluted; Śaṅkar is full of pollution.
Birth is polluted; death is polluted.
Chokhā says: there's pollution at the beginning and at the end.

Abhaṅg 282 (Kadam)

But although there is some of this strong, fierce language, Chokhāmeḷā and his wife at times do seem to acknowledge a sense of the cause of pollution being "a net" that catches those who do not acknowledge the god of the *bhaktas* or, in at least one *abhaṅga*, a previous birth. Chokhā's wife Soyrābāī can sing:

The pollution of the body
is only in the body.
So says Chokhā's Mahārī.

Abhaṅg 6

But she also acknowledges something quite different in this *abhaṅga:*

When I see you, O Nārāyaṇa,
No desire is left.
No distinction between any two is left.
All is pure within me.
There was a net of pollution
which gave way to the strength of the Name.
The cord of the four bodies is broken
Says Chokhā's Mahārī.

Abhaṅg 4

The *abhaṅga* of Chokhāmeḷā's that accepts his low status as a result of bad action in a previous birth is a puzzling one. It probably refers to an obscure Puranic figure, but whatever the reference, the message is clear, all too clear to today's descendants of Chokhāmeḷā:

> Pure Chokhāmeḷā, always chanting the Name.
> I am a low caste Mahār, Nīlā in a previous birth.
> He showed disrespect to Krishna, so my birth as a Mahār.
> Chokhā says, this impurity is the fruit of our past.
>
> *Abhaṅg* 76 (Kadam)

It is this last voice, acceptance of karma, that has, along with a lack of social equality in the bhakti movement itself, deprived Chokhāmeḷā of his place as a contemporary symbol of past importance and creative ability among the Untouchables of Maharashtra who come from his Mahār caste. Raidās is a hero to Chamārs of the North, and of their caste fellows the Chambhārs of Maharashtra as well. Chambhārs participate in the great bhakti pilgrimage to the center of the *panth* at Pandharpur, through their own palanquin in honor of Rohidās (Raidās or Ravidās), but there are only a few Mahārs who remain faithful *bhakta*s. The great majority have become Buddhists, and their loud and clear voices reject the idea that untouchability is anything but a social evil, and least of all is it a state achieved by a previous birth.

Chokhāmeḷā, however, *was* important as a symbol of Mahār courage and ability in the early days of the Mahār movement. Mahārs who had become *bhakta*s called themselves Chokhāmeḷāṣ instead of their caste name. A night school founded in 1912 by Mahārs in Pune was named in honor of Chokhāmeḷā. A leader of the Untouchable movement in Maharashtra early in the twentieth century, Kisan Fago Bansode of Nagpur, used the inspirational image of Chokhāmeḷā in many ways; this poem echoes the idea of Chokhāmeḷā as model:

> Chokhā went into the temple with courage
> Why do you, ashamed, stay so far away?
> You are the very descendants of Chokhā
> Why be afraid to enter the temple?[3]

Although Chokhāmeḷā and his family are rejected as models for the current-day movement activists, one wonders if they do not point to a capacity for song, a spirit of defiance, a grasp of reality, a yearning for equality, all qualities that mark the historically important Mahar movement and the current *dalit sāhitya* school of writing, which has added immeasurably to Marathi literature.

Harish Bansode, a contemporary *dalit* poet in Marathi, is one of the few modern poets in the Ambedkar movement[4] to recognize publicly the importance of Chokhāmeḷā. In a poem entitled "Gift to my Teachers," he acknowledges that

> The blood of Chokhāmeḷā
> runs through my veins.[5]

Only then does he go on to praise Dr. Bhimrao Ramji Ambedkar, the leader of the Untouchables until his death in 1956, and Mahatma Phule, a nineteenth-century non-Brahmin reformer.

Jayashree Gokhale-Turner, who quoted the verse of Bansode above, has shown in her article how even Harish Bansode along with all other *dalit* poets of the modern period has rejected bhakti (devotion) for *vidroha* (protest, opposition). Without disputing that interpretation at all, I think there may be a continuous line from Chokhāmeḷā to the current poets who disparage the very idea of bhakti as a useless piety, as in Namdeo Dhasal's bitter words that begin with the image of the Padharpur pilgrimage and end with prostitution on the Bombay seashore:

> Crumpled-paper-Pandurang-dindi goes on singing
> winding
> the sweet notes flute
> Juhu beach fragranced
> a quarter jingle jangles
> daughters wed between their thighs[6]

Dhasal is as harsh on the contradiction between belief and reality as Chokhāmeḷā was in his day. He rejects bhakti, but his very strength, courage, and imagination in using poetry as protest may owe a bit to Chokhāmeḷā's early example. The Mahār caste that produced the extraordinary voices of Chokhāmeḷā and his family also produced the first literary movement among Untouchables. That movement bears some debt to the stance and the ethos of the caste through the years, a caste which seems to own a creative urge that breaks out into poetry when there are ears ready to hear. The early bhakti period and the post-independence urge toward equality allowed that voice to be heard.

Notes

I am grateful to Mrs. Hemant Fanse, Mrs. Rekha Damle, Dr. Pramod Kale, Mr. B. S. Shinde, Dr. S. G. Tulpule Dr. P. N. Joshi and Mr. Jayant Karve for translating help at various times.

1. R. D. Ranade, *Pathway to God in Marathi Literature* (1933; Bombay: Bhavan's Book University, 1961), pp. 149–50. Ranade's classic has been recently republished as *Mysticism in India: The Poet Saints of Maharashtra* (Albany: State University of New York Press, 1983).
2. Irawati Karve, "On the Road: A Maharashtrian Pilgrimage," *Journal of Asian Studies* 22, no. 1(1962): 13–29. Republished in Eleanor Zelliot and Maxine Berntsen, eds., *The Experience of Hinduism* (Albany: State University of New York Press, 1988). The translation used here is chiefly by Maxine Berntsen.
3. Kisan Phaguji Bansode, *Pradip* (Nagpur: Jagriti Press, n.d.), p. 48. Translated by Lalita Khambadkone and Eleanor Zelliot.
4. "Ambedkar movement" is my term for the multifaceted movement among Untouchables led by Dr. B. R. Ambedkar which has had social, political, religious and literary effects upon society that are still felt today. See Eleanor Zelliot, *From Untouchable to Dalit: Essays on the Ambedkar Movement* (New Delhi: Manohar, 1992).
5. Jayashree B. Gokhale-Turner. "*Bhakti* or *vidroha:* Continuity and Change in Dalit Sahitya." In Jayant Lele, ed., *Tradition and Modernity in Bhakti Movements* (Leiden: E. J. Brill, 1981).
6. Namdeo Dhasal, *Golpitha*, translated by Jayant Karve and Eleanor Zelliot, with the assistance of A. K Ramanujan (Pune: Nilkanth Prakashan, 1973).

Bibliography

Joshī, Kāśīnāth Anant, ed. [1923] 1967. *Śrīsakalasantgāthā*, vol. 1. Compiled by Śrīnānāmahārāj Sakhare. Pune: Śrīsantwaṅgmaya Prakāśan Mandir. *Abhaṅg* references are to this volume, unless otherwise noted.

Kadam, Sa. Bha., ed. 1969. *Śrīsant Chokhāmelā Mahārāj yanche charitr va abhaṅga gāthā.* Bombay: Sa. Bha. Kadam. *Abhaṅga*s not found in the more easily available *Śrīsakalasantgāthā* are from Kadam's collection.

Nemade, Bhalchandra. 1981. "The Revolt of the Underprivileged: Style in the Expression of the Warkari Movement in Maharashtra." In *Tradition and Modernity in Bhakti Movements,* edited by Jayant Lele. Leiden: E. J. Brill.

Vaudeville, Charlotte. 1977. "Chokhamela, An Untouchable Saint of Maharashtra." In *South Asian Digest of Regional Writing*, vol. 6: *Bhakti in South Asian Regional Literature.*

Zelliot, Eleanor. 1981. "Chokhamela and Eknath: Two Bhakti Modes of Legitimacy for Modern Change." In *Tradition and Modernity in Bhakti Movements,* edited by Jayant Lele. Leiden: E. J. Brill.

The Avatar Doctrine in the Kabīr Panth

Uma Thukral

The word *avatar* refers to the act of descending *(avataraṇa)* from the higher, immaterial world to the lower, material world.[1] According to the *Bhagavad-gītā*, God periodically descends to earth in order to destroy the wicked, protect pure souls, and reestablish dharma.[2] According to the *Bhāgavata Purāṇa*, however, God's descent is not only for the sake of killing demons and saving the earth, but also in order to free from distress the living beings oppressed by having fallen into the intrigues of ignorance, desire, and desirous deeds, to display *līlā* worth hearing and thinking about,[3] and to make pure souls active on the path of bhakti.[4] Even after having descended into the material world bearing a concrete, sensible form, however, God does not become an ordinary human being. Unlike ordinary human beings, the avatar does not, by the instigation of fate, come into the world by the path of the birth canal, experiencing the pain of dwelling in the womb and a material body composed of the five elements.[5] The bodies that the avatars manifest are pure, divine bodies made from *sattva*. They assume these bodies in the world by their own choice and become manifest in supernatural fashion. This body is not born or destroyed. Rather, it is made manifest and then is withdrawn.[6] In the material world, the activities that the incarnated God displays are not the result of karma coming to fruition. They are simply his *līlā*,[7] which the *Gītā* calls divine karma.[8] Avatars are referred to in Vedic literature, but it is in the Purāṇas and in the environment of medieval Vaiṣṇava religion that the doctrine of avatar was especially developed.

The Purāṇas do not have one single opinion about the number of avatars. Some Purāṇas describe six avatars, other ten and still others fourteen. The most frequently mentioned avatars in the Purāṇas are Matsya (fish), Kūrma (tortoise), Varāha (boar), Vāmana (dwarf), Nṛsiṃha (man-lion), Paraśurāma, Rāma, Krishna, Buddha, and Kalki. Among these avatars, the stories of the *līlā* of Rāma and Krishna receive the most elaboration and popularity. Eventually the doctrine of the avatar comes to harbor cults characterized by worship of human beings and all sorts of external display. Because of the increasing mutual enmity as a consequence of various worshippers of avatars each considering their own cult to be the most worthy of worship, there was a decrease in the spiritual component of the doctrine of avatar and an increase in sectarianism. It is for this reason that Kabīr and others opposed the doctrine of avatar. Even after the opposition of *sant*s such as Kabīr, however, there was no lessening of popular support for the doctrine of avatar in Hindu society. Tied as they were to the speciousness of the doctrine of avatar, even writers in the Kabīr Panth gave Kabīr, the fierce opponent of the avatar doctrine, the form of an avatar. In the literature of the Kabīr Panth, particularly the literature connected with the Chhattisgarh or Dharmadāsī branch, the stories connected with the *līlā* of Kabīr's birth, death and life are nurtured in the soil of Puranic ideas about avatars.

In early compositions of the Chhattisgarh branch such as the *Garuḍ bodh* (about 1646 C.E.), the Kabīr Panth displays skepticism toward the idea of the "descending" of the ultimate reality (to which the Panth gave the name "Satyapuruṣ").[9] Moreover, in various other texts opposition to the doctrine of the avatars of Rāma, Krishna, and so on, is often expressed.[10] But from then on, as Kabīr began to be considered an avatar of the Satyapuruṣ, the Kabīr Panth in fact did not remain opposed to the avatar doctrine. As avatars conforming to traditional Puranic ideas, the Kabīr Panth also accepts the ten forms of Rāma, Krishna, and so on, but in comparison with the avatars of the Satyapuruṣ the traditional avatars are considered to be of an inferior and evil power. In the Kabīr Panth this power is given the name "Nirañjan."[11] Like the Satyapuruṣ, Nirañjan is also unmanifest and without attributes *(nirguṇ)*, but Nirañjan is counterfeit *nirguṇ*.[12] He is the creator of the whole of the creation endowed with the three *guṇas* and is also known as Kāl-puruṣ.[13] According to the ideas of the Kabīr Panth, those beings who worship Nirañjan and his sons (Shiva, Vishnu and Brahmā) and their avatars keep experiencing the pains of existence. They do not find release from the wheel of transmigration.[14]

According to the Kabīr Panth whenever living beings are oppressed, having fallen into the snare of the Kāl-puruṣ, called Nirañjan, then Kabīr "descends" in human form in order to liberate them.[15] For the sake of bhakti, he gives them instruction about the unmanifest, indescribable Satyapuruṣ.[16]

In the earlier texts of the Kabīr Panth, Kabīr is considered to be the son and representative of the Satyapuruṣ. In terms of his qualities, Kabīr is exactly equal to the Satyapuruṣ, and he comes to earth at the request of the Satyapuruṣ.[17] In the text called the *Jñān prakāś,* it is said that there is a connection as between the part and the whole, between the incarnated Kabīr and the Satyapuruṣ.[18] Nonetheless, in considering such a connection and in considering Kabīr as incarnated in the form of the son of God, the nature of the avatar in the Kabīr Panth seems to be inferior to that of the avatars of the Purāṇas, since the Purāṇas accept that Parameśvar himself was incarnated in the form of Rāma, Krishna, and so on. Probably for this reason, in later texts Kabīr is himself considered to be the Satyapuruṣ. According to the *Kabīr-Kṛṣṇa-gītā,* there is no other power above Kabīr.[19] He is the original creator.[20] The creator of creators, the true Sāhab (= Satyapuruṣ) himself became incarnate in the form of Kabīr.[21] In each of the four *yuga*s—the Satya Yuga, the Tretā, the Dvāpara and the Kali Yuga—Kabīr became incarnate on earth under the four names of Sat-sukṛt, Munīndra, Karuṇāmaya, and Kabīr respectively. The stories of their *līlā* are found in various texts associated with the Chhattisgarh branch of the Kabīr Panth.[22]

In order to make Kabīr a more perfect incarnation, his birth is given a supernatural character. Like the Puranic deities, Kabīr's birth is said to have not been from a woman's womb. He is said to have descended onto a lotus flower in the form of a ball of divine light.[23] According to the *Rāmānanda-digvijaya,* itself not a Kabīr Panthī text, Kabīr was manifested in the form of an avatar in another age from the semen of a lovelorn deity who was traveling in the sky. The semen fell onto a lotus leaf.[24] According to the Chhattisgarh branch of the Kabīr Panth, Kabīr's perceived body is not a destructible body created from the five material elements.[25] Rather it is the divine "body of desire" manifested for the sake of saving living beings without its having experienced the pain of being in a woman's womb.[26]

In the Purāṇas also the bodies of the deities are said to be of this sort. They are called bodies consisting of the pure sattva quality alone.[27] The Kabīr Panthī texts also mention several other special characteristics of Kabīr's immaterial body. For instance, his feet do not quite touch the ground and his body never sweats. According to the *Jñān sāgar,* Queen Indramatī recognized the deceitful Kālpuruṣ. (Nirañjan) on the basis of the absence of these characteristics when Kālpuruṣ had taken on the form and Vaiṣṇava dress of Kabīr. By these means the queen saved herself from having to go to the world of death.[28] According to the *Jñān prakāś*, Kabīr's seat rose above the ground and his body cast no shadow. On the basis of these characteristics Kabīr's disciple Dharmadās was able to recognize Kabīr even when he had disguised himself.[29] Such characteristics of the immaterial bodies of the gods are found in the classical Sanskrit epic, the *Mahābhārata*, where Princess Damayantī recognized the gods who had disguised themselves as Prince Nala during her *svayamvara* (choosing the groom) ceremony.[30] According to the Kabīr Panth, the body of Kabīr that the world saw in Banaras was not born nor died; it was made manifest and then withdrawn. Similarly to the way that Kabīr descended on a lotus leaf in the form of a ball of light, when his *līlā* on this earth was finished he withdrew in supernatural fashion. His "corpse" was covered with a sheet but afterwards his followers found nothing under the sheet except flowers.[31]

The Kabīr Panth has also given Kabīr's life story a Puranic character. In this way the Kabīr Panthī authors, by their own imaginative powers, associated Kabīr's life with several miraculous events and also made Kabīr the leading character in some popular Puranic stories, simply changing them a little in conformity with ideas and needs of the Kabīr Panth. As a result Kabīr makes a buffalo recite the Vedas.[32] He opposes the knife blows of Rāvaṇ with straw and defeats him.[33] He revives the dead bodies of Kamāl and Kamālī[34] and miraculously foils all the plots to kill him attempted by Sultan Sikandar.[35] In much the same way, in the *Bhāgavata Purāṇa* the avatar Krishna foils the plots of Kaṃsa. Likewise, Nirañjan time and again uses his demonic power to fight against Kabīr, who nonetheless remains unconquered in much the same way as the traditional avatars Rāma and Krishna.[36] Like the leading character of the *Garuḍa Purāṇa*, Vishnu, at the time of their entering a womb, Kabīr causes the *jīva*s (souls) to remember the true purpose of their taking birth in a human womb, liberation. The only difference is that here, in place of the *jīva* taking a vow to remember Vishnu and follow the Vaiṣṇava path, the *jīva* makes the vow to remember the Satyapuruṣ, perform the Chaukā-āratī ceremony, and be initiated in the Kabīr Panth.[37] Similarly, at the time of death Kabīr protects his own devotees from Kāl and shows them the way to go to his own world of liberation, Satyalok,[38] in much the same way that Shiva and Vishnu lead their own devotees to either Shivalok or Vaikuṇṭha.[39] Making a change in the Puranic stories, the Kabīr Panth says that the Pāṇḍavas' great sacrifice in the Dvāpara Yuga was completed with the help of Kabīr.[40] In the Tretā Yuga, Rāmachandra made, by the kindness of Kabīr, the bridge to Laṅkā.[41] In order to establish the Jagannāth temple in Puri, Kabīr helped King Indradyumna and created the idols in the temple.[42] According to these Kabīr Panthī texts, it was Kabīr who did all these things and not Vishnu, as various Purāṇas say.

Because of its considering Kabīr to be a divine, supernatural being and a full avatar of the Satyapuruṣ, the Kabīr Panth has imagined Kabīr's splendor to be comprised of *sattva guṇa* and has claimed that he is endowed with divine form and qualities similar to the splendor of the Satyapuruṣ. In all this, the influence of the Purāṇas can be clearly seen. In the Kabīr Panth, however, there is not found a clear theory of any divine essence such as the "pure *sattva*" which created the supernatural body—a concept one finds in the Vaiṣṇavā Purāṇas—but such a theory is certainly found in the Kabīr Panth in symbolic and somewhat altered form. The pure *sattva* of the Purāṇas is a symbol of a supernatural state endowed with serenity, munificence, peacefulness, and purity. Kabīr Panthī authors have selected the color white as a symbol of all these divine qualities. In Kabīr Panthī literature, the sattvic nature and the supernatural character of the Satyapuruṣ, of Satyalok, of each object of this world, and of the freed *jīvas* living in it is symbolized by the color white.[43] As a result, in the Kabīr Panth, Kabīr has been portrayed in the form of an image of graceful, divine sattva quality by means of a divine dazzling light and by adorning him with white clothes.[44] The portrait of Kabīr found in the Dhanauti monastery of the Kabīr Panth reproduced in Paraśurām Chaturvedī's *Uttarī Bhārat kī sant paramparā*[45] seems to have been created on the basis of the theory of the above-mentioned divine *sattva* form of Kabīr and on the basis of the influence of the avatar doctrine. In the portraits of Kabīr generally found on the first page of the books published by the Chhattisgarh branch of the Kabīr Panth, Kabīr is shown seated on a throne like a king, with prayer beads in his hand and around his neck, a royal umbrella over his head, and his head surrounded by a shining divine halo. Such portraits of Kabīr endowed with the attributes of divinity seem to have been created for the purpose of worship on the basis of sectarian sentiments. Thus the Kabīr Panth—while it accepts as its own first guru a Kabīr who opposed prayer beads, tilaks, image worship, and the avatar doctrine—has overturned Kabīr's ideology and not only produced portraits of Kabīr endowed with divine form and qualities, reflecting its claim that Kabīr was an avatar, but has also begun propitiation and worship of his portraits, statues, and holy relics (wooden shoes, throne, tomb) together with all the external ritual practices of the Vaiṣṇavas.

Now the questions arise, what was the aim behind the Kabīr Panth's establishing Kabīr as an avatar, and how successful was the Panth in achieving this aim? In fact the Chhattisgarh branch is an old branch of the Kabīr Panth. At the time of its founding it was seeking a way to spread the Kabīr Panth. In the South, for various reasons such as the presence of other sects and the big difference in language, the Kabīr Panth had no possibility of establishing a foothold. In the north-central parts of India a large part of the population was influenced by Vaiṣṇava dharma. In conformity with Vaiṣṇava dharma were the Kabīr Panth's doctrines of truth and nonviolence and its puritanism. Hence there was a strong inherent possibility of the Kabīr Panth's being accepted among the Vaiṣṇava sects. Nonetheless the proselytization of the Kabīr Panth was difficult in the absence of a rich and attractive literature such as that of *saguṇī* Vaiṣṇavas. Hence the Kabīr Panthī authors, for the sake of attracting converts, appropriated the avatar doctrine of the Purāṇas, which has proved itself to be so very popular, and created stories with the sort of events and roles associated with that doctrine. In these stories the excellence of Kabīr, the Satyapuruṣ and Satyalok was contrasted with the Puranic gods and goddesses, avatars, and cosmology. Whether or not this was successful in exalting Kabīr's personality, there is no doubt that by means of these fictions a separate personality was created for the Kabīr Panth, and the Kabīr Panth was able to find a place in the heart of the common people. It is certain that the Chhattisgarh branch of the Kabīr Panth created a widespread organization of its own followers that tried to establish Kabīr as a supernatural being, but intellectuals never accepted this superhuman form of Kabīr.

Many branches of the Kabīr Panth itself criticize the Chhattisgarh branch for this reason. Among these branches, the Burhanpur, Badahara and Allahabad branches are prominent.[46] These branches are followers of the *Pārakh* doctrine, and do not accept any such power as God or the Satyapuruṣ in the "form of the Ultimate Reality."[47] In their opinion the ten avatars of Vishnu are merely examples of the gradual evolution of life on earth and of the various states of mental development.[48] The clear opinion of the scholars of these branches is that we have no certain knowledge about Kabīr's birth and death or his mother and father, but we have no need of entangling the personality of Kabīr in a web of supernaturalness.

Notes

1. S. Radhakrishnan, *Bhāratīya darśan* (Delhi: Rājpāl and Sons, 1972), 2:691.
2. D. V. Gokhale, ed., *Bhagavad-gītā* (Pune: Oriental Book Agency, 1950), vs. 4.18.
3. *Bhāgavata purāṇa* (Gorakhpur: Gita Press, 1971), 1.8.32–35 and 10.33.37.
4. Ibid., 1.8.20.
5. *Kalyāṇ* [Gorakhpur], special number on Vedānta, pp. 291, 296, 297.
6. Ibid., pp. 291, 292.
7. Ibid., p. 291.
8. *Bhagavad-gītā*, 4.9.
9. *Garuḍ-bodh,* in vol. 5 of Yugalānanda Bihārī, ed., *Kabīr sāgar* (Bombay: Veṅkaṭeśvar Press, ca. 1953), p. 66.

जाकर कीन्ह सकल विस्तारा । सो साहब नहिं जग औतारा ।।
योनि संकट वह नहिं आवै । वह साहब तो अछय रहावै ।।
जहां लगै जो जग में आयै । तहं लगि सबही अंश कहावै ।।

10. *Svasaṃved bodh,* in *Kabīr sāgar,* 9:148.
11. Ibid., p. 171:

एक लक्ष अरू असी हजारा । पीर पैगम्बर को अवतारा ।।
सो सब आही निरंजन वंसा । तन धरि-धरि निज पिता प्रशंसा ।।
दश औतार निरंजन केरे । राम कृष्ण सब मांही बडेरे ।।

12. *Kabīr-Kṛṣṇa-gītā* (Bombay: Veṅkaṭeśvar Press, 1952), p. 100.

श्री कृष्ण वचन ।

निरगुण अजर कबीरा जिव तारा । सरगुण भक्त जो दस औतारा ।।
नकली निरगुण निरंजन राई । जिनके हम योहदार कहाई ।।

13. Paramānanda Dās, *Kabīr manśūr* (Bombay: Veṅkaṭeśvar Press, 1952), p. 65.

14. *Bhavataraṇ-bodh,* in *Kabīr sāgar,* 7:43–45, 47–48.
15. *Kabīr-Kṛṣṇa-gītā,* p. 9:

हम हैं अजर अमर घर वासी । जहँ सब जीव को घर सुखरासी ।।
जब-जब जीव निरंजन ग्रासी । तब-तब आय काटे यम फांसी ।।

16. *Svasaṃved bodh,* p. 149:

आदि पुरूष निहअक्षर जानो । देह धरि मैं प्रकट बखानो ।
गुप्त रहों नाही लखि पाया । सो मैं जग में आनि चेताया ।।

17. Paramānanda Dās, *Kabīr manśūr,* p. 20.
18. *Jñān prakāś,* in *Kabīr sāgar,* 4:57.

हम सों पुरूष सों ऐसी आही । जल तरंग अंतर रहई ।।
जिमि रवि औ रवि तेज प्रकाशा । तिमि मोहिं पुरूष अंतर धर्मदासा ।।
हमरी सुरति गहन चित लाई । तबही पुरूष पद दर्शन पाई ।।

19. *Kabīr-Kṛṣṇa-gītā,* p. 17:

कबीर के ऊपर और नहीं कोई । आप पुरूष कबीर है सोई ।।

20. Ibid., p. 37:

निरंजन तो तन धर-धर मूवा । आदि कर्ता कहो कैसे हूवा ।।
आदि कर्ता सो सत्त कबीरा । जो नहीं गले न जले शरीरा ।।

21. Ibid., p. 89:

सब करता के करता सब दाता के दातार ।
सकल मूल सत साहेबा सो कबीर औतार ।।

22. Paramānanda Dās, *Kabīr manśūr,* p. 178. See also *Kabīr-charitra-bodh,* in *Kabīr sāgar,* vol. 11.
23. *Kabīr charitra bodh,* p. 6.
24. *Rāmānanda-digvijaya* (Rajputana: Śrī Rāmānanda Sāhitya Mandir, 1947), chap. 5, vss. 20–26.
25. *Jñān-bodh,* in *Kabīr sāgar,* 7:36:

भग की राह नहीं हम आये । जन्म मरन ना बहुरी समाये ।।
त्रिगुन पांच तत्व हम नाहीं । इच्छा रूप देह हम आहीं ।।

26. *Svasaṃved-bodh,* p. 136:

गर्भवास कबहूं नहिं आवै । निज इच्छा नर तन दरसावैं ।।
हिन्दू मुसलमान नहिं सोई । बाल वृद्ध अरू युवा न होई ।।
दाया करैं देह नर धरहिं । जीव अन्नत कोटि लै तरहिं ।।

27. Bāladev Upādhyāy, *Bhāratīya darsan* (Varanasi: Śāradā Mandir, n.d.), p. 399.
28. *Jñān sāgar,* in *Kabīr sāgar,* 1:62–64.
29. *Jñān prakāś,* p. 21:

जिन्दारूप धरी प्रभु आये । वृक्ष एक तर आसन लाये ।।
आसन अधर देह नहीं छाया । अवगति लीला गुप्त रहाया ।।

30. *Mahābhārata* (Pune: B.O.R.I., 1942), *āraṇyake parvan* 3.54.
31. *Svasaṃved-bodh,* p. 170. *Kabīr charitra bodh,* pp. 6–7.
32. Kedāranāth Dvivedī, *Kabīr aur Kabīrapantha* (Allahabad: Hindī Sāhitya Saṃmelan, 1965), p. 21.
33. Paramānanda Dās, *Kabīr manśūr,* p. 188.
34. *Svasaṃved-bodh,* pp. 143–44.
35. Paramānanda Dās, *Kabīr manśūr,* pp. 278–82.
36. In this reference see the stories related to the cosmogony and four eras *(satyug, tretā, dwāpar* and *kaliyug)* in *Nirañjan-bodh,* in *Kabīr sāgar,* vol. 7; *Anurāg-sāgar,* in *Kabīr sāgar,* vol. 2; *Śvāsaguñjar,* in *Kabīr sāgar,* vol. 10; etc.
37. *Jagajīvan-bodh,* in *Kabīr sāgar,* 5:21–25.
38. *Bhopāl-bodh,* in *Kabīr sāgar,* 5:13–15; and *Amarasiṃha-bodh,* in *Kabīr sāgar,* 4:12–13.
39. *Skandapurāṇa* (Calcutta: Manasukharay Mor, 1959), *maheśvara-khaṇḍa, adhyāya* 2 (the story of King Śveta); *Nṛsiṃhapurāṇa,* Hindi trans. (Gorakhpur: Gita Press), pp. 30–31; and *Bhāgavatapurāṇa,* vss. 6.1.–2.
40. *Anurāg sāgar,* pp. 95–96.
41. *Lakṣmaṇ-bodh,* in *Kabīr sāgar,* 5:147–48.
42. Ibid., p. 141; also *Anurāg sāgar,* pp. 101–3. Compare with the story of *Indradyumn* in *Brahm-purāṇ* (vol. 2), *Vaiṣṇav-khaṇd, Purūṣottam-kṣetra māhātmyam* (Calcutta: Mansukharay Mor, 1960).
43. *Pañcha-mudrā,* in *Kabīr sāgar,* 8:219:

कमल अनंत पंखुरी छाजै । आदि पुर्ष जहाँ आप विराजै ।।
श्वेत सिंहासन श्वेत ही काया । श्वेत ही पुर्ष श्वेत ही छाया ।।
श्वेत छत्र शिर मुकुट बिराजै । भान अनंत शोभा तहाँ लाजै ।।
श्वेत चवर शीस फहराई । भान अनंत कला वहाँ छाई ।।

Ugra-gītā, in *Kabīr sāgar,* 8:70:

पुष्प दीप जहँ पुरूष स्थाना । आदि पुरूष जहँ बैठ अमाना ।।
श्वेतै दीप श्वेत विस्तारा । श्वेतै मंदिर श्वेतै द्वारा ।।
अजर हंस है श्वेतै भाई । सदा अनंद रहै सुखराई ।।

....

श्वेतै पान श्वेत पनवेरा । श्वेत सुपारी नरियर केरा ।।
श्वेत मिठाई कदली मेवा । अजर आरती हसंक भेवा ।।

44. Paramānanda Dās, *Kabīr manśūr,* p. 187.

45. Second edition (Allahabad: Bharati Bhandar, 1964). See first photograph on p. 171.

46. Kāśī Dās, *Nirpakṣa satya jñān darśan* (Burhanpur: Kabīr Nirṇay Mandir, 1947), pp. 94–105; and Abhilāṣ Dās, *Kabīr sandeś* (Allahabad: Pārakh Prakāśak Kabīr Saṃsthān, n.d.), p. 4.

47. Abhilāṣ Dās, *Kabīr darśan* (Allahabad: Pārakh Prakāśak Kabīr Saṃsthān, 1982), pp. 448–58; Dāmodar Dās, *Nispaksa jñān praśnottar* (Burhanpur: Kabīr Nirṇay Mandir, 1969); *Timir bhāskara* (Burhanpur: Kabīr Nirṇay Mandir, 1954); and other texts of this branch of the Kabīr Panth.

48. Guru Dayāl Sāheb, *Ekadaś śabda, saṭīk* (Burhanpur: Kabīr Nirṇay Mandir, 1954), pp. 333–34; and Dāmodar Dās, *Niṣpakṣa jñān praśnottar,* pp. 160–67.

The Vitality of the *Nirguṇ* Bhajan

Sampling the Contemporary Tradition

Edward O. Henry

Nirguṇ bhajan is a category of song recognized all across northern India, from Rajasthan (Srivastava 1974; Gold 1988) to northeastern Bihar (Hansen 1986, 22:1). *Bhajan*, in a narrow sense, means hymn or devotional song. *Nirguṇ* is the vernacular of the Sanskrit *nirguṇa*, which means "without form," and refers to a supernatural entity without personal traits, an attributeless divine. *Nirguṇ* is the opposite of *saguṇ*, "having form." *Saguṇ* bhajans concern anthropomorphic gods such as Krishna and Rām, and their activities. Actual references to the divine in the *nirguṇ* bhajans in eastern Uttar Pradesh, where the research being reported was carried out, are rare. These homiletic songs exhort nonattachment and devotion as means to salvation, often by depicting a man's death, aspects of the funerary rites, and family reactions as a blunt reminder of death's inevitability and the inescapable eviction of the soul from the body. (The homily is one type of bhajan in the taxonomy developed by Slawek in his wide-ranging study (see Slawek 1986, 168).

Ann Gold reports that in Ghatiyali, a village in Rajasthan where much of her fieldwork was carried out, there is a kind of rivalry between *nirguṇ* and *saguṇ* bhajan parties (singing groups) and "most persons, whether singing participants or not, will express a definite preference for one or the other" (1988, 102). But in at least some *kīrtans* (hymn-singing sessions) in eastern Uttar Pradesh *nirguṇ* bhajans are sung right along with the *saguṇ* bhajans (Slawek 1986, 250). The general public also hears the *nirguṇ* bhajan from street singers such as the wandering mendicants called Jogīs and from the blind singers who sing in the lanes and on the trains. Neither type of singer confines himself to the *nirguṇ* bhajan, but it predominates in the repertoires of both types. It is these repertoires that are sampled here.

This paper presents and discusses ten contemporary examples of the *nirguṇ* bhajan genre. It identifies and defines the principal metaphors and motifs of the songs, and demonstrates that although the motifs and metaphors found in the recently collected songs are with few exceptions the same as those found in the author's previous collection, dating from 1971 and 1978, new lyrics are being composed.

I had previously recorded songs from the blind men in 1971 and from the Jogīs in 1971 and 1978 (see Henry 1981 and 1988 for songs and discussion). I returned to India in December 1989, after an eleven-year hiatus, expecting the traditions to have gone the way of much cultural heritage in the age of industrialism, urbanization, and electronic media. There were indeed many changes in the rural area in which much of my research had been done: more people, more homes, larger schools, and tractors, tube wells, and television sets where before there had been none. But I found both traditions—the Jogīs' lane singing in the villages and the Sūrdāses' train singing—to be vital. I videotaped the performances of *nirguṇ* bhajans by both types of singers in December 1989 and January 1990. I recorded the Jogīs in their home village in Azamgarh District, and the two blind mendicants on trains traveling from Varanasi to Mau in eastern Uttar Pradesh.

Those Jogīs whose songs are presented here are not the ascetic Hindus that many villagers assume they are. In 1978 I visited their home village in Azamgarh District, where I learned that most belonged to a caste of Muslim laborers called Jogī, and took up mendicancy at certain times of the year (especially in the harvest season). The *nirguṇ* bhajans had apparently been a part of a Nāth and Buddhist heritage, and the caste had later converted to Islam without completely discarding that heritage (see Henry 1988 for more information about the Jogīs). Many of the songs are attributed to Kabīr, the medieval poet-saint of this region, and bear similarities to the other poetry attributed to him.

The blind mendicants who sing in the trains are not affiliated in any formal way, that is, they don't comprise a guild. Blind mendicants are addressed as Sūrdās after the blind sixteenth-century Vaishnava poet-saint of North India. In the nineteen-year span in which I have periodically recorded music in eastern Uttar Pradesh, they have always worked in the trains running on the Varanasi-Mau Junction line. I have observed others as far east as Darbhanga in north-central Bihar, and one is mentioned in one of Reṇu's short stories, which are set in northeastern Bihar (Hansen 1986, 22). Blind hymn-singing mendicants, who often accompany themselves on the *daph* (a small tambourine) are sometimes heard in the lanes of towns and cities as well. I recorded one such in Chapra in western Bihar and another near the palace-fortress of the maharaja of Banaras in Ramnagar, across the Ganges from Varanasi (heard on Henry 1981, A9).

The Song Texts

Like all of the *nirguṇ* bhajans, the first two songs are predicated on the idea that the soul leaves the body at death. Implicit is the assumption that the soul's reward is commensurate with the moral quality of the life just lived. The songs do not spell out the nature of that reward. Not to prepare for the eventuality of death and possible salvation by attending to devotions is to squander the precious gift of human birth. The first song was performed by Khalāmū Jogī and the second song by Rajaman Jogī, both of village Khalsa (inadvertently spelled *Khalisa* in Henry 1988) in Azamgarh District, the home village of all of the Jogīs whose songs are discussed here.

The first song is distinct in this collection by virtue of its being in modern Hindi-Urdu. I suspect that it was written by a professional song writer and learned either from the radio or from an inexpensive newsprint booklet. The second song is a standard among this group of Jogīs and I have collected several different versions of it (see Henry 1991). Like the first song it is concerned with not wasting the precious gem of human birth, the only chance to earn salvation. The enemy is *māyā*, which snares one in delusion like the sticky molasses catches the fly, and deceives like the nourishing-looking cottonwool pods whose contents prove to be only bits of down that float away in the breeze.

1

Hey, mind-traveler, you will have to leave.
You will have to vacate the body-house.
Can you take care of the rented quarters?
On the day the landlord evicts you,
You will have to pay the rent.
When the summons comes, there will be no bail,
Regardless of whether there is a deposit.
When you are arrested you will have to go.
Hey, mind-traveler; you will have to leave.
When the court of Yam Rāj [the king of the world of the dead] opens,

When the officer comes, what answer will you give?
You will have to burn in the fire of sin.
If you don't heed me, you will heed Yam Rāj.
[unintelligible]
Says the song-writer: a gem of this value is searched out in eighty-four lakhs [= 8,400,000] of rebirths.
Hey, mind-traveler, you will have to leave.
You will have to vacate the body-house.

2

Now someone squanders the diamond; you have to leave the world, brother.
Now someone squanders the diamond.
One day a wise saint will come.
One day a wise saint will come, one day, the diamond is sold at a high price.
Keep the precious, precious diamond with care; lock it up!
Keep the precious, precious diamond with care; you have to leave the world, brother.
The fly alights on the wet molasses; when his feet and wings are stuck, when there isn't the power to fly,
Then one will cry out, "Rām, Rām" and die. Now someone squanders the precious diamond.
You have to leave the world, brother.
Look, brother! The parrot remains in the red flowers of the cottonwool trees.
When he pecks it the cottonwool flies away.
In the heart of his heart he regrets it.
You have to leave the world, brother.
Says Kabīr, listen, brother sadhu, this stanza is salvational:
Without devotion there is no salvation; this birth is squandered.
Now someone squanders the diamond.

In the fourth song, performed by Jālīm Jogī, Kabīr warns that everything is left behind at death. In the third song, sung by Bīs Rām Jogī, the narrator desperately protests this loss of the phenomenal world at death. The third song is based on the metaphor of the bride removal stage *(gaunā)* of the wedding for death and funerary rites. The *kaṅgan*, "the string which is tied round the waist of the bridegroom and the bride at time of marriage" (Pande 1979, 4) is here a symbol of the death shroud. The phrase "Everyone is chanting *Rām nām*" refers to the customary chanting by pall-bearers of *Rām nām satya hai* ("The name of God is truth").

Gold asserts that from the point of view of the *nirguṇ* bhajans, "the snares of familial attachments are in fact doubly false. That is, they are not merely ephemeral in the face of time and mortality, but also hypocritical facades even for their limited duration" (1988, 108). Although they agree that close relations are not eternal, it is seen that the *nirguṇ* bhajans in eastern Uttar Pradesh are inconsistent in their view of the sincerity of kinship relations. In many there is nothing to indicate that the grief expressed at the death of a man is not genuine. In the third song relatives grieve as the corpse is carried away and cremated. The mother grieves for as long as she lives, and the sister (with whom a man's relations are stereotypically close in North India) cries six months. But the wife in this song cries for only three days. In the fourth song the relatives are shown abhoring the corpse, and we are told that the parents' interest is but a selfish one, but the wife's grief is deep and genuine—she is said to wash her face with tears. Likewise, in the seventh song the grief is not denigrated in any way.

3

Rām, how can I wear the *kaṅgan?* My home is slipping away [being left behind].
Mother cries as long as she lives; sister cries six months.
The wife of the house [cries] three days, she who is an outsider.
My home is slipping away; how can I wear the *kaṅgan?*
My home is slipping away.
Ahead goes the groom; behind comes the groom's party.
It plays no music; everyone is chanting *Rām nām;* my home is slipping away, how can I wear the *kaṅgan?*
You have to look toward tomorrow [?], beloved, be careful.
You have to consider today [?], beloved, they [will?] put the death shroud over your face.
How can I wear the *kaṅgan*, Rām, my home is slipping away.
Four yards of muslin and the bamboo palanquin will be ordered.
Five men will circumambulate and will light the fire like Holī; my home is slipping away.
From the time the poet has come into this world, everyone understands they have to go.

Wealth, riches—nothing will go with you, everything will be left behind.
My home is slipping away.
How can I wear the *kaṅgan*, Rām, my home is slipping away.

4

Yes, the soul leaves, the soul leaves the body. Why does the body cry? The soul leaves the body.
Why cry? The soul leaves the body.
Yes, as long as the soul remains in the pitcher, everyone welcomes you.
The soul leaves, the soul leaves. Everyone will abhor you.
They will abhor: "Take it away, take it away." The soul leaves. Why cry? The soul leaves.
Yes, mother and father have a selfish interest in you; your wife washes her face with tears.
Sister will cry, tearing her hair; brother will be sad; the soul leaves the body; why does the body cry?
The soul leaves the body an empty skeleton; it will reside in an auspicious place.
Says Kabīr, listen brother sadhu: nothing goes with you.
The soul leaves; why does the body cry? The soul leaves.

The fifth song was sung by a Sūrdās named Rājendra Prasād Gaur, a man of the Goṇḍ caste from Hurmujpur Halt, on the Mau line. The singer of the sixth song was Bīs Rām Jogī. These songs both employ the phrase *rāī rāī pāī pāī joṛ ke*—"grain by grain, cent by cent" to indicate the futility of scrimping—the parrot (soul) will leave the cage (body) regardless. The phrase is not found in any of the songs in the previous collection. The fact that it occurs in two songs recorded within weeks of each other suggests that both singers may have heard it elsewhere—perhaps on the radio. Both songs also admonish that loved kin will also be left behind.

5

Oh, what of saving bit by bit, cent by cent; the parrot will leave the cage and fly.
In the world a fair of illusion; not a cent will go with you.

All wealth will be left, thousands and millions; the parrot will leave the cage and fly.
The horse and elephant will remain in the stable.
The "ride" will be on a bamboo stretcher.
You will go with a red sari stretched over you; the parrot will leave the cage and fly.
Companion, friend, whoever [?], not grandson, great-grandson, mother, father or brother will go with you.
Everything will be stirred into the fire.
This whole life passes running silently.
[incomprehensible]
The parrot leaves his cage and flies.
Says Kabīr, listen brother sadhu, affection, wealth, the love of kin—all are left behind.
The parrot leaves the cage and flies.
What of saving grain by grain,
Oh, the parrot leaves the cage and flies.

6

Why save—grain by grain, penny by penny.
The parrot will leave his cage and fly away.
A palanquin of green bamboo was made.
They lift it to the shoulders; the world is left behind.
Now the parrot will fly and leave the body.
Four men will lift the stretcher; the head will be broken.
Now torn from all the relatives,
The parrot has left the body and flown.
Says Kabīr Dās, now listen brother sadhu.
Torn from relatives and the world left behind,
The parrot will leave the cage and fly away.

There are two problems in the seventh song. The identity of the bee is unclear. The song asks who will go with the bee, suggesting that it is a metaphor for the departing soul, but a subsequent line uses swan to refer to soul. In a *nirguṇ* bhajan translated by Gold, the bee stands for the egoistic mind (1988, 116–17) but in the song at hand nothing else supports that meaning. The assertion that sin and virtue do not endure is also confusing and is contradicted in the final three songs. It may have been a phrase garbled by the singer, or one my consultants and I misinterpreted. This was another song sung by Khalāmū Jogī.

7

Bee, who will go with you?
The time of birth everyone knows; people in all the homes celebrate.
The time of birth everyone knows; the time of death no one knows.
The swan flies alone.
Bee, who will go with you?
Grasping your leg mother cries; your arm your true brother. [2x]
Grasping your head your wife cries farewell to your body.
Bee, who will go with you?
Four men meet and carry your cot to the burning ghat.
Bee, who will go with you?
Five men will circumambulate and light the mouth. [2x]
Bee, who will go with you?
Says Kabīr, listen brother sadhu, this poem is truth.
Says Kabīr, listen brother sadhu, virtue and sin go with you.
Bee, who will go with you?

The last three songs all warn that the only aspect of life that remains after death is the reputation. The first of these also reminds that Vedic religion and wealth will not save anyone either. This was sung by Jalīm Jogī:

8

I don't realize, I don't realize; the soul will leave; I don't realize; the soul will leave.
The Ganga will go, and the Jamuna, whose water is pure, will go.
All the seven seas will go. All the seven seas will go [and] the nine hundred rivers; I don't go; the soul will go.
I don't realize, I don't realize; the soul will go.
Yes, the king who rules will go; the queen who gazes upon her beauty will go.
The Veda-reading pandits will go.
I don't go and the prideful; I don't go.
The sun and the moon, whose light is extraordinary, will also go.
Says Kabīr, listen brother sadhu:
Name and reputation remain; I don't realize.
Yes, I don't go; the soul will go.

The next song, by Rājendra Gaur, contains a plug for donations along with other ideas seen above.

9

So, brother, the wise man hits with knowledge, the hunter hits with an arrow.
From not subduing the senses, the body dies.
But arrogant egoism never dies, as was said by Kabīr.
People, why is there the treacherous bandit?
This body is but a guest of four days.
Don't be proud; one day you will go for sure.
For your going a bamboo vehicle is made.
This body is but a guest of four days.
You will make thousands, millions of rupees; you won't take even a cowry with you. [2x]
No matter how much you earn, it will all stay here.
Now there is made a red shroud for you to wear.
This body is but a guest of four days.
Keep the thought in your mind. [2x]
Think about donations to the poor. [2x]
Then this is wisdom for you to think about.
This body is but a guest of four days.
Four Kahārs [= men of the water-carrying caste] will lift the palanquin, and carry you to the burning ghat. [2x]
So your pyre can be lit at the burning ghat.
This body is but a guest of four days.
So Kabīr has sung and gone to heaven.
On this earth your mark has gone, a symbol of your good work.
This body is but a guest of four days.
People, why is there this treacherous thief?
This body of yours is but a house made of dirt.

The final song, by a Sūrdās calling himself Premchandra who said he was from Bilthra Road (in Ballia District), contains a unique motif. Although the song ends with a string of conventional metaphors, the first part of the song seems to describe a mystical experience. The palanquin that carries the newly married wife off to the home of her husband and his family is a conventional metaphor for dying and the departure of the soul to its divine home. But here the redness of the husband, palanquin, and bearers suggests a mystical experience: "Oh, in the dream, in the dream at night / I saw my husband in the dream. / The red palanquin came, the red bearers, the red-colored husband all made up. / Oh, I may enter that palanquin tonight." Such passion is not seen in other of the *nirguṇ* songs I have recorded and is somewhat reminiscent of both *saguṇ* bhakti and of *qavvālī*.

One Brahman friend from Bihar who helped me with the songs said these lines resembled lines from a poem attributed to Kabīr he had studied in college: "The redness of my red (God) / Wherever I see, there it is red./ I went to see the redness / I also became red." But I had recorded nearly the exact same lines quoted by my Brahmin friend in a *qavvālī* about the Sufi saint Lal Shabaz Qalandar, performed by an entertainment group singing in Moti Mahal, a restaurant in old Delhi, in 1978. One of the members of the group told me that the song had come out in a popular recording by the singer Aruna Leila of Bangla Desh. Apparently the lines in question comprise a floating stanza.

10

Ah, hey Rām, hey yogi, ho Rām.
Brother, sing the praise of Rām.
And oh, only then take rest.
The name of Rām is such a word
That even screwed up things will be straightened out.
Oh, in the dream, in the dream at night I saw my husband in the dream. [2x]
The red palanquin came, the red bearers, the red-colored husband all made up. [2x]
Oh, I may enter that palanquin tonight. I saw my husband in the dream. [2x]
The groom's party comes lined up to my door.
I see this and my heart is pounding.
My body is on fire tonight. I saw my husband in a dream. [2x]
This is the meeting, this is the meeting. [2x]
You won't get another human birth in this world.
Even if you prostrated yourself at the feet of your husband at this very time. I saw my husband in a dream in the night. [2x]
Oh, the fruit of your bad deeds and good deeds, all will go with you. [2x]
Oh, your reputation will stay and your body fall. [2x]
There will be a meeting with your lover in the night. I saw my husband in the dream. [2x]
Kabīr went to heaven saying this.
Oh, Prem Chandra is singing this *nirguṇ* song of Kabīr. [2x]
Having gotten this body, you have forgotten this. I saw my husband in a dream. [2x]
In a dream, hey, in a dream in the night, I saw my husband in a dream.

New Syntheses of Traditional Conventions

Of the twenty or so songs I recorded in this period, only one was textually more or less identical to any of the dozens of *nirguṇ* bhajans I had previously recorded. "The Precious Diamond," two different versions of which I had previously recorded, seems to be a standard in the repertoire of the particular group of Jogīs I happened to tap (see Henry 1991 for a comparison of the three versions). But all of the others but one were new (at least to me) syntheses of the same motifs and metaphors found in songs I had recorded in previous field research, reported in Henry 1988. As discussed in that study, the composition of folk songs such as these *nirguṇ* bhajans consists largely of the reassembly of standard metaphors and motifs.

There are five common metaphors in these *nirguṇ* bhajans. One of the most common is the *gaunā* or bride-removal rite, which likens the corpse's being carried off to the burning *ghāṭ* to a bride being carried off to her husband's home. The *gaunā* is thus a metaphor for death, with submetaphors of palanquin for the stretcher upon which the corpse is carried and *kaṅgan* or string tying bride and groom together in the wedding ritual for the death shroud. The second common metaphor is the bird (usually a parrot or swan) or bee for the soul with submetaphor of cage for the body. A third metaphor is the precious gem, representing human birth, and a fourth is the guest as a metaphor for the body. "A guest of four days" refers to a human birth and the four-*āśrama* theory. The four *āśrama*s are stages of a religious man's life in times past: student, householder, forest hermit, renunciant. The fifth metaphor, thief, stands for death.

There are numerous common motifs in the songs. No one song employs all of these, but most songs use several. They include the following:

1. The soul leaves the body.
2. You can't take wealth with you when you die.
3. The corpse is lifted onto a stretcher or palanquin and carried to the cremation grounds.
4. The relatives grieve.
5. The corpse is repulsive even to close kin.
6. The corpse is carried away and cremated.
7. This world is a tempting illusion *(māyā).*

8. Kabīr exhorts that . . .
9. Salvation requires devotion.
10. Only one's reputation survives death.

The metaphors and motifs are synthesized in various ways to create the songs. The following synopses of the songs illustrate the process.

1. You must realize that your soul will leave this body it inhabits and you are responsible for what happens to your soul.

2. Now someone squanders the diamond of human birth; don't be deceived by *māyā;* without devotion there is no salvation.

3. My home is slipping away. How can I wear the *kaṅgan?* All is left behind.

4. The soul leaves the body. Why cry? Everyone will abhor the body when the soul has departed. Says Kabīr: Nothing goes with you.

5. Why strain to accumulate wealth? This is a fair of illusion. Nothing will go with you. Affection, wealth, the love of kin—all are left behind.

6. Why strain to accumulate wealth? Your soul will leave this body; it will be torn from relatives and carried away for skull-cracking and cremation.

7. Bee, who will go with you? The fruits of virtue and sin go with you. Your relatives will grieve; five men will circumambulate the corpse and ignite the mouth.

8. I don't realize the soul will leave. Sun, moon, stars, and seas will go. The king, the queen, the Veda-reading pundits will go, but name and reputation remain.

9. This body is but a guest of four days, a house made of dirt. On this earth your mark is made, a symbol of your good work.

10. In my dream I saw my husband. In a red palanquin carried by red bearers was my red husband. I may enter that palanquin tonight. You won't get another human birth. The fruit of your bad deeds and good will go with you. Your reputation will stay and your body fall away. I saw my husband in a dream.

Two aspects of the content of the songs under study here distinguish them from my previous collection. One is an emphasis on a moral idea, the notion that after death, the only aspect of one's personhood that survives is reputation. This idea, found in only one song in the previous collection (Henry 1988, 164) is clearly seen in songs 8, 9, and 10: (8) *rah jāī hāī nām nisānī* (your name and reputation will remain), (9) *neke bādī leke jāye ke do nisān banal bāy* (on this earth your mark has gone, a symbol of your good work), (10) *nekiā nisān rehi ke dehawā giralā* (oh, your reputation will stay and your body will fall). The other departure from content previously seen is the primary motif of the last song, "I saw my husband in a dream," which seems to refer to a mystical experience.

Given that the content of the songs is so much the same, the amount of formal variation is surprising. Most of the songs are in Bhojpuri, but one is in Hindi-Urdu, and is more literary than the others. None share the same tune. Some are composed to tunes from entertainment genres like the *lok gīt, birāhā, qavvālī* or *kajalī.* These indicate that the composition has taken place recently and the genre is vital. Others are composed to tunes that appear to be used only for *nirguṇ* bhajans, and are probably older (see Henry 1991 for a study of the variation of melodic settings among *nirguṇ* bhajans and its significance).

I indicated in my previous study (Henry 1988) that the songs function to help people cope with a difficult environment by obliterating the value of the phenomenal world, depriving it of meaning, and by advocating bhakti practices that have the same effect. The strategies are expressed in the local sayings of local holy men: *yeh sab māyā kā khelwāṛ hai* (all this is but a plaything of *māyā*), and *bhajan karo* (do devotions!). In anthropologist Simon Ottenberg's 1989 study of the psychology of songs in an African ritual, he speculates that the songs are "healthy for human beings psychologically" (Ottenberg 1989, 73) in that song performances create for the listeners situations in which a beneficial free association can occur.

The listeners of *nirguṇ* bhajans, like the listeners to which Ottenberg referred, do not have to pay close attention; they have heard most of the content many times. As Wendy Doniger O'Flaherty stated about myth-telling in India, it is more communion than communication (O'Flaherty 1989). Unassailable is Ottenberg's assertion that while many ritual songs paradoxically appear "to deny individual belief and feeling for the uniformity of all," they "encourage individual reflection and emotion," "providing direction, scope, and associational grounds" (Ottenberg 1989, 72–73). But whether this rumination is ultimately beneficial to the listener would seem to depend very much on that individual's personality, religiosity, and present situation (see Loeffler 1988 for thoroughly documented research demonstrating the significance of individual religiosity). How are we to know that the songs don't lead some people into depressive episodes? But in Ottenberg's favor is Reṇu's story "The Messenger," in which the messenger hears a Sūrdās singer on a train (Hansen 1986, 22): "His mind became steadier hearing the Sūrdās's songs: 'I say Rāma! / Now the dream of the bride's family has come true. The palanquin has borne her to her husband's place. / Don't cry, mother, this is the course of fate.'" For some the *nirguṇ* bhajan bears a message of hope, the hope of relief in an afterlife.

In conclusion, I had returned to India after eleven years having heard of the consumer revolution and the television revolution, and I expected to find a changed culture. But for most of the people in the village lanes and the old trains pulled by steam engine, that is, the people of the poorer classes—who constitute the majority—things are much the same, and the messages of the *nirguṇ* bhajans are still all too pertinent.

Appendix: Transliterated Song Lyrics

1

re man mosāphirī (musaphir) nikalnā paṛegā
kāyā kūṭī khālī karnā paṛegā
bhāṛe ke kwārtar ko kyā tum sambhālegā
jis din jis din tujhe ghar ka mālik nikālegā
uskā kirāyā bhī bharnā paṛegā
āyegī noṭis jamānat na hogī
parle agar kuchh amānat na hogī,
ho karke kaid tumko chalnā paṛegā
re man mosaphir nikalnā paṛegā
jamarāj ki jab ādālat chaṛhegī pūchhegā
pūchhegā hakīm to tum kyā jawāb doge
pāpõ kī agnī mẽ jalnā paṛegā
merī mat mānõ to jamarāj manāyẽge
tere kam daṇḍ tujhko mār kar bhagāyẽge
kahe gīta bandā tune hīre ka aisā
lākh chaurāsī mẽ khoyegā sotā
re man mosāphirī nikalnā paṛegā
kāyā kūtī khālī karnā paṛegā

2

ab koi hīrā ratan gawāī jagat se jālan ho bhāī
ab koi hīrā ratan gawāī
aī ek dinā aī hāĩ koī sant vibheṣa (vibhekh) ek din aī hāĩ
koī sant vibheṣā ek din hīrā mahaṅg vikāī
hīrā ratan-ratan jatan se rākhau tālā kunjī lagāyī hāĩ
ek hīrā ratan-ratan jatan se rakhau tālā kunjī lagāī
jagat se jālan ho bhāī
gilai goṛ par makkhī baiṭhī
jab pā̃v pāyar lapaṭāī
gile goṛ par makkhī baiṭhī jab pā̃w pāyar lapaṭāī
jab uṛane kī śakti nāhī̃
tab rām-rām goharāī ke marī jāī ab koī hirā ratan gawāī jagat se
jālan ho bhāī
koi hīrā ratan gawāī
semar gā̃chh rahe lāl phulawā suganā dekh lo
bhāī mārat choñch rūwāh uchhie hiyai manahī
man pachhatāhī hīrā ratan gawāī jagat se jālan ho bhāī
hīrā ratan gawāī
kahat kabīr suno bhāī sādho i pad hai nirwānī
binā bajan mukhit na bani hāĩ
brithā janam gawāī
ab koi hīrā ratan gawāī jagat se jālan ho bhāī

3

rām kaise pahinab ram gahanawā mora naiharawā [spelled *nahiyarawā*]
chhūṭā jāī
mātā rowāī ab tak jivāī bahin rowāī chheh mās
ghar ke tiriyā tīn dinan ke jo hāĩ parāya waṭ [bat?]
morā naiharawā chhūṭā jāy kaise pahinab rām gahanawā
morā naiharawā chhūṭā jāy
āge āge dulhā chalat hai ab ta pichhe chalat hai barātī
ājan bājan kuchh nā bājai rām nām sab sāth
morā naiharawā chhūṭā jāy, kaise pahinab rām gahanawā
morā naiharawā chhūṭā jāy
kālh to tujhko dekhā pyāre [?] chale sambhal ke rāh
āj to tujhko dekhā pyāre [?] mukh par kaphanī ḍāl
morā naiharawā chhūṭā jāy kaise pahinab rām gahanawā
morā naiharawā chhūṭā jāy

chār gaj ki chāragjī maṅgāya aur bāsan ki ḍolī
pāñch bhāwar paikaramā karke phū̃kta āj se holī
jab se kavi yahī jag mẽ āye jag me bāye ajiyālā
dhan daulat kuchh na jāhī hāī̃ sab kuchh chhūṭā jāy
morā naiharawā chhūṭā jāy
kaise pahinab rām gahanawā morā naiharawā chhūṭā jāy

4

hā̃ nikalat prān hā̃ nikale prān kāyā kāhẽ roī nikale ho prān kāyā
kāhẽ roī nikale ho prān
hā̃ jab tak prān rhe chhaṭ andar swāgat kare sab koī
nikalat prān sab log chhinailāī̃ hā̃ nikale prān sab log chhinailāẽ lechal
    lechal hoī nikale prān kāhẽ roī nikale ho prān
hā̃ mātā pitā sukh swārath kesab tiriyā ā̃su mukh dhoī
laṭ dhuni dhuni ke wadhinā [?] roilī̃ bharuyā ker nisān nikale ho prān
    kāyā kāhẽ roī
hā̃ nikale prān khālī bhaī ṭhaṭharī maṅgal wās hoī
kahat kabīr suno bhāī sādho saṅgawā mẽ jālẽ nā tab koī
nikale prān kāyā kāhẽ roī

5

are kā hoī rāī rāī pāyī pāyī joṛi ke, uṛi jāī suganawā pijaṛawā ke chhoṛi ke
duniyā mẽ lāgal māyā ka melā saṅgawā mẽ jāī nā ekahu udhelā
sab dhan chhoṛi jāī lākhi karoṛ ke uṛi jāī suganawā pijaṛawā ke
    chhoṛi ke
hathī wah ghoṛā waidhal rai hāī̃ ghuṛasārī
bāsawā ke ḍoliyā par hoī hāī̃ sawārī
jaibā bhāī ye lāli raṅg chundariyā ke oṛhi ke
jāī suganawā pijaṛawā ke chhoṛi ke
sathī seghāṭī kehu kāme [?] nā āī nātī parānatī māī bāp aur bhāī
sab agiyā lagāī hāī̃ khori khorike
uṛi jāī suganawā pijaṛawā ke chhoṛi ke
ye sārā umariyā dauṛ chhup ke gawaula are ye srijanahār se neh na
    lagaula kuchh to kalyān kara prabhu se man joṛi ke
uṛi jāī suganawā pijaṛawā ke chhoṛi ke
kehat kabīr suno bhāī sādho mamta dhān nātā ye pyār jaibyā toṛi ke
uṛi jāī suganawā pijaṛawā ke chhoṛi ke ka hoi ye rāī-rāī joṛi ke
are uṛi jāī hāī̃ suganawā pijaṛawā ke chhoṛi ke

6

ka karbai rāī, rāī ab pāī pāī joṛ ke
uṛi jāī hāĩ suganā pijaṛawā ke chhoṛ ke
kache, kache basawā̃ ke ḍoliyā banāwāĩ
kanihā̃ pe uṭhāy lehlāĩ māyā moh chhoṛ ke
uṛ gailāĩ suganā ab ṭhandariyā ke chhoṛ ke
chār janā mil khāṭ uṭhawai phoṛ kehalāĩ khopāṛayā
ab sab nātā toṛ ke
uṛi gailāĩ suganā pijaṛawā ke chhoṛ ke
kahat kabīr dās ab suno bhāī sādho
jānā hai jagawā se sab nātā toṛ ke
uṛi jāi hāĩ suganā pijaṛawā ke chhoṛ ke

7

bhā̃warawā ke toharā saṅg jāī
āwat ke beriyā sab koī jān ghar ghar bajat badhāī
āwat ke beriyā sab koī jāne jāt ke beriyā koī na jāne
hans akelā chali jāī
bhā̃warawā ke toharā saṅg jāī
pāw pakari ke mātā rowe bāh pakari sag bhāī [2x]
keś pakari ke tiriyā rowe baduā kā hot bidāī
bhā̃warawā ke toharā saṅg jāī
chār jāne mili khāṭ uṭhaiye le mar ghāt pahuñchāī
bhāĩwarawā ke toharā saṅg jāī
pāñchhi jane parikaramā kari hāĩ muhawā mē āg lagāī [2x]
bhā̃warawā . . .
kahat kabīr suno bhāī sādho i pad hai nirbānī
kahat kabīr suno bhāī sādho saṅg mē̃ neki badi chal jāī
bhā̃warawā ke toharā saṅg jāī

8

ham nāhī̃ jānī he ham nāhī̃ jānī prān chali jāī ham nāhī̃ jānī
hā̃ gaṅgā jāī hai jamunā jāī hāĩ jinkar nirmal pānī
sāt samundar sab chali jāī hāĩ sāt samundar sab chali jāī hāĩ
nau sau nadiyā jhulānī ham nāhī̃ jānī prāni chali jāī
ham nāhī̃ jānī ham nāhī̃ jānī prāni chali jāī hāĩ
rājā jāī hāĩ rāj karne ke rūp nirkhet rānī

vedwā paṛhi ke paṇḍit jāī hāĩ logawā bhailāĩ abhimānī
ham nahī̃ jānī hāĩ
chānd bhī jāī hāĩ suraj bhī jāī hāĩ jinkar joti nirālī
kahat kabīr suno bhāī sādho
rah jāī hāĩ nām nisānī ham nāhī̃
hā̃ ham nāhī̃ jānī prān chali jāī hāĩ ham nāhī̃ jānī

9

ā to bhāī gyānī māre gyān se, vyādhā māre tīr,
satgurū māre śabd se, sale sakal śarīr
man nā mare tan nā māre mār jāye śarīr
as mamatā kabhī nā māre kahe dās kabīr
logawā kāhe bade ḍāku veimān banal bāy, veiman banal bāy
i ta dehiyā̃ chār din ka mehmān banal bāy
ki babuā mat karā garūr
a ek din jāye hoī jarūr
ki babuā mat karā garūr
a ek din jāye hoī jarūr
tohaṅke jaye khatin bās ka viman banal bāy
i ta dehiyā chār din ke mehmān banal bāy
dhan lākh karor kamāībā [2x]
kaurī saṅg nā leke jāībā [2x]
karbā ketno kamāī
sab kuchh ihawe rahi jāī
karbā ketno kamāī
sab kuchh ihawe rahi jāī
ab tohaṅke oṛhe khatir lalka ohar banal bāy
i ta dehiya chār din ke mehmān banal bāy
ta kailā jiyrā mẽ khyāl [2x]
karā garīban pe upkār [2x]
tohaṅke soche bade budhiyā bhāī gyān banal bāy
i ta dehiyā chār din ka mehmān banal bāy
chār kahār ḍolī uṭhāī [2x]
tohaṅke mar ghaṭ le pahuchāī [2x]
ki ojain jale bade chitā asamasān *[sic]* banal bāy
i ta dehiyā chār din ke mehmān banal bāy
to dās kabīr gāke swarg chalī gaile
aur ye dhartī par āpan gun chit gaināī
to dās kabīr gāke swarg chalī gaile
aur ye dhartī par āpan gun chit gaināī

neke badi leke jāye ke do nisān banal bāy
i ta dehiyā chār din ke mehmān banal bāy
logawā kāhẽ ḍākū beimān banal bāy
aur ī śaririyā raur mātī ke makān banal bāy

10

āh, e rām, ho, ho le jogiyā ho rām
āh e, to bhāī rām a nām guna gā kar ke
are karhū bhāī bīsrām
rām a nām kī aisī wānī
bigaṛal ban jātā hai kām
are sapanawā mẽ ho, are sapanawā mẽ ratiā dekhalī u balam ke sapanawā mẽ [2x]
lālī lālī ḍolā āī, lālī kā kahārawā lālī raṅg piawā ke sājal siṅgarawā [2x]
are jāī ke bāte lāl oharawā mẽ ratiā dekhalī balam ke sapanawā mẽ [2x]
sajī ke bārāt jabū āve morī duarawā
dekhā dekhā ke dharkelā hamarā jiarawā
are āg lagelā ehi tanawā me ratiā dekhalī balamū sapanawā mẽ [2x]
ihe bāte milinā, ihe bāte julanawā [2x]
or pir se nā hoī babūā jag milanā tanawā
abahū se gailā pia charanawā ke ratiā dekhalī balam ke sapanawā mẽ [2x]
are kartab kamāī sabu, saṅgawā mẽ jālā [2x]
nekiā nisān rehi ke dehawā giralā [2x]
holā pīā ke darśanawā mẽ ratiā dekhalī balam ke sapanawā mẽ [2x]
dās kabīr kahte gaile suradhāmawā
are premchandra gāve kabīr rāg nirgunawā [2x]
pāke bhuli gaile manus tanawā ke ratiā dekhalī balam ke sapanawā mẽ [2x]
sapanawā mẽ, ho, sapanawā mẽ ratiā dekhalī balam ke sapanawā mẽ

Acknowledgments

The field research upon which this article is based was supported by a grant from San Diego State University. I transcribed and translated the song lyrics with the help of village teachers and intercollege students. I would especially like to acknowledge the assistance of Paddm Kant Pandey, Tarun Kant Pandey, Rakesh Pandey, and Manoj Kumar Mishra.

In preparing the English translations for this report I consulted with Dr. Y. N. Sinha, originally from Muzzafarpur, Bihar (on the periphery of the Bhojpuri language region); his wife, Savitri Sinha, from Chapra, Bihar, in the heart of the Bhojpuri area; and their son-in-law, Dr. Braj Bhushan Pande, originally from Ballia District in eastern Uttar Pradesh, also in the core Bhojpuri region. Because the songs are mostly in Bhojpuri, with some Hindi, they were well qualified to assist in the translation, and I am grateful for the time and interest of all who took part in this research.

Bibliography

Gold, Ann Grodzins. 1988. *Fruitful Journeys: The Ways of Rajasthani Pilgrims*. Berkeley: University of California Press.

Hansen, Kathryn, trans. 1986. *The Third Vow and Other Stories*, by Phanishwar Nath Renu. Delhi: Chanakya Publications.

Henry, Edward O. 1981. *Chant the Names of God: Village Music of the Bhojpuri Speaking Area of India* [an LP recording]. Cambridge, Mass.: Rounder Records.

———.1988. *Chant the Names of God: Music and Culture in Bhojpuri-Speaking India*. San Diego: San Diego State University Press.

———. 1991. "*Jogis* and *Nirgun Bhajan*s in Bhojpuri-Speaking India: Intra-Genre Heterogeneity, Adaptation, and Functional Shift." *Ethnomusicology* 35, no. 2:221–42.

Loeffler, Reinhold. 1988. *Islam in Practice: Religious Beliefs in a Persian Village*. Albany: State University of New York Press.

O'Flaherty, Wendy Doniger. 1989. "Impermanence and Eternity in Indian Art and Myth." In *Contemporary Indian Tradition: Voices on Culture, Nature, and the Challenge of Change*, edited by Carla M. Borden. Washington: Smithsonian Institution Press.

Ottenberg, Simon. 1989. "The Dancing Bride: Art and Indigenous Psychology in Limba Weddings." *Man*, n.s. 24, no. 1:57–78.

Pandey, Shyam Manohar. 1979. *The Hindi Oral Epic "Loriki."* Allahabad: Sahitya Bhawan.

Slawek, Stephen Matthew. 1986. "Kirtan: A Study of the Sonic Manifestations of the Divine in the Popular Hindu Culture of Banaras." Ph.D. diss., University of Illinois.

PART III
POLITICAL ACTION

Interpreting Rāmrāj
Reflections on the "Rāmāyaṇ," Bhakti, and Hindu Nationalism

Philip Lutgendorf

> Incarnate Rām slew Rāvaṇ and his host in battle
> And returned to his city with Sītā.
> Rām became raja, Ayodhya his capital,
> And their merits are sung by gods and sages.
> But humble ones who lovingly recall the name
> Triumph effortlessly over the army of delusion
> And, lost in love, return to their own bliss,
> Free of all worry—by the name's grace.
> —Tulsīdās, *Rāmcharitmānas*, 1.25.5–8

A Contested Ideal

The man revered as the father of Indian independence, Mohandas Gandhi, was a devoted reader of the sixteenth-century Hindi epic *Rāmcharitmānas* (The lake of the acts of Rām"), an influential retelling of the *Rāmāyaṇ* story, and was fond of quoting from it in his conversations and speeches.[1] Though he studied the scriptures of many faiths, Gandhi once observed that he considered the *Mānas* (as devotees commonly abbreviate its title) to be "the greatest book of all devotional literature" (Gandhi 1968, 47), and even stated that he drew the inspiration for his Non-Cooperation Movement from an episode in which the epic's heroine, Sītā, though a helpless captive of the tyrannical Rāvaṇ, resists complying with his will (Gopal 1977, viii). A more obvious and pervasive borrowing from the epic, however, was of the term Rāmrāj—"the righteous reign of Rām"—which Gandhi frequently used to articulate his dream of an independent India, often equating it with or preferring it to the term *svarāj* (self-rule) used by other leaders of the freedom struggle (Bose 1948, 255). For Gandhi (1925, 295), Rāmrāj was "not only the political Home Rule but also *dharmaraj* . . . which was something higher than ordinary political emancipation. . . ." It was indeed Gandhi's invocation of such terms as Rāmrāj and *dharmarāj* and his quotations and homely anecdotes from the *Rāmāyaṇ* that enabled him to strike a sympathetic chord in tens of millions of Indians, especially those in rural areas, for nostalgia for Rām's mythical reign had long persisted, in Norvin Hein's words (1972, 100),[2] as "one of the few vital indigenous political ideas remaining in the vastly unpolitical mind of the old-time Indian peasant." Effective as it was, Gandhi's invocation of this centuries-old paradigm, and of the text through which it was best known, came under criticism from secularists who worried over some of the conservative, even reactionary passages in the poem—most notably, its confidence in the divine rightness of a rigidly stratified social hierarchy. Gandhi's reply to such critics was that he was concerned with the spirit rather than the letter of the text,[3] and this allowed him to come up with such startlingly unorthodox interpretations as the following, in which the epic's vision of a divine autocracy is transformed into a populist democracy through an appeal to the moral principle of self-abnegation (1932, 92): "Rāmrāj means rule of the people. A person like Rām would never wish to rule."

In the fifth decade after independence, Rāmrāj remains a much-used slogan in Indian politics, a signifier of social justice and material abundance that is predictably invoked by candidates in every parliamentary election and that sometimes figures prominently in party platforms. Yet not all who use the term share Gandhi's positive interpretation of its import. In *The Shadow of Ram Rajya over India*, an impassioned polemic that appeared in the aftermath of Prime Minister Indira Gandhi's period of emergency rule, journalist Prem Nath Bazaz argued that nationalist and Gandhian thought was indeed permeated by the notion of Rāmrāj, but that this notion had proven itself to be inherently reactionary, communalist, and undemocratic, and that its continued invocation could only lead India on a spiraling downward course toward violence, corruption, and ultimate dictatorship. "The bitter truth," wrote Bazaz (1980, 11), "is that dictatorship and authoritarianism are inherent in what the nationalists extol as ancient Indian culture." He contrasted the Rāmrāj paradigm with other "liberal and democratic currents" that he saw as historically present in Indian culture, for example, the *nirguṇ* devotional traditions of Kabīr and the *sants*.

Which, one may ask, is the real Rāmrāj—the Mahatma's perpetual wellspring of egalitarianism, or the journalist's stagnant reservoir of oppression? Although the observations of Gandhi and Bazaz are phrased in the language of twentieth-century politics, the debate they reveal is not a new one, for like the broader notion of dharma,

Rāmrāj has long been, in Wendy Doniger's memorable phrase (1978, xiv), "a problem rather than a concept"—a paradigm whose meaning has often been contested by conflicting interest groups. Moreover, debate over the interpretation of Rāmrāj is rooted in a paradox which runs through the *Rāmāyaṇ* tradition: an apparent dissonance between the letter and spirit of the epic that has allowed for its appropriation by both power wielding elites and disenfranchised lower orders. In the remainder of this essay, I will examine this paradox by considering some variations on the theme of Rāmrāj articulated by a number of texts and given concrete expression through a variety of sociopolitical movements, especially during the past century. Ultimately I will consider the question of whether the concept of Rāmrāj remains, in late-twentieth-century India, a fluid and contestable one.

Reigning Paradox

For the locus classicus of the concept, the modern scholar is likely to turn to the Rām story in its various literary avatars, and is equally apt to privilege the earliest of these—the Sanskrit poem *Rāmāyaṇa* attributed to Vālmīki (c. second–first century B.C.E.). An examination of relevant verses makes clear, however, that the cultural ideal of Rāmrāj owes little to the exegesis of specific literary passages. For although Vālmīki's epic does indeed include, at the end of its core narrative, a description of the condition of the kingdom of Ayodhya during Rām's lengthy reign, what is immediately striking about this passage is its brevity: less than ten *ślokas* out of some twenty-four thousand. Another influential *Rāmāyaṇ* text in Sanskrit, the *Adhyātmā Rāmāyaṇa* (c. fifteenth century) dispenses with the theme in a mere four couplets, and the medieval Hindi version of which Gandhi was so fond (and which most modern North Indians know best)—the *Mānas* of Tulsīdās—describes Rām's reign in only thirty-six of its roughly thirteen thousand lines.

The actual descriptions vary little among these three texts that span nearly two millennia and that differ in many other details of their interpretation of the story. All three sketch a formulaic vision of a utopia in which the most basic problems of human life have been transcended: beyond the achievement of social peace and harmony, old age and disease have been conquered, snakes and vermin no longer afflict people, robbery is unknown, and children never die before their parents or husbands before their wives.[4] The vision of a peaceable kingdom extends even beyond the human realm: all animals are said to live in harmony, trees to flower and bear fruit throughout the year, and clouds to yield rain whenever it is needed. A cool, gentle, and fragrant breeze, it is said, fanned Ayodhya continuously for eleven thousand years.

Perusing these passages, a modern reader may question how it is that Rāmrāj ever came to serve as a "political" ideal at all. The texts offer no practical or legalistic prescription for its establishment—in the sense that, say, the *Qur'ān* does for the establishment of Islam—because the *Rāmāyaṇ* (though often characterized by later commentators as a *dharmaśāstra* or "treatise on dharma") is not a collection of maxims or laws, but of acts or "characteristic behavior" *(charitra)*. Rāmrāj need not receive much verbal description in *Rāmāyaṇ* texts because it is assumed that its qualities are self-evident to the audience in the wider context of the story. It is the presence of Rām on the throne that is its defining feature, and the state of grace under which his people live is but an extension of his own personality and behavior. And since the epic itself constitutes an extended meditation on that personality and behavior, we may understand the whole of the *Rāmāyaṇ* to be, in a sense, an exposition of the nature of Rāmrāj. Rām's devotion to his understanding of dharma throughout the story establishes the parameters or boundaries of human behavior—*maryādā*, in the archaic sense of this important term (which also connotes dignity and social propriety); boundaries that, if adhered to, facilitate the boundlessly blessed state so tersely sketched by the poets. The vision of Rāmrāj inevitably depends on the understanding of Rām and his behavior, and here we must recall that the acts of Rām have been the subject of gradually evolving and at times conflicting interpretation.

Pertinent here is a distinction, which I shall examine further in a moment, between two aspects of Rām's character as an exemplar of dharma. We may relate these to the dual nature of dharma itself, which has from an early period been metaphorically compared to a *setu,* a term connoting both a "boundary"—a wall or dam—and a "connection" or bridge. The former meaning suggests its restraining, regulating character; the latter its expansive possibilities as a causeway to a further or higher realm.

In his analysis of the central themes of Vālmīki's Sanskrit epic, Sheldon Pollock argues that there exists a fundamental paradox between the explicit and implicit meanings of the story. Explicitly, the poem presents a vast meditation on dharma and on the nature of kingship, in which Pollock sees the reflection of historical processes occurring roughly contemporaneous with its composition—the coalescence of a system of hierarchical social organization and the rise of powerful hereditary monarchies. In its portrayal of an ideal kingdom under an ideal ruling family, the epic attempts to resolve problems of social competition and dynastic succession through an appeal to hierarchical order and submission to senior male authority (Pollock 1986, 16).

But there is another problem that the epic addresses only implicitly: that of the yearning of the individual (particularly within a rigidly hierarchical society) for autonomy and freedom. Insofar as Vālmīki offers any "solution" to this problem, it is Rām himself: a "spiritualized king" who transcends the limits of his Kṣatriya (warrior) class to incorporate the highest functions of the Brahmin order, who unites the city and the forest and the life-stages of householder and ascetic, and who reaches out with friendship and compassion to the lowly; a hero who contradicts expectations and oversteps conventional boundaries. According to Pollock, this characterization has profound implications (1986, 72):

> If, in his course of action, Rāma explicitly affirms hierarchical subordination, the spiritual commitment that allows for his utopian rule seems explicitly to oppose it. . . . Hierarchical life and the separation of "powers" that underpins it, which the poem elsewhere unambiguously attempts to validate, appears at the highest and critical level to be questioned, and a reformulation is offered in its place.

This reformulation has as its symbol the person of Rām: the divinized king whose role has expanded to fill both heaven and earth. This implicit understanding of Rām suggests the inevitability of his association with Vishnu, the "expanding" deity whose self-limitation in incarnate forms is the touchstone of his transcendence; the Kṣatriya guardian of this world who ultimately usurps the status of the absolute Brahman.

Another and not unrelated aspect of Rām's characterization was likewise to prove important in the subsequent evolution of his religious role: his portrayal as a suffering hero, whose strength of character is revealed through adversity. The unjust forest exile to which he willingly submits—*vanvās*—connotes suffering, and it is as a suffering God that medieval poets can invoke him (as Tulsīdās often does) as "brother to the wretched" *(dīn bandhu)*. The notion that Rām's trials manifest his true nature is eloquently expressed in a modern Hindi saying: "Only when Rām went to the forest did he become Rām."[5] The full implications of this understanding, and its relevance to my present topic, have been articulated by a renowned *Mānas* expounder, Rāmkiṅkar Upādhyāy, who has declared that Rāmrāj itself must be reckoned to begin not from the moment of Rām's installation on the throne of Ayodhya, but paradoxically, from the moment when he steps across its borders into exile (Upādhyāy 1983).[6]

Here we should recall a fact stressed by contemporary *Rāmāyaṇ* scholarship: that the epic of Rām, in the conception of its audience, has always been primarily a story and only secondarily a body of written texts.[7] Although individual authors, patrons, and communities have periodically aspired to cast this tale in enduring and authoritative form—the versions of Vālmīki, Kampan, and Tulsīdās, for example, have each functioned in this way in certain regions and periods—the multiformity of the narrative has always survived such efforts. Recognizing the distinction between story and text—and the primacy of the former over the latter—can help to clarify the seeming contradiction between the spirit and letter of Rāmrāj, for whereas rigid ideological prescriptions exist as specific passages in specific texts (and may be tempered by other passages in other texts or even, indeed, in the same one),[8] the "liberating" potential of the story exists more globally, at the level of what A. K. Ramanujan terms the "meta-*Rāmāyaṇ*," which encompasses a rich oral tradition of folk variants (Richman 1991, 33).

Two sets of writings from the medieval period, when the cult of Rām rose to prominence in many parts of India, illustrate the further articulation of the themes I have identified as central to the earliest extant *Rāmāyaṇ*. In a recent essay on "*Rāmāyaṇa* and the Political Imaginary in Medieval India," Pollock notes that despite the tremendous influence of Vālmīki's Sanskrit epic as a literary model and the story's presumed popularity as a folk narrative, there is no evidence that it played a significant role in either political discourse or cultic practice during the first millennium C.E. (Pollock 1991a, 4).[9] Beginning in roughly the twelfth century, however, certain kings in northern and central India began building temples to Rām, and a few went so far as to assert in their inscriptions that they *were* Rām incarnate—and these assertions often occurred in the context of polemic against Turkic and Afghan invaders from the northwest. Thus the Chalukya king Jayasiṃha Siddharājā (1094–1143) was identified (in Merutuṅga's c. fourteenth-century *Prabandhachintāmaṇi*) as an avatar of Rām, and was said to have achieved victory over the "*mlechchha* chiefs," in token of which he received a congratulatory emissary from King Vibhīṣaṇ of Lanka, Rām's immortal ally (Pollock 1991a, 23–24). Similarly the Sanskrit epic *Pṛthvīrājavijaya*, composed sometime between 1178 and 1193 by a court panegyrist of the last Hindu king of Delhi, used an explicit *Rāmāyaṇ* model to recount the campaigns of its hero against Muhammad Gorī—e.g., Brahmā appears before Vishnu to protest the presence of a *mlechchha* army on the shores of Pushkar Lake (whose holy waters are polluted by the soldiers' menstruating wives), and Rām, incarnating as Pṛthvīrāj III, takes a vow to slay these "demons in the form of men"; this king is later said to have restored "the riches and joys of *Rāmarājya* in the very midst of the Kali age" (Pollock 1991a, 26–28). Such examples can be multiplied, and according to Pollock (1991a, 29–32) they roughly parallel, chronologically and geographically, the course of Turko-Afghan expansion over northern and central India during the twelfth and thirteenth centuries.

In reflecting on why the *Rāmāyaṇ* became the metaphor-of-choice for embattled kings confronted with an expansionist alien culture, Pollock invokes certain features of Rām's *charit* that he has highlighted in his earlier writings: the fact that the epic presents a paradigm for both the divinization of a king and the demonization of an enemy (Pollock 1991b, 15–54, 68–84). A ruler who presents himself as upholding dharma partakes in the divinity of Rām, while outsiders who are held to imperil dharma assume the inhuman, perverse qualities of the epic's *rākṣasas*. From this perspective, the *Rāmāyaṇ* offered the only epic model suitable to the time, since the *Mahābhārata*'s darker vision of realpolitik presents a more ambiguous, Kali Yuga world in which evil is broadly diffused throughout society and the enemy ultimately proves to be one's kinsman.

The modest number of Sanskrit inscriptions, panegyrics, and ritual compendia cited by Pollock suggest one reading of the theme of Rāmrāj as an essentially conservative principle—a defense of a threatened order as interpreted by certain of its privileged representatives—which accords well with what I have earlier identified (again following Pollock) as a more explicit reading of the story. How widely this interpretation was shared by the broader population is open to question. Royal publicists may have eulogized a given monarch as Rām incarnate, but did his subjects subscribe to this identification? If Rāmrāj was a cherished ideal, it was also, realistically speaking, a tall order. Elite appropriation of *Rāmāyaṇ* themes presupposes the wide popularity of the story, and other elements in the population must have had their own interpretation of Rām and his virtues.

Although it is unfortunately impossible to determine whether late-twelfth-century peasants of the Ajmer region agreed that the "riches and joys" of Rāmrāj had been restored by Pṛthvīrāj III, an alternative interpretation of the story is indeed represented by another, and far more substantial, body of texts: the regional language *Rāmāyaṇ* epics. Although the period that saw the new royal preoccupation with Rām coincided roughly with that of the composition of the earliest of these, both ideologically and geographically these popular epics—which frequently incorporate folktales and local lore not found in the Sanskrit archetype—follow a different trajectory from that traced by Pollock for royal inscriptions and royally-patronized temples. Thus the earliest major *Rāmāyaṇ* in a local language, the great Tamil *Irāmavatāram* of Kampan, was composed in the extreme south, sometime between the ninth and twelfth centuries, and betrays no concern for political events occurring late in that period and far to the north. Instead, in both its poetry and theology, it shows the influence of the Ālvār poet-saints of earlier centuries, whose fervent devotion to Vishnu in the form of his human incarnations Rām and (more often) Krishna, emphasized themes of love, compassion, and universal accessibility. Kampan's Rāvaṇ is an arrogant and suitably demonic anti-hero, yet he is simultaneously humanized as a cultivated Dravidian monarch, and is ultimately redeemed, in death, by Rām's grace.[10] This bhakti orientation, which draws on the implicit reading of Rām as a suffering and loving God-man, will permeate later vernacular *Rāmāyaṇ*s, leading to an interpretation of the story that significantly expands beyond the dual paradigm of divine kingship and demonic otherhood so central to Vālmīkī.

To venture a broad generalization (which I will develop with a specific example shortly), the devotional *Rāmāyaṇ*s present a pietistic vision in which Rām's divinity entirely overwhelms his worldly kingship, so that his affinity to mundane rulers (especially during the present dark age) is downplayed or ignored. At the same time, the demonic nature of his opponents becomes, in many instances, allegorized as the consuming desire and egoism of worldly people, who can ultimately be purified by the arrows of his grace.[11] Of paramount importance to these texts is the universal accessibility of Rām, especially via his name, which is increasingly seen as a liberating mantra of greater power and efficacy than the Brahmin-mediated formulae of the Vedas. When bhakti-inspired poets, whatever their social background, emphasize Rāmrāj, it is likely to reflect the spiritual yearning of common people and so to be more in accord with what I have identified as an implicit reading of the Sanskrit epic.

The King and the Crow

Having made these general observations, I return to the treatment of Rāmrāj found in one of the most influential of the regional-language epics: the *Mānas* of Tulsīdās. The composition of this bhakti-saturated poem, which dates itself to 1574, occurred during the height of Mughal hegemony.[12] Yet despite the fact that its author was a classically educated pandit who spent most of his adult life in a pilgrimage center (Kashi or Banaras) that had occasionally suffered the visitations of Muslim iconoclasts, his writings betray little evidence of the cultural collision of the Brahmanical and Islamic worldviews. Indeed, the *Mānas* shows a striking absence of overtly political allusions, even in contexts in which one might expect some reflection on contemporary events—e.g., the poet's long diatribe (to be discussed below) against the evils of the Kali Yuga.

To suggest the predominant character of Tulsīdās's bhakti-inspired meditation on the theme of Rāmrāj, I will examine two passages from the *Mānas* in greater detail—passages that I believe are intentionally juxtaposed. Both occur in the seventh and final book, *Uttar kāṇḍ*, which, in keeping with the long tradition of seven-part *Rāmāyaṇ* compositions, is essentially an epilogue to the main narrative.[13] The first passage occurs about a quarter way into the final book, following the account of the hero's return to Ayodhya, his reunion with his faithful brothers Bharat and Śatrughna, and his consecration as king.

Vālmīki's account of Rāmrāj begins with a detailed inventory of the Vedic sacrifices performed by King Rām—*pauṇḍarīka, aśvamedha, vājapeya*, and so on—a kind of congealed kingly dharma in the worldview of the Sanskrit epic age, which sets the tone for the catalogue of meritorious fruits to follow. In contrast, Tulsīdās makes only formulaic mention of Vedic *yajñas* ("The Lord performed tens of millions of horse sacrifices" [7.24.1]), but introduces his account of Rāmrāj with a prolonged and touching scene in which Rām bids farewell to the beloved allies of his forest adventures—the lowly monkeys and bears and the impure Niṣād tribesmen, bridging the two passages with the verse:

> Observing Rām's behavior *(charitra),* the people of Ayodhya
> Exclaimed again and again, "Noble is the bounteous one!"
>
> 7.20.6

The most influential of twentieth-century *Mānas* commentaries, the twelve-volume *Mānas pīyūṣ* ("Nectar of the *Mānas*") reckons the account of Rāmrāj to begin with this farewell scene, and emphasizes the gracious compassion Rām displays toward his lowly cohorts as indicative of the tenor of his reign. The commentator points out that to admire virtuous deeds implies making an effort to reproduce them, according to the Sanskrit adage, "As the king is, so are his subjects" *(yathā rājā tathā prajā);* hence, he continues, Rāmrāj signifies the imitation *(anukaraṇ)* of Rām (Śaraṇ 1956, 12.169). By juxtaposing the account of Rāmrāj with this scene, Tulsīdās indeed appears to have given greater emphasis to social compassion than to ritual duty.

The ensuing account of Rāmrāj, as already noted, briefly sketches a world of perfect order regulated by the precepts of authoritative scripture:

> Everyone was devoted to his own duty
> According to class and stage of life,
> And ever following the Vedic path
> Was happy and free from fear, sorrow, disease.
>
> 7.20

> All men displayed mutual affection
> And, intent on scriptural precept,
> Followed their proper duty.
>
> 7.21.2

Yet under Rām's benevolent direction, this impeccable order, far from restricting human beings, produced a freedom hardly mundane at all—a world in which (echoing Vālmīki's account) even elemental limitations were transcended:

No one was stricken by untimely death,
All had beautiful and healthy bodies.

7.21.5

Forest trees ever blossomed and bore fruit,
Elephant and tiger dwelt in harmony.
Trees and creepers dripped honey on request,
Cows yielded milk at a mere wish,
The earth was always filled with crops,
The Kṛta age reappeared in the Tretā.

7.23. 1,5,6

The moon flooded the earth with nectar,
The sun offered just enough heat,
You asked the cloud and it released rain—
In the realm of Rāmchandra!

7.23

This vision of a utopia in which time itself is reversed—allowing the reappearance, during the second cosmic aeon, of the effortlessly blessed state of humanity during the preceding, Golden Age—resonates with one of the most persistent themes in Hindu discourse: the nostalgia for a lost era when Vedic wisdom was clearly understood, dharma firmly established, and humankind uniformly virtuous. Taken by itself, the description of Rāmrāj might seem a prescription for restoration of the past.

Yet this passage cannot be "taken by itself," for the *Uttar kāṇḍ* is far from over. In the remaining three-fourths of the epilogue, Tulsīdās boldly discards Vālmīki's narrative framework and, instead of recounting the birth stories of major characters and the tale of Sītā's banishment, weaves a tapestry of didactic tales that emphasize the preeminence of the path of bhakti in approaching Rām. To expound this theme, he introduces a new narrator and a new story-frame: one of the "four dialogues" *(chār saṃvād)* around which he has structured his retelling of the epic (Lutgendorf 1989). Here the inquirer is the solar eagle Garuḍa, vehicle of Lord Vishnu. Like the goddess Pārvatī and the sage Bharadvāj, who serve as questioners in earlier framing dialogues, Garuḍa becomes troubled by a doubt concerning Rām's godhood, occasioned by beholding the hero helplessly ensnared by a demonic serpent-weapon during the battle with Rāvaṇ: can this "limited" human being really be one with the Absolute (7.58)? To answer this question, Lord Shiva sends Garuḍa to the summit of the mysterious Blue Mountain, where, beneath an immense banyan tree, an immortal crow *(kāk)* named Bhuśuṇḍī ceaselessly narrates the story of Rām to a devout audience of birds (7.57.7).

One of the epic's most memorable characters, Kāk Bhuśuṇḍī appears to have been developed by Tulsīdās out of older *Rāmāyaṇ*-related lore.[14] According to the autobiography he recounts to Garuḍa, he is a spiritual seeker whose adventures span numerous rebirths, until he ultimately learns the story of Rām from the sage Lomaś, becomes a fervent devotee of the infant Lord of Ayodhya, and secures the boon of immortality. By angering the sage, however, Bhuśuṇḍī also incurs a curse to take on the form of a crow, the harsh-voiced, carrion-eating fowl whom Hindus despise as the "outcaste *(Chaṇḍāl)* among birds" (7.112.15). Though the sage later relents and offers to ease the terms of the curse, Bhuśuṇḍī accepts them gladly, presumably because the lowly crow form suits his hard-won devotional humility. Moreover, it gives him the freedom to fly to Ayodhya whenever, in the ceaseless round of the aeons, Lord Rām takes his Tretā Yuga incarnation there, and to witness with his own eyes the childhood pastimes of the Lord (7.75.2).

All of this seemingly carries us far from the core *Rāmāyaṇ* narrative and its concluding paradigm of an ideal polity. Yet even in the midst of devotional metaphysics, Tulsīdās retains his interest in mundane affairs, and so he makes Bhuśuṇḍī, in recounting his long chain of previous births, linger over one during a preceding Kali Yuga—the fourth age which, by Hindu reckoning, had again come full circle as that in which the poet and his audience lived. As in the "prophetic" verses describing the Kali Yuga common to many of the medieval Purāṇas,[15] this passage offers the poet a pretense for a critique of the evils he perceived in his own society. In this dark counterpart to the luminous vision of Rāmrāj described earlier, he portrays an age in which Vedic order has been overturned, resulting in a chaos of heresies and utter social corruption.

Religion is tainted by the Kali Age's filth,
The holy books become concealed
While hypocrites spin their own fancies
And promulgate numberless sects.

7.97a

There's no rule of caste or life-stages
And all men and women live opposed to scripture.
Brahmins sell scriptures, kings prey on their subjects
And no one obeys Vedic injunction.

7.98. 1,2

Brahmins are illiterate, greedy, lustful,
Reprehensible fools keeping low-caste concubines.
Śūdras mutter prayers, do austerities and fasts
And sitting on high seats expound the Purāṇas.

7.100.8,9

Even as, under Rāmrāj, the willing adherence of Rām's subjects to dharma produced a state of heaven on earth, so the refusal of the people of the Kali Yuga to adhere to scriptural precept results in the sufferings of an earthly hell:

Racked by disease, men find no pleasure anywhere,
Yet wallow in vain pride and enmity.
Their life span barely a dozen years,
They fancy themselves outliving an aeon!
The Dark Age makes all mankind desperate,
No one respects even sisters or daughters.
Without contentment, discrimination, detachment,
High and low are reduced to beggary.

7.102.3–6

This jeremiad, which goes on for some seventy lines (roughly twice as long as the account of Rāmrāj), may at first appear to be a strident call for restoration of the past, emphasizing how far society has fallen from its ideal standard. Such an interpretation, however, misses the full implications of this passage, which, significantly, the popular and ubiquitous Gita Press edition of the epic refers to as "the Eulogy of the Kali Yuga" *(kali mahimā)* (Poddar 1939). The heading is not facetious, for, paradoxically, the long diatribe against the dark age ends not with condemnation, but with praise, and with the promise of a new dispensation of grace, now accessible to all through the power of the divine name:

Listen, Garuda, the Kali age
Is the treasury of sins and vices,

Yet it has one great virtue:
Salvation may be had without effort!

The state attained in the first three ages
By worship, sacrifice, and austerity,
Truly is gained by Kali age people
By the name of the Lord.

7. 102a,b

The dark age has no compeer
For one possessing faith,
For by singing the pure fame of Rām
Liberation comes without exertion!

7.103

To be sure, the Hindi poet's powerful idealization of tradition is capable of eliciting nostalgia for the past, yet his insistence on carrying his narrative forward into the troubled present shows a recognition that the past is irretrievable; as one *Mānas* scholar in Banaras remarked to me, interpreting this passage, "In the Kali Yuga, the *dharmasetu* has been completely destroyed; it can never be rebuilt." According to this man's view, Tulsīdās's prescription for the ills of the age was not a reconstruction of the vanished order but a new, egalitarian expedient—not a Sanskritic Rāmrāj of the elite, but a *nāmrāj* (reign of the name), promulgated by a saintly crow and accessible to even the lowliest of human beings (C. N. Singh 1983).

I have discussed the *Mānas* at some length because of the extraordinary status which it has assumed during the past four centuries, and because its departures from the traditional *Rāmāyaṇ* narrative are not well known outside India. Although the Hindi poem retains much of the Sanskrit epic's explicit message of hierarchical subordination within family and society, it uses the ideology of bhakti to foreground and considerably expand on what I have termed the implicit subtext of the older story: its (spiritually) liberating and (socially) liberal dimension. Indeed, the tremendous emphasis given, throughout the poem, to the divine name—which Tulsīdās hails as "greater even than Rām himself" (1.23)—suggests that its author was closer in spiritual sensibility to the *sant* poets of the *nirguṇ* "school" of bhakti than is commonly understood.

The juxtaposition of conservative and liberal messages in a persuasive and accessible vernacular epic represented, in sixteenth century North India, a powerful new articulation of the paradox central to the *Rāmāyaṇ* tradition. Over subsequent centuries, a rising tide of manuscript and (later) printed editions, commentaries, and treatises documents the growing prestige of the *Mānas* among ever wider audiences, and its patronage by a range of caste communities and economic classes.[16] The research of Christopher Bayly and others has shown the importance of Hindu revivalism to the development of Indian nationalism and has noted that political ideas in nineteenth century India "were almost unavoidably expressed in terms of religious tradition, because this was the language of social comment" (Bayly 1975, 6). That the *Mānas* too became—with paradoxes intact—part of the language of social comment is demonstrated by the varied uses of its themes in nineteenth and twentieth century political movements, some examples of which I will now examine. For Rāmrāj has been viewed both as a harmonious but hierarchical order, in which the privileged confidently enjoy their status and the dispossessed keep within their limits, or conversely, as a kingdom of righteousness, in which the possibilities of freedom are made accessible to all.

Liberation by the Book

Not the least of the paradoxes associated with the *Mānas* is the fact that this text—the social teachings of which uphold the hierarchical order encoded in the Sanskrit term *varṇāśrarnadharma* (the system of classes and stages of life), advocate reverence for Brahmins, and express, at times, sharp censure of any claims to religious authority by those relegated to the rank of Śūdra or lower—should have been enthusiastically received by groups of low social and economic status, and adopted as an inspirational scripture associated with collective programs of "upward mobility." We can begin with the Rāmānandī ascetics who were probably among the earliest promulgators of Tulsīdās's epic and who eventually championed it as their primary scripture, identifying it as a "fifth Veda" that represented in the language of common people the distillation of the spiritual wisdom preserved in the Sanskrit scriptures of the past.[17] Rāmānandīs were considered among the most liberal of Vaiṣṇava ascetics, who took as their slogan a couplet attributed to their founder, Rāmānand: "Do not inquire of anyone concerning his caste or community; whoever worships the Lord belongs to Him,"[18] and who embraced relaxed policies on intercaste commensality and on the initiation of women, low castes, and even Muslims. Such policies appear to have contributed to their success, for by the nineteenth century they had replaced the Daśnāmī (Śaṅkarāchārya) order of sannyasis as the leading ascetic group in northern India and had assumed dominant roles in many pilgrimage centers and trade networks. Peter van der Veer has termed them an "open category" of ascetics, and has attributed their theological malleability and liberal recruitment policies, in part, to their adherence to the *Mānas*—a syncretic text which lends itself to divergent interpretations (van der Veer 1988, 84–85).

Even though in certain contexts (and following a pattern common to upwardly mobile groups within the Hindu hierarchy) the Rāmānandīs in later centuries showed increasing conservatism in matters of caste, this was sometimes little more than a formal acknowledgment of the standards of aristocratic and mercantile patrons or a bid for greater respectability in the eyes of established Brahmin teachers. In fact, Rāmānandīs—as well as their favorite text—continued to play prominent roles in movements intended to boost the prestige and power of low-status groups. During the late nineteenth and early twentieth centuries caste "uplift" movements, most commonly associated with claims to Kṣatriya status, were launched by a number of North Indian communities within the framework of what William Pinch has termed "a progressive, assimilative Vaishnava belief system" (Pinch 1990, 5). These communities ranged from relatively high socioeconomic groups like Babhan landholders (who claimed priestly status as Bhūmihār Brahmins—i.e., "Brahmins of the soil") and Kāyasths (a prosperous scribal and mercantile caste that was nevertheless classed as Śūdra by Brahmin legalists), to low-Śūdra and borderline-Untouchable communities like the Koirīs, Kurmīs, and Gvālās (a.k.a. Goālās, Ahīrs, Yādavs—the most populous *jāti* of Gangetic North India), each of whom would assert their descent from a Rājpūt lineage of the mythical past. Their religious preceptors were in nearly all cases Rāmānandīs, who had supplanted Śaiva Daśnāmī sannyasis and *nirguṇ* ascetics of the Nānak Śāhī (or Udāsī) tradition in ministering to the religious needs of these groups. The Rāmānandīs owed their success, according to Pinch (1990, 118), to their reputation for being ritually strict yet socially "assimilative," and to their offering "a new and radically different view of society wherein the strict hierarchy of *jāti* and *varṇa*, while still relevant, was decidedly softened." Pinch notes the adoption of the *Mānas* as a cherished and prestige-enhancing scripture by these groups, and his analysis of the Rāmānandīs' role echoes the paradoxical tension between order and transcendence that I have identified as characteristic of the Hindi epic.

The Rāmānandīs were hardly radical egalitarians in a late-twentieth-century secularist sense; their message was couched in what they themselves saw as an "orthodox" idiom, within what Pinch terms "the cultural constraints of Vaisnava morality" (1990, 186), and their influence on their patrons showed many features characteristic of what modern anthropologists term "Sanskritization"—thus, according to one British observer, they induced the members of "impure or vile tribes" to give up alcohol and meat eating and become known as *bhagat*s (i.e., *bhakta*s, Vaiṣṇava "devotees") (Pinch 1990, 116). Rāmānandī pamphlet literature, in explaining the debased and oppressed condition of the Hindu lower classes, generally focused on two scapegoats: the Brahmin religious elite and the Muslims; whereas the former could be reformed and co-opted (e.g., as priests managing caste-endowed temples) (Pinch 1990, 219), the latter remained irreducibly other, hence one effect of caste uplift movements in the early twentieth century was to sharpen the rhetoric of communalism (Pinch 1990, 169). Yet without sugarcoating the Rāmānandīs' motives or strategies, Pinch argues that these Vaiṣṇava ascetics successfully worked for enhanced economic and educational opportunity and self-respect for millions of North Indians whose aspirations were seldom given more than token acknowledgment by the predominantly high-caste leaders of the Indian National Congress.

Rāmānandī leadership came to the fore again during the Avadh peasant revolt of 1920–22, when thousands of tenant farmers on the vast estates of one of the Gangetic plain's most productive agricultural regions withheld rent and rallied in protest against oppressive landholders. "Law and order" deteriorated to such a degree that the British Governor of the United Provinces speculated that he was witnessing "the beginnings of something like revolution" (Pandey, 1982, 143). Yet the rhetoric of the agitators was not of revolution but of Rāmrāj, and their aim was not the overthrow of the state nor even of the state-supported system of revenue farming. Instead, they sought a return to an older order that had been disturbed by changes in the rural economy and by the depredations of a new class of absentee landlords—merchants and industrialists who flourished under the protection of British law. The most influential spokesmen for the network of Kisān Sabhās (cultivators' societies) which formed the organizational basis for the revolt were a pair of Rāmānandī sadhus, Bābā Rāmchandra and Bābā Jānakī Dās, who toured the region as itinerant *kathāvāchaks* (tellers of religious stories or *kathā*), peppering their discourses with quotations from the *Mānas* (Pandey 1982, 168–69). So important was *Rāmāyaṇ* symbolism to the movement that the establishment of the first Kisān Sabhā, in the village of Rure, was explained by citation of a half-line from the epic which could be interpreted to contain the name of that place.[19] For the first large-scale meeting of the movement in December 1920, the organizers selected Ayodhya, mythical capital of Rāmrāj, and mustered some eighty thousand supporters (Pandey 1982, 171). The slogan used by the organizers to assemble crowds of protesters was *Sītā-Rām kī jay!* (Victory to Sītā-Rām!), and to worried British officials, this common village salutation now came to represent "a war-cry . . . the cry of discontent" (Pandey 1982, 170–71). They responded with the full weight of the powers of the police and judiciary to suppress the revolt. Ironically, according to Gyan Pandey, though the leaders of the Indian National Congress initially backed the peasants' demands, they later withdrew their support, arguing that peasants and landlords (some of whom were prominent Congress patrons) should "forget their differences" and unite in a nonviolent struggle against the British, leaving political reform to the "natural leaders" in the Congress. In Pandey's analysis (1982, 188), this strategy represented "a statement against mass participatory democracy and in favor of the idea of 'trusteeship'—the landlords and princes acting as trustees in the economic sphere, Gandhi and company in the political." By April 1922, Bābā Rāmchandra was in prison and the revolt he had come to symbolize was effectively crushed.

The movements described thus far were aimed at bettering the lives of persons who, albeit scorned by the highest castes, were at least marginally incorporated within the fourfold *varṇa* order of Hindu society. For those regarded as outside this order—the Untouchables and tribals who are despised even by the lowest agricultural groups—Rāmānandī-style Vaishnavism, with its emphasis on sacred narrative and its endorsement (in theory at least) of *varṇa*-based hierarchy, would appear to have less to offer. Though a number of Untouchable saints have been claimed by Vaiṣṇava bhakti traditions, the majority of these, like the Chamār (leather worker) Ravidās, appear to have espoused a *nirguṇ* doctrine, placing their faith in a deity far beyond earthly forms and the power structures that tend to coalesce around these—a deity commonly invoked solely as an abstract and universally accessible name. Thus the Ravidāsīs reject caste Hinduism and its pantheon of deities "with attributes" *(saguṇ)*, preferring to worship their guru and the name through *nirguṇ*-oriented hymns (Hawley and Juergensmeyer 1988, 9–23).

Yet the *nirguṇ/saguṇ* division risks oversimplifying the picture where the utilization of the *Mānas* is concerned, for despite its rich iconography and conservative didacticism, this epic gives prominence, as I have noted, to the doctrine of *Rāmnām* (the name of Rām as the supreme mantra) and frequently uses Advaitin, yogic and *nirguṇ* terminology.[20] The Rāmānandī order too has long included among its adherents both *saguṇ*-oriented *rasik*s (savorers) who delight in richly decorated (and usually Brahmin-run) temples, and itinerant *nirguṇ*-oriented *tyāgī*s (renouncers) and *nāga*s (naked ones), who practice haṭha yoga, and worship Rām, Hanumān, and Shiva in the aniconic forms of rounded stones (van der Veer 1988, 107–29; 130–59). What has historically served to unify such disparate religious orientations has been a shared devotion to Rāmnām as both a symbol and a religious discipline *(sādhan)*, and to the *Mānas*—understood as imbued with Rāmnām—as an authoritative and power-bestowing scripture.

That Rāmānandī proselytization was not restricted to caste Hindus or even to Śūdras is illustrated by the Untouchable Rāmnāmī Samāj (Society of Devotees of Rāmnām"), founded in the 1890s by Parsurām, an illiterate leather worker of the Chhattisgarh region of Madhya Pradesh, who was allegedly cured of leprosy by a Rāmānandī and devoted the remainder of his life to spreading the ascetic's teachings concerning the glory of Rāmnām (Lamb 1991, 239). Although the practices of the sect centered on the rhythmic chanting of the name (and some adherents went to the extent of having it tattooed over their bodies) and thus differed little from those of other *nirguṇ*-oriented groups, the *Mānas* figured prominently in this practice as a symbol of scriptural authority, a copy of the epic being placed in the midst of a circle of chanters and its memorized verses periodically interjected into the chanting. As Rāmdās Lamb observes in his study of the Rāmnāmīs, the fact that the epic contains verses insulting to Śūdras and Untouchables, and a much larger number that are flattering to

Brahmins and other "twice-born" *(dvija)* groups, was initially overlooked by the Rāmnāmīs, possibly because they were illiterate and knew the epic only through selected verses learned from sadhus. Yet during the past century, as a growing number of Chamārs have acquired the ability to read the epic, the *Mānas* has retained its status among them and the number of verses memorized for liturgical purposes has steadily grown (Lamb 1991, 240–44). Indeed, Rāmnāmīs have developed a distinctive performance genre, the *ṭakkar* (quarrel), in which sect members well versed in the epic vie with one another in an exchange of quotations relevant to a particular theme, the whole exchange being ingeniously interjected into the context of group devotional chanting (Lamb 1991, 245–51).[21] Although Rāmnāmīs continue to venerate the *Mānas*, they also exercise freedom in interpreting its contents and even alter verses they find unacceptable (Lamb 1991, 244). None of this is unprecedented in the history of performance and interpretation of this epic—which, Lamb notes (1991, 251), is understood to combine the authority and sonic efficacy of *śruti* ("aural" revelation, encompassing the four Vedas and their appendages) and the narrative complexity and interpretive malleability of *smṛti* (the category of "lore" that traditionally includes much of the rest of Sanskrit literature)—but it serves as a reminder that the spirit of the *Rāmāyaṇ* can still appeal even to the most disenfranchised groups. The letter of the *Rāmāyaṇ* is another matter, however, and it is to those who cherish a less flexible interpretation of its social paradigm that I now turn.

Shoring up the Dam

The last two decades of the nineteenth century saw the proliferation of Hindu organizations that espoused political as well as religious aims, and that commonly identified themselves as adherents and protectors of an "immemorial tradition" or *sanātan dharm*—a term that, partly through the efforts of such groups, came into use throughout northern India to refer to the beliefs and customs of the majority of image-worshipping Hindus.[22] The most broad-based Sanātanī organization of the early twentieth century was the All-India Hindu Mahasabha (Great Assembly), founded in 1913 as a religious organization to complement the Indian National Congress, but which gradually became politicized in response to the allegedly pro-Muslim policies of the latter organization and eventually grew into an opposition party. In the aftermath of independence and the communal holocaust of partition (for which many Sanātanīs blamed the congress, which had "betrayed the Hindu nation"), the Mahasabha was joined on the scene by several parties that shared many of its objectives and that have been variously characterized as "communal," "conservative," "rightist," and "reactionary." Behind their various platforms lies a shared religiopolitical ideal that is often identified with Rāmrāj.

The most explicit articulation of Rāmrāj as a political goal came from the first of these parties to emerge after the achievement of independence: the Rām Rājya Pariṣad (Rāmrāj Party, hereafter, RRP), founded in 1948 by the energetic Swāmī Karpātrī (1907–82), a Brahmin-born leader of the Śaṅkarāchārya order of *daṇḍī* (staff-bearing) ascetics. A tireless religious activist whose name became a household word in Hindi-speaking regions, Karpātrī founded the Sanātanī newspaper, *Sanmārg* (The true path) in 1936, promoted the revival of large-scale Vedic sacrifices, and campaigned for the abolition of cow-slaughter, a cause also advocated by his older contemporary, Mahatma Gandhi. Unlike Gandhi, however, Karpātrī staunchly opposed the project of "Harijan uplift," and when a group of Untouchables, emboldened by the principles of the new constitution, dared to enter the Viśvanāth Temple in Banaras, Karpātrī declared its idol of Shiva to be irremediably polluted and collected funds to erect a new, "private" temple off-limits to Harijans (Tripathi 1978, 225).[23]

For its first test at the polls in the 1952 parliamentary elections, Karpātrī's party produced a forty-page manifesto "replete with Sanskrit quotations, moral exhortations, metaphysical subtleties, and even arguments for the existence of God. . . ." (Smith 1963, 464). Its evocation of Rām's reign—the model it wished India to emulate—resembled Tulsīdās's panegyric: "[E]very citizen of Rāmrāj was contented, happy, gifted with learning, and religious-minded. . . . All were truthful. None was close-fisted, none was rude; none lacked prudence; and above all, none was atheist. All followed the path of dharma" (Weiner 1957, 174). To recreate this utopia, the RRP called for a ban on cow slaughter and the sale of alcoholic beverages, advocated the rural system of barter *(jajmānī)* rather than a cash economy, and sanctioned the replacement of Western medicine with Āyurveda. Society was to function smoothly according to the immemorial *varṇāśrama* model, but lest it be supposed that this did not offer something for everyone, the manifesto recommended that sweepers, Chamārs, and other Untouchables be assigned "high posts" in sanitation departments and in the leather and hides industry. Though mocked by some English-educated intellectuals as a pack of "reactionaries and obscurantists" (Erdman 1967, 52), the RRP mustered some two million votes, including 14.2 percent of the vote in Madhya Pradesh and 9.4 percent in Rajasthan (Weiner 1957, 175).

Although the RRP lost ground in later elections and faded from the political scene, the attitudes reflected in its platform would prove more enduring. Also participating in the 1952 elections were the Hindu Mahasabha and the newly formed Bharatiya Jan Sangh—the ancestors, respectively, of the contemporary Vishwa Hindu Parishad (VHP) and the Bharatiya Janta Party (BJP). The Mahasabha secured four parliamentary seats with a manifesto advocating an "undivided India" (i.e., the annexation of Pakistan), cow protection, and Āyurvedic medicine. On social issues, it adopted a more reformist stance, advocating Harijan uplift and women's rights, but, as Howard Erdman has noted, such rhetoric can be misleading, since many Mahasabha supporters no more believed in the literal implementation of such ideas than their RRP counterparts did in those of Swāmī Karpātrī (Erdman 1967, 52). The Jan Sangh was founded in 1951 by Shyam Prasad Mookerjee, a former Mahasabha leader, but drew much of its support from the older Rashtriya Swayamsevak Sangh (National Service Corps, RSS) which was formed by a group of Maharashtrian Brahmins in 1925 on Vijaydaśamī, the day commemorating Rām's slaying of Rāvaṇ. The RSS rapidly expanded—by 1940 it claimed a nationwide membership of one hundred thousand—and all cadres were supposed to meet daily in local groups for calisthenics, military drills, and Sanskrit prayers; a regimen intended to foster devotion to what was vaguely termed "national religion and culture" (*rāṣṭrīya dharm evam saṃskṛti).*[24] A similar ideology later dominated the policy statements of the Jan Sangh. Its 1951 manifesto contained—in addition to calls for a ban on cow slaughter and for the promotion of Āyurveda—praise of Sanskrit as "the repository of national culture," and a decade later its platform continued to extol "the age-old scientific principles of social organization"—i.e., the *varṇāśrama* system (Weiner 1957, 176; Baxter 1969, 212–13).

The most successful of the early conservative parties was the Swatantra (Independence) Party, founded in 1959 by C. Rajagopalachari (a.k.a. "Rajaji"—former freedom fighter, chief minister of Madras, and author of popular adaptations of both the *Rāmāyaṇa* and *Mahābhārata*), who tried to steer a more centrist course and avoided blatantly communal rhetoric. Yet he defined "culture" *(saṃskṛti)* as "essentially the prevailing pattern of joyous restraint accepted by the people," called for the maintenance of dharma ("an organic growth which it is our duty to respect and which we should not treat as mere Indian superstition") and bemoaned the undermining of the caste system by "the impact of Western individualism and perverted movements of social reform" (Erdman 1967, 91). Rajaji's English-language ideology contains an element of euphemism, as Erdman astutely noted: "[I]n his analysis Rajaji uses the term dharma in a rather abstract fashion, but more relevant in popular Hinduism is the more 'earthy' notion of *varṇāśrama* dharma. . . . The former usage may be flexible, the latter is not, and in this sense . . . there is an element of 'disguised conservatism' which intrudes into Rajaji's approach" (Erdman 1967, 94).

The concept of *varṇāśramadharma* is indeed central to Sanātanīs' understanding of their tradition and is often invoked in oral discourse on the *Rāmāyaṇ*.[25] As a social agenda, the *āśrama* component—a reference to the ideal of life-stages—has no practical meaning,[26] but the *varṇa* portion carries potent ideological weight and its connotation of "color" remains a signifier for a wide range of class and caste prejudices. The essentially repressive meaning of *varṇāśrama* becomes clear from the circumstances in which it is commonly invoked; the fact that a Brahmin's son chooses to enter politics, industry, or, for that matter, sanitary engineering, does not elicit it; but the potential upward mobility of the sweeper, cobbler, or washerman provokes angry cries. In this context, Rajaji's emphasis on "joyous restraint" acquires a more authoritarian overtone; restraint, joyous or otherwise, is ever urged on the oppressed by their oppressors.

In the face of complex economic and social challenges, rightist leaders consistently invoked a familiar battery of emotional symbols—Rām, the cow, Mother India—urging rich and poor Hindus to "forget their differences" and unite to face an enemy who was always without—Muslims, Pakistanis, Christians, the West. Writing on the early Jan Sangh and Hindu Mahasabha, Myron Weiner observed: "Their emphasis was on cultural questions—Sanskritized Hindi as the national language, a ban on cow slaughter, their opposition to the Hindu Code Bill, and their charge of favoritism toward Muslims by the government—these were the key issues for both parties, not land reform and other economic questions" (Weiner 1957, 213). The essential elements of one interpretation of Rāmrāj were present in the rhetoric of all the rightist parties, regardless of whether the slogan used was *Rām rājya* (RRP), *dharma rāj* (Jan Sangh), *Hindū rāṣṭra* ("Hindu nationhood"—used by the Mahasabha), or *Bhāratīya maryādā* ("Indian national morality"—the slogan of the Swatantra Party): an authoritarian government with a militaristic stance, strict adherence to a "dharma" defined by the ruling elite, and the denial of religious and cultural pluralism.

Contestable No More?

Since the mid-1980s, public debate over the message of the *Rāmāyaṇ* and its political implications has been carried to a new level of intensity, in part due to the televised serialization of the epic and to the contemporaneous (and some say, not unrelated) emergence of revivified rightist parties that use *Rāmāyaṇ* themes in a bid for mass support. At the same time, growing disillusionment among the middle classes with the official secularism of the ruling Congress and widespread disgust at its manipulation of communal issues precipitated an upsurge of militant Hindu nationalism that carried these parties to their greatest political successes since independence, and provoked a nationwide debate over the future direction of Indian politics.

Although specific metaphors varied from region to region (e.g., in Maharshtra, the Shiv Sena or "army of Shiva" was the most active rightist party), the symbol with the most dramatic nationwide impact was an image of Lord Rām imprisoned in a padlocked cage, which was transported throughout the country in 1985 by the VHP, an allusion to the longstanding lockout of pilgrims from Rām's reputed *janmabhūmi* (birthplace), the Babari Mosque in Ayodhya. While the government considered Hindu and Muslim claims to the site, the image graphically dramatized the VHP's claim that the state gave preferential treatment to minorities at the expense of the "Hindu majority." Even after the Center's decision, in February 1986, to open the Ayodhya mosque to Hindus—a concession that sparked bloody rioting in many parts of the country—the VHP continued to press for the demolition of the mosque and the erection of a huge temple in its place, embroiling the nation in a rancorous dispute which eventually toppled a central government.

Unrelenting pressure from rightist groups over the Janmabhūmi issue culminated in the complete destruction of the mosque on 6 December 1992, by a Hindu mob, an event that stunned the nation and was soon followed by riots in cities as distant as Jaipur, Bombay, and Bangalore.

The most horrific consequence of these developments was the great upsurge and geographic proliferation, especially in the wake of the Ayodhya agitations of 1990 and 1992, of "communal violence"—a euphemism that conceals the fact that in nearly all the most brutal episodes the victims were overwhelmingly Muslim: individuals, families, and, in some instances, whole communities, murdered by rampaging mobs of Hindu youths, assisted, in certain documented (but often suppressed) instances, by local or provincial police (Kishwar 1990, 12–13).

That *Rāmāyaṇ* episodes and, indeed, specific verses from the *Mānas*, were sometimes invoked by participants in these terrible events is beyond dispute. The fact that the hate-filled ravings of BJP firebrand Uma Bharati (e.g., "Do not display any love. This is the order of Rām!")[27] represent a grotesque contradiction of the teachings of Tulsīdās is rather beside the point; they were widely circulated on audio cassettes and were persuasive enough to win her a seat in Parliament in the aftermath of the Ayodhya controversy. The new militancy and its related obsession with machismo influenced iconography as well: in some VHP posters the lotus-eyed and softly-rounded Rām of earlier devotional art was replaced by a superhero armored with Bruce Lee musculature, posed in warrior stance with drawn bow, an unchallengeable avenger for an imagined community of politically "impotent" and angry Hindus; in Maharashtra, he was reduced to his weapon alone—cocked with an upward-pointed arrow, like James Bond's magnum—which served as the Shiv Sena's symbol in the 1990 by-elections.

Does the meaning of Rāmrāj remain negotiable in the age of mass-mediated politics? Or has the appropriation of the concept by rightist groups, with their rabid publicists and increasing access to sophisticated communications technology, foreclosed on more liberal readings? Ironically, during the same decade when folklorists and historians of religion and literature—mainly outside India—were freeing themselves from a text-based model to recognize the multiform diversity of the *Rāmāyaṇ* tradition,[28] a number of prominent Indian intellectuals and social critics, confronted with the grim realities described above, were voicing warnings of an opposite process: a narrowing of interpretation in the direction of a univocal reading of the *Rāmāyaṇ*. Some of these arguments appeared in response to the phenomenally successful television serial *Rāmāyaṇ*, directed by Ramanand Sagar, which aired on India's state-run television network, Doordarshan, for eighteen months during 1987–88. The serial, although incorporating many *Mānas* verses and permeated with a sentimental devotional mood, represented a major new *Rāmāyaṇ* text, presented in Hindi prose and utilizing the visual conventions of the Bombay cinema. Though avidly consulted by an unprecedented regional audience estimated at one hundred million viewers, Sagar's *Rāmāyaṇ* was roundly condemned by prominent English-language critics, not solely for its alleged slow pace, melodramatic acting, and visual kitsch, but as a more ominous portent of government imposition, through a persuasive new technology, of a hegemonic "received text" that would obliterate the multiple strands of the *Rāmāyaṇ* tradition. Thus historian Romila Thapar, writing in *Seminar*, warned of "an attempt to expunge diversities and present a homogenised view of what the *Rāmāyaṇa* was and is" an effort that would necessarily entail "the marginalising and ironing out of other cultural expressions" (Thapar 1988, 72,74). Similarly, sociologist Ashish Nandy charged that the serial "impoverishe[d] all the imagination and fantasy which is associated with the *Rāmāyaṇ*," and concluded that, after the television version, "There is no scope for new interpretations" (cited in "The Ramayan": 14–15).

Yet interpretations—new and old—abounded, both during and after the airing of the serial, offering compelling evidence for the continuing role of the *Rāmāyaṇ* in public discourse. Although it may be true, as many complained, that the timing of the serial was politically motivated—part of Rajiv Gandhi's cynical (and unsuccessful) attempt to "play the Hindu card"—no elite critic seems to have noticed the fact that the television *Rāmāyaṇ* was itself far from being "univocal." The product of a team that included government bureaucrats, movie moghuls, pandits, and devoted reciters of the *Mānas* (the latter category interpenetrating the former three), the television serial, like the written epic of Tulsīdās, was a syncretic text that tried to offer something for everyone, incorporating messages of "national integration" and communal harmony, and foregrounding women's roles in a manner common to folk retellings but rarely encountered in written texts (Lutgendorf 1990). The popular response to the serial, though overwhelmingly favorable, was nuanced as well: the details of weekly installments inspired diverse and often conflicting interpretations as they were discussed and debated in countless homes, shops, and tea stalls.[29]

The complexities of the *Rāmāyaṇ*'s entanglement with contemporary Indian life, as well as the continuing possibility—even under the full assault of the VHP's dharmic Rām(bo)—of a more liberal reading of the story, are eloquently revealed by Madhu Kishwar's impassioned essay, "In Defence of Our Dharma," which appeared in the journal *Manushi* in 1990. A Delhi-based activist prominent in the women's movement and in work on behalf of the urban and rural poor, Kishwar undoubtedly surprised some readers by disclosing her admiration for Tulsīdās's *Mānas* and recalling the "outrage" she had felt in college, when sophisticated fellow students at Delhi University mocked her for reading this "symbol of backward-looking religiosity fit only for semi-literate grandmothers" (Kishwar 1990, 3). Kishwar asserts that "the BJP-RSS-VHP Combine" has cynically adopted *Rāmāyaṇ* motifs for the purpose of capturing state power through "the politics of revenge" (ibid.), yet she is equally critical of "the secularists among the western educated elite," whose internalization of colonial standards in education and culture has "produced generations of people alienated from and ignorant of India's traditions of culture and learning" (ibid., 2-3). Indeed, Kishwar asserts that it is ignorance of the *Rāmāyaṇ*—not allegiance to it—that makes modern youths embrace the rightists' cause (ibid., 3); like Gandhi, she selectively quotes *Mānas* verses emphasizing brotherhood and nonviolence (ibid., 3, 9, 12),[30] and insists on the preeminence of a reading of Rām rooted in bhakti piety (ibid., 7):

> We need to redeem Rām as a religious figure, religious in the sense of representing a revered moral, ethical code and as an embodiment of rare spiritual ideals which have inspired generations and generations of people to upright lives in this land. The appropriation of Rām by sectarian politicians to perpetrate communal massacres pours contempt on Rām, who in popular imagination stands as a symbol of love, compassion, self-sacrifice, and steadfastness to duty. The Rām we imbibed as children from our parents bears no resemblance to the BJP-RSS incarnation.

Charging that the VHP is an essentially political rather than religious organization, Kishwar remarks that "their dharma is nationalism, not Hinduism. Their inspiration comes from Hitler, not from Rām" (ibid., 5). That the VHP and its Janmabhūmi movement can in fact best be understood as modern nationalist phenomena—manifestations of the distinctive "religion" which arose in Europe during the last century, in part as a replacement for older networks of religiopolitical allegiance—is argued at greater length by Peter van der Veer in his contribution to this volume. Such an understanding indeed helps to explain the dissonance between the rhetoric of the neo-Hindu right and that of the earlier literature of bhakti. Tulsīdās's "imagined community" (to borrow Benedict Anderson's useful phrase)—constantly invoked throughout the *Mānas*—was neither linguistic nor regional, nor even "religious" in the twentieth century sense (since *yavanas*—i.e., Muslims—were also said to be saved by the power of Rām's name); rather it was the boundless circle of "good people" *(sujan samāj, sant samāj)* who were devoted to the Lord's name and acts. The limits of this constituency were not determined by geography or time, and no territorial claims were made for it. For although pilgrimage places such as Ayodhya, Prayag, and Chitrakut were indeed celebrated as gathering places, such locales ultimately served (in the poet's well-known metaphor) to connote the faithful themselves: "a Prayag circulating throughout the world . . . accessible to all, everyday, in every land" (1.2.7, 12). Despite its ostensible commitment to a *saguṇ* deity, possessing alluring attributes and enmeshed in a complex narrative, the *Mānas* epic leaves no doubt that Tulsīdās put his ultimate faith in an abstraction: the divine name, which he viewed as the sole refuge of human beings in this dark age. In contrast, the Rām Janmabhūmi movement, rooted in nationalist ideals of "Mother India" as a Hindu homeland, favors an agenda of concretized reclamation and restoration: by "taking back" the mosque site in Ayodhya and constructing a huge temple there, its votaries claim that they will "make firm the foundation of dharma" in a restored Rāmrāj, establishing a microcosm for their planned "Hindu nation."[31]

The gulf that separates Hindu nationalist rhetoric from premodern discourse has been noticed by a number of observers. Already a quarter century ago, Erdman observed that, whereas Hindu rightists claimed to speak for an immemorial tradition, their authoritarian program in fact represented "a considerable departure from traditional Indian norms and institutions," for these always implicitly recognized the gulf between real and ideal and settled for a negotiated compromise and parceled authority (Erdman 1967, 35). Similarly, Jan Heesterman attributes this disjunction to a nationalist "tradition of modernity" with its own powerful truth claims (Heesterman 1985, 9):

> Its distinctive feature is . . . the total identification of the mundane with the transcendent order. As the sovereignty ascribed to it makes clear, the modern state cannot be transcended. . . . Hence the similarity of the Brahmanical and the modern tradition. However, the difference is equally obvious. There is no more room for a countervailing order. Modernity, then, means the integration of the mundane and the transcendent orders into one explosive reality.

To Kishwar too, the rightist insistence on a monopolization of loyalties—one nation, one language, one religion—suggests a Semitic or Christian worldview (the matrix that gave rise to nationalism), rather than one incorporating the diversity of paths characteristic of most traditional visions of dharma (Kishwar 1990, 10).

The ongoing contest of *Rāmāyaṇ* interpretation, now waged against the harsh backdrop of late-twentieth century India's ongoing crises of overcrowding, scarce resources, and corrupt leadership, seems to call for more than a neutral scholarly nod. As a student of the *Mānas* epic and its commentarial tradition, I can state that Kishwar's interpretation of that poem, at least, is closer to my understanding of its predominant message. For Tulsīdās, the heavenly state of Rāmrāj could be brought to earth in only two ways: by Rām himself or by his name. The vision of transcendence realized in concrete terms was set by the poet in a remote epoch and made dependent on the catalyzing presence of an incarnate avatar; transcendence in mundane time, however, was made immanent and personal, dependent only on an accessible and salvific name. It is surely an irony worthy of the Kali Yuga that this name—which Gandhi is said to have uttered when he fell to a rightist assassin's bullet—should now be routinely invoked to justify discrimination, hatred and murder.

Notes

All quotations from the *Rāmcharitmānas* are based on the popular and widely available Gita Press edition (Poddar 1939). Numbers refer to the subsidiary book *(kāṇḍ)*, stanza (understood as a series of verses ending with a numbered couplet in *dohā* or *sorațhā* meter), and individual line within a stanza. Translations are mine unless otherwise noted.

1. Throughout this essay I use the term *Rāmāyaṇ* to refer to the broad tradition of oral and literary retellings of the Rām story; the transliterated Sanskrit title *Rāmāyaṇa* refers only to specific literary works so named (e.g., the *Rāmāyaṇa* of Vālmīki, the *Adhyātmā Rāmāyaṇa*).

2. The more recent work of "subalternist" historians, among others, challenges Hein's assumption that Indian peasants possessed "vastly unpolitical" minds. See, for example, the works of Pandey (1982) and Pinch (1990).

3. E.g., "Tulsīdās had nothing to do with the Rām of history. Judged by historical test, his *Rāmāyaṇ* would be fit for the scrap heap. As a spiritual experience his book is almost unrivalled, at least for me. . . . It is the spirit ruling through the book that holds me spell-bound" (1925, 111).

4. Both Sanskrit versions note the absence of widows under Rāmrāj, presumably because husbands never died before their wives. Conversely, then, one supposes that in each generation women typically died before men—a curious fact of Rāmrāj demographics that, like India's most recent census data, flies in the face of biological expectations. One can only trust that, unlike the situation which prevails today, under Rām's benevolent rule this prodigy was achieved without recourse to female infanticide, nutritional and medical deprivation, overwork, abuse, and dowry murder.

5. The original makes a pun, playing on the identical spelling of the word "forest" (*van* or *ban*) and the stem of the verb "to become, be made" *(ban jānā): jab Rām ban gayā, tab hī Rām ban gayā.*

6. Significantly, this leads Rāmkiṅkar to the further argument that the "first citizen" of Rāmrāj is in fact Kevaṭ, the Untouchable boatman who ferries Rām's party across the Ganges.

7. For a recent statement of this position, see Richman 1991, especially Richman's "Introduction" (pp. 3–21) and the contribution by A. K. Ramanujan, "Three Hundred *Rāmāyaṇas*" (pp. 22–49); see also Thiel-Horstmann 1991.

8. A good example occurs in the third book of the *Mānas;* after slaying the demon Kabandh, Rām lectures him (now freed from a curse and in the form of a *gandharva*) on the necessity of showing respect to Brahmins: "Though he curses, beats, and berates you, / A Brahmin should be adored—thus sing the holy." (3.34.1; translation by Linda Hess). A mere fifteen lines later, he praises the devotion of the female untouchable Śabarī by declaring, "I recognize only one relationship: devotion. / Caste and lineage, virtue and status, / wealth power, family, merit, and intellect— / a man possessing these, yet without devotion, / resembles a cloud without water" (3.35.4–6)

9. This essay has recently been published as "Rāmāyaṇa and Political Imagination in India," *Journal of Asian Studies* 52, no. 2 (1993): 261–97.

10. I do not mean to overlook the possibility that one of the backgrounds against which Kampan wrote was the hegemony of the imperial Cholas, whose occasional military forays into Sri Lanka sometimes inspired inscrip-

tional and architectural evocations of *Rāmāyaṇ* episodes; however, the preeminence of bhakti themes in Kampan precludes any reading of the Tamil epic as simply an allegory of Chola history.

11. E.g., after introducing Rāvaṇ and his minions and detailing their sins, Tulsīdās has his narrator (Shiva) remark, "O Pārvatī, consider all creatures whose conduct is such to be demons" (1.184.3).

12. Interestingly, Tulsīdās's floruit coincided with another significant elite appropriation of the *Rāmāyaṇ*: the Emperor Akbar's commissioning of a Persian illuminated translation that rendered the great epic not simply into the official language but also into the iconographic vocabulary of the Indo-Muslim court, an act of patronage that Pollock sees as a royal effort to bridge the cultural strait between Hindu and Islamic elites and perhaps to reduce the "otherness" of the Mughals in the eyes of their Rājpūt allies (Pollock 1991a, 46). Tulsīdās, too, was concerned with bridge-building and cultural conciliation, though of a different sort—between Vaiṣṇava and Śaiva orientations, between *nirguṇ* and *saguṇ* Vaiṣṇava traditions, and between Advaitin intellectual philosophy and bhakti emotionalism.

13. Note that whereas Vālmīki appends his description of Rāmrāj (which itself concludes the main narrative) to his sixth book, *Yuddhakāṇḍa*, thus allowing the seventh to become a true (and stylistically uneven) "epilogue," Tulsīdās (in one of his rare departures from Vālmīki's narrative sequence) moves the account of Rāmrāj into his (more coherent) seventh book, highlighting its juxtaposition with the Kāk Bhuśuṇḍī narrative I discuss below.

14. Bhuśuṇḍī's first appearance (under the name Bhuśuṇḍā, identified as an immortal being) may have been in one of the stories preserved in the c. twelfth-century *Yoga Vāsiṣṭha*, a series of rambling metaphysical meditations framed as a dialogue between Rām and his family guru, Vasiṣṭha (see Venkatesananda 1984, 276–87). His prominent treatment in the framing narrative of the *Mānas*, however, has been explained by the tradition that there existed an esoteric *Rāmāyaṇ* attributed to him and known to Tulsīdās. A voluminous Sanskrit text calling itself *Bhuśuṇḍī Rāmāyaṇa* has been published in two volumes by B. P. Singh (1975), who argues that it is an authentic, early medieval text. Other scholars, however, regard it as probably postdating the Tulsīdās epic, and as the product of a sectarian author within the *rasik* or aesthetic-erotic tradition of the Rāmānandī order (see also Singh 1980).

15. E.g., the various treatments of the *kali varjya* theme (discourses on "things prescribed during Kali Yuga") found, for example, in *Liṅga* 1.40; *Vāyu* 32, 57-58; and *Bhāgavata* 12.2 (I am grateful to Frederick Smith for these references).

16. On the rise to prominence of the *Mānas*, see Lutgendorf 1991, esp. 61–64; 133–37; 254–67; 420–26.

17. As early as the first decade of the seventeenth century (i.e., within

forty years of the composition of the *Mānas*) the Rāmānandī Nābhā Dās, residing in Galta, Rajasthan, hailed Tulsīdās as the reincarnation of Vālmīki, and accorded him a place of honor in his hagiographic "garland of devotees," the *Bhaktamāl* (Rupkala 1909, *chhappay* 129:756). This citation—significantly, from a distant geographic center—indicates the reverence the Banaras poet must have enjoyed in Rāmānandī circles even during his lifetime.

18. This saying is inscribed over the gateway to the fortress temple of Hanuman Garhi, the principal seat of Rāmānandī *nāgā* ascetics in Ayodhya (cited in Pinch 1990).

19. The line is *rāja samāja virājata rure* (1.241.3), which occurs in the context of Sītā's *svayamvar* (bridegroom choice), at which Rām and Lakṣmaṇ "appear resplendent in the assembly of kings." However, by reading the adjective *rure* (resplendent, beautiful) as a proper noun, the line can be ingeniously construed to mean "the royal assembly appears in Rure," thus implying that the brothers visited the village. This kind of playfully strained interpretation of *Mānas* verses is common in oral exegesis (see Lutgendorf 1991, esp. 147–48, 187, 221–31).

20. E.g., such recurring epithets for Rām and Vishnu as *arūpa*, "without form"; *anāma*, "nameless"; *nirañjan*, "faultless, unblemished"; and the use of the yogic technical term *kaivalya* for "liberation." In the introduction to the first volume of the *Mānas pīyūṣ*, Añjanīnandan Śaraṇ notes that Tulsīdās has sometimes been accused, by *saguṇ* Vaiṣṇavas, of being an Advaitin.

21. *Ṭakkar* appears to be a modern revival of a once more widespread art of agonistic religious performances, e.g., the eighteenth-century traditions of Lāvanī and Khyāl (see Hansen 1992, 65–70).

22. On the development of the *sanātan dharm* identity, see Lutgendorf 1991, 360–71.

23. Like many of Karpātrī's highly publicized actions, this was sensational but ultimately ineffectual, since the new shrine is rarely visited by worshippers, whereas the "polluted" one continues to thrive as the city's principal temple.

24. The Sanskritized diction of the phrase carries an ideological weight that is lost in English translation. Its implications are conveyed in the writings of RSS "supreme leader" Golwalkar, e.g.: "The non-Hindu peoples in Hindustan must either adopt the Hindu culture and language, must learn to respect and hold in reverence Hindu religion, must entertain no idea but those of glorification of the Hindu race and culture . . . or may stay in this country, wholly subordinated to the Hindu nation, claiming nothing, deserving no privileges, far less any preferential treatment—not even citizen's rights"; M. S. Golwalkar, *We or Our Nationhood Defined,* 4th ed. (Nagpur: Bharat Prakshan, 1947), pp. 55–56, cited in Baxter 1969, 31.

25. One sometimes encounters the claim that *varṇāśramadharma* is the

"real essence" of the *Mānas;* e.g., this is declared by Swāmī Karpātrī in his introduction to Vijayānand Tripāṭhī's three-volume *Mānas* commentary (Tripāṭhī 1980, 1:i). Similarly, a wealthy Banaras Brahmin, prominent in the patronage of *Mānas* performances, once explained to me rather confidentially: "God, Rām, bhakti—the truth is, you can leave all that aside. The essence of Gosvāmī-jī's teachings is a certain *social genius.*" Although our conversation was in Hindi, the italicized phrase was in English—a coding that emphasized its euphemistic intent.

26. Not even Swāmī Karpātrī, who was fond of quoting from the law book of Manu, would have been inclined to introduce legislation forcing, say, a middle-aged male to pack up and leave for the Himalayas (in accordance with the life-stage of *vānaprastha* or "retirement to the forest") "when he sees . . . the sons of his sons" (*Mānusmṛti* 6.2).

27. A translation from a speech marketed on cassette (quoted in Kishwar 1990, 4).

28. E.g., Thiel-Horstmann 1991 and Richman 1991. Both volumes were based on conferences and panels organized during the 1980s.

29. Although it is not possible to do justice here to the complexity of the serial and its reception, I have argued elsewhere that critics' fears of an electronically imposed "hegemonic text" may reflect assumptions about the impact of television that have been uncritically adopted from Euro-American discourse, as well as misunderstanding of the vitality of the contemporary *Rāmāyaṇ* tradition (Lutgendorf 1990, 171–76).

30. Kishwar makes no mention of verses that castigate women and Śūdras or appear to advocate martial solutions (e.g., the verse, much used by the VHP, wherein Ram vows "to rid the earth of demons"; 3.9).

31. Interview with RSS volunteer at Babri Masjid (Rām Janmabhūmi), Ayodhya, April 1990.

Bibliography

Baxter, Craig. 1969. *The Jana Sangh*. Philadelphia: University of Pennsylvania Press.

Bayly, Christopher A. 1975. *The Local Roots of Indian Politics*. Oxford: Clarendon Press.

Bazaz, Prem Nath. 1980. *The Shadow of Ram Rajya over India*. New Delhi: Spark Publishers.

Bose, Nirmal Kumar. 1948. *Selections from Gandhi*. Ahmedabad: Navjivan Publishing House.

Erdman, Howard. 1967. *The Swatantra Party and Indian Conservatism*. Cambridge: Cambridge University Press.

Gandhi, Mohandas K. 1968. *An Autobiography; or, The Story of My Experiments with Truth*. Translated by Mahadev Desai. Ahmedabad: Navjivan Publishing House. First published in Gujarati in 1927–29.

———. 1925. *The Collected Works of Mahatma Gandhi*. Vol. 28. New Delhi: Publications Division, Government of India.

———. 1932. *The Collected Works of Mahatma Gandhi*. Vol. 49. New Delhi: Publications Division, Government of India.

Gopal, Madan. 1977. *Tulasi Das: A Literary Biography*. New Delhi: The Bookabode.

Hansen, Kathryn. 1992. *Grounds for Play: The Nautanki Theatre of North India*. Berkeley and Los Angeles: University of California Press.

Hawley, John Stratton, and Mark Juergensmeyer. 1988. *Songs of the Saints of India*. New York: Oxford University Press.

Hein, Norvin. 1972. *The Miracle Plays of Mathura*. New Haven: Yale University Press.

Heesterman, J. C. 1985. *The Inner Conflict of Tradition*. Chicago: University of Chicago Press.

Kishwar, Madhu. 1990. "In Defence of Our Dharma." *Manushi* 60:2–15.

Lutgendorf, Philip. 1989. "The View from the Ghats: Traditional Exegesis of a Hindu Epic." *Journal of Asian Studies* 48:272–88.

———. 1990. "Ramayan: The Video." *The Drama Review* 34, no. 2:127–76.

———. 1991. *The Life of a Text*. Berkeley and Los Angeles: University of California Press.

Pandey, Gyan. 1982. "Peasant Revolt and Indian Nationalism." In *Subaltern Studies*, edited by Ranajit Guha, 1:143–97. Delhi: Oxford University Press.

Pinch, William Ralph. 1990. "Being Vaishnava, Becoming Kshatriya: Culture, Belief, and Identity in North India, 1800–1940." Ph.D. diss., Department of History, University of Virginia.

Poddār, Hanumān Prasād, ed. 1939. *Śrī Rāmcharitmānas*. Gorakhpur, U.P.: Gita Press.

Pollock, Sheldon I., trans. 1986. *Ayodhyākāṇḍa*. Vol. 2 of *The Ramayana of Valmiki*. Princeton: Princeton University Press.

———. 1991a. "Ramayana and the Political Imaginary in Medieval India." Unpublished manuscript.

———, trans. 1991b. *Aranyakāṇḍa*. Vol. 3 of *The Rāmayana of Valmiki*. Princeton: Princeton University Press.

"The Ramayan." 1987. *The Illustrated Weekly of India*. 8–14 November.

Richman, Paula, ed. 1991. *Many Ramayanas: The Diversity of a Narrative Tradition in South Asia*. Berkeley and Los Angeles: University of California Press.

Rūpkalā, Sītārāmśaraṇ Bhagvānprasād, ed. 1909. *Śrī Bhaktamāl*. Lucknow: Naval Kiśor Press.

Śaraṇ, Añjanīnandan, ed. 1925–56. *Mānas pīyūṣ* (Nectar of the Manas). 12 vols. Ayodhya: Mānas pīyūṣ kāryālay.

Singh, Bhagvatī Prasād, ed. 1975. *Bhuśuṇḍī Rāmāyaṇa*. 2 vols. Varanasi: Vishvavidyalay Prakashan.

———. 1980. "*Bhusundi Ramayana* and Its Influence on the Medieval Ramayana Literature." In *The Ramayana Tradition in Asia*, edited by V. Raghavan, 475–504. New Delhi: Sahitya Akademi.

Smith, Donald E. 1963. *India as a Secular State*. Princeton: Princeton University Press.

Thapar, Romila. 1988. "The Ramayana Syndrome." *Seminar* 353 (January): 73–75.

Thiel-Horstmann, Monika, ed. 1991. *Contemporary Ramayana Traditions: Written, Oral, Performed*. Wiesbaden: Otto Harrasowitz.

Tripathi, Bansi Dhar. 1978. *Sadhus of India*. Bombay: Popular Prakashan.

Tripāṭhī, Vijayānand, ed. 1980. *Śrī Rāmcharitmānas: vijaya ṭīkā*. Calcutta: Indian Development Trust.

Upādhyāy, Rāmkiṅkar. 1975. *Mānas-muktāvalī* (Necklace of *Mānas*-pearls). Calcutta: Birla Academy of Art and Culture.

———. 1983. Tape-recording of oral *kathā* delivered at the Lakṣmī-Nārāyaṇ Temple, New Delhi.

van der Veer, Peter. 1988. *Gods on Earth*. London: Athlone Press.

Venkatesananda, Swami, ed. and trans. 1984. *The Concise Yoga Vāsiṣṭha*. Albany: State University of New York Press.

Weiner, Myron. 1957. *Party Politics in India*. Princeton: Princeton University Press.

The Politics of Devotion to Rāma

Peter van der Veer

The notion that Hinduism has only recently become "politicized" is a false one. "Politicization" and "depoliticization" of something called "religion" are notions that belong to a discourse of modernity which invents a sharp distinction between two spheres of action: religion and politics. This is a discourse of secularization, developed in the European Enlightenment, which assigns religious faith to the private domain as a matter of personal beliefs without political consequences. The political aspect of religion is often seen as a transgression of what religion is supposed to be.[1] A widespread idea is that religious people should not fight each other, but live in harmony. When confronted with violent conflict between religious communities outsiders often deplore the "politicization" of religion. There is a prevalent notion that this kind of violence also violates the "original intent" of the message of the founder of their religion or of god himself. Another version of this view is the argument that violence between religious communities has nothing to do with religion, since it is *really* economical and political competition which fuels it. This discourse which makes a sharp dichotomy between *real* religion and "politicized" religion can be located, by and large, among the well-meaning, well-educated, "responsible" individuals in society. Those who perpetrate the violence are often characterized as "fanatic" members of mobs led astray by their "irresponsible" leaders.

This general discourse is also the background to many scholarly interpretations of religious politics and violence. In the case of Hinduism, two instances come to mind immediately: the Cow Protection Movement of the nineteenth century and the current Ayodhya affair. Protection of *Gau Māta* (Mother Cow) became one of the most important issues of an incipient Hindu nationalism between 1880 and 1920. The Cow Protection Movement demanded a ban on cow slaughter from the colonial government. Failing that, it attempted to prohibit physically the slaughter and sacrifice of cows. The movement created not only a rift between Hindus and the British, but also between Hindus and Muslims, since the latter acted as butchers and used the cow also as sacrificial victim in their celebration of Bakr-Id. The organizational aspects of the movement as well as the violent agitation and riots connected to it have been very well studied by historians. Much less attention has been given to the Hindu love for Mother Cow and the protection of her body. Modern historians do not go as far as the colonial observers of the movement in assuming that religion is only the smoke screen for political agitation, but the emphasis on organization does imply an assumption that Mother Cow is simply a rallying symbol for the mobilization of the Hindu community. Its function is to serve the struggle for independence with the rather unfortunate side-effect of Muslim alienation. What is left out of consideration is why people would want to die and kill for the protection of cows. Much of the research begs the question what the cow's body meant to the Hindu protectionist. In an interesting way the denial of the significance of that question perpetuates the colonial view that religious beliefs should not be a matter of politics.

In terms of scope and significance I see the current Ayodhya Affair as the successor of the Cow Protection Movement. In 1984 the Vishva Hindu Parishad (VHP) started a campaign to remove a mosque, built in the sixteenth century, from a place which it considered as the birthplace of the god Rāma. While this campaign was initially not very successful, the VHP continued to put pressure on politicians which resulted in a decision of the District and Session Judge of Faizabad on 14 February 1986 that the disputed site should be opened immediately to the public. This decision triggered off communal violence all over North India and on 30 March 1987, Muslims staged in New Delhi their biggest protest since independence. The mosque was open for the Hindu public then, but its future was still contested. The VHP demanded that the mosque be demolished and a Hindu temple be built in its place. The Muslim Babri Masjid Action Committee demanded the opening of the mosque for prayer and removal of the image. It argued that the mosque should be regarded as an unalienable place of Islamic worship under the authority of the Wakf Board, whose sanctity should be protected by the state.

After the decision by the Faizabad judge the temple-mosque issue has been taken up increasingly up front by the Indian political parties. It played an important role in the elections of 1989. Although even the leader of the Congress Party, Rajiv Gandhi, insisted in a rally in Faizabad/Ayodhya that he supported the VHP case, the issue was made absolutely central by the Bharatiya Janata Party (BJP), a party with a long history in Hindu nationalism, which was to gain considerably in the elections. At least from this point onwards and probably already from 1986 the political agenda of the BJP cannot be separated from the religious agenda of the VHP. There is a direct coordination of rituals, agitation and political maneuvering by a high command of BJP, RSS and VHP. There is in fact an important overlap of functions. Vijaye Raje Scindia is a vice president of the BJP and a leader of the VHP; L. K. Advani and A. B. Vajpayee are leaders of the BJP, but have a background in the RSS; an important leader of the RSS, Manohar Pingle, has the VHP in his portfolio. It is also important to note here the extent to which the VHP leadership draws on the experience of retired members of the higher echelons of the Indian bureaucracy, such as former directors-general of police, former chief judges, former ministers and so on.

From September 1989 the VHP engaged in the worship of bricks of Lord Rām *(rāmśilā)* in villages in North India and the organization of processions to bring these sacred bricks to Ayodhya for building a temple on Rām's birthplace in place of the mosque of Babar. It is estimated that some three hundred lives have been lost in connection with these building processions. The most heavy casualties were found in Bhagalpur in Bihar where the Muslim population was almost wiped out. Ultimately, the VHP was allowed to lay its foundation stones in a pit outside the mosque on so-called undisputed lands.

In August 1990, Advani, the leader of the BJP, decided to start a procession from Somnath to Ayodhya, through ten states with as its goal the construction of the temple on 30 October. This initiative met with great enthusiasm all over the country. Members of a recently established Youth Branch of the VHP, the Bajrang Dal, offered a cup of their blood to their leader to show their determination. All this set a kind of time bomb which ticked with every mile taken in the direction of Ayodhya. Mulayam Singh Yadav, the chief minister of Uttar Pradesh, in which state Ayodhya is located, took a vow that he would not allow Advani to enter Ayodhya and indeed, before 30 October, Advani was arrested in Bihar. This did not prevent Advani's followers' march to the mosque, but they were stopped by police firing. Nevertheless, the action by the Government resulted in its loss of the BJP's support in Parliament and its subsequent fall on 16 November.

The VHP has continued its agitation with a highly effective video- and audiocassette campaign on the happenings in Ayodhya on 30 October. It claims that thousands have been killed by the police and that evidence is suppressed. Martyrs have been cremated and their bones and ashes are taken in ritual pots *(asthi-kalāśas)* through the country before immersion in sacred water. In the general elections in May and June 1991, the BJP gained again considerably and has become the second party in India after the Congress Party.[2]

Even more importantly, the state government of Uttar Pradesh came into the hands of the BJP, which meant that the Ayodhya site came under the direct authority of a party that had vowed to demolish the mosque and build a temple. I think it is fair to say that the BJP tried for a period to diffuse the matter in order to avoid a direct confrontation with the central government, which was controlled by the Congress Party. For example, the BJP's president, Murli Manohar Joshi, organized a march on Kashmir *(ektāyātrā)* to focus attention of Kashmir rather than on Ayodhya. However, it has become clear that the Vishwa Hindu Parishad is not under the control of the BJP, and it has continued to put pressure on the BJP to fulfill its election pledge. Despite some efforts by the central government to get talks under way between the VHP and the All-India Babri Masjid Action Committee, the mosque was attacked by a large crowd of Hindus, unhindered by the police, in December 1992. In this attack the mosque was totally destroyed. This led the central government to depose the state government of Uttar Pradesh and several other state governments controlled by the BJP. It also put a "ban" on the RSS, VHP and other communalist organizations. The central prime minister, Narasimha Rao, declared that the government would rebuild the mosque. Despite these actions, riots flared up all over the country, most notably in Bombay and Calcutta. More than a thousand people were killed during the first week of these riots. In addition, Hindu temples in Pakistan, Bangladesh and Great Britain were attacked by Muslims in retaliation. In Bombay renewed riots, fomented principally by the Shiv Sena, broke out in January 1993.

What concerns us here is the fact that the direct connection between the VHP, the BJP and the RSS leads many people within India and outside of it to think that *in fact* the Ayodhya issue has nothing to do with religion and everything with politics. A regular comment in liberal newspapers in India is that the BJP is playing the "Hindu card" and that the Hindutva program of Hindu nationalism is a travesty of real Hinduism. This popular distinction between real religion and unreal religion is brought on a somewhat theoretical level by the Indian thinker, Ashis Nandy, in a contribution to a volume on violence in South Asia.[3] I will summarize his argument at some length, since it makes explicit some of the main assumptions of one level of public discourse in India.

Nandy argues that religion in South Asia has split into two, faith and ideology:[4]

> By faith I mean religion as a way of life, a tradition which is definitionally non-monolithic and operationally plural. I say "definitional" because unless a religion is geographically and culturally confined to a small area, it has as way of life, in effect, to turn into a confederation of a number of ways of life which are linked by a common faith that has some theological space for the heterogeneity which everyday life introduces. . . .
>
> By ideology I mean religion as a sub-national, national or cross-national identifier of populations contesting for or protecting non-religious, usually political or socio-economic interests. Such religions-as-ideologies usually get identified with one or more texts which, rather than the ways of life of the believers, then become the final identifiers of the pure forms of the religions. The texts help anchor the ideologies in something seemingly concrete and delimited, and in effect provide a set of manageable operational definitions.

According to Nandy, three trends have tended to reinforce religion-as-ideology. Firstly, the modern (colonial and postcolonial) state has a bureaucratic necessity to divide populations in neat categories and thereby creates an arena in which these so divided groups are pitted against each other. Secondly, "evangelical Anglican Christianity" has engendered an eurocentric perspective on the "older faiths of the region" with a set of clear polarities (p. 71): "centre *vs.* periphery, true faith *vs.* its distortions, civil *vs.* primordial, and great traditions *vs.* local cultures or little traditions."[5] Thirdly, Nandy sees secularism as an ethnophobic and ethnocidal force in South Asia that wants to destroy both religion-as-faith and religion-as-ideology, but is much more compatible to religion-as-ideology. Both are ideological forces that work against the fluid definition of the self as a configuration of selves that is prevalent in South Asia.

Of course, Nandy, as a fervent antisecularist, is well aware of the fact that secularism implies the separation of politics and religion. He follows Gandhi in seeing religion and politics as inseparable. Gandhi advocated not secularism as a solution to violence between religious communities, but religious tolerance:[6]

> Gandhi used to say that he was a *sanatani*, and orthodox Hindu. It was as a *sanatani* Hindu that he claimed to be simultaneously a Muslim, a Sikh and a Christian and he granted the same plural identity to those belonging to other faiths. Traditional Hinduism, or rather *sanatan dharma*, was the source of his religious tolerance. . . .
>
> Urban, westernized, middle class, Brahmanic, Hindu nationalists and Hindu modernists often flaunt Gandhi's tolerance as an indicator of Hindu catholicity but contemptuously reject that part of his ideology which insisted that religious tolerance, to be tolerance, must impute to other faiths the same spirit of tolerance. Whether a large enough proportion of those belonging to the other religious traditions show in practice and at a particular point of time and place the same tolerance or not is a secondary matter. Because it is the imputation or presumption of tolerance in others, not its existence, which defines one's own tolerance in the Gandhian worldview and praxis. That presumption must become the major source of tolerance for those who want to fight the new violence of our times, whether they are believers or not.

There are a great number of elements in Nandy's argument which are interesting illustrations of Enlightenment discourse. The most striking is, of course, his opposition of religion-as-faith to religion-as-ideology. Faith is a way of life, pluralistic in nature. It allows for social and cultural heterogeneity. One may give Christianity or Islam as examples of those "faiths" that are found in very diverse populations. Nandy's essay, however, primarily concerns India and therefore he wants to demonstrate that Hinduism as *sanātan dharma* is a "faith," because it has a view of the person as not fixed and stable, but as a fluid configuration of selves. Moreover, Hinduism is essentially tolerant. A "real" Hindu is a religious pluralist like Mahatma Gandhi who granted the same pluralism to other faiths. Hindu nationalism, on the contrary, is religion-as-ideology. It is singular and intolerant. Its purpose is to mobilize social groups for political and economical purposes. It is the ideology of the murderers of Gandhi. In the case of Hinduism the opposition is between *sanātan dharma* and *Hindutva.*

While Nandy wants to save traditional Hinduism from the attacks of modernity, his own account is thoroughly "modern" and itself a product of what he attacks. The idea that "real" religion or faith is essentially tolerant and pluralistic can only arise in a period in which religion becomes a limited sphere, separated from politics, economics and science. In the Enlightenment it arises in the seventeenth century as a solution to the problem of Christendom's internal sectarian wars. The notion that Hindu faith unifies a number of different ways of life raises the question what this unification means. When it means that, basically, people's ways of life are not formed by their adherence to a particular set of religious doctrines and practices, then we have a perfect example of what is otherwise called "secularization." It is absolutely stunning to see that Nandy uses the term *sanātana dharma* for this unideological, tolerant "faith." In the nineteenth century the term *sanātan dharma* came to stand for "orthodox Brahmanic Hinduism," a specific "ideological" formation intended to protect "traditionalist" values from attacks by reform movements, such as the Arya Samaj. It is precisely this formation that can be seen as the main ideological source for Hindu nationalism. Gandhi clearly gets as many ideas from it as his murderers.

Instead of *sanātan dharma*, we often find the term *varṇāśrama-dharma* in Hindu sources before the nineteenth century. It is a more specific term that refers to the division of society in four estates *(varṇa*s), hierarchically ordered, and to the division of life in four stages. This Brahmanical ideology is constantly invoked as the "law and order" of society that has to be protected by the Hindu king, the *dharmapāla.* Dharma is directly related to the state, to Hindu kingship. The plurality and heterogeneity about which Nandy speaks is thus ordered in a specific hierarchical way, leaving Untouchables, Muslims *(yavana*s) and Christians *(mlechchha*s) outside the system. There is indeed some kind of tolerance for the plurality of ways of life involved here, since every species has its separate dharma.

Following Paul Hacker, I would argue that "tolerance" is a poor term for what should rather be seen as a kind of hierarchical relativism.[7] This finds an expression in forms of social inequality, but also in the well-known Hindu idea that there are many paths leading to God, as well as that there are many gods. The underlying conception here is one of hierarchy. The many gods and paths are manifestations of the One who is formless. Some of these manifestations are higher than others. Moreover, they perform different functions in a hierarchical order. A god for every season, as it is sometimes said about Hinduism. I would submit that the underlying idea is that from a certain chosen perspective all other "paths" do not have to be denied as heretical, but that they are seen as inferior and thus as catering to inferior beings. It is clear that we are here in a different conceptual universe than the one Nandy refers to when he speaks about "plurality," "heterogeneity" and "tolerance."

What we find in Gandhi's political philosophy is an interpretation of Hinduism's hierarchical relativism. One might consider it as a hierarchical relativism which includes other religions within its "faith." Therefore, a *sanātanī* Hindu like Gandhi can indeed claim to be simultaneously a Muslim, a Sikh, and a Christian. Nandy's argument that this kind of pluralism is "granted" or "imputed" to those belonging to other faiths is very significant. It is not that these elements are already "naturally" there; they are presumed to be there, since these other faiths are simply forms of the same religious essence. Ultimately, this kind of view is a neo-Vedānta inflection of European discourse on "tolerance." All religions are included in the Vedānta, the spiritual "essence" of Hinduism in its philosophical form, as in the famous formula of India's philosopher-president, Sarvepalli Radhakrishnan: "The Vedānta is not a religion, it is religion itself in its most universal and deepest significance."[8] It is a perspective that is certainly rejected by many Hindus, Muslims and Christians, but from this perspective they are seen to be not really religious, but fanatical pursuers of religious difference. The tolerance of which Nandy is an advocate wants to transform diverse religious traditions into something modern, which explains why so much of this particular argument resembles the discourse of the state, both colonial and postcolonial.

Nevertheless, it is important to understand the ways in which the colonial and postcolonial state impinge on India's social formations. Nandy is absolutely right in arguing that the modern state needs bureaucratic clarity and uniformity and that modernity stimulates certain processes of homogenization which in turn engender new heterogenizations. And, indeed, Christian missionary activism has led to revivalist reactions which have political and religious consequences, so that people are forced to identify themselves with one religious group or another in ways we do not find up to the eighteenth century. However, this should not lead us to a romanticization of either the precolonial past or the religion of the common folk. It should lead us to rethink the politics of religion and its transformation in the modernizing process. There were substantial and politically significant differences between Hindus and Muslims before the colonial period and, sporadically, they led to political violence. The basis for these differences have to be understood before we can move on to grasp the nature of their transformation in the era of nationalism.

Nandy's distinction between "faith" and "ideology" resembles in some respects a distinction between "faith" and "belief" made by the leading historian of religion, Wilfred Cantwell Smith.[9] In a meandering account of Buddhist, Muslim, Hindu and Christian notions of "faith," Smith makes a case to distinguish between different forms and systems of religious belief on the one hand, and faith, an attitude of "personal, sincere, authentic involvement," on the other. Faith precedes and transcends religious traditions and it is faith that links people who adhere to different traditions. Faith is a universal, human quality and its recognition brings people together. It is a capacity "to see, to feel, to act in terms of, a transcendent dimension."[10] Smith locates "faith" in the Islamic instance as a central category of thought *(iman)*. It is a form of "knowing" rather than "believing." "Believing" in the modern sense involves a lack of certitude and a neutrality as to correctness. In that sense Muslims do not "believe" that the *Qur'ān* is the word of God; they "know" that it is the word of God; they have faith *(iman)*. From this follows that someone who has no faith in fact commits the sin of refusing to accept this knowledge. He commits *kufr* (infidelity) while someone who is a "polytheist," who believes in many gods, is someone who perversely associates other beings with God.

In the Hindu instance, Smith locates "faith" in the term *śraddhā*, which he glosses as "putting one's heart to the Truth." There is a transcendental knowledge *(jñāna)* and an existential faith *(śraddhā)* which are as tightly connected as in the Islamic case. Finally, Smith also recognizes the same connection between knowledge and faith in the traditional Christian concept of *credo*.

Smith sees himself engaged in an enterprise which tries to construct "faith" as a comprehensive notion uniting the different religious forms in which it appears in human history. He argues that this notion of "faith" is under attack from the secularizing discourse of "modernity," which equates belief and "faith," and sees it as an individual option without social consequences and certainly not as "knowledge." This is an important and useful observation, but Smith is not aware of the extent to which his own account has its roots in the attempts made in seventeenth-century Europe to produce a universal definition of "religion." According to Asad, "[W]hat later came to be called natural religion defined in terms of beliefs (regarding 'transcendental power'), practices (ordered 'worship'), emotions (a sense of the 'sacred'), and ethics (a code of conduct based on 'rewards and punishments after this life')—was now said to exist in all societies."[11] Smith is, of course, three centuries removed from these earliest attempts, and his search for the essential, transcendental core of natural religion is certainly subtle and learned, but still the project remains very much the same: to come up with something universal, abstracted from concrete practices and attitudes authorized by specific doctrinal traditions. One may, of course, argue that there is a concept of "faith" which underlies Islamic *iman*, Hindu *śraddhā* and Christian *credo*, but the historical fact remains that there are specific doctrines and practices connected to these concepts, and that these unify groups of the "faithful" as against the "infidels." The politics of inclusion and exclusion are directly tied to doctrinal debates about orthodoxy and cannot be divorced from them. Ultimately "faith" is produced by social forces, however "personal" or "human" one may declare it to be.

I would therefore submit that these arguments—which make a distinction between "faith" and "ideology" or "belief"—depend on a discourse of modernity with which both Nandy and Smith are clearly uncomfortable. This kind of distinction can only be made at a point in history in which there is a powerful discourse which says that religion is not essential to everyday politics and economy and that religious beliefs should not divide us and when they do they are wrong. While we can recognize that this kind of liberal discourse on the limits of religion derives from the Enlightenment, we have now to come to grips with the fact that there are a number of political-religious movements, such as the VHP, which are not converted to that discourse. If the way in which they construct a political religion is not "modern," what is it? "Traditional" perhaps? To counter such an unfruitful opposition of "tradition" and "modernity" it might be helpful to have a brief look at the long-term transformations of the relation between "religion" and "politics" in one important Hindu cult, that of Rāma.

The Political Cult of Rāma

Rāmachandra, the hero of the *Rāmāyaṇa*, is the son of King Daśaratha of Ayodhya. He has the right to succeed his father, but because of a palace intrigue he is exiled. On his return from exile he becomes the king of Ayodhya and rules according to dharma. At the same time he is also God, namely an incarnation of Vishnu. He is therefore a god-king. This is, of course, well known. What is perhaps less known is the extent to which Rāma's kingly divinity made the Rāma cult suitable for appropriation in Hindu kingship. Hans Bakker shows that the Yādava kings of Vidarbha in the thirteenth century C.E. not only actively supported the expanding bhakti cult of Rāma, but almost equated court ritual and temple ritual: "the idol being handled as a living king, the king treated as a deity."[12] That this phenomenon is not only found in Vidarbha under the Yādavas and that it is not limited to the Rāma cult is shown by the following quotation from Burton Stein, whose work has concentrated on medieval South India:[13]

> Sovereignty is conceived as shared between powerful humans (Rajas) and powerful divinities (Devas); the sovereignty of neither is complete; the sovereignty of both, together, is perfect. Those who fall under the sovereignty of both kings . . . and gods comprise a community of reverence and worship. This is a conception of community which occurs at every level of South Indian society from the village to the whole kingdom. . . . Worship is constitutive of (it establishes or creates) community; the sovereignty of great humans . . . and gods is realized in worship events, or ritual performances, of a public kind in which all of any corporate whole (family to kingdom) express membership and in which all witness as well as compete for the honors which alone can be distributed by powerful personages and divinities.

Very important for the understanding of the current Ayodhya affair is the connection between the Guptas, the Rāma cult and Ayodhya. According to Bakker, the fictional Ayodhya of the *Rāmāyaṇa* came to be identified with the important North Indian town of Saketa during the reign of the Guptas in the fifth century C.E.[14] The Guptas removed their capital from Pataliputra to Saketa, which they decided to name "Ayodhya." The Gupta kings Kumāragupta and Skandagupta styled themselves devotees of Vishnu, and Skandagupta took the title of

Vikramāditya. He liked to compare himself with Rāma and it was a dominant theme in the Gupta court that the Guptas continued the glory of Rāma's dynasty and had restored the capital of Rāma to its ancient glory. After the reign of the Guptas, the town fell into insignificance, but not into oblivion, thanks to its recognition as Rāma's place. On the eve of Muslim expansion in North India, Ayodhya contained several temples. Local tradition has it that king Vikramāditya (Skandagupta?) "rediscovered" the birthplace of Rāma and built a temple on it. This would then have been the temple allegedly destroyed by a general of Babar, who built a mosque on the now disputed site. Whatever the historical value of the local tradition, the connection between Rāma's divine kingship and Hindu kingship is clearly a crucial one in medieval India.

These observations about the Rāma cult and Hindu kingship could easily reproduce the logic of Hindu historical narrative by arguing that, after the Gupta period Hindu state and society decayed and suffered from a long period of Muslim and later British domination. According to this narrative only Hindu majority rule, established by Hindu nationalism, could restore the ancient glory of Hindu state and society. In Hindu nationalist discourse there is an enormous pride in India's ancient civilization, whose rediscovery was in fact largely based upon orientalist writings. The Muslim period is generally portrayed as one of darkness and tyranny, while the British period had at least the redeeming aspect of allowing Hindus to find their true excellence again.

This communalist periodization that leaves Indian history with some ten centuries of decline completely ignores the fact that Hindu traditions of the nineteenth century are heir to the preceding centuries and not to some ancient, pre-Islamic Hindu civilization of orientalist fancy. It also does not acknowledge the important contributions Muslims and the Islamic heritage have made to Indian history.[15] I will certainly not try to counter this account of Indian history in detail within the span of this short article. What I would like to stress, however, is the obvious fact that there has been a history between the Guptas and the nineteenth century, and that in that history the Rāma cult was not "depoliticized," as some may want to have it. "Renouncers" were important agents in that history, and it is one of the confusions of the modern mind to see them as, by definition, "apolitical." Let me give a short and somewhat oversimplified account of the agency of the Rāmānandīs in the centuries preceding the age of nationalism.[16]

The most important element in the spread of a particular kind of

Rāma cult in North India has undoubtedly been the sixteenth-century Hindi rendition of the *Rāmāyaṇa* by Tulsīdās. This text has become the basis for both popular and theological interpretation of the Rāma cult. Although Tulsīdās was probably not a Rāmānandī himself, his story has been much promoted by the Rāmānandīs, who spread from Rajasthan to other parts of North India during the sixteenth century. In the seventeenth and eighteenth centuries the Rāmānandīs had established themselves in holy places connected with episodes in the Rāma story, such as Janakpur in the Nepalese terai, and Ayodhya and Chitrakut in Uttar Pradesh. Although the monks settled in Ayodhya at the beginning of the eighteenth century, Ayodhya became the main center of the order only in the nineteenth century. Rāmānandīs now form the majority of the population and are the main actors in the current Ayodhya affair on the local level.

The success of the Rāma cult from the sixteenth century onwards is part of a larger historical process in which bhakti has come to define modern Hinduism. As I have outlined elsewhere, bhakti sects are often described as religious movements, especially developed and eminently suited for practice by the lower classes, namely Śūdras and women: those who are not entitled to read the Vedas or to understand Brahmanical philosophy.[17] Emphasis is given to a structural opposition between the egalitarian values of the bhakti sects and the hierarchical ones of the caste system which is assumed to be underpinned by Brahmanical ideology. This kind of interpretation has a Hindu nationalist version that tries to explain the success of the Rāmānandīs in North India. The best-known verse attributed to Rāmānand, the legendary "founder" of the Rāmānandī sect, enjoins: "Do not inquire from anyone his caste or community; whoever worships Vishnu belongs to Vishnu." The social openness of the Rāmānandīs has often been interpreted as the Hindu answer to the conversion of Hindus to Islam under Muslim rule.[18] Similarly, the organization of the Rāmānandīs and Śaivas in military bands is often seen as the protection of Hindus from Muslim oppression.

Both the general interpretation of bhakti by historians of religion and anthropologists and the communal interpretation by Hindu historians have to be rejected. The Rāmānandīs are divided in three suborders, separated by different forms of secondary initiation. To become a Rāmānandī sadhu one has to choose a guru who performs the initiation. Having become a Rāmānandī sadhu, he may choose to be initiated in one of three suborders: *tyāgī*s, *nāga*s or *rasik*s. The different religious practices in these suborders are related to differences in social organization that have consequences for the relation between these suborders and the rest of society.

The *tyāgīs* follow a program of ascetic disciplinary practices and focus on the accumulation of *tapas*. They lead a peripatetic life in monastic groups *(khālsā, jamāt)*. Their mobility provides the basis for both social independence and open recruiting. They are organized around "big men" who are able to marshal the resources for feasts *(bhaṇḍārā)*. The *nāgas* are "fighting" ascetics devoted to wrestling and military training and organized into armies *(anī)* and regiments *(akhāḍā)*. They have developed out of the itinerant groups of *nāgas* and protect their brethren, especially during the great bathing festivals. This was not a protection against Muslim attacks, but against rival ascetic orders. The main struggle was between Śaivas and Vaiṣṇavas. In the eighteenth century they controlled the pilgrimage routes, which doubled as commercial routes. As long as they had a military and commercial role, their recruiting was as open as that of any military group in this part of India.[19] The practices of the *rasiks*, part of a ritual theater based on an aesthetic *(rasabhāva)* philosophy, result in an organization as a sedentary suborder living in temple communities. While the ritual practices of *tyāgīs* and *nāgas* are in various ways focused on the body, the *rasik* practices focus on image worship. They are very restrictive in terms of caste and dominated by Brahmans.

We can easily discern that there is not one essential meaning of the bhakti phenomenon with a set of easily identifiable social consequences. Rather, there are within one order, specializing in Rām bhakti, different religious orientations with different social consequences. To mention only one aspect, the establishment of image worship and temple ceremonies is often thought to be a crucial aspect of bhakti's openness to the lower classes. The contrary is true for the case we have just discussed. *Nirguṇ* Rām and the Rām mantra may be considered to have inclusivist consequences, while the celebration of *saguṇ* Rām in images of Rāmachandra has exclusivist consequences.

The communalist interpretation of Rāmānandī open recruitment policies is also totally unfounded. In fact, there can be little doubt that the expansion of the Moghul Empire had a very stimulating influence on long distance trading networks which were, to a considerable extent, in the hands of *tyāgīs* and *nāgas*. Moreover, we have ample evidence that Shaivite *nāgas* served in the armies of the Nawabs of

Awadh in the eighteenth century, enabling some of them to become the major condottieri of their time.[20] Their Rāmānandī counterparts established themselves in Ayodhya in the eighteenth century with explicit assistance from the Nawabs. Safdar Jang (1739–54) gave land to Abhayarāmdās, abbot of the Nirvāṇī akhāḍā, for building Hanumangarhi, which is now the most important temple in Ayodhya. The removal of the Nawabi administration first from Ayodhya to Faizabad and then to Lucknow is often interpreted as the liberation of a Hindu sacred place from Muslim oppression in Hindu historical writing. Clearly, the contrary is the case, since Ayodhya rose as a Hindu pilgrimage center in direct relation with the expansion of the Nawabi realm and with direct support from the Nawabi court.

The linkage between Rāma's divine kingship and Hindu kingship remains an element in the Rāma cult also after bhakti gained an unprecedented centrality in Hindu religiosity. In the North the claim to descend from Rāma remained a powerful aspect of Rājpūt ideology. This element led a great number of rajas to make considerable investments in temples and *ghāṭs* in Ayodhya during the nineteenth century. For dynasties such as that of the Bhūmihār rajas of Banaras, investment in the pageantry of the Rām Līlā was an important aspect of their legitimacy. Much of this, however, collapses in the twenties and thirties of the twentieth century. The role of patrons of religion is then taken over by business groups, such as the Marwaris. Both ex-aristocrats and Marwaris have come to play a significant role in supporting the nationalization of the Rāma cult.

The notion that the kingdom of Rāma provided one with an ideal model for the nation-state was taken to some extreme length in a marginal Hindu party, the Rāma Rajya Parishad, founded by Swāmī Karpātrī (1907–82). In a 1952 party manifesto Rāma's glorious reign is invoked: "Every citizen of Rāmrāj was contented, happy, gifted with learning, and religious-minded. . . . All were truthful. None was close-fisted; none was rude; none lacked prudence; and above all, none was atheist. All followed the path of dharma."[21] While Karpātrī did not have much success with his adventure, it is important to note that the notion of Rāmrāj was also important in the political philosophy of Ashis Nandy's hero, Mahatma Gandhi. In Gandhi's view, based on his reading of Tulsīdās, Rāmrāj was "not only the political Home Rule but also *dharmarāj* . . . which was something higher than ordinary political emancipation."[22]

It is indeed fairly typical for Hindu nationalism that it allows for a wide divergence of political interpretations of religious concepts. There is a vast gap between Karpātrī and Gandhi, but still they are operating within the same discourse, which cannot be very appealing to those who are outside of the Hindu fold. It is the particular strength of the VHP that it articulates aspects of the state-religion rhetoric of Karpātrī and Gandhi at a conjuncture in which the "secular multiculturalism" of Nehru's Congress Party appears to be failing.

Conclusion

When one tries to understand the politics of Hindu nationalism, one has to acknowledge that indeed this is a "modern" phenomenon. Nationalism is a discourse that originates in Europe in the eighteenth century and becomes universally dominant in the nineteenth and twentieth centuries. The Hindu version connects a vision of a Hindu nation-state with an imagination of a pre-Islamic past of that nation-state. What gets lost in this essentialization of the past is the historical transformation of Indian social formations. Hindu nationalism clearly owes more to the colonial than to the Gupta period.

However, to understand Hindu nationalism with its Hindutva as something "modern" does not imply that a "traditional," "apolitical" faith of the common people either precedes or coexists with it. The arguments of Ashis Nandy and Wilfred Cantwell Smith are thoroughly "modern" in their denial of the fact that true faith has political implications that are, from a humanistic point of view, not very nice. The faithful are just as intolerant as the modern, secular state is. One of the peculiar features of Hindu nationalism is that it attributes "tolerance" to Hinduism and uses this attribution as a political argument against those who are "intolerant," such as Muslims (with their "holy war") and Christians (with their missionary activities). It should be understood that this notion of "tolerance" itself belongs to a discourse that leads to political violence.

Finally, I would suggest that the argument that the followers of Hindutva are not truly religious is a political one about orthodoxy. There is no objective, transcendent criteria to distinguish "true" from "false" religion. Also in this case orthodoxy is decided by the relative power of the parties involved in its debate.

Notes

1. My analysis here has been informed by Talal Asad's introduction to "Religion and Politics," a special number of *Social Research* 59, no. 1 (1992).

2. I have written extensively about the Ayodhya affair and the Vishva Hindu Parishad in "'Hindu Nationalism' and the discourse of 'Modernity': The Vishva Hindu Parishad," in Martin Marty and Scott Appleby, eds., *Accounting for Fundamentalisms*. Chicago: University of Chicago Press, forthcoming

3. Ashis Nandy, "The Politics of Secularism and the Recovery of Religious Tolerance," in Veena Das, ed., *Mirrors of Violence* (Delhi: Oxford University Press, 1990), pp. 69–94.

4. Ibid., p. 70.

5. Ibid., p. 71.

6. Ibid., p. 91 (emphasis in the original).

7. For a thorough discussion of Hacker's argument, developed in a number of articles written between 1957 and 1977, see Wilhelm Halbfass, *India and Europe* (Albany: State University of New York Press, 1988), pp. 403–18.

8. Quoted in Halbfass 1988, 409.

9. Wilfred Cantwell Smith, *Faith and Belief* (Princeton: Princeton University Press, 1979).

10. Ibid., p. 12.

11. Talal Asad, *Religion and Politics,* 4

12. Hans Bakker, "Throne and Temple: Political Power and Religious Prestige in Vidarbha," in Hans Bakker. ed., *The Sacred Centre as the Focus of Political Interest* (Groningen: Egbert Forsten, 1992), pp. 83–101.

13. Burton Stein, ''Mahanavami: Medieval and Modern Kingly Ritual in South India," in Bardwell Smith. ed., *Essays on Gupta Culture* (Delhi: 1983), pp. 89f., quoted in Bakker, "Throne and Temple."

14. Hans Bakker, *Ayodhya* (Groningen: Egbert Forsten), pp. 26f.

15. See Partha Chatterjee, "History and the Nationalization of Hinduism," *Social Research* 59, no. 1 (1992): 149.

16. See for details, Peter van der Veer, *Gods on Earth* (London: Athlone, 1988).

17. Peter van der Veer, "Taming the Ascetic: Devotionalism in a Hindu Monastic Ordel,'' *Man*, n.s. 22 (1987): 680–95.

18. One could give many examples of this argument, which has also become accepted in some Western scholarship, but a very clear case is made in B. P. Simha, *Rāmbhakti meṃ Rasik Sampradāya* (Bālrāmpur: Awadh Sahitya Akademi, 1957).

19. See Dirk Kolff, *Naukar, Rajput and Sepoy* (Cambridge: Cambridge University Press, 1990).

20. See Richard Barnett, *North India between Empires: Awadh, the Mughals and the British, 1720-1801* (Berkeley: University of California Press, 1980).

21. Quoted in Philip Lutgendorf, *The Life of a Text* (Berkeley: University of California Press, 1991), p. 385.

22. Quoted in ibid., p. 380.

Social Identities, Hindu Fundamentalism, and Politics in India

Susana B. C. Devalle

> Late at night,
> through streets reeking of gunpowder,
> dodging through obscure lanes,
> and bypassing death,
> his father came back.
> The son never returned.
> —Subhas Mukhopadhyay, "Coming Home"

Some of the scholars who are currently studying the various phenomena generally grouped together under the label "fundamentalism" insist on the need to privilege religious aspects over questions relating to the formulation of social identities and politics. In my opinion, however, events in the world today force us precisely to study these social and political questions in more detail. What has been termed "ethnic" and "religion based" acts of violence, which in some cases have been perceived as overlapping phenomena, have intensified worldwide and acquired an international dimension. These circumstances have become a cause of worry not only in the countries where they occur, but also at the political and academic levels in central Western societies where ambitious projects to study them were set up at the end of the 1980s, and where representations of ethnic and religious confrontations in the media have translated into the decontextualized association of certain non-Western peoples and cultures with "terrorism" (see Said 1988). Of late, the appeal to religion and to divine sanction in order to legitimize political actions, particularly those of an aggressive kind (like war), has become part of the discourse of international politics. During the Gulf War of 1991, for instance, political discourses which incorporated moral/religious elements proved to be a handy resource for the United States' government as well as for leaders in the Asian context. This war also showed the alarming capacity of modern military technology to portray violence as if it were independent of human will, and the role of the printed and electronic media in shaping public opinion and consciousness. In India as well, we can see the modern media performing this role, as they fueled the latest communal confrontations.

The current situation in South Asia has a specificity and, at the same time, is not unique. It shows features that place it in a wider framework worldwide in which violence has entered as a component of political culture. The assertion of variously expressed social identities has also become salient. On the one hand, identity assertion often appears to question the configuration of the modern nation-state. On the other, identity assertion—for example, the strengthening of racism and exclusivism in ultranationalisms and some kinds of fundamentalisms—seems to be a reaction to the negative effects of the present attempt to impose a new global economic order. Furthermore, economic uncertainty has combined with the diffusion of values that support hard competition, individualism and the alleged natural dominance of "the strong" over "the weak." This undermines values centered on equality, solidarity and sharing. This response to the current situation as experienced in various contexts around the world, is multivocal, its expressions ranging from ethnic-based movements that put forward the right to diversity to fundamentalisms and ultranationalisms that stress exclusivity and the elimination of diversity.

The world appears to be passing through a *time of high density* characterized by an increased tension between deep socioeconomic and political transformations and the forces tending to check them. These latter forces can either ensure historico-cultural maintenance and reproduction (as with ethnicity) or attempt to gain wider spaces over the totality of public and private life (traditionalist and conservative ideologies, communalism, "fundamentalisms," ultranationalisms). At present, this tension is significantly marked by violence.

Our present epoch may be qualified as one of crisis experienced at multiple levels worldwide. In this general situation, the feeling of belonging to a community—be it based on linguistic, religious or/and ethnic commonalities— for some has become the only firm and undisputed certainty (see Hobsbawm 1991). As Björkman has said: "[R]eligious fundamentalism replaces questions with answers, doubts with certitudes, rootlessness with stability. . . . [R]evivalism . . . promises restitution to an earlier, better age. Under conditions of disruptive modernization, it is no surprise that people succumb to the temptations of fundamentalism" (1988, 2). L. Caplan, on the other hand, stresses the modern character of fundamentalism, saying "it constitutes a response to events and conditions in the *present* . . . [being] a symptom of perceived threat or crisis" (1987, 5; italics in the original).

The feeling of belonging, based on exclusive group identity, often acquires a millenaristic connotation in which one's own community is conceived as that of "the chosen ones" by opposition to all others, who are considered to be "the enemies." The social project is delineated in terms of the attainment of a new social and moral order of which only "the chosen ones" will benefit. These kinds of social projects, in which fundamentalisms and ultranationalisms appear to share some elements, eliminate the possibility of tolerance and compromise with respect to other communities, and may allow or promote—as is happening now—the exercise of violence against all those "outside the fold." Meanwhile, on the political terrain we are presently observing, in the Asian as well as in the Western contexts, that group identity and culture-bound issues are replacing the politics of class among some social sectors (see Rudolph 1992, quoting Inglehart's *Culture Shift . . .* 1990). Although this may seem to be an increasingly widespread phenomenon, the important question to be answered is in which specific social and economic contexts and in which social sectors has this phenomenon manifested itself, since it has not permeated the political practice of all social sectors.

After considering the present situation in India and some common misconceptions regarding religious and ethnic identities and the way in which they are being asserted, I want to briefly examine the phenomenon of communal violence and the impact of what has been called a "Hindu fundamentalist" ideology in India, taking into account the modifications that have taken place in political culture and in state practices during the last decade. The events of 20 May 1991, in which the Congress Party (I) candidate was assassinated, and the violence of the last elections add new diacritics to the political "text" of present-day India.

Culture, Religion, and Politics

The increase in the number and virulence of communal riots in India appears to have been, especially since the watershed of 1984, a constant of the eighties. In the process, this constant feature has acquired a dynamic that remains operative today. In the present situation, many appraisals of the phenomenon tend to underplay considerations about the nature of the state and the conception of the nation in contemporary India, and to ignore the fact that the state has increasingly taken recourse to coercive practices and abandoned the search for consensus.

Unsolved contradictions existing from the inception of the independent state in India, the continuation of some administrative modalities, and the preservation of fixed social taxonomies on the basis of caste and ethnic ascription inherited from the colonial system, influenced political practice after independence. In order to foster a firm macronational unity—undoubtedly instrumental during the anticolonial struggle—class conflicts were submerged and not confronted, and the existence of regional and ethnic diversity was underplayed. Religious differences, meanwhile, were underlined. The colonial creation of administrative units on the basis of the often arbitrary delimitation of territories, was bequeathed to the new ruling sectors after independence. These in turn rephrased this administrative creation as the abode of "the Nation." Thus, the postcolonial state has come to act as the true and sole interpreter of the nation(s) and communities it embraces. Ultimately, in the statist conception of the nation, state and nation become one, an "imagined community" to use B. Anderson's term (1983), a community in which the various nations/identities/histories it may include are subsumed. These are the grounds on which ethnoregional assertion has emerged in India.

Following the efforts to impose a constructed "national" unity in a context marked by social, ethnic and religious diversity, two contradictory strategies have been followed. On the one hand, diversity has been underplayed in the name of national integration. On the other, differences based on "racial," ethnic or religious grounds have been reinforced in social and political practice. We see in India the coexistence of the ideology of Indian unity with cataloguing devices and popular representations of social diversity on the basis of constructed ethnic and caste ascriptions. At the same time, the secularist ideal coexists with a religious idiom in the political practice of the ruling classes. In the course of the eighties, this last circumstance has led to a widespread communalization of electoral politics. The clearest evidence of this process could be observed during the 1984/85 electoral campaign of the Congress Party (I). The antecedents of this process are to be found in the practice adopted by the Congress Party (I) of looking for votes in one or other community according to the party's needs at different points in time. Muslims and subaltern sectors were the "card" played by Indira Gandhi after 1969 and up until the Emergency, when this support became eroded. Since 1980, it has been the Hindu petty bourgeoisie who have been approached to win their electoral support. The inclusion of the communal element in the politics of the then ruling party, with the connivance of the ruling classes, contributed to the violent riots of the first half of the eighties (Moradabad, Biharsharif, Meerut, Baroda, Pune, Sholapur, Bombay-Bhivandi), in which the communally biased attitude of the security forces (particularly of the police) was evident. It also contributed to an increasing polarization of the Hindu and Muslim electorates. The Delhi communal violence of 1984 against the Sikh community falls within this pattern. This frequent use of communal tactics by parties that profess to be secular favored a further development of communalist organizations and parties (like the BJP, the VHP and the RSS). The situation of social dislocation that these organizations have helped to create since August 1989, and particularly around the feared date when *kar sevaks* were to storm the disputed sacred space at Ayodhya, make them feel strong enough to consolidate the grounds of a Hindu platform on the basis of a fundamentalist ideology and the practice of terror.

In 1989, the Congress Party (I) and Rajiv Gandhi did not hesitate to again use the same communal tactics of the 1984–85 electoral campaign. Then the visual assault of electoral propaganda on the voters by means of huge sensationalist posters with images of a bullet-ridden and bleeding Prime Minister (Indira Gandhi) lying in the "arms" of North India (the Hindu-Hindi belt), acted as "an ellipse of language . . . an anti-intellectual weapon . . . [that] tend[ed] to spirit away 'politics' . . . to the advantage of a 'manner of being', a socio-moral status . . . [and] offer[ed] to the voter his own likeness, but clarified, exalted, superbly elevated into a type" (Barthes 1980, 91, on electoral appeal). In 1989, the candidate himself (Rajiv Gandhi) took the place of iconography, combining his presence, a pro-Hindu message and the appropriation of a now strong symbolic space: Ayodhya. The booty sought was the Hindu vote. The price that people had to bear was increasing and widespread communal violence instigated by the VHP, a fundamentalist organization.

Although totally different in their nature and aims, both ethnic movements and fundamentalisms have grown out of the contradictory situation of living under a state that proclaims its secularism and the diversity of Indian society, and that counts on the leadership of professed secular parties, in a reality marked by divisive political violence. In common perception, ethnic movements and fundamentalism are sometimes placed together, aided by confusing adjectives such as "separatist," "secessionist," "antisocial" and "antinational." For some communities, religion—the central category to define fundamentalism—may serve, together with other elements (mostly a consciousness of historical permanence, language and often territory), as one of the pillars of ethnocultural identity. The case of the Sikhs in Punjab, of Muslims in Kashmir and other ethno-regional assertions reveal varied (historico-cultural) dimensions of composite identities. Only some sectors of the community that is stressing its identity before the state in a situation of perceived or real threat—like among the Sikhs—may turn to a fundamentalist ideology to further their cause. In both ethnicity and fundamentalism, the aim is to recover or conquer social and political spaces. The nature and objectives of ethnic movements and fundamentalism, however, radically differ. The most important difference lies in the fact that ethnic (including the religious marker) assertions focus on the affirmation of diversity, while fundamentalist ideologies negate the right to diversity. In fundamentalism as well as in ultranationalism, this negation reaches the point of discarding the fragile attitude of "tolerance" in order to pursue the annihilation of perceived *enemies* both within as well as external to the community in which it arises.

Fundamentalism, contrary to one of its main supporting themes—that of defending a given religious tradition (conceived as the "only," "true" one)—assaults the traditions from which it claims to derive, violates the history and beliefs of the community whose interests it claims to defend, distorts the past, and chains the present to this distortion. Fundamentalism may be seen in some cases (like in the Sikh case) as an attempt to reinforce the identity of a community that feels socially endangered by means of the "invention of a tradition" (see Hobsbawm and Ranger 1983). When combined with the demand for autonomy, it stands in opposition to the state conceived as an unitarian nation-state. On the other hand, to understand the rise of what in India has been labeled the "fundamentalism" or "revivalism" of the so-called majority community, a constructed massive Hindu community, one has to look for other explanatory elements.

It is well known that the separation of religion and politics in South Asia is often problematic This fact in itself begs for a more refined definition of the Western notion of secularism in societies like India that have adopted it as an integral part of their states. The problem, however, resides not so much in the close relationships of religion and politics nor in the existence of religious diversity, but in the phrasing and purposes of the religious idioms used in political practice, particularly in the case of fundamentalist ideologies. The interpretation that official discourse gives to secularism and the confrontation between this secularism and the political practices developed particularly by the ruling classes, the tension between secularism as an ideology and the actual process of secularization, and the nature of the forces that resist this process should be subjected to close analysis (see discussions in Rai 1989, Nandy 1990, Mohanty 1989, and Kumar 1989).

Hindutva is a key concept in Hindu fundamentalist ideologies that has become recently salient, but its appearance dates back to the early twentieth century and to the notion of India as the nation of Hindus alone *(hindū rāṣṭra)*. Depending on the different interpretations of the notions of community and of "nation," and the variations in the constructions of Self and Other, Hindu discourse has suffered changes in the course of the present century until it acquired its modern militant form, which also shows variations in interpretation (see Pandey 1991b: 2997–3009). These variations mostly refer to issues of inclusivity/exclusivity in the notions of community and "nation." While people of different religious ascriptions (such as Sikhs and Jains, or even those "converted" or "reconverted" from "foreign" religions) may fall under the criterion of inclusivity, and while the place of "Untouchables" and *ādivāsī*s (the so-called "tribals") in Hindu society has been a debated issue, the definition of the Other seems to have been always clear: the Muslim community (there are, however, other noticeable exclusions, as pointed out by Pandey [1991b, 3000–3001, 3003–5]). At present, Hindutva is an ideology that exalts a certain version of the "religious, racial and cultural identity" of "the Hindus" as an assumed "majority community." As such, it negates not only the basis of a society that defines itself as a democracy but also the plural basis of Hinduism, all this set in a social context in which diversity is the norm.[1] In fact, Hindutva and Hinduism stand in opposition. What happens when the so-called majority, a dangerous creation of the elites in a position of dominance, is presented as the supporter of a fundamentalist ideology like Hindutva?

Hindutva is in reality an ideology appealing to a minority belonging to the upper caste and petty bourgeois ranks of Indian urban society, who feel that they hold an unstable socioeconomic position while they attempt to ascend the social scale. Once traditional privileges were curtailed and these sectors found that Western education did not necessarily translate into special political positions, this minority started to perceive popular demands and mobilizations with socioeconomic aims as a threat to their ambitions. Already in 1984 a dangerous equation emerged, which was then tapped by the Congress Party (I): nation = state = Congress Party = Hindu nationalism (Devalle 1985). The real threat to the established political authority of upper-caste Hindus were the peasant, *dalit* and *ādivāsī* mobilizations of the last two decades, ethnic and regional self-assertions, and lately, the recommendations of the Mandal Commission endangering the virtual upper-caste Hindu monopoly over government jobs. These threats were perceived as signs of impending doom by the Hindu elite. In the process, the identification of the Indian nation with the Hindu nation—an equation the BJP, the VHP and the RSS have sought to exploit in the political terrain—was added to the picture. Furthermore, this conception of the Indian nation has been forged *in opposition* to one of its existing components: the Muslim community. This definition of the Indian nation and its identity is based on an oppositional confrontation of the communities that constitute the plural national society. In conjunction with other elements—exclusivism, intolerance towards diversity, and violent social practices that aim at "ethnic purification"—this definition places present Hindu fundamentalism close to the ultranationalisms we have seen lately reemerging in other parts of the world, most notably in Europe.

Hindutva is an ideology based on a censored and reformed Hinduism whose origins can be traced to the reform movements of the nineteenth century. Reformed Hinduism was born in the context of the cultural colonialism called "Westernization," partly as a result of the rejection of the actual expressions of popular Hinduism. Hindutva's perception of Hinduism is elitist. Furthermore, its points of reference in relation to an "original" religious background are shallow. To support its defense of a "religious, racial and cultural identity" of "the

Hindus," Hindutva has had to deal with the history and culture of the community it proclaims to represent. This has been done by molding to their advantage or inventing history and culture. For instance, Hindu fundamentalists maintain that it was only the Hindus that sacrificed themselves in the anticolonial struggle, and they attempt to erase from collective memory the instances of collaboration of the Hindu elite with the British colonizers.

The opportunity to launch a Hindutva interpretation of the past and of religious tradition came with the development of the Babri Masjid/Ram Janmabhumi issue since 1986. This issue turned into a tragedy that plunged many parts of India into communal violence, the effects of which continue to this day. The issue provided the ideologues of Hindutva with symbols and rituals with which to move popular feelings, and an opportunity to mold scraps of history and legend into an "invented tradition" that fed the communalist imagination. Invented traditions aim to establish a legitimizing continuity with the past, not to understand historical discontinuities and the evolution of social contradictions. Through the creation of an invented past, new versions of identities become possible. Communities were conceived of as ideal brotherhoods, however easily such conceptions could be dismantled in any objective examination of the history of these communities. This process of historical examination, however, is unthinkable from a fundamentalist position. Central to the VHP's case is the claim that the mosque has been built in what is now modern Ayodhya over a temple commemorating Rāma's birthplace (that is, if he was really a historical figure). According to historians, this claim is based on an early nineteenth-century British construction of historical evidence around Babar's assumed anti-Hindu activities in the area (see Noorani 1989). In this way, although fundamentalists use historical arguments, they do so in an uncritical fashion, finding legitimation to their position on grounds of faith.

The dispute that started in the mid-eighties, instead of being left to the judiciary, became a "Hindu card" in the hands of the Congress Party (I) to offset the "Muslim card" used when passing the Muslim Women's Bill. In this way, the manipulation of electoral politics, communalism and fundamentalism have become interwoven in one of the most dangerous ways since independence. While October-November 1984 was an ominous instance of widespread bloodshed, this time with the Sikhs as victims, 1989 and after—with Muslims as the main victims—

showed how political culture in India could create a deluge of violence encouraged by a politically weak leadership and the political ambitions of Hindu "fundamentalist" organizations and parties.[2] In reality, the span between 1984 and 1993 is all part of the same disquieting story.

The Reality of Violence

Descriptions of present-day "Hindu fundamentalism" sometimes speak of it as if it were a disease: it is "contagious" and can "infect" whole areas (see the Indian press). Inadvertently, considering the extension and nature of political violence in recent times, such a view ends up perceiving communalism and fundamentalism as autonomous forces beyond human creation and control. It is precisely the inclusion of the practice of terror in communal and fundamentalist tactics, aided by representations of the "irrationality of the crowd," that makes these phenomena appear as if they were autonomous

The painful memories and the images of horror of the political drama of 1947 have been revived in the last decade, this time in a drama carefully performed in the heart of India. The *theater of terror,* a kind of continuing social drama, which has been enacted during three years in India as a prolegomena to the violence that followed, had several objectives, mostly defined by their extreme nature: to cause terror, not just fear; to be repetitive, not to appear as finite; to pervade the social fabric; to inculcate in its victims feelings of humiliation and subordination to those who wield force. This *theater of terror* very easily can give way to the actual *practice of terror,* as in the unchaining of the sequence of riots that we observe today in India. Through the *theater* and the *practice of terror,* those involved attempt to pervade the whole area of lived experience in order to make it lived dominance and lived subordination (Devalle 1992). It is at this point when violence seems to acquire an autonomous inertia.

Regarding the behavior of crowds, the riots after 1989 that have spread across North, Central and Western India show that they have not been a sudden and "irrational" outgrowth of a situation of confusion, but the outcome of planned and organized actions: the BJP and the VHP considered the riots to be an effective means to raise a social consciousness about Hindutva. This was the role played by the riots that accompanied and followed the *rath yātrā* (pilgrimage, lit. "chariot journey") of the BJP, a journey that covered a distance of around eleven thousand kilometers, all this happening in the midst of the government's silence and with the security forces adopting a partisan attitude. More recently, this was the prevalent position adopted before the pre-announced renewal of activities of the *kar sevaks* organized by the VHP and the BJP that led to the destruction of the mosque at Ayodhya on 6 December 1992. This in turn led to widespread rioting in many cities and towns.

Social and political violence—like in communalist riots, fundamentalist and ultranationalist confrontations—is supported by meanings and values. This is a violence that needs to become public and, through the appropriation of the public domain, to permeate private life. It has also to become "legitimate," not a difficult task in the South Asian situation where the state itself and the superordinate sectors, invoking the "legitimacy" of repressive means, have resorted with increasing frequency to coercion, punishment, and terror to reproduce the given hegemonic order (see Tambiah 1990, 743). Among the meanings and values at the back of the last period of riots (1989–93), considered to be the most serious among Hindu-Muslim confrontations since 1947, are the conceptions of (1) superiority/inferiority, (2) violence as "a right" of certain social groups, (3) a constructed "object of violence," and (4) the perception of the "objects of violence" as dangerous elements.

The Muslim community has been constituted as the "object" of the present violence and constructed into an "enemy" to be eliminated, either from the geography of India or physically. Thus the slogans that raised suspicions about the Indian Muslims' patriotism and prompted them to leave for Pakistan (for instance: "India is for Hindi-speaking Hindus; Muslims must go to Pakistan," seen in Bhagalpur, Bihar, in 1990), and the general Hindu perception of Muslims as backward, illiterate and "fanatics."

In the construction of the "object of violence" and in encouraging this violence, the printed media performed a key role acting as a source of Hindu propaganda, of the diffusion of rumors that led to further violence, and of the distortion of facts (see, for instance, Ramaseshan 1990, on the Hindi press in Uttar Pradesh). There is evidence, as well, that shows that the widespread riots were electronically engineered. According to witnesses' reports, inflammatory messages were distributed by audiocassettes from *pān* shops, passing cars, and from unknown places in the middle of the night. These cassettes were part of the scenography on the stage of the *theater of terror*. The visualization of symbols and the historization of legends have had their space on television as with the regular telecasting of the series dramatizing the *Rāmāyaṇa* and the *Mahābhārata*. Although the series were consciously written in a noncommunal way, they became a way of constantly nurturing popular collective imagination with elements working towards the construction of a version of "national" Hindu identity. The effects of these teleseries have to do not with the original noncommunal intention but with issues of content—confronting the variegated and rich spectrum of popular regional and local versions with a "national" standard version of the epics—and with issues of context. It is in this last respect where, as L. I. Rudolph has recently pointed out (1992, 1495), "the mega-serials in conjunction with the outlook and practice of the Vishva Hindu Parishad and other 'national' Hindu organizations, open the way contextually to communalise the series."

The "utterly Other" in Hindu fundamentalist minds—the Muslim community—has become the target, as Padgaonkar puts it, of "the nation's accumulated fears, frustrations, anger and disillusionment." The satanization and terrorization of the Other has resulted at present in the humiliation and victimization of the Muslim community, and in revolting mass killings. This conception of the Other in Hindu fundamentalist hands may lead to further violence and create pressure (by terror and/or by undermining their economic base) to have Muslims leave the country, a substitute for their physical elimination by genocide.

Concepts and Realities

The often careless application of concepts of Western origins like fundamentalism, not to mention others like secularism, democracy and development, that appears in current analyses of the phenomenon under discussion, may lead us to unwanted distortions in the understanding of issues concerning the expressions of collective social identity in the Asian context.

Is fundamentalism appropriate to qualify Hindutva? In terms of a scriptural authority to guide its project, it relies heavily on textual authority: the Vedas, medieval digests of Hindu law, and Tulsīdās's *Rāmcharitmānas*. In all these texts justifications for a prejudiced attitude against women, Untouchables, and Muslims can easily be found. The emphasis put on legends (understood by Hindu fundamentalists as "history"), and public collective rituals and their repetition (processions, collective events that grow into symbols like *rath yātrās* and *kar sevaks*, or the offerings of human blood during the *rath yātrā*), point at sources that have been instrumental in the reinforcement of identity. However, this new tradition in the process of amalgamation may prove to be difficult for the fundamentalists to maintain under their strict control. Perhaps this is the reason why, for the purpose of imposing their ideology, the supporters of Hindutva have engaged in widespread violence engineered not only to cause fear but terror through threats of elimination made to the community targeted as *the enemy*. The historical and cultural arguments the supporters of Hindutva brandish seem to be too weak to back social practices that may attract a wider and willing acceptance of such an ideology.

Looking at Hindu communalism, in their discussions on fundamentalism, some Indian analysts (Grewal and Tuteja 1990; S. Sen Gupta 1991) associate it with fascism, another category of Western origins and application. The extrapolation of concepts and categories outside the contexts in which they were generated will not necessarily clarify phenomena like those that have come to be known as fundamentalisms in the Asian framework. Several characteristics seem to be the basis for placing Hindutva in the category of fascism: the attempt to impose a social order and moral code, which would not be subjected to discussion, by force; the "racial" justifications to pinpoint the "enemies" to be eliminated; a reinforcement of patriarchal values; and the ritualization of collective actions resulting in depoliticization. However dangerous Hindutva appears to be for the political culture in India, the overall political, economic and social context does not seem to provide yet sufficient justifications to qualify it as fascism, possibly because its adherents have not up to now attained substantial political power or control of the state. We see instead the reinforcement of quasi-traditionalist and ultraconservative ideological positions, with veiled and overt racist overtones. There are also disturbing signs about how civil rights are understood in the present context (see Banerjee 1991, 100). J. V. Deshpande (1991, 851) has regarded "militant Hinduism" as any "civil disobedience . . . accepted as an standard part of the political activities . . . in the country." In other words, killing and terror may end up being understood as manifestations of civil rights.

What is evident is that "Hindu fundamentalism" has become a

political instrument in India, one that has strong appeal among the semi-Westernized, urban, petty bourgeoisie who feel betrayed by the promises of economic development and threatened by the forces that defend equality for all. The tapping of existing communal tensions by the ideology of Hindutva has created an explosive combination in present-day India: frustrated ambitions of the lower-middle social sectors in conjunction with the interests of the upper castes and ruling classes, in a situation of confusion in formal politics, of a deepening economic crisis, and a weakening of state hegemony.

Recently, the "fundamentalist" ideology of the BJP-VHP-RSS attempted to fill up the vacuum in the relations between the state and civil society.[3] Of late, violence and the *practice of terror* are threatening to take over the terrain of political culture. It cannot be forgotten, however, that the political discourses being uttered today in India are more numerous and more diverse than the one expressed in "Hindu fundamentalism." Popular mobilizations among peasants, laboring people in general, *dalits*, *ādivāsīs* and women, and ethnoregional movements speak a different and powerful language within the codes of a dynamic political culture.

Notes

1. As Frykenberg has remarked: "No country nor region in South Asia has ever had a 'majority' as such. Neither in terms of caste, community, ethnicity, or religious identity, has there been such a thing as a 'majority'.... [T]he conjuring up of this concept can be seen as nothing more than another attempt by one elite minority or coalitions of elite minorities to dominate all others" (1988, 38–39; see also Björkman 1988, 4 ff.).

2. The destruction of the Babri mosque on 6 December 1992, and the lack of opportune and decisive actions on the part of the central government have been considered "the most shameful event that has taken place in the country since independence" (A. M. 1992, 2625) and have dealt a severe blow to India's secularism and democratic character. The wave of arson, killings and violent confrontations among Hindus, Muslims and partisan police forces spread throughout the country, acquiring extreme virulence in Congress-ruled Bombay. The removal of the BJP-led governments of Rajasthan, Madhya Pradesh, Uttar Pradesh and Himachal Pradesh and the banning of some communalist organizations have done little to stop the reproduction of the communalist ideologies that have permeated the Indian polity.

3. A disquieting consequence has been the international developments

around this issue, the first of them having been the pro-Hindu forum inaugurated in Britain in August 1989, addressed to the Hindu resident community, that surprisingly won the support of British Labour members of Parliament. By introducing further divisiveness in the immigrant community in Britain, this new development adds to the current situation of ethnic discrimination. Recently, the destruction of the Babri mosque and the subsequent anti-Muslim violence in India have further internationalized the issue. Violent reactions occurred in parts of the Arab Emirates, Pakistan, Bangladesh and Afghanistan, and even in Great Britain (Derby). The call of the Islamic fundamentalists of Pakistan for a holy war against India adds a new element to the existing tensions between both countries.

Bibliography

A. M. 1992. "Calcutta Diary." *Economic and Political Weekly* 27, nos. 49–50:2625–26.

Andersen, W. K., and S. D. Damle. 1987. *The Brotherhood in Saffron: The Rashtriya Swayamsevak Sangh and Hindu Revivalism*. Boulder and London: Westview Press.

Anderson, B. 1983. *Imagined Communities: Reflections on the Origin and Spread of Nationalism*. London: Verso.

B. M. 1992. "New Delhi: A Trap for the Left." *Economic and Political Weekly* 27, nos. 49–50:2629–30.

Banerjee, S. 1991. "'Hindutva': Ideology and Social Psychology." *Economic and Political Weekly* 26, no. 3:97–101.

Barthes, R. 1984. *Mythologies*. London: Paladin.

Bharti, I. 1989. "Bhagalpur Riots and Bihar Government." *Economic and Political Weekly* 24, no. 48:2643–44.

Björkman, J. W. 1988. "The Dark Side of the Force: Notes on Religion and Politics." In *Fundamentalism, Revivalists and Violence in South Asia*, edited by J. W. Björkman, 1–19. Riverdale: Riverdale Company.

Caplan, L., ed. 1987. *Studies in Religious Fundamentalism*. Albany, New York: State University of New York Press.

Das, V., ed. 1990. *Mirrors of Violence: Communities, Riots and Survivors in South Asia*. Delhi: Oxford University Press.

Deshpande, J.V. 1991. "Misreading 'Militant Hinduism'." *Economic and Political Weekly* 26, no. 13:851–52.

Devalle, S. B. C. 1985. "India 1984: La Violencia Comunalista como Estrategia Politíca." *Estudios de Asia y Africa* 20, no. 4:646–78.

———. 1992. *Discourses of Ethnicity: Culture and Protest in Jharkhand*. New Delhi: Sage.

Dogra, B. 1990. "Bhagalpur: Communal Violence Spreads to Villages." *Economic and Political Weekly* 25, no. 3:145.

Engineer, A. A. 1989. ''Communal Frenzy at Indore." *Economic and Political Weekly* 24, nos. 44–45: 2467–69.

———. 1991. "Making of the Hyderabad Riots." *Economic and Political Weekly* 26, no. 6:271–74.

———. 1990. "Communal Riots in Recent Months." *Economic and Political Weekly* 25, no. 40: 2234–36.

———. 1990. "Grim Tragedy of Bhagalpur Riots: Role of Police-Criminal Nexus." *Economic and Political Weekly* 25, no. 6: 305–7.

———.1991. "The Bloody Trail. Ramjanmabhoomi and Communal Violence in UP." *Economic and Political Weekly* 26, no. 4:155–58.

Frykenberg, R. E. 1988. ''Fundamentalism and Revivalism in South Asia." In *Fundamentalism, Revivalists and Violence in South Asia,* edited by J. W. Björkman, 20–39. Riverdale: Riverdale Company.

G. P. D. 1992. ''Communalism: Beyond Political Parties." *Economic and Political Weekly* 27, nos. 49–50:2627–28.

Grewal, D. P., and K. L. Tuteja. 1990. "Communalism and Fundamentalism: A Dangerous Form of Anti-Democratic Politics." *Economic and Political Weekly* 25, no. 47:2592–93.

Hobsbawm, E. 1991. "The Perils of the New Nationalism." *The Nation* 253, no. 15:537, 555–56.

Hobsbawm, E., and T. O. Rangel, eds. 1983. *The Invention of Tradition.* Cambridge: Cambridge University Press.

Kumar, K. 1989. ''Secularism: Its Politics and Pedagogy." *Economic and Political Weekly* 24, nos. 44–45:2473–76.

Mohanty, M. 1989. "Secularism: Hegemonic and Democratic." *Economic and Political Weekly* 24, no. 22:1219–20.

Nandy, A. 1990. "The Politics of Secularism and the Recovery of Religious Tolerance." In *Mirrors of Violence*, edited by Veena Das, 69–93. Oxford: Oxford University Press.

Noorani, A. G. 1989. "The Babri Masjid-Ram Janmabhoomi Question." *Economic and Political Weekly* 24, nos. 44–45:2461–66.

Pandey, G. 1991a. "In Defence of the Fragment: Writing about Hindu-Muslim Riots in India Today." *Economic and Political Weekly* (Annual Number) 26, nos. 11–12:559–72.

———. 1991b. "Hindus and Others: The Militant Hindu Construction." *Economic and Political Weekly* 26, no. 52: 2997–3009.

Rai, A. 1989. "Addled Only in Parts: Strange Case of Indian Secularism." *Economic and Political Weekly* 24, no. 50:2770–73.

Rahul. 1992. "On 'Modernity' and its Victims." *Economic and Political Weekly* 27, no. 19:1031–32.

Ramaseshan, R. 1990. "The Press on Ayodhya." *Economic and Political Weekly* 25, no. 50:2701–4.

Rudolph, L. I.1992. "The Media and Cultural Politics." *Economic and Political Weekly* 27, no. 28:1489–96.

Said, E.W. 1988. "Identity, Negation and Violence." *New Left Review* 171:46–60.

Sathyamurthy, T. V. 1991. "State and Society in a Changing Perspective." *Economic and Political Weekly* 26, no. 6:303–8.

Selbourne, D. 1979. "State and Ideology in India." *Monthly Review* 31, no. 7:25–37.

Sen Gupta, B. 1991. "People, Parties and Power." *Economic and Political Weekly* 26, no. 15:937–39.

Sen Gupta, S. 1991. "Sexual Politics of Television Mythology." *Economic and Political Weekly* 26, no. 45:2558–60.

Srinivas, M. N. 1991. "On Living in a Revolution." *Economic and Political Weekly* 26, no. 13:833–35.

Sundaram, R. 1992. "Modernity and its Victims." *Economic and Political Weekly* 27, no. 9:459–64.

Tambiah, S. J. 1990. "Reflections on Communal Violence in South Asia." *The Journal of Asian Studies* 49, no. 4:741–60.

The Times of India. December 1990; February 1991.

LIST OF CONTRIBUTORS

Susana B. C. Devalle is a professor and researcher in the Center of Asian and African Studies of El Colegio de México. Her books include *Discourses of Ethnicity* (1992), *La diversidad prohibida* (editor, 1989), *Multiethnicity in India* (1980), and *La palabra de la tierra* (1977).

Daniel Gold is a professor in the Department of Asian Studies of Cornell University. His books include *Comprehending the Guru* (1988) and *The Lord as Guru* (1987). He has also contributed to M. Marty's *Fundamentalisms Observed* (1991).

Roxanne Poormon Gupta recently received a doctorate from Syracuse University with a thesis on the Kīnā Rām movement.

John Stratton Hawley is a professor in the Religion Department of Barnard College of Columbia University. His books include *Songs of the Saints of India* (coauthor, 1988), *Saints and Virtues* (editor, 1987), *Sur Das* (1984), *Krishna the Butter Thief* (1983), *The Divine Consort* (coeditor, 1982), and *At Play with Krishna* (1981).

Edward O. Henry is a professor in the Anthropology Department of San Diego State University. He is the author of a book on Bhojpuri folk music, *Chant the Names of God* (1988). He has also published several articles and produced a recording on the same topic.

Mark Juergensmeyer is a professor in the Sociology Department of the University of California at Santa Barbara. His books include *The New Cold War?* (1993), *Radhasoami Reality* (1991), *Songs of the Saints of India* (coauthor, 1988), *Fighting with Gandhi* (1984), *Religion as Social Vision* (1982), and *Sikh Studies* (coeditor, 1979).

David N. Lorenzen is a professor and researcher in the Center of Asian and African Studies of El Colegio de México. His books include *Kabir*

Legends (1991), *The Kapalikas and Kalamukhas* (1972, 1991), and *Religious Change and Cultural Domination* (editor, 1981).

Philip Lutgendorf is a professor in the Department of Asian Languages and Literature of the University of Iowa in Iowa City. He is the author of *The Life of a Text* (1991), a book about *Rāmacharitamānas* performance.

Harjot Oberoi is a professor in the Department of Asian Studies of the University of British Columbia. He is the author of *The Construction of Religious Boundaries* (1994), a historical study of Sikh tradition, and has contributed to M. Marty's *Fundamentalisms and the State* (1993).

Joseph Schaller is an assistant professor in the Religion Department of Carleton College in Northfield, Minnesota. He recently received his doctorate from the University of California at Berkeley with a thesis on the modern followers of Ravidās.

Michael C. Shapiro is a professor in the Department of Asian Languages and Literature of the University of Washington in Seattle. He is the author of *A Primer of Modern Standard Hindi* (1989) and has published several articles on Sikh literature.

Uma Thukral is a visiting professor in the Center of Asian and African Studies of El Colegio de México. She is the author of several articles on the literature of the Kabīr Panth and is a cotranslator of Anantadās's *Kabīr parachaī* (1991).

Peter van der Veer is a professor in the Centre for the Comparative Study of Religion and Society at the University of Amsterdam. Previously he taught at the University of Pennsylvania. His books include *Religious Nationalism* (1994), *Orientalism and the Postcolonial Predicament* (coeditor, 1993), and *Gods on Earth* (1988).

Eleanor Zelliot is a professor in the History Department of Carleton College in Northfield, Minnesota. Her books include *An Anthology of Dalit Literature* (coeditor, 1992), *From Untouchable to Dalit* (1992), and *The Experience of Hinduism* (coeditor, 1988).

INDEX